Felix Salten
Man of Many Faces

Studies in Austrian Literature, Culture and Thought

General Editors:

Jorun B. Johns
Richard H. Lawson

Beverley Driver Eddy

Felix Salten
Man of Many Faces

ARIADNE PRESS
Riverside, California

Ariadne Press would like to express its appreciation to the Bundesministerium für Wissenschaft und Forschung, Vienna for assistance in publishing this book.

Library of Congress Cataloging-in-Publication Data

Eddy, Beverley D.
Felix Salten : man of many faces / Beverley Driver Eddy.
   p. cm. -- (Studies in Austrian literature, culture and thought)
Includes bibliographical references and index.
ISBN 978-1-57241-169-2 (alk. paper)
   1. Salten, Felix, 1869-1945--Criticism and interpretation. I. Title.
PT2637.A52Z64 2010
833'.912--dc22
                          2010026831

Cover Design
Beth A. Steffel
Photo of Felix Salten
Courtesy of Deutsches Literaturarchiv, Marbach

CONTENTS

Introduction

Although Felix Salten was, in many respects, an outsider in the Vienna that he loved, and although he eschewed politics, few men's lives have been so closely interwoven with the rise and decline of that imperial city. As a Jew, he was both a major contributor to the city's cultural ascendancy and a victim of its fall. He was born in 1869, at the start of Vienna's building boom and its rise as a dominant center of world culture, and he died in 1945, when the city lay collapsed in the ashes of the Second World War. He was neither born in Vienna nor did he die there, but he loved the city with rare intensity and believed that he could be happy nowhere else.

Salten understood the complexities and contradictions of Vienna better than the vast majority of its citizens. When he was a child, he wandered throughout the city and its suburbs, sneaking onto the grounds of the imperial city palace, passing through the hallways of fancy apartment buildings as shortcuts from one city street to the next, exploring alleyways and stairwells in the poorest working-class districts beyond the old city walls, dreaming and playing on the Turkish redoubts, scampering through the vineyards of the outermost suburbs, and hiking into the Vienna Woods, where he could look down exultingly onto the city that was spread at his feet. As he got older, he explored the cultural offerings of the city, attending its art gallery openings, indoor and outdoor concerts, opera and theater productions, and salon gatherings. He went bicycling out from the city around the Prater Park and to neighboring villages and ate and drank in the downtown coffeehouses, in the Sacher and Imperial Hotels, and in both the rustic and the fashionable restaurants on the city outskirts. From his earliest childhood, he made it his business to observe and note all that he could, frequently by making himself invisible to others, and he used these talents to become one of the great word portraitists of his age.

An old friend recalled a typical Salten scene: he saw him sitting on a park bench in the public Volksgarten, his dog at his side, watching the crowds that swarmed past him "with eyes that missed nothing."[1] Salten maintained that he was able to read "small novels" from the faces that he studied and, in an essay entitled "Junge Frauen" (Young Women), he gave several examples of this ability, writing, for example: "There is another one. A few years ago she raved about everything imaginable. She painted and sang, wrote poetry and worked clay, and had a Botticelli hairstyle. Now she complains about domestic servants and plays poker."[2] He offered similar observations and analyses of political figures, emigrants, members of the royal family, actors, musicians, the elderly, and the unemployed, capturing their essence through a few deftly drawn observations; not without reason is one book of his essays entitled *Das österreichische Antlitz* (The Face of Austria).

Just as he sat largely unnoticed, quietly observing the Viennese who lived and moved around him, so he studied the wildlife in the Austrian fields and forests, noting individuality of character, whether grouse, rabbits, or fish. Upon seeing a young roebuck, for example, he wrote: "There! A buck nears us with proudly raised head, with high steps of Spanish syncopation. His solemn stride, his 'Here I am!' bearing could create a sensation. Sure enough, his antlers have six points, but the beams are thin, the points scarcely remarkable. This youthful gentleman has a fine future, seems to know his own promising talents and is proud of them. We content ourselves with the pleasant sight."[3]

When Salten became a writer, his ability to blend with and move in all levels of society served him in good stead. He had seen how the various classes of society lived. He had visited their places of entertainment, their homes, and their churches; had attended murder trials, court balls, and parliamentary gatherings; looked in on city morgues and royal funerals. All became fodder for his pen. Like many of his contemporaries, Salten felt that Vienna was unique among European cities in that its soil was drenched with music. The highest praise that he could give a writer was that his literary production was filled with the harmonies of Schubert, Strauss, and Lanner. In his later years, Salten would produce "pictures from the concert hall," portraying the character – and the idiosyncrasies – of many of the musicians who performed in the city.

Despite dismal childhood poverty, Salten began at an early age to be aware of the Habsburg royalty. When he was ten, he visited the courtyard of the imperial palace and saw Franz Josef – who, at 49, still had blond hair – and his wife Elisabeth pass close by in the imperial coach. At about this same period, he sneaked into Easter services in the imperial court chapel, where he saw the knights of the Golden Fleece assembled and where he gazed upon the emperor and his son, Crown Prince Rudolf. When Salten was in his twenties, he became the friend and confidant of Leopold Ferdinand, the disgruntled Archduke of Tuscany. In his thirties, he helped rescue the Princess of Coburg from a mental institution.

Salten watched as Karl Lueger, the populist mayor of Vienna, spouted his anti-Semitic rhetoric, and he studied the paradoxes in his character. He reported on the horrors of the First World War and on the sacrifices and sufferings of the citizens of Vienna. He saw the influx of thousands of Jewish war refugees from Galicia, and pled in his newspaper columns for charitable donations to ease their desperate plight. He viewed with unease the foundation of the Austrian republic, the rise of German nationalism, Dollfuss's assumption of emergency powers, and, finally, the Anschluss (annexation) of Austria by Nazi Germany. After the Anschluss, Salten remained in Vienna for nearly a year, hoping that he could outlast the madness of Nazi domination. Eventually, he was forced into exile, where he died, six months after Hitler's suicide in a Berlin bunker.

When Salten wrote about these tumultuous days, he focused not on political issues and parties, but rather on the effects they had upon Vienna's cultural institutions and on its citizens. He tried – through a lifetime of work as a journalist, critic, novelist, playwright, theater director, and president of the Vienna P.E.N. Club – to win acceptance as a preeminent representative of Viennese culture, but several forces conspired to deny him the recognition that he worked so hard to achieve: the pen of the social satirist Karl Kraus, whose thirty years of attacks on Salten in his journal *Die Fackel* created an enduring image of a poorly educated and corrupt journalist; anti-Semites who, early in his career, attacked his cabaret as the obscene expression of "foreign" culture and, decades later, denied him a German-reading public and drove him into exile; and the Walt Disney studios, which substituted Disney's name for Salten's on three of his novels, destroyed their Austrian ethos, and eliminated their core ideas.

Perhaps there is an even stronger reason why Salten remains today an unseen or shadowy image among his friends and contemporaries, Arthur Schnitzler, Hugo von Hofmannsthal, Hermann Bahr, and Richard Beer-Hofmann: he is extraordinarily difficult to pin down. There is some truth to Karl Kraus's claim that Salten was chameleonlike, willing to write in every genre, in every style, and on every subject. Some of his writings are, quite frankly, sentimental hack work, produced for a perceived market under the pressure of time. Others are poetic gems. Many of Salten's contemporaries considered him an unreliable ally. Salten frequently appeared to contradict himself, and even his closest friend, Arthur Schnitzler, was disturbed by his apparent hypocrisy. This criticism has endured. How, people ask, could a man who killed over two hundred roebucks in his lifetime write a sensitive work like *Bambi?* How could a man who wrote a weekly column for Theodor Herzl's Zionist newspaper follow a path of appeasement toward the Germans immediately after the Nazi book burnings? How could a man who is now renowned primarily for his lyrical nature stories for adolescents pen the most notorious piece of child pornography in the German language?

For many, the answer is to denigrate Salten, to regard him as a man of little substance or character, a traitor to the Zionist cause, and a writer of inferior abilities. Some proclaim him a man of so little talent that he could not possibly have written the erotic classic *Josefine Mutzenbacher*, while others maintain that he was incapable of writing anything other than children's literature and child pornography. Such comments are ill informed and do Salten a great injustice. From 1906 to 1938, Salten was regarded both as an authoritative voice on Vienna's cultural scene and as a graceful stylist whose miniature portraits of kings, actors, writers, and musicians brought those figures to life and shed light on their character, their talents, and their vulnerabilities. These pieces are invaluable documents of a past age.

One should, in short, not dismiss Salten because of his elusiveness and uneven literary production, but examine him instead for his deeper consistencies. Salten is, in his complexity, a remarkable representative of the city that he loved, a man whose inner conflicts epitomize the contradictions of his age. The very criticisms leveled against Salten can be leveled against Vienna, and one might ask: how could a city of refinement and culture participate so enthusiastically in two world wars? How could a city that gave so many rights to its Jewish citizens outdo even Germany in its zealous persecution of them? How could a city promote the best in classical music and at the same time revel in winehouse schmalz? Vienna, like Salten, is full of contradictions and apparent hypocrisies.

Salten made every effort to succeed in Vienna and, when he was depressed, sought refreshment in the forests that encircled it. In these woodlands, his powers of observation gave him full control as a naturalist and hunter, a situation he could never quite replicate in Vienna, where he was sovereign yet vulnerable, first rewarded, and then abandoned by the city that he loved.

In this book, I examine the many facets of Salten's character within its Viennese context and attempt to reconcile the inconsistencies and contradictions that I find there. Wherever possible, I use Salten's own words to describe the influences and events that shaped him and the conflicts in which he became enmeshed, in the belief that the benefits to be gained by study of Salten's own views outweigh the advantages of more sober scholarship. For similar reasons, I will frequently cite statements made by Salten's friends and enemies. All translations from the German are my own unless noted in the endnotes. Similarly, all letters, diaries, and previously unpublished materials cited throughout the work are from the Felix Salten Estate/Lea Wyler Archives in Zurich unless another source is given. This includes typescripts of the letters that Salten wrote to Schnitzler.

All citations from Salten's published writings, his books, essays, and newspaper feuilletons, are identified in the endnotes by title only. Full information as to publishers and dates is given in the final bibliography. This is also true for my other endnote citations.

This book could never have been written without the considerable assistance and encouragement of Salten's granddaughter, Lea Wyler, and the support of her ROKPA International staff in Zurich. Ms. Wyler opened the Salten collections to me and encouraged me at every turn. I owe many others a great debt of gratitude: Gregory Ackermann and Iris Bruce for generously sharing materials with me; Silke Becker and Inga Wagner of the Deutsches Literaturarchiv, Marbach; Dorothy G. Knaus of the Division of Special Collections and University Archives at the University of Oregon; Gotthelf Wiedermann of the Cambridge University Library; B. Stadler of the Staatsarchiv des Kantons Zürich; Wilhelm Urbanek of the District Museum of Alsergrund; Wolf-Erich Eckstein from the records office of the Israeli Religious Community in Vienna; Renate Mercsanits of the Wasa Gymnasium; Gerda Morrissey of the Stefan Zweig collection at SUNY-Fredonia; Scott Daniels of the Oregon Historical Society; and Günter Sellinger of the city archives of Stockerau. I am also grateful to the staff members at the Österreichische Nationalbibliothek (including the Österreichisches Literaturarchiv and Bildarchiv), the Österreichisches Theatermuseum, the Wiener Stadt- und Landesarchiv, the Archives of the Verein für Geschichte der Arbeiterbewegung (in Vienna), the Harry Ransom Center at the University of Texas at Austin, the Lilly Library at the University of Indiana in Bloomington, the Rare Book and Manuscript Library Collections of the University of Pennsylvania, and many individuals, including Evelyn Adunka, Jens Baufeldt, Charlotte Berry, Peter Michael Braunwarth, Barbara Gable, Norbert Goll, Christel Gnirss, Angela Karasch, Hanna Klessinger, Jennie Knox, Joan Links, Walter Pagler, Evelyn Schlag, and Regina Wonisch. I am particularly grateful for the financial support given to me by the Research and Development Committee of Dickinson College and for the moral support of my husband, Truman.

Chapter 1: Family Influences

"I am not a Hungarian,"[1] he wrote, and "I was not a Jew when I was a boy."[2] Felix Salten might well have added, "I am not Sigmund Salzmann."[3] Clearly, he liked to think of himself as his own man, as one who had not only been shaped but who had also constructed himself in his adoptive hometown of Vienna. He was born in Hungary, in Pest, on September 6, 1869, but his family (father Philipp Salzmann and mother Marie née Singer, brothers Emil, Ignaz, and Theodor, and sisters Katherine and Rosalie) moved to Vienna when Salten was just over three weeks old. He grew up in – one could even say with – the imperial city and, as a feuilletonist for the city's leading newspapers, perceived himself to be not only part of that city but also its authentic voice. Salten pointed out, "My parents spoke only German. I went to school in Vienna. And I do not understand the Hungarian language."[4] His lifelong nemesis Karl Kraus continually reminded Salten, however, that his background was both Hungarian and Jewish, and, in truth, Salten paid frequent visits to his father's family in Mischkolcz, capital of the Hungarian county of Borsod, where several generations of the family had been rabbis.

Salten seldom admitted it, but, as important as Vienna was in shaping his personality, his loving but irascible father appears to have been an even greater influence. For, although Salten resisted his father from an early age and escaped the world of business for a life in literature, although he officially changed his name from Sigmund Salzmann to the nom de plume that established his reputation in his adopted city, many of his actions, many of his dreams, seem to have been influenced – both in accord and in revolt – by Philipp Salzmann, a passionate and talented man whose own dreams and actions had been doomed to failure.

In his prime, Philipp Salzmann was a strong, sturdily built man with chestnut hair, a ruddy, pockmarked face, and a trimmed full beard, an exuberant dreamer with endless self-confidence, a hearty laugh, and occasional outbursts of inexplicable temper. Salten was almost overwhelmed by his father's vitality and effusiveness; he was never able to establish a spontaneously loving relationship with him the way his younger brother Géza did. In spite of their differences though, Salten would in later years acknowledge the "enormous impact" of his father's personality and the "indissoluble bond" that united them.[5] Before Salten's birth, Philipp Salzmann had been an engineer with a solid income and a good middle-class home in Budapest, but he had given that up upon his discovery of some apparently rich coal fields and decided to pursue his dream of making a fortune in coal mining. It was this dream, which had already led to his first failure in Hungary, that brought him to Vienna in search of new investors. In October 1869, the family settled into a comfortable apartment in the inner city.

Philipp Salzmann's plan to pursue riches through the mining of coal deposits made sense, although the decision to give up regular employment in pursuit of this dream proved to be his undoing. During this period of industrial expansion, hundreds of middle-class immigrants from the east joined rural workers pouring into Vienna in hopes of improving their financial situations; Jews came in especially high numbers after Vienna granted them full citizenship in 1867. The city was embarking on a big building boom, tearing down the old city fortifications, filling in the old moat, and constructing the Ringstrasse, which became an architectural, albeit somewhat stodgy, showcase consisting of a state opera house, two court museums, a parliament building, a new town hall, a new university, and the new Burgtheater. The city itself was entering a risky period of economic speculation, expanding its borders even while the old Empire was shrinking, embellishing its palaces at the same time it was struggling to pay for two disastrous wars against Prussia and Italy. Men like Salzmann were stimulated by the visible signs of the city's growth and by the promise of future wealth, as new factories were planned for the suburbs with improved and expanded railway lines to service them. It seemed a particularly opportune time to invest in coalmines.

Unfortunately, Philipp Salzmann, like many citizens of Vienna, fell victim to overeager speculation. On May 9, 1873, just nine days after the city opened a grand world exhibition to tout its splendors, the Vienna stock market crashed. Many citizens, including Philipp's investors, lost large portions of their fortunes. The timing of the stock market crash gave the first blow to Philipp's plans but not the final one, for, as it turned out, Philipp's personality was badly suited to the world of business. According to his son, he was both virtuous and gullible, which is a deadly combination in an entrepreneur. He was an enthusiastic salesman, but his enthusiasm led him to enter into risky business dealings, and he was cheated by various business partners over and over again. His son wrote, "He dug again and again, for years, for decades, had to leave off when his investors pulled back peevishly, had to go on the lookout again for new business partners, had to start all over. Three times I saw him collapse in disappointment during all those years, three times I saw him pull himself together and then, as an adult, I watched how this man, beaten down by misfortune, aged and weakened, had to give up just short of his goal."[6] Philipp would, in fact, recover a portion of his lost fortune after Salten was grown and even contribute some money to his children, but this success never altered Salten's lasting impression of his father's having been destroyed by circumstances beyond his control.

Salten was six when his father suffered one of these complete economic collapses, and the family was never able fully to recover. By that time, Salten's younger brother, Géza, had raised the number of children to seven. The Salzmanns had to auction off their furniture and most of their possessions and move into a crowded two-room apartment in the suburb of Währing, in what is now the city's eighteenth district. It was in this setting that Salten's resentment against his father grew, and he began to see his father with ever more critical eyes. Philipp Salzmann did not drink nor did he socialize beyond the family, but Salten faulted him for his constant promises of future wealth and for his unwillingness to let his older sons prepare for careers so that they might assist in contributing to the family income. Instead of enjoying the riches that his father promised, Salten saw only how the family descended deeper and deeper into poverty, and he reacted with shame and anger. He recalled that neither he nor any of his siblings ever received a single book or toy from their father, although Philipp promised that he would more than make up for this neglect when his coalfields started producing. The rebellious son saw how his father was generous to a fault with potential business partners. Philipp never gambled at cards or horses, but his business ventures were just as risky as the gaming table, and they all seemed doomed to failure. Whenever one of his ventures collapsed, he took to his bed for several weeks, then pulled himself together, reiterated the old promises to his family of prosperity to come, and went out to search for new business partners.

As a boy, Salten often reacted to his father's authority with defiant recalcitrance, deliberately ignoring his orders and his rage. Still, his father never struck him; on at least one occasion, after Philipp had recovered from his furious outburst over Salten's refusal to obey him, he tenderly ruffled Salten's hair and called him his "stubborn little *pojazer* (clown)."[7]

As a man, Salten came to appreciate his father's optimism, despite the disappointments that inevitably followed. At Easter in 1918, when all Vienna was suffering hunger and want caused by the First World War, Salten recalled his father's method for cheering the family:

> When, on a high holiday, he was seated with his wife and seven children around the table on which there was nothing to eat, he began to speak about the future, about a splendid future, of course, which most certainly had to come, whose approach was in fact already imminent. He could describe it all in loving detail; he could make plans about how they would furnish the flat, how well off they would be, in such a lively manner that the children also began to bring up all their desires and all their longing.

Philipp's optimism proved contagious. He actively encouraged his children by listening to their wishes and debating the quality and reasonableness of each. Recalling these days, Salten remarked, "I am firmly convinced that one cannot spend a holiday in any better fashion than by thinking about a finer future," adding, "Let us hold to this: this future will surpass all our expectations."[8]

Despite the fact that the men in his family had trained as rabbis for generations, Philipp Salzmann was not a practicing Jew. Instead, he aspired as a European liberal "to a vague pantheism, that was bound by no religious rules or traditions," believing "passionately in the reconciliation of human beings, in the cessation of spitefulness between peoples, in the assimilation of the Jews into the community of nations." He described all church ritual as "outdated nonsense."[9] Salten remembered that he and his siblings said evening prayers but that they hadn't any idea to which god they were praying. Philipp Salzmann did return to the Jewish faith late in his life, but Salten was by then long out of the family home and had already reconciled himself to his Jewish heritage.

In looking back on his father's life, Salten wrote:

> He was altogether passionate, and enthusiasm was the only thing that kept him going .... [H]e hadn't the trace of a businessman in his being. He, who lived in the rosy clouds of illusion, he, the gullible man, the man cheated a hundred times, he, who was cruelly mistreated and misunderstood, was without a homeland in this world. He, whose great loving soul longed to give his wife and his children the gifts of good fortune, was always left facing his family with empty hands.[10]

The most obvious lesson that Salten learned from his father, besides an acquired sense of indomitable optimism, came in response to Philipp Salzmann's negative example. Philipp had "given up safe daily earnings before I was born," Salten remarked. In contrast, "I began, even as a ten-year-old, to honor the regularity of daily work, to consider earned income important, however modest it was, and to hold a stroke of luck and the expectation of a stroke of luck in hostile, fierce contempt." He also learned from Philipp "to meet every failure standing, to look directly into the frightful face of every catastrophe," adding, "never have I been given a wind at my back, never an effortless piece of good luck."[11]

In this last statement, Salten reveals a streak of self-pity that did little to endear him to his colleagues. This was *not* a legacy from his father, although it certainly came about as a result of Salten's poverty-stricken circumstances.

One negative attribute that Salten acquired from his father was a hair-trigger temper, which got him into trouble numerous times, especially during the early part of his career. He had the good sense to hold on to his journalistic work as a source of steady income through most his life but, like his father, sometimes got involved in risky financial endeavors and, again in reaction against his impoverished childhood, was constantly trying to live beyond his means.

Other positive influences that Salten inherited from his father included generosity to friends, a drive to improve his family's living situation, a liberal, cosmopolitan world view, and a genuine religiosity free from all denominational doctrine. But perhaps the most important lesson that Salten learned from his father was survival. Salten suffered verbal attack, slander, and humiliation but continued on his course. He acquired great agility at adapting to circumstances, seeking out new jobs, writing in new and different genres. Although he shared his father's optimistic beliefs in the future, he balanced this optimism with a more realistic point of view. Salten declared that at no time in his life did he understand his father's greatness more than when he and his brothers carried Philipp Salzmann's coffin to the grave in April 1905. "Five sons carried their father, who had had the confidence, the optimism, the courage to bring seven children[12] into the world... He did not conquer existence, that's true. Still, or because of that, he stands in my memory as a touchingly heroic figure. Because in the struggle for existence one needs above all confidence, optimism, and courage."[13]

Whereas Salten's father provided him with personal attributes and tenets, it was the maternal side of the family that gave Salten his first openings to culture. Marie Singer had married Philipp Salzmann when she was eighteen. She and her sister Retti had been raised in a world of music and theater. Marie sang not only the old folk songs but also operatic arias from *Aida*, *Rigoletto*, *Martha*, and *Ernani*. Salten remembered her singing all day long, as she cooked, made beds, darned, and knitted. She also entertained the children by declaiming the great monologues from Schiller, Grillparzer, and Raimund. Her performances were extremely emotional, and when she performed comic dialogues, the children howled with delight. It is quite possible that Salten wrote his short story "Die Mutter der Sängerin" (The Singer's Mother), 1909, in tribute to his mother, since he portrays there a woman held back from a possible singing career by poverty and the demands of her family.

Salten noticed how the family home had a strict patriarchal structure – that his father never listened to the mild suggestions and warnings of his wife and that, as a result, she learned to keep her opinions to herself. She was a slight, slender woman who always wore a gentle smile. Salten said of her, "She was considered a beauty and probably was one, with her high, clear brow, her noble, narrow nose ..., her soft, innocently smiling eyes that were deer-brown in color."[14] She wore her jet-black hair in braids wound tightly around her head. Salten noted that she was the realist in the family and that her dramatic flair for parody delighted her husband. Salten felt that, by parodying others and in making embarrassingly frank comments to guests, his mother was seeking an outlet for her frustration over her husband's irresponsible business ventures. If this is true, Philipp Salzmann never noticed it. She always deferred to his opinion, and he, in turn, showered her with praise. Philipp loved his wife "like a bridegroom and a little in the fashion of a troubadour." He declared that she had a "silver face, [whose] light brings joy into my life." He called her "You lovely kindness"and "You fulfillment of my dreams." Salten said he was especially pleased when Philipp called her "You soul of my soul."[15]

In spite of this obvious love, in spite of the fact that Salten's parents had "an unusually happy marriage," Salten always had a guilty conscience towards his mother, who endured so much and grew old so quietly. Salten wrote:

> How often, as a grown man, have I rocked this tiny, tender, fragile woman consolingly on my knees, just like a child. And like a child, she laid her head on my shoulder to cry. This woman, who had such a joyful heart, who had so much talent for happiness, was silenced and made a patient sufferer by a merciless fate. And she wept as fervently, as softly and devastatingly, as she once had so charmingly laughed.[16]

Salten himself was a little slow to develop real empathy for the suffering of others, but such empathy was perhaps his greatest legacy from his long-suffering mother.

Marie's sister, Retti, never allowed herself to be defeated by her fate, and she always remained a bright presence in Salten's memory. She and her husband, Romeo Lamberg, were among the family's closest friends in Vienna and, for a brief period, Retti and the Lamberg son shared the Salzmanns' living quarters. Uncle Romi, with his long white sideburns and beard, was not particularly child-friendly, and Salten interacted with him rarely. Retti Lamberg, however, was a "radiant woman" to the young Salten, and he preserved a vivid memory of her holding him in her arms and bending down to sing to him the coda of a Strauss waltz. "What magical laughter this woman had," Salten exclaimed, "how talented she was at picking herself up when being kicked by a gruesome fate, to give herself over to raucous joy with us children and to awaken loud rejoicing all around her. She could tell stories tirelessly, carried away by the force of her fantasy, by the intensity of her memories, by the power of her still active hopes."[17]

Ironically, some time before Salten's birth, the Lambergs had suffered a greater financial ruin than Salten's family had. Uncle Romi had owned a large villa in the Viennese suburb of Baden and had had servants, horses, and a coachman until he embarked on a futile lawsuit against Baron Nopesa, the Empress Elisabeth's powerful court chamberlain. The suit dragged on for years until the Lambergs lost all that they had and were reduced to living in a two-room apartment in Währing, within easy walking distance of the Salzmann home. Salten saw a distinction in the living conditions of the two families, however, demonstrated by the closed door to the Lambergs' building. The Salzmanns lived in a noisy proletarian building, where the door to the street was always open, but Aunt Retti and her son lodged in a home of the petty bourgeoisie, where privacy and quiet manners were still the norm. One of the Lambergs' neighbors was the elderly niece of the opera composer Albert Lortzing. Salten noted how this impoverished spinster maintained elegance in dress and manner and wrote that she taught him to do the same, without regard to his financial circumstances. Aunt Retti also preserved the elegance of her earlier days: "She retained the airs and the free superiority conferred by opulent wealth, even in the long years of her hopeless misfortune. And she possessed great inner nobility and the rich and pure soul of a girl, assets which she would not allow to be taken from her, however hard her fate."[18] With her encouragement, Salten adopted similar airs.

After Uncle Romi's death – Salten was nine at the time – the Lamberg home became Salten's favored retreat from family cares. Aunt Retti retained her innocent enthusiasm and good humor even after her husband's death by focusing her loving attention on their only child, Josef. Josef Lamberg was eighteen years older than Salten; he was "ravishingly beautiful, in spite of the fact that he had lost an eye as a boy and wore a black eye patch." He made a living as a piano teacher and was also the composer of many lieder, a cantata, and a string quartet. Salten always maintained that if his cousin "had, in wise modesty, decided to write operetta music, he would have become as rich as he was poor in his old age." He and his mother lived in their small apartment in perfect harmony. They laughed and joked constantly with one another and shared their confidence in better days to come. Salten spent many happy hours in this house of music, calling them "the richest hours, the happiest days" of his childhood.[19] While Josef played, his mother busied herself in the kitchen, preparing small treats for the boys, keeping her son's clothes neat and clean. Josef would call to her when he had written a new composition and she would hurry in to the piano to listen and admire, and when Josef was absent, she and Salten would sing Josef's compositions together.

The hours spent with the Lambergs were decisive for Salten. Here he heard a true artist play the great piano repertoire: Beethoven's piano sonatas, the symphonic studies of Schumann, Handel's air and variations, and Schubert's German dances. But, Salten said, there was more: "Not just the classical piano literature, but also, later, whenever my memory returned to the room ringing with music and wafting with carefree, easy talent, and to Aunt Retti and her handsome son, I finally understood how great artistry can be wasted and how an incomparable maternal devotion helps one to overcome even that."[20]

The young Salten had a fine singing voice and enjoyed singing with his mother, with his Aunt Retti, and with his siblings. The Salzmanns used music as an opiate to help them forget the gnawing hunger that so often plagued them. Looking back years later, Salten wrote, "I remember the narrow, impoverished parlor of my childhood, crowded full with my siblings, with male and female friends, reverberating with song, and through song freed from the bitter poverty that otherwise filled the house."[21] This was, Salten felt, uniquely characteristic of Vienna, where song and chamber music filled the rooms of rich and poor alike.

The Salzmanns needed the solace of music in their home, for their difficulties were not only financial. Salten's brother Theodor was mentally retarded, and, although he was a remarkably cheerful and loving child, he was a burden because of his inability to master even the alphabet at school.[22] The family suffered a worse misfortune when Salten turned thirteen – one that permanently banished music from the Salzmann home. Like Salten, his sister Katherine had nurtured some resentment towards her father because of the family's poverty. She, who "had a deep heart, rich in understanding," who was "peculiar, of strong character and, despite all her reserve, still incredibly kind and sometimes tender as well," was studying to be a teacher, but in February 1883, in her eighteenth year, she took to her bed with tuberculosis and in August she died. "She fell," Salten wrote, "as victim of her sleepless nights of work, as the first victim of the miserable conditions that prevailed in our paternal household." [23]

Salten's parents did little to alleviate their children's anguish over this calamity. Philipp disappeared from the house completely and didn't return until after his daughter had died. Marie suffered a complete collapse shortly before Katherine's death, and for a time the children were convinced that they would be losing their mother as well as their sister. Marie managed to pull herself together, however, and to return to watch at her daughter's bedside. But her attitude had changed; Katherine's death was proof to Marie that the family's misery was irreversible and that better days were not around the corner, as Philipp had so often promised. Although she would learn to laugh once more, Marie never sang again. The hole created by Katherine's death made an irreparable rupture in the family unit. Even sweet-tempered Theodor left the family for a time to try, without success, to become a butcher's apprentice. Young Salten, who was already having difficulties at school, now spent more time at the free library, escaping drab reality by fleeing into the world of literature. And he learned, for the first time, what it meant to be a Jew in Vienna.

Chapter 2: Environmental Influences

Salten's earliest memories stretched back to his comfortably bourgeois home in Alsergrund, Vienna's ninth district. This district was still developing when, in 1872, the Salzmann family moved there from Taubengasse, in the inner city.[1] It was a popular area for liberal Jewish families and, after Leopoldstadt, housed the city's second largest concentration of Jewish citizens. Numerous hospitals had long been located here, but most of the district's living quarters were only being built at the time of the Salzmanns' arrival. Elegant apartment buildings were being constructed close to the city Ring, while new construction further out towards the city Belt (the Währinger Gürtel) housed those of lower social standing.

The Salzmanns lived in a newly built apartment building at what is now Wasagasse 18;[2] Salten remembered their having fashionably dark mahogany furniture in their spacious dining room and enjoying the services of a cook, a chambermaid, and a rather dour nursemaid. Alsergrund bordered directly on the city's first district, and the family had easy access to its shops and to its cultural offerings either by foot or by taking the public horse tram that departed from Alsergrund's Votive Church to circle around the Ring, past all the new state buildings that were being erected during the 1870s and 1880s and were growing even as he was. For Salten "these gigantic structures that were forming, this incomprehensibly slow progress, this scarcely noticeable growth" were "unforgettable like all impressions from earliest childhood."[3] He retained especially vivid memories of going with his mother and sisters to concerts in the Volkspark that were directed by Johann Strauss's somewhat theatrical brother Eduard. Salten delighted in jumping up close to the conductor and mimicking his every move, much to Strauss's annoyance and to the amusement of the crowds. Young Salten was unself-conscious and outgoing with no fear of expressing either his delight or his annoyance with strangers, thereby revealing early on a critic's disregard for public approval. He behaved badly towards two members of royalty who were friendly towards him but became good friends with an elderly woman who attended these concerts and visited her often in her home. His stubborn disapproval of her manner of knitting, her placement of pictures, and her refusal to allow him to try to play upon a miniature horn might, he said, have led to the end of their friendship. This breakup was doubtless expedited by Philipp Salzmann's 1876 bankruptcy and the family's forced move to the Vienna suburbs.

For Salten the move out beyond Vienna's city borders was a sudden but not cataclysmic event, despite the fact that the nurse-maid, cook, and chambermaid were let go and most of the family furniture was sold. The Salzmanns moved into a crowded apartment in Theresiengasse[4] in the Viennese suburb of Währing, where the sudden squalor of the family's living conditions provided a sharp contrast to the bourgeois comforts they had known. As Salten put it, "In Währing we had no cook, for there was only rarely something to cook. A dining room too was unnecessary because often we simply couldn't get anything to eat. It was a real calamity, a complete plunge into the depths." Still, the young Salten seems to have been impressed most by the novelty of his new life; his sense of family shame developed later, "when I turned ten, twelve, fourteen years old and learned how bitter poverty tastes."[5]

Salten's childhood recollections of Währing were contradictory: he saw it both as a rural paradise and as a crowded proletarian ghetto. This was a time when large apartment buildings – Miets-kasernen – were replacing the shabby one-story homes scattered throughout the district, and both kinds of housing could be found in close proximity. In one of his many newspaper articles, he portrayed this suburb as a garden of paradise, writing:

> [Währing] lay outside [Vienna], before the solid walls of stone behind which the city was entrenched, and began only a good piece behind the enormous wooden gate with which one could close off the old "defense line." From the city side [Währing] could be reached only through the single escape hatch that this line left open. I clearly remember the country lane that began behind the tollgate and led homeward. [There were] fields and meadows everywhere. And on the other side of them stood the first houses of Währing, like good acquaintances with friendly faces. From the bright streets one quickly came into the open air everywhere. A few steps away from the church, up the

old Neugasse, past the half-dozen "cottage" villas that people still enjoyed mocking, and you were on the Turkish entrenchment [*Türkenschanze*], could stroll through high-growing crops, through vineyards and fallow fields … and simply be in the country. And all of Währing was a small, half-rural community.[6]

With its mix of rural countryside, English-style estates, and poor working-class dwellings, Währing was a world apart from Vienna proper, but for the young Salten, it held greater charms than the city, and throughout his life he was never able to recall the district without waxing nostalgic for the open fields and the gently rising woodlands that led through Pötzleinsdorf up into the Vienna Woods. For if Salten had, during the first six years of life, been oriented towards the entertainments of the city, his new orientation was to the nature that lay beyond it. This was the Vienna of Franz Schubert, and Salten, his mother, and his siblings often sang the songs from Schubert's *Die schöne Müllerin*, songs that were a paean to the bliss of nature and the joys of domestic life. During their first years in Währing, everyone in Salten's family retained Philipp Salzmann's strong sense of invulnerable optimism, and they clung together as a strong family unit, even in their greatly reduced circumstances.

Young Salten set out to explore his new environment with enthusiasm. He ran through the narrow streets, peeked into windows, and inhaled the smells of horse stalls, tanneries, and breweries. One of his favorite spots was the pub Zum Bierfach, where Schubert had once, on a dare, written a song upon the tavern menu. Young Salten sneaked into the garden of this pub to sit in the shade of its chestnut and linden trees and to the door of the restaurant to gaze adoringly at the two daughters of the pub owner, who, at twelve and fifteen, were "much, much older than I," and were his first unrequited loves. Despite their double chins, he wrote, "I considered them the most perfect, most wonderful feminine creatures in the whole world. Whenever I saw them, my pulse began to hammer away; I felt that I was a miserable being, not worthy even to breathe in the presence of such ideal figures." Since the Salzmann family frequently had to go hungry, the odors of "roasts, cakes, and strudel" that poured out from the pub kitchen undoubtedly lent the young girls additional charms.[7]

But Salten also got to know another, more sordid side of Währing. The town was filled with people whose behavior puzzled and confused him. His family lived in a noisy and crowded apartment house, not in a rural cottage. It was one of the many three- and four-story structures built in the proletarian suburbs; like these, it had an elegant facade that mimicked the fashionable houses of the inner suburbs, but it had none of their interior amenities. It was filled with tiny, overcrowded apartments; the walls were badly insulated, and one could hear neighbors' angry rows and drunken laughter. On his way to and from school, Salten was often a witness to cruel behavior and to passive suffering. He looked through a cellar window to see a loutish father reach into a crib to strike a crying infant, then turn away with a "tormented, guilt-ridden expression." He saw a pretty maid beaten by her woman employer while the neighbors watched and laughed. For the first time, he saw grown men raise their fists and fight each other.

An observatory was being built in the town's Cottage district, and Salten was often the beneficiary of bread given to him by an elderly couple who lived in a small hut on the property. One morning the two were found murdered. Young Salten did not fully understand or mourn their deaths but regarded them instead as "something interesting and mysterious."[8] At about the same period, he pushed through a crowd of bystanders to see the bloody victim of another killing. Again, he was more interested in than horrified by the sight. The murderers were never found.

When he was several years older, however, young Salten not only saw a murder in progress, he even knew the killer. He had been accustomed to visit the Währing market on his way home from school and became acquainted with a butcher's helper named Leopold, a jovial young man much loved for his joking with the women vendors. One day, however, Salten saw Leopold fly into a rage against the butcher, lift an axe, and forcefully strike the older man between his shoulders. At that point, Salten recalled, Leopold "stood there, half insane, perhaps in this moment even completely insane. His anger had gone, his power faded. Every drop of blood was wiped from his face. [He was] a despairing, a destroyed man. He began to run." Salten remarked about this and about his earlier experiences with abuse and suffering, "Today I have, of course, long been aware that all these events were really not important. [They were] small local events such as occur daily and hourly in every city." To the schoolboy, however, the murder on the market-place was extremely shocking and "caused me to lose the light-hearted cheerfulness … that had filled me until then."[9]

At about the same time, young Salten encountered a neighbor-hood bully who enjoyed cuffing and tormenting him whenever he saw the smaller boy out by himself on the street. One day, how-ever, "something snapped," and Salten turned on his tormenter and fought him furiously until he had him on the ground and was able to beat him "unmercifully." From that day on, he stated, he was conscious of his own power.[10]

Salten found a perfect refuge from the pent-up anger of the working classes in the site of the Turkish entrenchments that lay just outside of town: "The Türkenschanze was quite near. … At that time everything was open fields, vineyards, and sand pits." Sal-ten heard his first larks there: "I lay there in the grass for hours, looking up at the tiny speck high in the blue ether. This small heart up there in the air, the small throat, which poured down melodi-ousness, tunefulness, and jubilant joie de vivre, was a great miracle to me; it had the power to make me happy and to move me to tears."[11] He and his friends played around the old powder houses and, in exploring the recently excavated mass grave of Turkish sol-diers from the second Turkish occupation, he found numerous relics – buckles and crescent pins – that he carried home as treas-ures.

In late August of every year, soldiers were sent to Währing to conduct maneuvers on the Türkenschanze. They were housed with families in town, and young Salten rushed out each morning to watch their maneuvers:

> I ran breathlessly back and forth between the divisions so as not to miss anything …. The color-ful uniforms in the green field, the white bands on the caps of the "enemy," the gold bands of the of-ficers, the flashing of the swords, trumpet signals, roll of drums, shouts of orders, now and then a horseman galloping up so that clods of earth flew

under the horse's hooves, and then the shooting,
the firing of weapons that lashed at our nerves,
the fumes of powder, blue and gray, that lingered
in heavy clouds upon the fields.

Perhaps the greatest joy was lying in bed at night and listening
to the sound of a horn playing the military curfew:

> This energetic, slightly melancholic tune
> moved me; it excited and calmed me at the same
> time. That it is Austrian in its deepest coloration,
> in its innermost nature, was something I did not
> yet understand. But later certain verses by Eichen-
> dorff or Lenau awakened in me quite involuntarily
> the memory of those childhood evenings when,
> before falling asleep, I listened to the flugelhorn
> blow curfew, first from far away, then ever closer,
> finally fading off into the distance again. ... Schu-
> bert and Eichendorff, Lenau and Lanner, or Jo-
> hann Strauss, still other voices of this place and
> voices that received a breath of inspiration from
> this place, conjure up all by themselves this piece
> of earth on which I was a child.[12]

The landscape around Währing was indeed drenched in music,
and it was here that the young Salten acquired his identity as an
Austrian. As a boy he often ran past Josef Lanner's birthplace and
past Schubert's and Beethoven's overgrown graves in the old
Währing cemetery. He was about seven or eight when he first met
the composer Anton Bruckner out by the Schottentor; they sometimes took walks together and Salten even went with him to the
Ausgustiner church to hear a Bruckner mass without suspecting
that this friendly older man was its composer nor that, when he left
Salten for the duration of the concert, he was the man who was
playing the church organ. Salten listened to the performances of
street musicians, heard music pouring out of open windows and
restaurant gardens on warm summer evenings, and until the dark
days following his sister's death, his own home rang with music as
well. As his cousin Josef Lamberg would point out to him many

years later:

> A Beethoven, a Brahms had to come to Vienna because of those mysterious seeds which fill the air here and which seem to wait simply to fall into the soul of an artist in order to emerge from it again as those immortal works which make its masters so infinitely endearing. You can settle wherever you wish, because *you* [sic] are full of these seeds. You have inhaled them from your childhood right up into your maturity, and exile cannot prevent them from bursting into bloom.[13]

The move from Alsergrund to Währing had taken Salten out of a predominantly Jewish culture and into a predominantly Catholic one. Since Philipp Salzmann's cosmopolitan views never dictated religious doctrine, his wife, Marie, made an arrangement with the authorities at the Währing Volksschule (elementary school) that Salten, the only Jew in his class, be allowed to participate in catechism lessons. Young Salten, grandson of a rabbi, became an enthusiastic student of the Catholic faith, won prizes for his mastery of the catechism, collected cards of saints' pictures, and attended Sunday services at Währing's St. Gertrude's church, where he sang Schubert's *German Mass* as part of the student boys' choir. It was only after four years of diligent study of Catholic doctrine that Salten learned that he was shut out from full participation in the Catholic faith:

> In the fourth grade, when the boys who were considered mature enough were chosen to go to confession and communion, the priest selected me as well. But the schoolmaster turned red [and] whispered something softly into the priest's ear, whereupon the priest stroked my hair and said in a friendly way, "Well… perhaps another time." With that, I was sent back to my seat.
>
> "Another time" never came. Small as I was, I did not suspect that in that second I had been sent back to my Jewish roots.[14]

In spite of this rejection, Salten continued to attend church services and throughout his life found comfort in reciting the words of the Catholic rosary. He generally got along well with his classmates; like most boys he participated in the occasional schoolyard fight, where he compensated in spirit for slightness in stature. He also began to take notice of the fairer sex. Some of his early crushes were merely an idealization of feminine beauty, such as his crush on the beautiful blond woman who lived with her husband in the apartment next to his. One early love went unspoken: on his way home from the Hernals Gymnasium (secondary school), Salten passed a little girl each day in the street. They exchanged smiles at each meeting, but no words ever passed between them. "She was a small, poorly dressed girl, perhaps eleven years old," Salten recalled. She "had her brown braids wound tightly around her head and, with her somewhat broad facial features and her large, soft, dark eyes, resembled a child saint."[15] Because they never spoke, Salten never knew her name, but he created his own name for her, Veronica, because that was the name of the street (Veronikagasse) on which he always met her. One day, however, she was gone, and Salten never saw her again. One can reasonably assume that the sudden disappearance of this innocent young girl led to speculation on Salten's part, and that his memory of "Little Veronica" inspired the 1903 novella that bears her name.

During his early years at the Hernals Gymnasium, now known as the Hernalser Gymnasium Geblergasse, Salten was still an innocent, as demonstrated by his reaction to the obvious affection shown him by a pretty young chambermaid who served in an apartment on the first floor of his building. One day when she was alone in the apartment, she called Salten in, took him to her room, cradled him in her arms, and began to kiss him. "Strong resistance stirred within me. No! I wasn't such a little baby as that!" He fought with her until she released him and pushed him petulantly out of the apartment. Some time later, she left her service in the apartment building and she too vanished from Salten's life. His interests turned from girls to handiwork and to poetry. He delighted in working with a fretsaw, trying to build pipe stands and watch holders, but despite this newfound passion, "I didn't achieve anything except that I got swollen eyes and a bad cough from the wood dust."[16]

Adolescence was a difficult period for Salten. Not only was he increasingly affected by the family's poverty, but he was oppressed by passions and cruelties he did not fully understand:

> I didn't wander around the streets of Währing any more, thirsting for adventures and addicted to people. Now the lonely hikes began: to the wilderness of the Krotten Brook, to the Wallriess trenches, to the Pötzleinsdorf Woods, to the hillside meadows of Schafsberg. And soon came my first poems, my first novellas, and my first "Observations," for which I must forgive myself with the same smile with which I forgive other childish impertinences.[17]

Salten was becoming increasingly aware of his Jewishness: "For a while I remained a pious Catholic. But at the grammar school it quickly became clear to me that I am Jewish." The gymnasium was a "proletarian gymnasium"; a later pupil at the school, Eugen Hoeflich (Ben-gavriêl), recalled how unfair it seemed to him "that the powerful Christian majority of pupils [there] crusaded against the laughably small heap of Jews."[18] Salten claimed that his detachment from Christianity occurred "without any severe crises,"[19] but his unpublished memoirs suggest differently. There he recalled a school chum who tore his pants on his way to school and, to escape his father's beating, told the school director that Salten had caused the accident by deliberately tripping him and causing him to fall. As Salten remembered it:

> When I brought forth evidence to protest that this was a lie, [the school director] looked at me disdainfully and said, "Faced with the decision whom to believe, you or the son of the district judge, I don't hesitate for a moment." He didn't hesitate for a moment, either, to declare me a shameless liar and to sentence me to sixteen hours of detention. My father was supposed to approve

this judgment and confirm my lying nature. My father knew that I was not capable of lying, but he also knew about the position of a Jewish child in society and so, with a pained smile, gave me the required signature.

But the claim that I was a liar stuck to me at school.

When other teachers began, rather routinely, to refer to Salten as a liar, his parents felt it necessary to transfer him and his younger brother Géza to the Wasagymnasium, where half his class was Jewish. The damage, however, had been done. Salten had already lost his "illusions from the nice times in elementary school" and had become "a real devil and a wild ruffian." [20] It did not help that he was forced to repeat a grade. The teachers "embittered and demoralized" him. Of one he wrote that he never observed in this teacher "a single action that rose above the freezing point" but witnessed instead "an outbreak of anger that verged on uncontrolled rage and completely swept away one unhappy classmate from the school, as well." His German teacher "understood the subject that he was supposed to teach only very unsatisfactorily" but "understood superbly how to humiliate somebody with biting sarcasm." This teacher caused Salten's mother great consternation when he told her that her son had a "depraved nature." [21]

The final straw for Salten came when a Latin teacher misgraded Salten's paper, and, when Salten protested, accused him of having cheated by correcting the error after the fact. This was a repetition of the false accusation Salten had endured at the Hernals school, and "there was no appeal, there was no way to prove the truth, no possibility of clearing myself." Many years later, Salten would recall that moment and "the horrible, feverish feeling that was a mixture of pallid fear, rebellion, hurt, burning shame, and powerlessness," adding that the only thing the school ever gave him was a deep distrust of justice and of human kindness. [22] He published a number of articles critical of the teaching methods of his day and spoke out on behalf of schoolchildren's demands for less authoritarian and more relevant instruction. Stefan Zweig, who attended the Wasagymnasium several years after the Salzmann boys' departure, apparently shared Salten's views in this regard when he wrote, "We felt instinctively that there was nothing more of importance to be learned from [the school] and that in many of the subjects which interested us we knew more than our poor teachers."[23] Neither Salten nor his brother Géza were outstanding pupils, and both were frequently absent from their classes. They did not remain in the school for long. Salten later told his daughter that they "couldn't go to school any more because [we] had no shoes,"[24] explaining that, because they had only one pair between them, they could attend classes only on alternate days. Although the story of the shoes may be somewhat exaggerated, a number of disastrous events had indeed converged within the twelve-month period that preceded their departure from the school. On the home front, their sister Katherine had died, family finances had worsened, and the Salzmanns had been evicted from their apartment and were moving from one cheap hotel to another. Salten recalled that, after leaving the Wasagymnasium, "Without supervision, without school, I was in danger of going completely to the dogs. I was kept on track by reading the classics in a free library."[25] He began work on a novel: "I began writing a book, but hid this bold undertaking from my parents and siblings as if it were a misdeed (which it really was)."[26]

For a brief period, Salten took to visiting the dissecting rooms in the morgue of the city's large Allgemeines Krankenhaus (General Hospital). There he would slip through the halls and study both the fresh and the dissected corpses that were on display. Later in life he would suppress most of these images. Those that remained always created in him "the same cold dread as before." In trying to analyze his behavior at that time, Salten noted that "it is probably the horror and the resistance that I wished to muster up against this horror that drove me to seek out such a sight."[27]

Salten's father now found it necessary to allow his children to find jobs and help support the family. Philipp's oldest son, Michael Emil, found work in the insurance field, probably with the assistance of a distant cousin of Philipp's, who was named Moskovic and served as director of the Phoenix Insurance Company. In addition, Salten went to Moskovic's office once a month to receive a small dole of money as his contribution to the family income. Then, as soon as he turned sixteen, Moskovic hired him as a policy

writer. Now Salten continued leading the double life he had begun
at school: performing the daily drudgery of office work by day and
exploring Vienna's inner city at night.[28] Parts of Salten's short story
"Die Wiener Straße" doubtless refer to this period in his life, when
he rebelled against his family's poverty by rubbing shoulders with
the wealthy:

> I have observed that it was through these
> walks in these young years that many characteris-
> tics were developed in me. The Burgplatz (Castle
> Square), for example, Graben, Kohlmarkt [streets],
> there I gradually got a sense for manners, quite in-
> voluntarily, an inclination toward better modes of
> living, and a certain sensitivity regarding ordinari-
> ness and tastelessness. ... When I had left my of-
> fice and eaten, I ran into the city to see the spar-
> kling life there. ... My joy in luxury was awakened
> more and more each day. And I needed only to go
> walking to enjoy this luxury.[29]

The manners that Salten acquired in the city streets were dictated, in part, by the actors of the city's venerable Burgtheater. As
his younger colleague, Stefan Zweig, remarked:

> In the court actor the spectator saw an excel-
> lent example of how one ought to dress, how to
> walk into a room, how to converse, which words
> one might employ as a man of good taste and
> which to avoid. The stage, instead of being merely
> a place of entertainment, was a spoken and plastic
> guide of good behavior and correct pronuncia-
> tion.[30]

By buying the cheapest tickets, Salten was able to watch performances from the gallery of the old Burgtheater, where he saw all
the great performers of the day; he even acquired an autograph
from the great actress Charlotte Wolter, which he kept throughout
his life as a treasured souvenir. In addition to the theater, Salten
went to free concerts and art exhibits. In this manner he continued

his autodidactic education and developed a passionate interest in the city's newest cultural trends. And he soon made the first important friendships with other would-be poets.

Chapter 3: Man about Town

The insurance business proved to be the salvation of the Salzmann family. Salten and his oldest brother, Emil, now provided the family with its first stable income, and it was they who enabled the family to end at last its move from hotel to hotel and, in 1888, to establish a more permanent residence in Alsergrund at Stroheckgasse 13.[1] They were joined for a time by a cousin, Hugo Salzmann, who was also employed at Phoenix.

By now the Salzmann brothers had acquired a deep love for the arts. Emil had a special fondness for music, while the youngest brother, Géza, was more interested in sculpture. Ignaz, like Salten, favored literature and had pretensions to being a poet. According to Salten, Ignaz was the reason for his adoption of a pseudonym for his own literary endeavors. Ignaz "created verses quite in the manner of Heine, witty and ironical, which he read aloud at home, whereupon he was celebrated by the family as a genius." Salten, who found this effusive praise repugnant, began writing under the name "Felix Salten" "in order to hide from my relatives."[2]

This story may be true, but it was also extremely common at the time for poets – especially Jews – to adopt pseudonyms.[3] Salten was probably inspired in part by a friend, another ambitious young poet named Felix Biedermann, who adopted the pseudonym Felix Dörmann before going into print. The two met when they were in their midteens. At the time, Salten had a schoolboy crush on a young girl named Mizzi von Stankowitz, and one evening, when he went to her home, he saw her standing at the window with a young man "with large eyes and a mouth twisted with mockery." His jealousy faded quickly when he learned that Felix Dörmann was Mizzi's cousin and that he, despite their proximity in age, "seemed to be far beyond this [Salten's] kind of platonic idolization." Salten admired his worldliness and recalled that Dörmann soon "acquired so much influence over me that I soon forgot the path to Mizzi's in Kreuzgasse and sat for many hours with Dörmann in his apartment."[4]

Because he had lost his father when he was a small boy, Dörmann was not much better off financially than Salten was, although he did manage to complete a semester at the University of Vienna, where he enrolled in courses in French, English, and Indian religions.[5] Both Dörmann and Salten published their first poems in a journal entitled *An der schönen blauen Donau*. This was the first of the new literary journals willing to give its pages over to a rising generation of promising Austrian writers, and it did so without espousing a single literary program, as some later journals were to do. From 1886 through 1889, Dr. Paul Goldmann headed the biweekly journal in collaboration with his uncle, Fedor Mamroth. Goldmann was himself a young man, having assumed codirectorship of the journal when he was twenty-one years old. It was thus only natural that he would become the discoverer of new talent by encouraging writers of his own generation.

Salten beat Dörmann by getting his first poem into print in 1888, with three more appearing the following year. These poems, with the titles "Ohne Wunsch?" (Without Desire?), "Wann ruht der Geist?" (When Does the Mind Rest?), "Resignation," and "Der Unbesiegbare!" (The Unconquerable!), are rather undistinguished efforts, more aphoristic than lyrical, although their content says a good deal about Salten's moral attitude as a teenager toward the transitory nature of pleasure and the limitations of the ambitious mind. His "Ohne Wunsch?" is, in fact, an elaboration of Faust's wager with Mephistopheles that the Devil might have him if he should say of any pleasurable moment, "Please stay, you are so wonderful!"[6] Salten elaborated on the claim that complete pleasure is impossible, observing:

> You wish for only a few minutes
> To find complete contentment?
> ...
> The hesitant wish 'Oh, that it might remain so!'
> Can never be avoided.[7]

Similarly, in "Wann ruht der Geist?" his restless spirit ponders the unanswerable question,

> When does the mind rest, does it rest with you in the grave?
> Does it move on alone into a better land?

After resigning himself to the fact that moments of delight fade: "Oh, do not hope for a return / Of that which once caused your breast to swell,"[8] he reflects that even when "The mind ... has with splendor grasped / That which may happen eons from now – / It can never control its own fate of the very next day."[9] A fifth poem, published in 1890 to honor the sixtieth birthday of the Austrian prose artist Marie von Ebner-Eschenbach, is most remarkable for the fact that, through his praise in this poem of Ebner-Eschenbach's "truth transfigured by art,"[10] Salten won the honor of meeting the distinguished writer and receiving her personal thanks for his poetic tribute.

Although Salten beat Dörmann by two years in getting a poem into print, Dörmann quickly overtook him as the dominant poet. 1890 was, in fact, a breakthrough year for both young writers: Dörmann wrote the verses that were published in the volume *Neurotica*, making his name as the "official" poet of the Young Vienna group of writers [*Jung-Wien*], while Salten, quietly and unknowingly, revealed his strength as a writer of animal tales.

Salten's first published piece of prose fiction, "Der Vagabund, eine Hundegeschichte" (The Vagabond, a Dog's Story), tells of an apparently homeless dachshund that the narrator adopts on a holiday in Graz. This light tale, in which the narrator's wife tells him from the very beginning that the dog is untrainable, reveals not only Salten's remarkable powers of observation but also his strong empathy with animals. When, for example, the narrator asks the dog how it can find pleasure rolling in the dirt, the dog "calmly raised his head and looked at me – all the while wagging his tail rhythmically – ... as if he wanted me to understand that precisely *that* was a special enjoyment that I could not understand."[11] Because of this attitude, the dog resists baths until it is clear that he cannot get away; Salten anthropomorphizes the dog as he describes its behavior:

> And how he submitted! With the stoic calm with which the ancient Romans covered themselves with their togas as they awaited death. Without moving, he ... let himself be soaped, rubbed, scrubbed, and dipped – he didn't make the slightest effort to escape my hands. With an endlessly resigned expression, he accepted the showers and rinses that were given him, and when I dried him off and laid him on the floor wrapped in towels, all the while speaking to him encourag-

ingly, he stared apathetically into space.[12]

When the narrator tells the dog that he will be returning with him to Vienna, where he will have to learn city manners, "Daki lowered his head so that his long ears fell forward and stared thoughtfully at the floor." Finally, when the dog is able to, he escapes: "like some mad creature, the lackadaisical Daki was already galloping away in the far distance. With his short legs, he seemed by every leap from the pavement to bound up like a rubber ball; ... his back was bent into a half circle – thus he flew off, far away, and I soon lost him from view." [13]

Salten was already a passionate dog lover and kept both a pet dachshund and a hunting dog for most of his life. He would return many times to the empathetic portrayal of dogs, most notably in *Der Hund von Florenz* (The Hound of Florence), which he first conceived soon after the turn of the century but did not publish until 1923. During all these years, Salten identified himself – as did the hero of the novel – with the dog in this evolving tale.

It was perhaps Salten's dog that first attracted the attention of the young doctor Arthur Schnitzler when the two would-be writers met in Paul Goldmann's office in late 1890. Like Salten, Schnitzler brought his first pieces to Goldmann; to protect his medical position, he signed them "Anatol." Schnitzler, a handsome man with striking blue eyes and reddish hair and beard, remembered their meeting this way: "As I [was] visiting Paul Goldmann in the editorial office of the *Blue Danube*, I [met] a very young, slender man with whiskers in a rather old Viennese style, with a hunting dog named Hex at his feet. An animated conversation soon [developed ...]."[14]

Salten was slightly shorter than Schnitzler, with a round, beardless face that served to emphasize his appearance of youthfulness. He was taken at once with Schnitzler, seeing in him, "a young man whose radiant beauty, heightened by an indescribable expression of mental power and human goodness, captivated me immediately. ... We went away together and our friendship began from that day."[15] Just as instant attraction had drawn Salten to Dörmann, he was now drawn to Schnitzler: "Schnitzler's free manner of speaking about God and the world, which frequently tended to mockery, was foreign to me and captivated me at once. The fact that Schnitzler was seven years older than I made a tremendous difference at that time. He was mature, experienced, and in addition held a socially and materially privileged position."[16]

Schnitzler, who appears to have been attracted by the younger man's open admiration of him, by his ambitious drive, and by his entertaining discourse, quickly made Salten his confidant. Theirs was a friendship that would be frequently tested and often strained, but never broken. Particularly during the early years of their friendship, Schnitzler's secure financial situation as assistant to his father in the Vienna Polyclinic Hospital enabled him to come frequently to Salten's rescue with small loans – and Salten was often in financial difficulties, covering, as he was, not only his own expenses but often those of his family as well. In the fall of 1890, he was holding essentially two jobs: continuing his full-time job in the Phoenix Insurance Company while also working as chief literary critic for the *Allgemeine Kunst-Chronik*, an "Illustrated Journal for Art, Handcrafts, Music, Literature, and Theater," published by Dr. Wilhelm Lauser, a distinguished cultural historian and editor of the daily newspaper *Neues Wiener Tagblatt*. One of Salten's new friends from this period, the poet Richard Specht, has preserved a picture of Salten as a young man "who, with impetuous energy, was just breaking into this [literary] world and taking hold of everything, work, people, books, never to let them go, eager to learn and fertile at the same time, always ready to enter the battle with life and always strong enough to bring it to its knees."[17] Salten was very much a young man of action, and saw the world as one "of struggle, of storms and regeneration." "Not 'let us therefore drink' but rather 'let us therefore fight, help – act!' is the watchword," he cried.[18]

Salten's own willingness to help had already led him into a previously unknown world of drugs and addictive sex. Apparently impressed by the young man's ambition and reliability, a wealthy man named Moritz Schwarz hired Salten to help his son Karl withdraw from his morphine addiction by controlling his injections. Despite his parents' reservations, Salten readily took over the task of monitoring Karl's behavior but soon discovered that the assignment was well beyond the powers of an eighteen-year-old. Karl, six years Salten's senior, secretly helped himself to a hidden stash of drugs and even held Salten hostage with a gun until he agreed to accompany him on a drug rampage. After a frightful bout with cocaine, which had been prescribed by his physician as a cure, Karl finally made the effort to withdraw, but his behavior was still wildly irrational, and his mistress asked to share Salten's bed at night since she was now afraid of her lover. Karl eventually shot himself, and the mistress, Berta Karlsburg, quickly transferred her affections to Salten. She was, in Schnitzler's words, "an operetta singer of notoriously bad reputation,"[19] who, Salten recollected, had "already passed through many hands [and] was twice as old as I."[20] She was, "although not my first, destined to be my most important lover. Young boy that I was, I got to experience everything through her, sensuality, jealousy, delight, and torment, all frightfully mixed."[21]

The relationship lasted for well over two years, and for several months Salten seriously considered marriage. To facilitate their meetings, he rented a furnished room in Währing close to the house that Berta shared with her mother. Philipp Salzmann was deeply concerned that his son not give up his ambitions, writing him, "Your good Mama and I have, as you know, nothing against your marrying B., but see to it, my child, that you first establish your existence. The way you are heading now, my child, is, in my view, not the right one."[22] The relationship continued at a high pitch until Salten caught Berta betraying him with another man. After suffering severe pangs of rage and jealousy and after contemplating whether "to wound or to kill" her, he settled, he recorded later, on "simply writing her a letter" in which he broke off the relationship.[23] Berta was not so easily discarded and returned to Salten's flat with a revolver that she fired at him: "It was a theatrical shot intended to frighten me, and the bullet lodged up above me in the doorframe. I remained firm; I had suffered enough."[24] Although Salten began to seek pleasure from other women, he continued to suffer for many weeks after the breakup. His father took him along on a business trip to Mischkolcz; from there Salten wrote to Schnitzler of his attempts to heal himself from his passion and of the anguish that still befell him. In one letter, for example, he wrote, "My relapse is quite inexplicable but still no less violent. The way I am suffering here is horrible. The only help for me is driving. ... It is a blessing, I tell you, when one is so tormented that he would like to scream out loud and he has two horses and a whip in his hand."[25]

Salten's inauguration into the world of physical passion and pain now made him an equal with Dörmann and the older Schnitzler, both of whom had had – and continued to have – numerous affairs during this period. While still emotionally entangled with Berta, Salten penned two poems that she inspired. Both suggest that Salten was not only emulating Dörmann's life style but also adopting his theme of the degenerate femme fatale, without, however, reaching Dörmann's level of poetic artistry One poem, bearing the title of the ancient Greek courtesan "Laïs," asks the question:

> Do you believe he who rested in your arms
> Can ever forget you,
> His enjoyment of indiscrete pleasures,
> His possession of your sweet body
> And the fire of your kisses?

> He bears these wounds for life,
> This unfortunate man.
> His longing and all his yearning
> Are directed to you, who *gives* so freely
> And cannot *love* in return.

The second, entitled "Mephistophela," envisions the dead mistress, commenting:

> Now you descend to decay,
> You ravenous woman,
> With a heart that derides everything,
> With a body greedy for love.

He closes, again in an agony of unrequited love:

> I would like to claw your grinning skull
> Out from its musty grave:
> A terrible memento
> Of the coming, comfortless night.

By the time of his breakup in August 1891, Salten was no longer working at the Phoenix Insurance Company. He had accumulated many missed days of work during his failed attempt to wean Karl Schwarz from morphine, and when his father's cousin left his directorship post at Phoenix, Salten was fired. Fortunately, he retained his post at the *Kunst-Chronik*,[26] but he was now partially dependent upon the fortunes of his father, who had found new investors and was attempting, once again, to get his coalmines going.

In the spring of 1892, Salten was called up for military duty. He found the entire business of examining and processing recruits dehumanizing. One "is treated like the moronic cobbler, the drunken bricklayer's assistant, arrogant inspector, etc. etc. [Number] 1529 – the cobbler, – 1530 – the bricklayer's assistant, – 1531 – me, 1532 – the inspector. And so on.... The bricklayer's assistant will presumably live longer than I, and the inspector will probably betray me with my mistress because he has a much more auspicious nose than I do." At the end of the day, to his great relief, Salten was "freed forever from 'a citizen's finest duty'" and felt "as if I had just received myself as a present."[27]

For the next decade, Salten kept up an active, mostly uncommitted, sex life. "I permitted myself every imaginable freedom," he confessed years later; "If my parents had a pretty chambermaid, I simply had to sleep with her." He began a relationship with "a very well-situated married woman"[28] and rented quarters in the city for their rendezvous. "And with the owner of this house, whose breasts I took hold of once in the dark without intending to, only to discover that they were very lovely breasts, I slept again and again."[29] It appears that, during this period, Salten, Dörmann, and Schnitzler were competing with one another in their erotic conquests. Salten acquired at least three of Schnitzler's lovers – the doctor's former patient Josefine Lydia von Weisswasser, the operetta singer Mila Theren, and the popular stage actress Adele Sandrock, and Salten told Schnitzler how another of his conquests had asked, as she lay at Salten's side, "I wonder who my next lover will be? Probably Dr. S."[30] Schnitzler recorded a dream that reveals just how closely he and Salten were entwined in their many erotic adventures, especially in regards to Salten's taking Schnitzler's lovers off his hands:

Dream: Salten has murdered a woman: it is [his lover Berta] Karlsburg, Jeanette [Heeger, my lover] ... by turns. He comes out of the house .... "It's been done." Two policemen [are] in front of the house. I [say]: "Discovered!" – He: "It is settled; I will say she came in to me through the window"; [he] goes into the house to turn himself in, impresses me. I, fearful: witness – then they will discover the murdered woman was my mistress earlier; suddenly the caretaker runs from the house (mine, in woman's clothing), says, pale with horror: "You cut up the belly of one of them" – I take a walk along the lake, very fearful.[31]

Salten and Schnitzler included one another in evening meals with their mistresses and discussed them all thoroughly with one another. Typical of this is Schnitzler's diary entry for December 24, 1893: "Conversation with Salten as to how people (I) [sic] are quite different in the different adventures they are conducting at one time. In respect to Mz., I am always sentimental and feel 'faithful'; regarding Diltsch, I am adventurous and experimental; in respect to Jenny, abandoned and lecherous, in regard to the child Else, harsh, superficial, heartless."[32] These liaisons were, for the most part, short-lived and occasions for some bragging. Felix Dörmann boasted, after a visit to Berlin, that he had slept with sixty-five women, a number that even Schnitzler found questionable.[33] And, when Schnitzler told Salten about the birth of a nephew, Salten boasted, "I knew that you had a little nephew, but that cannot impress me, since I have two daughters!"[34] Years later, Salten would note how his relationships with women during this period were rooted in "desire" that arose "from below," adding, "But men cannot live with women, or women with men, whom they desire in *this* way. One can *live* only with someone whom one loves as a *whole*, with all one's heart."[35] Many of the girls with whom he and his friends had casual affairs were the *süße Mädel* (sweet girls) made popular by Schnitzler in his dramas and short stories; they were "corrupt [but] without sin, innocent without being virgins, quite sincere and a little bit deceitful," and all eventually settled down into satisfactory bourgeois marriages.[36] Recalling the friendship and the erotic adventures of the three young men, the magistrate Alfred Pick would ask Schnitzler some twenty-five years later, "Who invented the term *süßes Mädel*, [you], Salten, or Dörmann?"[37]

Casual relationships between the sexes were possible only in a "new" society where middle-class morals were freer, the women more emancipated, and the men less morally responsible than in the age that preceded it. Nevertheless, in most of these same middle-class circles, the old moral laws still applied, especially those regarding the sexual purity of their woman, and this created an atmosphere of willful hypocrisy. Nowhere is this more evident than in Salten's long-term relationship with a young socialist named Charlotte (Lotte) Glas, a woman who was politically engaged and sexually emancipated. She was open with her family about her political activities but determined to preserve an image of purity at home. Salten met her at the home of the journalist Dr. Paul Wertheimer and was immediately captivated. "She was not very pretty but very intellectual," he recalled. "She didn't have any prejudices [and] was a socialist of the strictest observance …. Our relations very quickly became intimate."[38]

The two lovers made a pact with one another – that theirs would be a union without obligation, that either party could break with the other if his or her feelings for the other faltered. From the beginning, Salten took advantage of his "free" relationship with Lotte to explore other avenues of passion, even taking up for a while with Lotte's sister, Emma. The young Karl Kraus was friends with Salten at this time and even shared Salten's quarters for several weeks after a falling-out with his father; Kraus was genuinely fond of "Red Lotte"[39] and was appalled by Salten's apparent indifference to her. Things came to a head when Salten was staying with Kraus in Ischl in the summer of 1894. There Salten had begun a summer romance with a married woman when he received a telegram from Lotte, saying that she was coming to Ischl and asking him to meet her at the train station. Salten asked Kraus to meet Lotte instead and to tell her that Salten was off on a mountain-climbing trip and would be returning directly from there to Vienna. Kraus believed Salten's story himself until, after Lotte's tearful departure from Ischl, Salten, who had been a hidden witness to the scene, stepped forward to meet "the horrified Kraus."[40] Kraus's sense of morality was deeply shaken, especially since Lotte had come to Ischl with two disturbing messages: first, that she was pregnant and second, that she had been sentenced to three months in prison for insulting the Habsburg royal family in one of her speeches. The friendship between the two men was now irreparably broken. Kraus was determined to protect Lotte by keeping track of Salten's love liaisons, his increasing debts, and signs of his exorbitant lifestyle. Even Salten would admit later that during Lotte's pregnancy he "lived off the fat of the land, wore very elegant clothes, rode in a fiacre through the Prater Park and bought various luxury items,"[41] despite the heavy debts he ran up in doing so.

To his credit, Salten behaved correctly towards his pregnant mistress. By deliberately writing her letters that advised her to turn from socialism, he was able to visit her in the home of the prison director rather than behind prison bars. Lotte was desperate that her family not know of her pregnancy, and so when Lotte was released from prison – and her pregnancy was beginning to show – Salten arranged for her to go to Munich, at her request, to have the child there. "Now," Salten recalled, "there was no thought of abandoning her, none of our earliest agreements counted anymore; I had to stand by her and I did it gladly."[42] He took on all the expenses, including the rental of a small apartment in Munich. Then, when Lotte decided that she wanted to give birth to the baby in Vienna after all, he brought her back to the city in the late spring of 1895, took her in a closed carriage to a private part of the Vienna Birthing Clinic, paid 500 crowns for her secret confinement for six weeks, and more for the birth and his baby daughter's upkeep in the country with an elderly nursemaid. He and Lotte resumed their relationship, which "acquired wilder and wilder sexual forms"[43] and was often broken by angry arguments on both sides.

Their daughter was sickly from the beginning. On August 1, Salten wrote a letter of remarkable aesthetic detachment to Schnitzler, telling him of her death:

> As the old woman who brought me the news
> sat in tears at my editorial desk and I thought
> about the trip with Lotte to Gerasdorf, about the
> little cemetery, the wreath that we'll take with us,

and the cross that we will buy there, I found myself thinking right off how splendidly this all suits the novella form. Beer-Hofmann will say it is his [work], "Child." Much of that is in it, but it is still something quite, quite different, when one considers Lotte's personality, the Munich affair, and our present relations.[44]

Salten would, in fact, use part of the story of Lotte, in much altered form, in his novel *Die klingende Schelle* (The Tinkling Cymbal) some twenty years later. There he would, like Richard Beer-Hofmann before him, present a devastating portrayal of his generation of young aesthetes and their casual attitudes towards love and death.

After their daughter's death, Salten considered his bond to Lotte loosened, but he didn't break with her immediately, in defiant opposition to Kraus perhaps, since Kraus now not only told Lotte about Salten's deception of the past summer but also warned her that Salten was intending to break with her when she went to visit him in Salzburg in late August. Salten didn't actually break with Lotte until the following January, but even then they kept up a casual intimacy until May, when Lotte moved to Berlin. As for Salten: "These dissolute affairs, flophouses, hotels, sleeping with different women … ended when I met my future wife."[45]

Chapter 4: The Coffeehouse Clique

When Salten entered the coffeehouse scene in 1890, he was following a long Viennese tradition. Ever since their establishment some two hundred years before, Vienna's coffeehouses had served as a center for cultural and political discourse. Because even the earliest coffeehouse owners made newspapers available to all their customers, these establishments immediately drew a more intellectual crowd than that which frequented the city's beer and wine halls. In addition to newspapers, billiard tables were almost immediately added to the inventories of the coffeehouses; these provided a more "aristocratic" recreational activity than the bowling lanes in the city's pubs.[1]

Because of its location directly across the street from the old Burgtheater, Café Griensteidl was a favorite haunt of the theatrical crowd. The young Arthur Schnitzler was a frequent guest; he was familiar with many of the theater's actors and singers through his father, a laryngologist who treated performers with throat problems. Despite much of the contradictory literature that suggests that Schnitzler was a participant but not the center of the Young Vienna writers, it was he who formed its original nucleus and drew other writers to his table: Salten and Dörmann, Richard Beer-Hofmann, Gustav Schwarzkopf, and the young Hugo von Hofmannsthal.

This circle of young writers brought with them a healthy respect for older Austrian writers such as Marie von Ebner-Eschenbach and Ferdinand von Saar; at the same time, they were eager to explore new methodologies for tracing the subtlest movements of the human soul. It was a somewhat elitist group, suspect among much of the Viennese citizenry because of its predominantly Jewish membership. These young writers were sons of idealistic fathers who had grown up in a liberal culture and found careers as professionals and as successful businessmen. They had believed fervently in the possibility of full integration into Austrian society, but in the 1870s and 1880s, the city had gone through a period of violent economic upheaval, and a rising tide of anti-Semitism had shown this younger generation the limitations of successful assimilation. These sons now turned in rebellion to the arts and were determined to look behind societal facades for deeper truths. For Salten, it was a great step upward to be part of a rising elite of young literary figures. When Hermann Bahr entered this circle in 1891, this group of writers was already referred to as "Young Vienna" or "Young Austria," and Schnitzler and Hofmannsthal were its acknowledged stars. By then the Burgtheater had new quarters on the city Ring, and Griensteidl had been transformed from a gathering place for a predominantly theatrical crowd to the city's primary literary café. Griensteidl offered its customers, in addition to a wide selection of newspapers, plenty of paper and writing implements, and a full set of Meyer's *Conversationslexikon* (Popular Encyclopedia). It was a masculine club and distinguished itself accordingly from the more organized society salons run by such renowned women as Bertha Zuckerkandl, Princess Pauline von Metternich, Dr. Eugenie Schwarzwald, and Josephine and Franziska von Wertheimstein. Women were welcome in the coffeehouse only when brought to Griensteidl's "smoky, noisy, dimly lit room" by their male companions.[2] There were no invitations and no planned program; regulars came together to play cards and billiards, to gossip, and to debate the virtues and failings of the latest work of art or literature. "Wonderful conversations" were carried on there, ranging from the significant to the seemingly trivial – "an old man's accident, gossip about a girl, knotting one's tie, the tone of an actor, the color of a cloud above the Minoriten Church."[3] Richard Specht recalled that the circle was dominated by the conversational "grace" and "bravura" of Hofmannsthal, Schnitzler, Salten, Beer-Hofmann, and the nimble-witted musician Leo Van-Jung and that "thoughts and insights bubbled up" at their table.[4] It was a time, Salten recalled, when "I, as a matter of course, regarded everything from a literary standpoint, books and people and all of life," whereas, as a mature man, he would learn "to measure all of life's appearances against only life itself."[5] The circle of young writers around them ebbed and flowed; soon would-be writers were drawn to Griensteidl to see and be seen at its tables. By the mid-1890s the reputation of the coffeehouse became "so international that there wasn't a foreign poet or literary figure who failed to come to Griensteidel during a visit to Vienna."[6] Stefan Zweig was a restless pupil at the Wasagymnasium who came to Griensteidl to see precisely those writers who were *not* taught in the literature classes at school; the young aspiring actor Karl Kraus was similarly drawn to the circle and became particularly close to Salten and to his younger brother Géza, who was studying to be a sculptor at the Vienna Academy of Fine Arts. Other, often occasional, participants in this loose Griensteidl circle of the 1890s included Paul Goldmann, Eduard Michael Kafka, Jacques Joachim, Richard Specht, Julius Kulka, Heinrich von Korff, Victor Léon, Franz Herold, Friedrich Fels, Friedrich Schik, Gustav Schwarzkopf, Otto Erich Hartleben, Falk Schupp, Paul Horn, Karl Maria Heidt, Ferry Beraton, Felix Holländer, Robert and Georg Fischer, C. Karlweis, Karl Federn, Carl von Torresani-Langenfeld, Adalbert von Goldschmidt, Leopold von Andrian-Werburg, Peter Altenberg, Leo Hirschfeld, Leo Ebermann, Emil Mark, Max Pollandt, Michael Georg Conrad.[7] "The most varied people joined our circle," Salten recalled, "as sweet-toothed observers, so to speak. We were taken very seriously by some; we were derided by others with true Viennese irony. It was a matter of defending oneself, of returning blows with blows, and it happened only occasionally that the jolly disputes derailed into hot temper and serious consequences."[8] As the crowds at the table grew, they moved into the billiard room. Even this was scarcely big enough for the crowd of onlookers who came to gawk, and the literary debates became more heated when a group of German nationalist writers also began frequenting Griensteidl, and the Schnitzler/Bahr circle had to defend itself not only "against mockery and sneering doubts, but also against evil intent, maliciousness, and simple narrow-mindedness."[9]

When Hermann Bahr entered the group in late April 1891, the circle was a good deal smaller, but it was far from inactive. Eduard Michael Kafka, founder at age 21 of a journal entitled *Moderne Dichtung* had already moved his headquarters from Brünn to Vienna, where Jacques Joachim now served with him as co-editor; this was the first journal to propagate the new Austrian literature actively to the larger world, thereby making Kafka, in Bahr's words, the "prophet" of Young Austria.[10] Not coincidentally, Bahr's essay "Die Moderne" (Modernity) appeared in the journal's first issue. Most of the young writers who had first appeared in Paul Goldmann's journal now appeared in the pages of *Moderne Dichtung* and in its successor journal *Moderne Rundschau*. Salten published an editorial essay here, as well as a short story entitled "Nuance," a tale about a femme fatale constructed solely of her lover's internal reflections about her; its style reveals Schnitzler's profound influence on the younger writer during this period. Hermann Bahr exclaimed that Kafka's journal was the first to show its readers that there was an Austrian art form independent of Germany, "independent in growth, in power, in character, and in splendor," adding that it was left to himself, Hermann Bahr, to use his "courage, audacity, [and] joy in paradoxes" to "proclaim it aloud" to the world.[11]

Shortly before Bahr's move to Vienna in 1891, the Young Vienna group made its first official appearance in mid April at a late dinner held to honor Henrik Ibsen on the occasion of Max Burckhard's production of Ibsen's play *The Pretenders* at the Burgtheater. Kafka was the main organizer of that evening's tribute, which featured poems by Felix Dörmann and Richard Specht. Salten was, along with Kafka, part of Ibsen's welcoming committee; both young men felt deep veneration for Ibsen as the first playwright to revolt against the Victorian literature of the past by treating forbidden subjects and showing the harsh reality behind society's comfortable facades.

Bahr felt that Ibsen had placed Austria's new literature into his hands. Bahr had traveled widely in Europe, but was particularly influenced by two decisive years spent in Paris. By the time he came to Vienna, Bahr was twenty-eight years old; he had already rebelled against the art of the Naturalists and was proclaiming the new art of the French symbolists, impressionists, and decadents. Bahr introduced the term "modernity" for the young Austrian authors whom he met at Griensteidl and became their most ardent champion. Richard Specht called him "the voice of youth, the eternal man of 'tomorrow,' bubbling with life, power, and high spirits, with something of the Latin Quarter, something of Daudet, yet completely Hermann Bahr, the Austrian."[12] As the programmatic voice of the young authors, in his role as essayist and critic in the Vienna press, Bahr declared the "defeat of naturalism" [*Überwindung des Naturalismus*] (1891) and became an ardent champion of not only the Young Vienna writers but also the modernist painters, especially Gustav Klimt. Bahr was frequently ridiculed for the way that he switched titles for the literary trends he claimed to have "discovered," variously identifying the Young Vienna literature as "symbolist," "decadent," "satanic," "aesthetic," and "impressionistic." Karl Kraus, who was first an enthusiastic participant in Bahr's circle, would later make Bahr his chief whipping boy, commenting that "without him, many a young non-talent would have perished and been forgotten."[13]

Despite Bahr's efforts to define and categorize them, Salten and his fellow writers did not always fit Bahr's program of a single, unified literary movement; their bonds were more of association than of aims. These writers all had healthy egos, and there were frequent strains and rivalries among the group, especially among those who shared not only ideas but sexual partners. When the young Lou Andreas Salomé was invited to the circle in 1895, she was struck by the unusual "competition of love and ambition" that she found there, although she was impressed at the same time by the nature of the "male friendships that acquired a special and quite exquisite form."[14]

The closest friendships developed between Arthur Schnitzler, Felix Salten, Richard Beer-Hofmann, and Hugo von Hofmannsthal; in October 1891, Schnitzler noted in his diaries that "Loris [Hofmannsthal], Salten, Beer-Hofmann, and I are already regarded as a clique."[15] Beer-Hofmann, an independently wealthy Jewish dandy who "wore a different flower in his buttonhole every day" to reflect his varying moods,[16] was, in Richard Specht's view, "a sort of Viennese Oscar Wilde."[17] Because of his "charming eloquence" and "thoroughly penetrating bright mind," Salten dubbed him the circle's "patron of understanding," adding, "His first novella 'Camelias' was admired by all of us as a rare jewel."[18]

Salten wrote, "Loris, the not yet sixteen-year-old schoolboy Hugo v. Hofmannsthal ..., won the rapture of all of us. Not just the formal, musical beauty of language in Hofmannsthal's verses [in the verse play *Gestern* (Yesterday)] but also their profound unity of thought affected us like a kind of noble intoxication."[19] Hofmannsthal had "the allures of a prince" and his voice revealed an "aristocratic pride" and "steely iron will."[20] The boy Hofmannsthal was accepted by his three elder companions as their superior. Salten recalled that it was only when they happened to see Hofmannsthal among his schoolmates that they were reminded of his youth. Schnitzler and Salten memorized Hofmannsthal's poems and recited them to one another on their walks together in the Vienna Woods. Schnitzler regarded Hofmannsthal as a boy genius, noting, "I find it absolutely reasonable that people consider Loris the most significant of us ...."[21]

In 1893 Hofmannsthal paid literary tribute to his friends in a prologue to his drama *Der Tor und der Tod* (The Fool and Death). In it he wrote of the "four famous, great, completely unknown poets" who as "friends" met regularly on Sunday afternoons to socialize and to read to one another their works in progress.[22] He described Schnitzler as a doctor who played everything from "children's songs" to "solemn church fugues" "on a tiny artificial spinet";[23] Beer-Hofmann as a puppeteer who performed pantomime dramas for his friends with his collection of marionettes; and Salten as the owner of "a beautiful, slim, flaxen-haired hunting dog" that, when awakened from a troubled dream, gazed "gratefully" at his master "with large moist eyes."[24] He described the four friends as nobility (Salten is referred to as "Don Ferrante") and as aesthetes. He tells how he buys a bouquet of red roses, which he tosses into the room where Schnitzler and Salten await him, and how, as he walks along with Beer-Hofmann, he searches for the name "of that beetle, whose gold-green, sparkling blue wing covers he could compare to the dome of St. Charles [Church] ... for he loved these similes."[25] All four, Hofmannsthal wrote, "knew ... that the excitable soul is like a short burst of strings in the dark hand of life."[26]

Salten also made light mockery of his and Hofmannsthal's aestheticism in an unpublished fragment from these years:

> Loris says, etc., "I imagine it so (sitting while he speaks in Schnitzler's desk chair, foot over the arm. Hand gesture). Pastels, clouds of incense, stalks of lilies to the left and right and, gleaming through the cloud of incense, a beautiful woman's face, or the opposite: stalks of lilies to the left and right and behind the clouds of incense me (Loris), one of the armor-clad angels at Paolo Cagliari's tomb."
> *Sch.* If Schwarzkopf were here, he would maintain that you conjured up the whole image for me in order to get to Paolo Cagliari's tomb.
> *Loris:* (suddenly sniffing indignantly.) What is this smell here? It is nothing like it should be, not

like the room of a *garçon* who is doctor and author at the same time, not even like *Bohème*. It should smell differently here, of bandage material, of patrons, women's perfume, and all kinds of cigarette tobacco.

Sch. und *S.* tell Loris that they've talked all night, it is a pity, how *vieux jeu* it expands into dawn.[27]

Although the four men gathered nearly every Sunday at Arthur Schnitzler's home, their friendships were always of a cautious, critical nature, and Salten never felt completely at ease among them. Schnitzler didn't like to be touched and maintained the formal *Sie* when addressing his friends. During these early days of their friendship, Salten noted how Hofmannsthal "understood ... completely how to maintain a cool sense of personal distance in the midst of the most turbulent intellectual companionship"; only in his written correspondence "did he become warm, did he become affectionate."[28] Richard Beer-Hofmann refused to use the term "friendship" at all, saying, "Friends? We are really not friends – we simply don't make one another nervous."[29] Salten commented some thirty years later, "The subdued warmth with which we socialized and which always gave the impression of coolness, even of coldness, remains strange to me even to this day."[30] It was a generation, he commented, that "was particularly careful to keep a distance. In its manner of tackling and living life, there was an elegantly artistic culture of taste, strangely mixed with a feeling of social tact of the most extreme vigilance and with the meticulous concern to protect oneself and one's composure under all circumstances."[31] Members of the larger circle had a tendency to downgrade each other behind their backs: Hofmannsthal, for example, complained of Felix Dörmann's body odor and Bahr commented in his memoirs that "Even back then I had to defend Salten against the whole world, as I still do today."[32] Even though Schnitzler maintained his contacts with Salten, Hofmannsthal, and Beer-Hofmann throughout his lifetime, he subjected these friendships to frequent, critical scrutiny, as when he wrote in his diary, "My friends: impossibility of complete intimacy: with Loris [Hofmannsthal] because of intolerance, with Richard [Beer-Hofmann] because of affectation, with Salten because of unreliability,"[33] and "In our dealings Salten is definitely the most pleasant [of my friends]; I like him very much, especially when I am together with him personally, [but] if I miss seeing him for a few days, reflection, particularly on his unreliability, disturbs the picture."[34] Reflecting further on Salten, Schnitzler wrote, "My relationship to him is also not a completely clear affair. Or to anyone at all. We are all namely such egoists. And all of us sensitive, all of us mistrustful. [These are] relationships with [an] occasional emphasis of friendship."[35]

Salten felt at a distinct disadvantage in Griensteidl's select circle because his friends not only had the benefit of a higher education but were "all well off and able to live without a care." Within Salten's circle, Beer-Hofmann, in particular, set himself up as a fashion critic, and Salten, still mindful of the lesson learned as a boy when he saw the carefully maintained silk dresses worn by Albert Lortzing's impoverished niece, tried desperately to match his new friends' wardrobes. These were men who "could permit themselves trips to Venice or Paris and summer vacations in the Salzkammergut" while he alone had to support himself though the pieces he wrote for the Vienna papers.[36]

Indeed, Salten's efforts to live in grand style nearly cost him his friendship with Arthur Schnitzler. Schnitzler had long wondered how Salten was able, especially with his high level of indebtedness, to maintain an elegant life style, noting that "with a salary of 60 Gulden from the *Allgemeine Zeitung* he buys himself an umbrella at Rhodek for 24 Gulden."[37] Then, in the summer of 1892, Schnitzler made the unpleasant discovery that Salten had acquired some of his spending money by selling some expensive books that he had "borrowed" from Schnitzler's library. When Schnitzler confronted him, Salten at first tried to hide the theft but then confessed and wrote Schnitzler a "half sincere, half repentant letter" of apology. To Salten's great relief, Schnitzler was remarkably forgiving; the friendship was restored quickly, in part because of Schnitzler's need for "a confidant."[38] Unfortunately, however, Schnitzler also began from this point to regard his friend with clear mistrust.

Occasionally, Salten was able to visit one of his friends rent free; in this manner, he was able to spend part of the summer of 1892 with Richard Specht's family in Unterach am Attersee and to stay with Karl Kraus in Ischl in the summer of 1894. In 1893, however, while his friends were off on their summer vacations, Salten returned to work in an insurance office in order to pay off some of his debts.

Still, the foursome met regularly and read to one another from their works in progress. Schnitzler recorded carefully in his diary the reception that his works received and his reactions to the newest pieces by Hofmannsthal, Beer-Hofmann, and Salten. Occasionally other poets – Felix Dörmann, Leo Ebermann, Heinrich von Korff – came to read to this smaller group, while the circle of listeners widened frequently to include Gustav Schwarzkopf, Richard Specht, or Leo Van-Jung. Over time, however, only the core clique remained solid, in large part because the relations between the four extended far beyond Griensteidl. They dined together, visited the Prater Park, took long walks together, and met at the theater. Whenever they were together, they spoke "about everything": "About God, about the world, about the relationship between the sexes, about the position of parents in relation to their children, the husband in relation to his wife, about sports, about gymnastics, about dance, about painting, about music, about the social order."[39] Salten recalled, "The better part of my existence was spent in the company of these friends …. I spent the happiest hours with them not just in Café Griensteidl …, but on walks and in particular when we gathered at Arthur Schnitzler's or at Richard Beer-Hofmman's."[40]

Salten shared Beer-Hofmann's love of dogs and Schnitzler's passion for sports. Cycling – and later tennis – became Salten's main sources of relaxation. He frequently took long bicycle trips with his brother, with Schnitzler, and with Hermann Bahr. The rising young novelist Siegfried Trebitsch first met Salten because of a common interest in bicycling, and soon Trebitsch could be counted among Salten's closest friends. Trebitsch recalled that "Salten was actually the first to say – as he did quite unexpectedly as we were cycling side by side from the Krieau [in the Prater Park] back into town: 'I should like to get to know something more of your writings. And I like having young poets read aloud to me. I am very fond of doing so myself.'" Salten, Trebitsch noted, "knew many more literary people than I did"[41] and introduced him to others in the Griensteidl circle.

Salten's relations with the young Karl Kraus were decidedly more complex. Kraus, or "little Kraus"[42] as he was called by the Griensteidl clique, was the same age as Hofmannsthal, but unlike Hofmannsthal, he was not taken seriously by the Young Vienna writers. Despite his efforts to participate as their equal, his views were "irksome"; according to one biographer, he "was regarded as a Thersites" and "only just tolerated."[43] The situation did not improve when, in 1893, Kraus suffered an embarrassing failure as an actor in a production of Schiller's *Die Räuber* (The Robbers) that the group attended. At first, Kraus reviewed the Young Vienna writers positively, but he soon became critical of the poets with the "feinen Nerven" (sensitive nerves)[44] who, he felt, were retreating from the great issues of the day into their own overly aestheticized, self-absorbed world.[45] Kraus rebelled against Bahr's pro-French leanings and looked to Berlin for literary currents more to his taste; Gerhart Hauptmann's play *Die Weber* (The Weavers) was his great passion, and, wherever he could, he gave public readings of it. Kraus continued to come to Griensteidl, but he soon adopted a mocking tone within the circle. His first falling out with Salten reveals this when he writes: "I sought your company because I recognized you as a reasonable, tasteful, talented human being. But I also got to know you as a man of great affectation; it is bad to be affected, it is annoying to affect the role of an affected person – I wonder if you have always done the latter?" Kraus added, "Have I occasionally struck an extremely unelegant, 'unartistic' tone in this letter? Have I? But you will forgive me! After all, a bourgeois, an average man, is speaking to a 'modern person with the sensitive mind and secrets of quite an exquisite nervous system.'"

The immediate cause for Kraus's sarcastic rebuke in this letter was his discovery, in Ischl, that either Salten or his brother, Géza, had apparently expressed to others their annoyance over Kraus's frequent, unannounced visits to their flat and, worse, that one of them had declared that Kraus was "quite without talent," that he "writes well, the way every educated person does, but as to whether there is anything special about it ...." Kraus complained, "I have been laughed at while I was away: Little Kraus wants to found a newspaper! Haha!" adding, "When ... I am attacked as a writer I can do nothing about it; I can't forbid people to make judgments." If it had been Salten, and not his brother, who had spoken this way, however, this was a serious matter: "Then I realize that you have lied to me frequently by saying *the opposite* at times." Kraus's complaint about Salten – that he praised people to their face while attacking them behind their backs – would be taken up by several of his friends as time passed and Salten acquired real power as a literary and theater critic; although people enjoyed his company, they distrusted him and feared his reviews. In this particular case, the problem between Salten and Kraus was satisfactorily resolved, and their uneasy friendship restored.

During the early 1890s, all the young moderns were struggling to get into press and onto the stage. Like *Moderne Dichtung*, *Moderne Rundschau* was of short duration; in December 1891, it ceased publication, informing its readers of the rise of an organization, *Freie Bühne für den Entwicklungskampf der Zeit*, that would carry on the battle of the journals by now providing not only a journal but also a stage for the young modernist playwrights who were being neglected elsewhere. This organization was modeled after the Freie Bühne in Berlin; E. M. Kafka was its head, with Jacques Joachim as secretary. Salten was on its governing board, along with Bahr, Hofmannsthal, Schnitzler, and Beer-Hofmann. In the group's earliest meetings, there was discussion of putting on performances of Schnitzler's *Das Märchen* (The Fairy Tale), Gerhart Hauptmann's *Das Friedensfest* (The Peace Dinner), and Strindberg's *Der Gläubiger* (The Creditor). Eventually, however, Bahr's influence prevailed, and the group agreed upon Maurice von Maeterlinck's drama *L'Intruse* (The Intruder), as translated and directed by would-be poet and painter Ferry Beraton. Its premiere was scheduled for April 11, 1892, in the Rudolfsheimer Volkstheater. Because Salten neglected to take the play to the proper censorship office prior to this premiere, the production was postponed, and Salten was subjected to "violent reproaches" from his friends.[46] The delay – and ensuing publicity – proved beneficial, however, and at its opening some three weeks later the company moved into a larger theater to accommodate the demand for tickets.

It was a short-lived triumph for the Vienna Freie Bühne. As Salten put it, "While [we] were still debating whether Ibsen, Hauptmann, or Strindberg should have the first word, the doors of the Vienna stages suddenly sprang open, and Ibsen, Hauptmann, and Strindberg were played at three theaters." Within three years, plays by the Young Vienna authors were also being accepted for production by the established stages "and the 'Freie Bühne' had, in the end, become rather superfluous."[47] Nor did the publication of the Viennese journal *Freie Bühne* take root. Wilhelm Bölsche took over its direction, but Salten, like many others, transferred his loyalty to Dr. A. Bauer's *Wiener Literatur-Zeitung*, which also actively promoted Vienna's new young authors. In 1893 this journal changed its name to *Neue Revue* and added more non-literary topics. Salten continued contributing to the pages of this journal, and in October of this same year, acquired steadier work by becoming a prolific critic and feuilletonist for the daily *Wiener Allgemeine Zeitung*, a paper with a much larger readership.

With this move, Salten stepped firmly into journalism as a necessary source of steady income, and literature became a luxury. Indeed, all the major players of the Griensteidl circle were now establishing niches for themselves. In 1894 Hermann Bahr co-founded the weekly newspaper *Die Zeit* and served as main editor of its cultural section. In the same year, Hofmannsthal passed his state exam in law at the University of Vienna, then took a year's leave to serve in the Sixth Dragoon Regiment of the Austrian army before continuing his university studies. He had already become acquainted with the German poet Stefan George and his poems were appearing regularly in George's *Blätter für die Kunst* (Pages for Art). In 1894 Kraus, who had changed fields from law to the study of philosophy and German literature, was writing for the Berlin newspapers.

Arthur Schnitzler opened his own medical practice in 1893. He also saw the first stage productions in Ischl and at the German Volkstheater in Vienna of his plays *Abschiedssouper* (Farewell Dinner) and *Das Märchen* (The Fairy Tale); in October of the following year, Max Burckhard accepted Schnitzler's *Liebelei* (Flirtation) for production at the Burgtheater, and Schnitzler was finally taken seriously as a playwright. And in 1893 Richard Beer-Hofmann published the volume *Novellen* with his stories "Das Kind" (The Child) and "Camelias."

Salten was also writing short works of prose fiction, although it would be a number of years before any appeared in book form. He continued reading his works in progress to his friends; Schnitzler was often encouraging, noting about one, "Progress. Maupassant's influence very beneficial,"[48] and, about another, "Interesting idea, the development frequently weak."[49] Because Schnitzler, Beer-Hofmann, and Salten often treated similar themes and employed similar techniques of narrated monologue in their works, Schnitzler was somewhat protective of "his" terrain, as when Salten read a finished work to him and Schnitzler "objected to its being published since it simply paraphrases my 'poor girl.'"[50] Another Schnitzler theme that Salten adopted was bereavement; in 1894 Schnitzler wrote "Der Witwer" (The Widower) and Salten "Der Hinterbliebene" (The Bereaved One).

In general, critics were not positively disposed to the Griensteidl circle of young writers. Franz Blei referred to them as "callow" "high-school students";[51] Peter Altenberg, who had been discovered and promoted as a writer by Schnitzler and Beer-Hofmann, published a "somewhat perfidious attack" on his former friends,[52] and Edmund Wengraf bemoaned the fact that "gravity and thoroughness do not thrive in the coffeehouse atmosphere."[53] Hofmannsthal appeared to be the least affected by these critiques. He referred to one as "mockery by anonymity," asking Schnitzler if one such piece had been written by Kraus. He added, "I would be happy if such things would be written much more often and if caricatures were drawn of us. This will certainly keep increasing as we become better and more courageous."[54] As one of the inner circle, Salten was a strong advocate of the Vienna modernists, but he was at the same time exceedingly critical of those "literary parasites" at the Griensteidl tables who claimed membership by producing offensive writings that they claimed were influenced by Nietzsche or Ibsen.[55]

The strongest and most enduring attack on the Griensteidl circle came from Karl Kraus, who, as early as 1893, had railed to Schnitzler that he "hated this false, fabricated 'Decadence'" with its "posturing, sick, masturbated poetry."[56] He launched his attack in a four-part essay published in the new journal *Wiener Rundschau* between November 15, 1896, and January 1, 1897. The editors of the journal were careful to state that these articles were being published only because they were "clever" and "of current interest," adding, "We emphasize ... the fact that we in no way identify with the standpoint of the author."[57] These essays, to which Kraus gave the title *Die demolirte Literatur* (The Demolished Literature), were a mockery of the Young Vienna writers. They made Karl Kraus's name as satirist and went through five printings as a separate pamphlet. The occasion for these articles was the necessary demolition of the Griensteidl coffeehouse in order to construct an enlarged entry to the Royal Court across the square. Kraus's first segment began with irony-laden nostalgia for the café, with its lack of fresh air and daylight, its rich supply of magazines and newspapers, and its importance for the literary life of Vienna, but his mockery soon turned directly to the Young Vienna writers, especially their leader, Hermann Bahr, whom he portrayed as a man eager to play Goethe to a herd of young Eckermanns. Kraus mocked Bahr's introduction into Austria of "artistic greats" whose names were known to Bahr alone since he "had often read them on Spanish theatrical posters or even on Portuguese street signs"[58]; Kraus also copied and mimicked Bahr's "strangely ornate and artistically elaborate non-German."[59]

In the second segment of his essay, Kraus continued his attack on his former friends, whom he found pretentious and "so easy to please that they hope to make do their whole lives with a couple of Viennese sentiments,"[60] men whose art was characterized by "ever recurring sentimental delusions."[61]

He let Schnitzler off relatively easy, although he derided him as one who knew how "to preserve a calm modesty of delusion": "Too good natured to be able to approach a problem, he has for all time cobbled together a tiny world of men about town and working-class girls to rise only occasionally from these depths to false tragedy."[62] But Kraus's most virulent attack was saved for part three of his essay, in which he assailed Salten for plagiarism, ignorance, and a bad writing style. Salten, he wrote, was "a parvenu of gestures, who has observed everything in his literary table companions and owes them his knowledge of the most important posturings."[63] "One must imagine his production in this way," he wrote, "that he, as a kind of informant of nuances, has all of his more accredited friend's [Schnitzler's] ideas in safekeeping and therefore is allowed to use every tenth one." As for his work as a theater critic: "He first asked a policeman for the location of the theater whose traditions he was determined to combat";[64] and for his art criticism: "He had Muther's 'History of Nineteenth-Century Painting' sent to him as a review copy and thus became an art critic."

Next Kraus turned to a harsh critique of Salten's style: "As an ironist, he has always stood on his own quotation marks [literally: "little goose feet"]." "Some foreign words seemed so new to him that he believed he had to try using them again and again." In reference to Salten's limited education, he added, "Perhaps he emphasize[s] a bit too strongly the joy after only four grades of mastering expressions that are usually learned only in the senior year." He attacked Salten for mixing up the dative with the accusative. "In the beginning, he had to battle against the resistance of the typesetters, who ... like to correct ... that which is the most individualistic expression of an artistic personality," Kraus jeered, but "his talent prevailed. He could now live it up, and he is recognized even in his unsigned articles." [65] After citing examples of these errors and then mimicking them in his own writing, Kraus closed his discussion of Salten by saying, "the stage successes of his friends have intoxicated him; now the goal of all his effort is: to be performed!"[66]

Die demolirte Literatur was Kraus's first popular success. In this work, Kraus never mentioned any writer by name, but he gave enough clues to make it a simple matter for the public to recognize the figures he was mocking. What made the satire even more effective, however, was the kernel of truth in each of his critiques. Bahr was stung by Kraus's questioning his mastery of European literatures; Schnitzler remained highly sensitive to the criticism that his works always revolved around decadent dandies and "sweet girls." Salten was the only one of the circle to reciprocate, and his attack on Kraus became the stuff of legend.

As Salten told it, Kraus's article in the *Wiener Rundschau* was simply the last of a whole series of personal assaults that included stalking and even verbal attacks against Salten's future wife. As thanks for taking Kraus into his home, Salten said, he had been rewarded with "a lot of hostility, evil slander, and mean gossip."[67] On the evening of the day that this latest attack appeared, Salten walked into Griensteidl, where Kraus had a niche seat in a corner of the billiard room, crossed the room, and slapped him twice in the face. Schnitzler noted that this attack "was greeted with delight from all sides."[68] Kraus sued Salten for bodily harm and Salten's attorney predicted that he would be arrested. Instead, the waiter and many of the Griensteidl customers disputed Kraus's claims that he had been attacked from the rear and that he had had no opportunity to defend himself; Salten recalled that the waiter even added that "he, like all the others in the coffee house, could have held me back but felt that Karl Kraus had richly deserved the [two] blows."[69] Salten was sentenced to a relatively minor fine of twenty florins.

Kraus's verbal attack was doubtless motivated by what he considered Salten's lack of personal and professional integrity. Salten's assault may have been applauded by his friends and colleagues, but it earned him the enmity of a rising circle of Kraus admirers. Indeed, seen in retrospect, Kraus may even have emerged the victor, for Salten's blows confirmed for Kraus's readers that he had been entirely accurate in his description of Salten's failings. Kraus not only succeeded in ridiculing Salten where he was the weakest, in his educational background and in his tendency to follow his better-situated friends wherever they might lead him, he also gave fuel to Salten's newspaper rivals by suggesting that he had neither the background nor the writing skills necessary for being a credible critic.

Chapter 5: Finding His Niche

Salten had begun his journalism career as a literary critic, but when he joined the *Wiener Allgemeine Zeitung* in 1893, he was hired primarily to write art and theater reviews. After Julius von Gans-Ludassy became chief editor of the paper in 1894, Salten's position was formalized as Burgtheater critic and feuilletonist. As a journalist and playwright, Ludassy was sympathetic to the Young Vienna writers, and he gave Salten considerable freedom. In addition to reviewing art exhibits, theater productions, and a limited number of literary works during his first two years at the paper, Salten composed a poem mocking the anti-Semitic Wilhelm von Hammerstein's departure from the conservative German newspaper *Kreuzzeitung*,[1] responded to a Nietzsche parody by composing his own, and editorialized about the directorships of the main theaters, about writers who compose nothing but aphorisms, and about cuts in governmental support of the arts. He also wrote of his suspicions that some published "prison letters" were actually composed by the writer who praised them. While he was in Munich tending to Lotte Glas's pregnancy, Salten sent back an article describing his visit to the studio of the artist Franz Stuck, along with three reviews of art exhibits in that city. Finally, in 1895, his short story "Heldentod" (Death of a Hero) appeared in the paper's New Year's issue, and on two Sundays at Whitsunstide, his collection of sketches entitled *Quer durch den Wurstelprater* (All Around the Prater Park) were printed.[2]

These two literary works reveal a lot about the delays that were frequently to occur between Salten's initial composition of a piece and its final publication in book form. "Heldentod" first appeared in a collection of short stories entitled *Der Hinterbliebene* (The Bereaved One) in 1900.[3] As for *Quer durch den Wurstelprater*, this work lay on his desk until 1911, when it was published with photographs by Emil Mayer.[4] In this later work, the basic 1895 text remained the same in nineteen of the entries, although several sentences were added to fill out the sketch "Der Wurstel" (The Puppet Theater), describing the audience of the puppet play. One of the original episodes, "Velocipede Circus," was omitted, probably because this entertainment was no longer part of the park offerings. The book also included seven new sketches: about drunkards, waiters, young lovers, a dance hall,[5] an all-women's orchestra, and men and women selling treats in the park. Throughout his lifetime Salten retained this habit of publishing works many years after their original composition. Frequently, as in the case of "Heldentod" and many of the pieces in *Wurstelprater*, Salten's newspaper sketches were incorporated, virtually unchanged, into a book of stories or essays. But, as is also the case with *Wurstelprater*, sometimes Salten's pieces lay dormant in his study for many years, then underwent revisions and additions before appearing years later as "new" works. And finally, some, like "Der Vagabund" appeared only in journals and newspapers and never attained permanence as part of a bound volume.

Salten's 1895 works indicate that he was already acquiring a fine eye for drawing character. The old colonel of "Heldentod" is not a stereotypical Radetzky-type hero but rather a somewhat grumpy man who realizes that heroic acts are not acts of free will but of despair. *Quer durch den Wurstelprater* is full of easy dialogue written in the rich Viennese dialect of the day. Salten doesn't look down on the park's performers and visitors but shows instead unsentimental empathy and understanding for such varied types as the deep-sea diver whose boyish dreams of swimming in coral seas have been reduced to submerging himself in a tub of dirty water for people's entertainment, and the aggressive ruffian who picks fights with everyone in the park and then cries out in frustration to the police who have come to restore order, "When I go to the Prater, I should be allowed to amuse myself."[6]

Most of Salten's attention during the 1890's, however, was focused on his work as theater and art critic. As an art critic, he championed the works of the Düsseldorf and Munich painters of the Secession and urged the Austrians to study and emulate their works. He attended the openings of the annual art academy exhibitions and had special praise for the artists who were to form the core of the Vienna Secessionist movement in 1897. He proved in his art criticism to be as independent in his judgments as he was in his literary reviews, paying tribute both to the most promising younger artists as well as to the greatest of the older, established painters and sculptors, such as Adolph Menzel, Hans Makart, and Victor Tilgner, commenting, "At every collection of fleeting and coincidental achievements, one should exhibit some single, immortal piece of art as a yardstick."[7] Salten railed as much against the younger artists whose work he found lacking in talent or vision as against older artists who refused to develop and change with the times. He did, however, review his brother Géza favorably in his critique of an 1896 student exhibition of the Academy of Fine Arts, noting that Géza's sculpture *Lions at Play* revealed "great study and comprehending observation" of these animals.[8] Although Salten rejoiced at the fading of art that depicted great historical events, he was unhappy with many of the sentimental genre pictures created by younger Austrian artists. What he sought in fine arts, literature, theater, and music was art that gave the public insight into its common humanity.

Theater provided a two-fold opportunity for making a deeper statement on the human condition, first through the text of a play, then through its performance on stage. During the late nineties, Salten immersed himself thoroughly in all matters relating to the theater. In 1896, for example, in addition to reviewing some twenty-five productions at Vienna's leading theaters, he wrote six portraits of actors, as well as essays critical of the director of the Deutsches Volkstheater, of the appointment of a German director to manage the troubled Raimundtheater, and of the application of an anti-Semite to become director of the new imperial Jubiläumstheater. He also commented on the choice of plays and actors at various theaters, actors' low salaries, and other critics' (bad) reviews of plays. Salten had not only become a critic to be reckoned with but also a vocal opponent of a number of theater directors, fellow writers, and journalists.

Unfortunately, Salten's journalistic attacks, as well as his volatile temper, brought him into frequent conflicts. He not only created a number of enemies but also was forced to participate in several "affairs of honor." This was not an unusual occurrence: both his friends Richard Beer-Hofmann and Siegfried Trebitsch had been involved in a number of duels. Trebitsch considered this form of "chivalrous settlement" often "nothing but a disguised taste for brawling or mere vengefulness" but also pointed out that dueling "was at that time obligatory in the upper-middle and upper classes."[9] By the 1890s, dueling had filtered down from the aristocratic, military, and student classes – those entitled to bear arms – to members of the bourgeoisie, often through an individual's attainment of "rank" through a university degree or through service in the army reserves.[10] Salten had neither a degree nor a military rank, but through his prominence in the press, he had apparently earned the right to duel and was declared *satisfaktionsfähig*, or "eligible to seek satisfaction." During the 1890s and early 1900s, then, Salten was involved in a variety of conflicts, some of which were settled by judicial means, some through the mechanism of the duel. In the summer of 1894, Salten was brought to court and forced to pay a fine for an attack on another man; it is unclear who instigated the attack and whether it was verbal or physical.[11] The following year, Salten accused the journalist Otto Frischauer of plagiarism in a judicial case that was finally settled to both men's satisfaction. In 1896, however, an "affair of honor" between Salten and the young journalist Leopold Jacobson[12] became so heated that it could be settled only by a duel with sabers to be fought until one of the parties reached a state of "incapacity for [further] fighting."[13] The men fought for three rounds before Jacobson received a wound severe enough to end the duel and to effect a reconciliation. Salten showed up at the coffeehouse the next day with a "light wound to the head." Schnitzler called the entire affair "stupid and bestial," caused by "journalistic gossip," but confessed, "Nevertheless, I always feel a little bit of envy toward him who has fought a duel."[14]

Given Salten's history, Karl Kraus could not have been terribly surprised when Salten slapped him in the face after his verbal attack on Salten appeared in the *Wiener Rundschau* in December 1896. By this time, the animosity between the two men had reached such a pitch that Kraus was unwilling to let Salten off for this "tertiary offense"[15] merely with the payment of a small judicial fine. Instead, he hired a relatively unknown writer named Arpad Sor[16] to provoke Salten to another physical attack and then to challenge him to a duel.[17] Sor began with a letter to the editor of *Wiener Rundschau* in which he suggested that Salten had made "a physical attack on an unsuspecting man" (Kraus) because he lacked both the wit for a verbal response and the courage for a duel[18] – a letter that Schnitzler called "a hypocritically silly invective" against his friend.[19] When this letter drew no response, Sor went to Griensteidl, apparently with the sole purpose of instigating an attack. He deliberately shoved Salten, who turned around sharply, striking him with his elbow. Sor shouted out "Rascal!" and headed for the exit. Salten followed and struck him in the face while Leo Van-Jung attempted to intervene, telling Sor, in reference to both his written and physical provocations, "You got what you deserved, now leave!" Instead, the two men traded insults and Sor loudly challenged Salten to a duel.[20] Representatives were named – Salten first called on Leo Van-Jung[21] and Richard Beer-Hofmann to serve as witnesses and asked Siegfried Trebitsch and Julius Sternberg to act as seconds. In the end, the entire matter was dismissed because a prior claim against Sor rendered him "ineligible for [demanding] satisfaction." In a futile attempt to preserve his image, Sor sported a bandage when he appeared in public the next day in order to create the impression that the duel had actually occurred.[22] Salten never again participated in a duel but sought justice instead through the courts and through the Honor Council of the city's Concordia Association of journalists and authors. Although Kraus would continue mocking Salten in his journal *Die Fackel* for the rest of his life, Salten never again got involved in either a legal case or in an affair of honor against him,[23] a decision made somewhat easier by his refusal ever to read anything that Kraus printed.

When Salten began his career as drama critic at the *Wiener Allgemeine Zeitung*, the Deutsches Volkstheater, founded in 1889, was already flourishing as a popular alternative to Vienna's imperial Burgtheater, and Adele Sandrock was its indisputable star attraction. When Arthur Schnitzler's *Das Märchen* (The Fairy Tale) had its premiere there in 1893, Sandrock played the lead, and Schnitzler and she began a tempestuous love affair. Salten was frequently with the two at the theater or afterwards at dinner or at the coffeehouse, and in 1895, at about the same time as Sandrock moved from the Volkstheater to the Burgtheater, he, too, had an affair with her, while keeping Schnitzler fully informed of all that transpired between them. After a fleeting bout of jealousy over Sandrock's infidelity, Schnitzler confessed to his diary, "I cannot help myself, I am actually grateful to him."[24] Neither Schnitzler nor Salten had an exclusive, lasting relationship with Sandrock.[25] Instead, Salten soon became smitten with the woman who was to become his wife.

Ottilie (Otti) Metzl was also an actress, albeit one of the lesser players at the Burgtheater. The family name had been shortened from Metzeles; her father, Moses Metzeles (Moritz Metzl) was an insurance inspector in Prague; her mother was Louise Wiener Metzeles, Moses' second wife. She was born on March 7, 1868, making her a year and a half older than Salten; she had grown up with five half-brothers and sisters and one full brother named Richard, who was older than she. Like Otti, Richard pursued a stage career, and the two were especially close.

In his reviews for the *Wiener Allgemeine Zeitung*, Salten mentioned "Fräulein Metzl" only five times, since she played primarily small secondary and supporting roles in the Burgtheater productions. There he noted that she had been miscast by being given a male role in an Otto Ludwig play,[26] that she and the actress Lotte Medelsky "spoke with poetic effect" in their roles as elves in Hauptmann's *Die versunkene Glocke* (The Sunken Bell),[27] that in Hauptmann's "Hannele" she was one of three angels who "speak wonderfully,"[28] that she played Titania in Shakespeare's *Midsummer Night's Dream* "with beautiful, heartfelt gestures and with an exquisite treatment of the verse,"[29] and that she participated in the first night's reopening of a newly enhanced Burgtheater by playing a minor role in a play co-authored by Hugo Wittmann and Theodor Herzl.[30]

As Salten recalled it, and as his reviews ultimately prove, he was first attracted to Ottilie Metzl not by her fame but by her voice, writing, "At the Burgtheater, her bell-like voice spoke the first and last verses of *Faust* unforgettably for those who had the good fortune to hear her."[31] One evening, as he was leaving the theater, "a young woman stormed past me, up the stairs to the boxes, and I stopped to look after her, for it was an actress at the Burgtheater whose voice had always enchanted me. Beer-Hofmann … whispered to me, 'That is a Jewish girl from Prague!'"[32] In no time at all, Salten began seriously courting her. Schnitzler remarked on how quickly this courtship followed Salten's breakup with Lotte Glas: "I have the impression he needed only to turn the page, so to speak, to move from Lotte to Frl. M."[33]

Otti was especially close to Wilhelmine Mitterwurzer, one of the older actresses at the Burgtheater, and she urged Otti not to get involved with Salten. One reason, doubtless, was Salten's reputation for sexual promiscuity; another may have been the common notion that Salten was concerned only with his own advancement and was incapable of commitment. When Otti refused to break with Salten, Frau Mitterwurzer insisted that she bring Salten to her, so that they could get better acquainted.[34] This occurred and, in the summer of 1896, when Salten and Otti were on a bicycle trip to the Attersee, they spent a congenial day at Frau Mitterwurzer's home, and Salten was able to establish a firm friendship with the older woman.

Salten continued to have numerous liaisons during his extraordinarily long courtship of Otti Metzl, but he also recognized the more serious nature of their relationship. When the two traveled together, they slept in separate rooms, and Otti was careful to avoid any situation that might suggest to outsiders the extent of their intimacy. Salten appreciated having a woman friend of exquisite taste and noble character. She was, he said, "a rare, very distinguished person of … artistic sensibilities, of sure, unerring judgment, of the noblest mind."[35] In May of 1897, Salten wrote Schnitzler, "Bicycling and Miss M. fill my spare time." He had traveled with Otti to Riva, on Lake Garda, where he could finally say, "a decisive turn has been taken [in our relationship]. This makes me feel better and calmer, and gives my life fullness again, since I haven't loved anybody for a long time."[36]

During this same period, Salten came to terms with his Jewish heritage, in large part through reading and working with Theodor Herzl, a prominent Viennese playwright and journalist now fighting for the establishment of a Jewish homeland. Salten never forgot the day in 1896 when Herzl burst into the offices of the *Wiener Allgemeine Zeitung* to deliver a copy of his pamphlet *Der Judenstaat* (The Jewish State). Until that moment Salten had regarded the 36-year-old Herzl with admiration and not a little envy as the arts editor and Paris correspondent for the prominent newspaper *Neue Freie Presse*, one whose essays were "little masterpieces" because he "had an eye for tiny but characteristic details, and he understood the magic of opening up wide perspectives into the world through the peephole of the tiniest of them."[37] Now, however, Herzl had taken on the Zionist cause, and instead of being merely a brilliant "man of the pen," he "became a man of deeds."[38] Salten read Herzl's pamphlet, and it made him "willing to love my Jewishness."[39] He was "enflamed" by Herzl's "figure" and "humanity" and commented, "his willingness to sacrifice and his courageous conviction obliged me and every honestly sentient being to stand by him and commit to Israel."[40]

Herzl's pamphlet was well timed, as there was a pronounced increase in anti-Semitism in Austria between 1895 and 1897. The highly political and obviously biased Parisian trial of Alfred Dreyfus had first awakened Herzl to Zionist activity, but the situation of the Jews in Vienna had also become more volatile. The Jewish population in Vienna had risen from 40,000 in Salten's birth year to 118,000 by 1890,[41] and it had acquired a good deal of influence in business, law, medicine, banking, journalism, and the arts. These upper middle-class Jews were associated with liberal politics, and, as a consequence, anti-Semitism arose primarily among conservative clerics under the leadership of August Rohling, and the pan-Germanist party under Georg von Schönerer, which had been created in protest against the infusion of East European immigrants into the city. University students also showed a new anti-Jewish bias when the Waidhofen association of German and Austrian university fraternities adopted a resolution in 1896 declaring all Jews to be without honor and therefore unworthy of participating in a duel.[42] Arthur Schnitzler declared that it was impossible at this time, "especially for a Jew who was in the public eye, to ignore the fact that he was a Jew, since other people didn't, not the Christians and even less the Jews themselves."[43]

Still, many of Vienna's Jews did not share Herzl's passion for a new homeland. Herzl found most of his followers among the Eastern Jews, while the city's liberal, middle-class Jews preferred to believe that the current wave of anti-Semitism would subside. Karl Kraus, for one, believed that Zionism actually served the anti-Semitist cause by proclaiming the differences between Jews and Austrians, thereby making them racially incompatible with European society.[44] But Kraus was not alone. In Salten's circle, Richard Beer-Hofmann was the only one to applaud Herzl's pamphlet, exclaiming enthusiastically, "Finally we have someone again who does not resignedly bear his Jewish heritage as a burden or misfortune but is instead proud to be the legitimate heir of an ancient culture."[45] Schnitzler regarded Herzl's Zionism with mild amusement while Salten's editor at the *Wiener Allgemeine Zeitung*, Julius Ludassy, denounced Herzl's text as "a piece of desperate insanity."[46]

Many who ignored the rise of anti-Semitism in Vienna sought comfort in the actions of the emperor. Emperor Franz Josef was personally revolted by the anti-Semitism that kept breaking out in his capital. He once walked out of a theater when a popular anti-Semitic song was performed,[47] and he refused to acknowledge the anti-Semitic Karl Lueger's election as mayor of Vienna until public demonstrations and the intercession of Pope Leo XIII forced him to do so. As Salten recalled it, when Herzl brought his pamphlet to the newspaper office, "the whole editorial staff mocked him." "I alone aligned myself with him," he later boasted and "even became friends with him, inasmuch as one could with Herzl."[48]

This alignment was occasioned by Herzl's bold pronouncement that Jews had no cause to be ashamed of their race. In Philipp Salzmann's day, anti-Semitism had focused primarily on religious differences, and many people of that generation had believed that they could fully assimilate into Austrian society by downplaying their religious heritage and even by seeking baptism as Christians. Many of Salten's contemporaries still clung to this belief, even though it was becoming increasingly apparent that the new wave of European anti-Semitism emphasized racial rather than religious differences. This shift in attitude made it virtually impossible for Jews ever to fully integrate into European society.[49] Salten, who suffered all his life under the stain of childhood poverty, anti-Semitic slurs, and an aborted formal education, now discovered under Herzl's tutelage that he could be proud, rather than ashamed of his Jewish heritage. And, just as Salten's participation in the Young Vienna circle had turned him from a cultural outsider to a member of a literary elite, so his newfound pride in his Jewish heritage rescued him from the stigma of being a social outcast among his Aryan neighbors.

Salten's new Zionism, like Beer-Hofmann's, was rooted in ethnic pride, rather than in a desire to participate actively in the founding of a Jewish state. And, whereas Beer-Hofmann responded to this newfound pride by adopting the Jewish faith, Salten chose to speak out for the Jewish cause. When Herzl established *Die Welt*, a weekly newspaper for Vienna's Jewish readers, Salten was the only member of the Young Vienna circle to join the venture as a regular contributor. For nearly a year, he wrote a column called "Die Woche" (The Week), in which he commented on instances of anti-Semitic prejudice and violence throughout Europe. Salten peppered these pieces with ironic commentary not only on Aryan actions but also on the over-eagerness of middle-class Jews to be accepted as the equals of their persecutors. When, for example, several Viennese Jewish lawyers were made judges, Salten commented, "How greatly surprised the ministry was when these gentlemen suddenly produced their new baptismal certificates, which was something that no one had required of them!"[50] In his weekly columns, Salten reported on the Alfred Dreyfus case in France and on anti-Semitic actions taken in France, Malta, Romania, Poland, Algiers, Germany, and Russia. He allowed that England and Austria were friendlier to the Jews than most European nations but pointed out that the air in Vienna was also polluted with anti-Semitic rhetoric.

In describing cases of discrimination at home, Salten drew a clear distinction between Vienna's comfortably middle-class Jews and the impoverished Jews who were so often the victims of racial violence. He also emphasized the delusional nature of those Jews who were trying so eagerly to assimilate fully into Viennese society, citing examples of anti-Semitic thinking that affected all Jews. He noted, for example, that the press frequently put exclamation marks after the names of Jews in order to distinguish them from the names of Aryan citizens, that Jews were banned from contributing to certain charitable organizations, that complaints were made about the Jews making too much use of the city's charity hospitals, and that several newspapers that listed Austrian playwrights made a distinction between "Germans and – 'those writing in German.'"[51] He reported on the anti-Semitic statements made by Vienna's mayor, Karl Lueger; by Georg von Schönerer of the German Nationalist Party; and by many other representatives in Parliament. His conclusion was straightforward: "The Jews see that they cannot please others, either when they have good fortune or when they suffer a calamity. Perhaps they will try at some point to please themselves for once, just for variety's sake."[52]

By writing for Herzl's newspaper Salten developed a strong sense of his own Jewishness. At the same time, he took care to keep his authorship a close secret. Erwin Rosenberger, who eventually succeeded Salten as author of the weekly column, noted that Salten "did not wish to be publicly identified with the column," while Isidor Schalit remarked, "He didn't sign his articles. He never came to the editorial offices; he sent his manuscripts by messenger to Herzl's private address."[53]

Later Salten declared his position more openly and published in this same paper a five-part series on *Das Theater und die Juden* (Theater and the Jews), a three-part series treating the anti-Semitism to be found in Houston Stewart Chamberlain's seminal work *Die Grundlagen des neunzehnten Jahrhunderts* (The Foundations of the Nineteenth Century),[54] and a harsh critique of the anti-Semitic work *Israel*, which a French countess had published under a pseudonym; he identified himself as the author of these pieces with the initials "F.S." In addition, he signed two articles on the topic "'Echt jüdisch': Bekenntnisse" ("Clearly Jewish": Confessions) "F. S–n." In these he confided how, until recently, the phrase "clearly Jewish" had caused him to feel guilty and to hide from his own Jewishness: "For years I fled this phrase, for years it followed me and tracked me down wherever I was hoping to enjoy a brief respite." He was, he said, not alone: "In my flight I had many companions who all ran away in pure fear and tried to hide behind the shrubbery of foreign ways and foreign attributes," adding, "We sang 'Watch on the Rhine' with enthusiasm in our voices and fear in our hearts; we drank and drank, and when we got sick from it, we thought it was the Jew in us who balked against the alcohol, and then we drank still more. I am glad that I have escaped from these preserves."[55] This was Salten's first public declaration of his allegiance to Zionism and one that he never recanted.

Salten had begun to make his name through his theatrical writings, and Otti Metzl gave him previously unknown insights into the actors' lives at the Burgtheater. She had been given a theatrical contract after having proven herself at her debut engagement at the City Theater in Olmütz, now Olomouc in the Czech Republic, and at engagements with theaters in Marienbad and Linz. She had come to the Burgtheater in 1891, but in five years had not been given parts that would allow her to develop her skills. Her most frequent roles were as servant girls and pages; she also played a surprisingly large number of smaller male roles because of her deep voice. Her confinement to smaller roles was true of many loyal players at the theater. Salten now made these "small players"[56] the subject of one of his feuilletons. During their years of employment at the Burgtheater, he wrote, these players gradually gave up on getting any grand roles. Their repertoire shrank and they grew too old to move on to other theaters. After spending ten years or so at a court theater, the theater owed them more than a small pension or, worse yet, a firing.

Salten was developing a stable relationship with Otti, but he remained depressed about his own professional achievements. His friends were moving on and achieving the kinds of literary success about which he was still dreaming. He was growing uncertain about his own talents or lack thereof and was himself feeling like a "small player" in the world of literature. Dörmann, Bahr, Specht, Schnitzler, Hofmannsthal, and Beer-Hofmann all had books in print, whereas his pieces had appeared only in the more transitory media of newspapers and literary journals. Furthermore, he felt that his relationships with Hofmannsthal and Beer-Hofmann were foundering. In May 1897 he noted that he saw Hofmannsthal rarely and when he did, they never discussed anything except bicycles, while his contacts with Beer-Hofmann were limited to games of poker.[57]

He had a collection of short stories that he had put together the year before, including "Heldentod," "Hinterbliebener," "Flucht" (Flight), "Cocotte und Kellner" (Coquette and Waiter),[58] "Begräbnis" (Burial), "Der Hund" (The Dog), "Die Hochzeit auf dem Lande" (The Country Wedding), and "Die Confirmandin" (The Confirmand). He had asked Schnitzler to show them to Samuel Fischer, who was Schnitzler's and Hofmannsthal's Berlin publisher. But Salten was also plagued with self-doubt. He wrote Schnitzler:

> All my desires are now concentrated on bringing something to fruition. If that could happen, I would be considerably more settled. But you can't imagine how much I suffer from a feeling of insignificance as soon as I imagine my work finished and printed and out there among all the rest of art that exists. It is the most depressing feeling, and I am paralyzed, as it were, when I begin to calculate in how many respects I am dispensable in everything that I would like to do, or could do.[59]

Salten continued to publish stories in the newspapers:

"Fernen" (Distances) in the Christmas issue of the *Wiener Allgemeine Zeitung*, "Der Hinterbliebene" in the weekly *Die Zeit*. The story Salten identified as "Der Hund" may refer to his very first published tale, "Der Vagabund," which had been published in 1890 and which never was included in a Salten book. Similarly, "Die Hochzeit auf dem Lande" never appeared in book form, unless under another name. "Die Confirmandin" waited to be published in a separate volume in 1902 as *Die kleine Veronika* (Little Veronica). Salten remarked, "Things are going strangely for me with my work. So much that is all mixed up, so many new prospects for old materials, so many new plans, have seldom occupied my mind at once. And if my feeling of great irrelevance did not prevent me, I would probably make faster progress."

Salten's depression was caused, in part, by health problems. He was plagued by painful, recurring bronchial infections and had convinced himself that he would not live past thirty-five: "It is as if I had to complete everything in these eight years that are left to me, as if then I would be on schedule. ... [T]he old bronchitis, which will eventually attack my lungs, my work projects, my love life, everything seems as if it could not hold out beyond that day in March 1905."[60]

This conviction spurred Salten to enormous activity. In June 1899 he was given editorial control over a literary insert called *Wiener Allgemeine Rundschau* that was part of *Wiener Allgemeine Montags-Zeitung*, a new publication by the *Wiener Allgemeine Zeitung*. He approached Schnitzler, Hofmannsthal, Goldmann, Schwarzkopf, and Hirschfeld to assure their participation. Schnitzler offered him his *Liebesreigen* (Round Dance of Love), and, despite its scandalous content, both Salten and his publisher, Dr. Julius Szeps, were willing to fight to get the state censors to approve its publication.[61] Almost immediately, however, Salten's insert ran into difficulties when subscribers complained that it was too "literary." Szeps was inclined to heed his subscribers' complaints, and Salten was worried that his reputation would suffer if the paper failed. The paper lasted, in fact, only six months, but these six months stretched Salten to the limit as he struggled to fill the *Rundschau* pages with quality pieces by a variety of authors. This struggle, Salten confessed, "brings no pleasure to me nor to Dr. Szeps nor to the subscribers."[62]

Still, Salten acquired an impressive list of contributors. Paul Goldmann, Gustav Schwarzkopf, Siegfried Trebitsch, Richard Specht, Hugo Salus, Karl von Levetzow, Georg Hirschfeld, Fritz Freund, and Franz Karl Ginzkey became regular contributors; Salten also published work by Strindberg and a good many French writers, including Maupassant, Maeterlinck, Georges Courteline, Pierre Beber, Alphonse Allais, Auguste Germaine, Marcel Prevost, Jean Reibrach, and Charles Quinel, as well as the English writers W. C. Morrow, Anthony Hope, and John Ruskin.

When these contributions were not enough to fill the *Rundschau* pages, he included his own works: the short stories "Sedan," "Flucht," "Das Manhardzimmer" (The Manhard Room), and "Begräbnis" – all stories that would appear in his first published book – made their first appearance in the *Wiener Allgemeine Rundschau*. He wrote a series of dramatic scenes: "Ihre Herkunft" (Her Background), "In der Garderobe" (In the Dressing Room), and "Ein Engagement" (An Engagement), which he identified as being "aus einem Schauspieler-Roman (from an Actor's Novel)."⁶³ This work never appeared in book form.

In addition to these acknowledged works, Salten published a number of pieces under pseudonyms. For his story "Lebenszeit" (A Lifetime), which would appear under his own name in his first collection of short stories, Salten hid behind the letters "F. F.," while for the one-act play "Ein Tag" (One Day), which would appear under his own name in 1902,⁶⁴ he used the pseudonym "Leopold Heinwerder," and, for his one-act play "Die Einzige" (The Only One), "Martin Martin." While these two pseudonyms are provable as belonging to Salten because of later printings of the works under his own name, it is reasonable to assume that the other works signed by author "F. F." or "ff" – the two dramas published under the title "(Geschichten) aus dem Leben des Herrn Snob" ([Stories] from the Life of the Gentleman Snob)⁶⁵ and a short story entitled "Der Condukteur" (The Conductor) – as well as a play by "Xanrof" and short stories by "Nadja" and "Popeia" all came from Salten's pen. He was almost certainly the author of two short stories without author identification: "Der Kranz" (The Wreath) and "Ein Duell." Both appeared in the final issue of the *Wiener Allgemeine Rundschau* on December 18, 1899. The crux of the former story, which deals with the issue of reconciliation between a

72

wife's murderer and her lover, would reappear in inverted form in his novel *Die klingende Schelle* (The Tinkling Cymbal), 1915, while in the latter he ridiculed dueling by revealing that his fictional participants had forgotten the cause of their duel and that one of them, fearful of the damage that might be done to his nose, was afflicted in the middle of the duel with an uncontrollable fit of sneezing.

At the *Wiener Allgemeine Rundschau*, Salten had rich opportunities to hone his satirical skills. Each week he produced a segment of the paper entitled *Wurstel-Theater*, in which he took on people and events of his day: the anti-Semitic mayor Karl Lueger for his ignorance of literature, the Countess Prokesch-Osten for her badly thought-out charities, Adele Sandrock for her desire to tackle the role of Hamlet, the distinguished critic Max Kalbeck for his ignorance about the music of Richard Wagner, Otto Brahm for calling the actor Josef Kainz a "Caesar" in the art of acting,[66] a reporter for the *Arbeiter-Zeitung* for gorging himself at a banquet while mouthing the words of the workers he was supposed to be representing, Pastor Josef Deckert for winning the Salvator medallion despite his support some years earlier of particularly vile anti-Semitic slander, and the actor and theater manager Karl Blasel for his declaration that he would "restore" burlesque to the Viennese stage. He returned again and again to his favorite whipping boy, Paul Schlenther, Director of the Burgtheater, for his failure to bring good productions of the classics, for miscastings, for delays in openings, and for neglecting his duties to spend evenings carousing with actors and friends.

Salten devoted the most space in his *Wurstel-Theater* to the reopening of the Dreyfus case after exonerating evidence seemed to absolve Dreyfus of the espionage charge that had led to his imprisonment on Devil's Island. However, since the newspaper was not uniquely Jewish, Salten used his pen to expose foolishness and prejudice in all quarters of Viennese society, not just in Jewish and anti-Semitic circles.

Although the *Wiener Allgemeine Rundschau* folded in December 1899, Salten was now able to look forward to his first book publication. His volume *Der Hinterbliebene* (The Bereaved One) appeared in 1900 with Fritz Freund's Wiener Verlag; it included the first five pieces he had originally intended for a book in 1896, with the addition of "Fernen," "Sedan," and "Lebenszeit." These last two stories featured animals and were unsentimental statements about the brevity of life. "Sedan" told of a sparrow's death on the field of battle. The more interesting one, "Lebenszeit," described the struggle of a fly to survive a cold night by flying to a candle set out upon a window sill. The window is closed; the fly batters against the glass in rage, then sinks to the sill and dies just as dawn is about to appear on the horizon. It has been noted that in both these tales, Salten used modernist techniques for portraying varying states of consciousness but that he was unique among the members of the Young Vienna circle in that he applied these techniques to dumb animals.[67]

If Salten had, as Schnitzler suggested, learned from Maupassant in writing his story "Begräbnis," "Lebenszeit," with its dying fly, and "Sedan," with its reckless sparrow, show a remarkable affinity with the tales of Hans Christian Andersen.[68] Salten was an admirer of Andersen, saying, "[He] made animals so accessible to us. ... The dung beetle, the ducks and chickens, the house cat, the watchdog, the snails. But not at all in a sentimental fashion," adding, "He doesn't try at all to teach anybody anything. At least he doesn't let it show."[69] Salten would not recognize his own similar ability to portray the fears and joys of animals for many years. Perhaps his fellow authors were responsible for this; neither Schnitzler nor Hofmannsthal nor Beer-Hofmann seems to have recognized this special talent of Salten's or even given it much attention.

Chapter 6: Attempts to Conquer the Theater

Even as Salten struggled to save the *Wiener Allgemeine Rundschau* and to publish his first collection of short stories, his thoughts were turning more and more to the stage and to what he might accomplish there. In "Das Theater und die Juden," a series of articles that he published in Herzl's *Die Welt* from March through July 1899, Salten had reflected on how Jews could – and did – contribute to the stage from their unique position as only partially assimilated outsiders in Austrian society. This perspective made Jews particularly adept at observing and critiquing the society around them; it was a special talent that made Jews remarkably successful as actors – and as critics. As playwrights, too, Jews could comment with insight and clarity on the contemporary scene. What they lacked, he said, was a sense of national history. Their fathers and grandfathers had been newcomers to the Austrian empire; they had achieved middle-class success but were not yet accepted as true Austrians. He postulated that it would take another two generations before Jews would be rooted deeply enough in the Austrian soil to be able to write great and enduring Jewish works for the stage.

Nevertheless, Salten was determined to play a more prominent part in the city's theatrical life. As a critic he had of course made it his business to ground himself thoroughly in the theater's history and traditions. In 1901 he published a long essay entitled *Wiener Theater 1848-1898*[1] in which he traced the turbulent history of the Vienna stages during the fifty years that followed the Austrian revolution. Over half of this essay discussed the Burgtheater, its traditions, its directors and their accomplishments and/or failures, and the actors and actresses who were notable during this fifty-year period. The rest of the essay did the same for Vienna's for-profit theaters. Salten was now in his late twenties; he was an acknowledged authority on the theater and his reviews had an impact on the Vienna scene. But he was eager to do more. In 1897 and again in 1899, he tried getting financial backing so that he could acquire the directorship of the city theater in Teplitz, a spa town close to the German border in what is now the Czech Republic. This theater leased the position of director to qualified applicants, and, although Salten was a finalist for the position in 1899, he was ultimately rejected and the dream died.

A larger crisis arose for both Salten and Otti Metzl in 1898-99 when a new director came to the Burgtheater. Max Burckhard had been the theater's director since 1890, but he was replaced in 1898 by Dr. Paul Schlenther, a move that Salten had at first endorsed with enthusiasm.[2] Unlike Burckhard, who had come to the Burg with little to no theatrical experience, Schlenther had been involved in Otto Brahm's founding of the Free Stage in Berlin and had been an early champion of Gerhart Hauptmann and the naturalist writers in his position as drama critic for one of Berlin's major newspapers, the *Vossische Zeitung*. Burckhard had, to be sure, brought productions of Ibsen and Hauptmann to the stage of the Burgtheater; he had also hired Adele Sandrock and given her the female lead in Schnitzler's *Liebelei*. But Salten felt that the theater had become somewhat tired and stodgy under his directorship, the stars of the theater were aging and were not being replaced quickly enough with younger actors, and Burckhard was bringing mediocre productions of mediocre plays in order to satisfy the various cliques that had become powerful in recent years.

In spite of these complaints, Salten began to have second thoughts after Burckhard was forced to resign abruptly because of a play that he had written attacking the tastes of "good society" and after a clique of actors conspired to bring in Schlenther to replace him. In an essay in February 1898, Salten paid tribute to Burckhard's hard work, his genius in bringing Friedrich Mitterwurzer – and recently Josef Kainz – to the theater ensemble, his rich productions of the old classics, and his premieres of newer naturalist and symbolist plays. Burckhard, he now said, was a man of "high intelligence," well suited for the "truly Austrian politics of compromise," who had grown into his role and become "really a good director."[3] In hindsight this belated tribute to Burckhard was a portent of trouble to come with Schlenther's rise to the position of Burgtheater Director.

Salten was ostensibly cautious in evaluating Schlenther's first four months at the theater. "One must be perfectly fair to him so that he cannot speak of prejudicial opinions if he is dismissed at some time," Salten wrote, with tongue partially in cheek, noting, "He came to Vienna under difficult circumstances" at midseason, to a theater beset by revolt, intrigue, and rancor.[4] Nevertheless, the Vienna critics were nearly unanimous in their displeasure with the way Schlenther had been selected for his position, and in the months that followed, Salten, in particular, became increasingly critical of his work. He bemoaned Schlenther's clumsiness in driving the admittedly temperamental actress Adele Sandrock from the theater in October; in November he remarked that even Josef Kainz's presence was not enough to breathe new life into the theater. He began to refer to Schlenther as "this Prussian,"[5] and when the actress Katharina Schratt, the Emperor's much-loved confidante, left the theater in 1900, he editorialized, "it is a sad sign for the current rule at the Burghteater, when so pleasant and good-natured a woman gives up her profession in disgust."[6] He attacked Schlenther for having served as an apostle for Ibsen and Hauptmann during his years as critic in Berlin but then producing inferior plays by Gustav von Moser and Koppel Elfel when he came to Vienna. What one could not have predicted, he wrote, were Schlenther's "dependence on Berlin," "the sacrifice of the Burgtheater's leading position" in Europe, and its "entrance into competition with our city's for-profit theaters."[7]

Salten soon had a deeply personal reason for hating Schlenther. As he would tell the story in later years, "When I ... sharply attacked this gentleman, he sent two actors from the Burgtheater to warn me that he would make an 'example' of my [future] wife" unless Salten moderated his attacks. In response Salten "in no way stopped [his] attacks, but simply sharpened them." Schlenther then did as he had threatened. He "fired [Ottilie Metzl] just short of the date of her eligibility for a pension."[8] Otti was frantic since she now had no income and no opportunity to practice her art. If indeed her firing was a punishment for Salten's newspaper attacks, it was a successful one, since it forced postponement of the couple's marriage until Salten could get on a more stable financial footing.[9] And Salten would have to wait another eleven years for Schlenther's dismissal.

In truth, Salten's finances continued to be in a desperate state. He had spent a good deal of money covering Lotte Glas's pregnancy; in addition, demands were constantly being made on him by members of his family, and he continued to live beyond his means. Again and again, Salten borrowed money from his friends, then had to borrow more to cover payments on the old loans. December 1899 was a particularly low point. Even though he had taken the step of acquiring his own apartment in Hietzing,[10] he continued to pay rent on his family's quarters. And he had yet to publish his book of short stories, he and his future wife were unable to get positions in the theaters, and the *Wiener Allgemeine Rundschau* had failed. Salten had hoped to help Otti by gaining the directorship of the city theater in Teplitz; when that plan fell through, she managed to get an engagement with Vienna's Raimund Theater in the fall of 1900. She continued to work at this theater, often in larger and more interesting roles than she had had at the Burgtheater, until 1903, when she became visibly pregnant with her first child.

Salten had, in the meantime, acquired a good deal of practice dealing with dramatic form: first in the many short, gripping dialogues he crafted for his satirical column *Wurstel-Theater* in the *Wiener Allgemeine Rundschau*; then in the three portions of the *Schauspielerroman* (Actor's Novel) that he published in that paper – dramatic scenes that portrayed both the enticements and the hazards of the theater for a young girl eager to pursue a stage career. This was a theme he had treated several months before in an editorial about the "Tugendbund," an organization of ballerinas that had joined together to fight against the misuse of male power in the theater, and he would return to a variation on this theme in his first full-length play, *Der Gemeine* (The Common Soldier), published in 1901 with Fritz Freund's Wiener Verlag.

In Salten's *Schauspielerroman*, the moral problems faced by the young heroine were created by her agent; in *Der Gemeine* they are caused by a conflict between the moral demands of the young girl's strait-laced fiancé and the seductive connivings of an aristocratic army officer. The conflict comes to a head when the fiancé is drafted and thereby separated from his sweetheart. After several weeks of trying to heed his demands that she remove herself from the vaudeville theater at which her mother and her brother are employed, she follows her own desires and the urgings of her family and goes on stage as a singer. There she attracts the attentions of an officer who tricks her into coming alone to his room, where he hopes to seduce her. Chance brings the girl's fiancé to the officer's room; finding her there, the soldier draws his gun and kills her, then throws the pistol at the officer's feet and says that he is now willing to obey orders.

The play has a rich array of characters, from stage performers to both city and rural residents, to army recruits, to army officers, and all speak in the language and dialect of their class and locale – a naturalistic feat that shows that Salten's finely tuned powers of observation included aural as well as visual acuity. There are no true villains in the play except for the villainy of differing values. Circumstance also plays a major role in the tragedy: it is the hero's required military service that separates him from his fiancée and causes her family to regain its influence over her. And it is only by chance that he is asked to serve the young officer on the evening that the officer manipulates the young singer into visiting him in his private rooms.

Still, Salten's implicit critique of the military draft and the decadent power of its aristocratic officers caused the Austrian censorship bureau to bar Salten's play from production in Vienna. The report claimed that scenes such as the attempted seduction of the heroine "are actually unthinkable in the Austrian officer corps" and could "have a provocative effect and make the officer class contemptible." It did, however, acknowledge that this was "certainly not the intent of the author, who had the human aspect of the problem in mind" and "does not know very much about military affairs."[11] The German censors apparently did not have the same concerns as their Austrian counterparts; Salten's play debuted at Berlin's *Neues Theater* on November 25, 1902, followed closely by a production in Munich. It would have to wait until May 1919 before it could be performed on a Vienna stage.

Salten had, he said, composed *Der Gemeine* and the one-act play "Schöne Seelen" (Lovely Souls) "under the prodding of my then fiancée."[12] "Schöne Seelen" was a stage version of his short story "Das Manhardzimmer" (The Manhard Room), which tells how an acclaimed actress, long a regular in a fine restaurant's *chambre séparée*, gets into conversation with her discrete, middle-aged waiter and how the two of them decide to wed and open their own establishment. This play became a staple of the German theaters, playing in Berlin, Chemnitz, Hannover, Nürnberg, Zwickau, Breslau, and Hamburg before opening in Vienna in December 1905 at the Lustspieltheater in the Prater Park.

Salten's next theatrical endeavor was a particularly daring one: he determined to introduce a Viennese version of Ernst von Wolzogen's Berlin cabaret *Buntes Theater* or *Überbrettl* to hometown Vienna audiences. Wolzogen, who had opened his literary cabaret in January 1901, was motivated by rather elitist idealism; by bringing "genuine artists, poets, composers, actors and singers" to his stage, he hoped to create a theater for the average man that would raise the standards of the many varieté or vaudeville theaters then prevalent in Europe.[13] Its songs, dialogues, marionette plays, and pantomimes would be of high artistic quality and would ennoble as well as entertain the public. Salten saw this as a projection of the ideals that had driven the Vienna Free Stage experiment of 1891 – an opportunity to introduce talented Young Vienna writers, composers, and artists to a broader public.

He should have foreseen problems in introducing a modernist literary cabaret into Vienna at this time. His failure with the *Wiener Allgemeine Rundschau* had demonstrated that the public was not yet ready for works that were "too literary," and, indeed, something of a backlash had arisen against the so-called degeneracy of the modernist writers and artists. This had come about rather suddenly when Karl Lueger's Christian Socialist party had defeated the Liberals in 1895. In 1897 the charismatic Lueger became the highly popular mayor of Vienna – a post he would hold until 1910. His platform speeches were overtly anti-Semitic, and in the minds of many of his followers, the terms "Young Vienna" and the "Secessionist movement" became synonymous with "perverted Jewish art." Still, Salten went ahead with his plans to found Vienna's first literary cabaret and gave it the name *Jung-Wiener Theater zum lieben Augustin*, or "Poor Augustine's Young Vienna Theater." By combining in this title the name of a cultural movement with that of a legendary folk hero who drank heavily and thereby survived the horrors of the plague, Salten announced his program of popular acculturization and satire. He counted on the active support of those writers who had contributed to his *Wiener Allgemeine Rundschau* and also on actor, artist, and musician friends for a continuing influx of material and performers.

In seeking appropriate texts, music, and performers for his opening performances, Salten cast a wide net, traveling to Budapest, Prague, Munich, Zurich, Paris, Cologne, and Frankfurt to persuade artists to contribute works to the cabaret or to appear on its stage. He found two men willing to help underwrite the endeavor: Joseph Simon and Karl Luterstrasser became his business partners, and Simon, who was the brother-in-law of Johann Strauss, also contributed his *Theater an der Wien* as a venue for the performances. Salten, who was as woefully ignorant of financial dealings as his father, agreed that Simon, Luterstrasser, and he would have an equal share of all profits, but he neglected to make these partners liable for any financial losses the venture might incur. He signed on Hugo Felix as music director and the secessionist artist Kolo Moser as stage and costume designer. Herman Bahr agreed to write works exclusively for Salten's theater, and Hofmannsthal began work on a pantomime intended for performance there.[14] Salten announced in September that Bahr would be joined by other writers such as Ludwig Ganghofer and Max Halbe as masters of ceremonies, but this plan was never realized, due to the short life of his theater.

Salten's ambitions were probably too lofty from the start. "The presentations are intended to be humorous, light, with a satirical hook but should always be taken seriously," he wrote.[15] The serious purpose of Salten's proposed entertainments undoubtedly created artistic tensions in the vaudeville world that could be resolved only with difficulty. He hoped to use the Wagnerian concept of totality – *das Gesamtkunstwerk* – to enlighten his audiences through a multitude of songs, pantomimes, shadow plays, and dramatic sketches, and to make poetry accessible through music and dance. Familiar folk songs of high caliber would provide variety throughout the program.

The opening program went through several changes before it reached its final form, and Salten had to make several last minute substitutions. It appears that even some of Salten's friends were skeptical about the success of the endeavor, in part perhaps because of the articles in several newspapers that predicted disaster even before the opening. Still, Salten managed to enlist the popular actress/songstress Hansi Niese for several musical numbers, and the controversial German poet Frank Wedekind joined the program at the eleventh hour to perform some of his ballads. In addition, Salten introduced composer Franz Lehar to the Viennese public in a duet entitled "Der windige Schneider und seine Liebste" (The Unreliable Tailor and His Beloved) and brought some new musical settings of Ludwig Jakobowsky's poems by Ignaz Brüll. These acts were framed by two longer works: Robert Schumann's cantata *Des Sängers Fluch* (The Minstrel's Curse), which opened the evening's entertainment and had at its core a ballad by Ludwig Uhland, and a musical number by Georges Fragerolle entitled *Ahasver* (i.e., The Wandering Jew) that was performed at its close. *Ahasver* had been transformed into a shadow play by means of the artist Henri Riviere's zinc silhouettes and colored glass projections, and the production had been a big hit at the Parisian cabaret *Le Chat Noir*. Salten was confident that by including such an established Parisian hit the program would end on a high note.

A particularly rowdy audience gathered for the opening on November 16, 1901. Although the performers had their paid claques in the audience to cheer those numbers in which they appeared, Salten's enemies made up the noisiest claque, loudly booing and hissing throughout the more experimental numbers. It was, Bahr reported "a real battle between parties, both of whom seemed at times to lose their heads."[16] Things came to a head with the *Ahasver* number, when, Bahr noted, "all at once everyone seemed to have a coughing fit for exactly as long as 'Ahasver' was being performed."[17] It was soon clear to everyone that the evening was a failure. Even generous critics noted that there was not much of "Young Vienna" in the evening's program. At the last minute, the premiere of a Strauss waltz had had to be canceled, and several substitutions had to be made in casting. Max Burckhard, himself now a theater critic, commented sadly on "what kind of blunders can befall even so experienced and solid a critic as Felix Salten …, when he makes the first step from the solid ground of theory over to the shaky boards of reality."[18]

The critics were especially hard on the evening's longer works. *The Minstrel's Curse* was attacked both on questions of quality – some said it was one of Schumann's weakest works, composed shortly before his descent into madness – and for its casting of an older man in the role of the young troubadour. Although the work is anti-monarchal and portrays the rise of a new social order, no reviewers mentioned this critical aspect in their reviews. Political concerns were quite a different matter, however, with Fragerolle's *Ahasver*. While more objective reviewers justifiably criticized the fact that the projected illuminations were too small for a thousand-seat theater and that the off-stage singers could not be understood by the audience, voices from more reactionary circles leveled harsh anti-Semitic attacks not only against this work but against the entire evening. *Die Deutsche Zeitung* referred repeatedly to Salten as "'Director' Salten, more accurately Salzmann," and claimed that by the end of the evening the room reeked of bordello and tavern; it expressed particular moral outrage at the sight of a "skinny, stark-naked Jewess [dancer] named Sartori, who was clothed only in gauze."[19] The *Deutsches Volksblatt* summarized the entire evening as "Jew beginning, Jew ending, Jew everything!"[20]

The newspaper critics were nearly unanimous in their condemnation of Frank Wedekind's performance of his ballads. Salten recalled one particularly negative line published in the *Neue Freie Presse*: "A Mr. Wedekind sang songs by idiots for idiots."[21]

The *Wiener Allgemeinge Zeitung* stood by Salten. It published a defense of the theater[22] in which it traced the history of the literary cabaret back to eighteenth century France, then attempted to explain why it was timely to have a theater such as Salten's that was so well suited to "the complex psychology of modern society" and to literature's and art's "impressionists, intimists, … symbolists, and mystics." Salten, it claimed, tried with his theater "to create a new forum for the modern alliance of poetry, music, dance, and mood colorings." It was, it admitted, an attempt that "was not quite successful." But "a program cannot prevail right away, not with its first performance." It expressed confidence that someone like Salten, who "assimilates with such sensitivity the artistic enunciations of the age and knows how to interpret them with such understanding in his activity as critic" would also understand how "to smooth the path for [the] popularization of modern atmospheric values."[23]

Salten's undertaking continued to be plagued by attacks in the press, however. His old nemesis Karl Kraus had a field day attacking the entire endeavor in his journal. The main focus of his attack was on Hermann Bahr and Siegfried Löwy, since the two had had good words for what had clearly been a failed premiere. Kraus chuckled over the theater's having been named for the folk hero Augustine, noting that the chorus to the song "Alas, poor Augustine" is "All is lost." He assailed Löwy for insisting in his November 17 review that the premiere had been a "decisive artistic success": "Never in a shorter time period has an artistic start become more popular than that which recently met its artistic death at the same time."[24] In an effort to save his theater, Salten dropped

Frank Wedekind and the *Ahasver* number from the program and added Siegfried Trebitsch's translation of Georges Courteline's "Sein Geldbrief" (His Money Order). It did not help. The *Jung-Wiener Theater zum lieben Augustin* shut down after only seven performances. Salten noted, "The hatefulness of the newspapers went so far as to keep bringing notices about how empty the theater was and how the whole concern should officially be shut down." In truth, the size of the theater had, from the first, been an impediment to the intimacy demanded of cabaret performances. Salten called his cabaret "the greatest failure of my life." Admitting that this failure was "certainly not undeserved," he complained that, unlike the Berlin press, which had treated a failed opening of Max Reinhardt's *Schall und Rauch* theater "with great consideration," "the bearing of the [Vienna] newspapers seem[ed] to me … much too harsh and much too biased and hostile."[25]

Salten's last public statement regarding his experimental cabaret came in January 1902, after "all opinions had been expressed."[26] He began by acknowledging that "Young Vienna" was a misleading title for his cabaret's opening program but insisted that the theater would have rapidly become a venue for both established and newer names among Vienna's writers and composers. He pointed out that Hofmannsthal, Hugo Salus, Ernst Lothar, and Hermann Bahr had signed on as established writers, along with the younger talents Fritz Freund, Willi Handl, and Leo Heller. Similarly, the more-established composers Ignaz Brüll, Alexander von Zemlinsky, Carl Michael Ziehrer, and Salten's cousin Josef Lamberg were on board, as were the younger talents Rudolph Braun, Franz Lehar, and Arnold Schönberg. He defended his selection of the Schumann work for the premiere, pointing out that a weak Schumann work was superior to the music regularly offered on the vaudeville stage. And although he acknowledged errors in the staging of *Ahasver*, he defended its selection.

Salten's strongest defense was of Frank Wedekind's songs and performance style and of Kolo Moser's stage designs. Both were on the cutting edge of modernity, he insisted, and both had been unjustly reviled by the Viennese press. Years later he would note, with some satisfaction, that Franz Lehar was performed for the very first time in Vienna on his stage.

Salten's reputation had taken a beating; he was now so heavily in debt that he could not see the end of his financial obligations. Once again he had to call on friends for assistance. Siegfried Trebitsch was particularly generous in helping him pay off his more immediate debts. As for Salten's emotional state, "I went to the theater and wrote the cheekiest articles that I could compose. ... I stuck to my old principle of showing the world a smiling face and an elegant jacket."[27]

Salten now retreated to journalism and the writing of fiction. He had published the novella *Die Gedenktafel der Prinzessin Anna* (Princess Anna's Memorial Plaque) in the journal *Insel* in 1901;[28] it came out in book form with the Wiener Verlag in 1902. This satiric tale is set in Renaissance Italy, where Salten could safely attack the tyranny of royal rulers; it tells of a hypocritical duke who, returning late at night from a tryst with a young bourgeois girl, sees his sister leaving the residence of one of his cadets. Enraged, he hires a sculptor to chisel and mount a tablet on the cadet's door saying *"In diesem Haus wurde Prinzessin Anna entehrt"* (Princess Anna was dishonored in this house). The drunken sculptor forgets the correct verb and chisels instead the word *"entjungfert"* (deflowered). This simple act creates a sensation and ultimately a quiet revolution of sorts: the sculptor declares that the tablet will bring in sightseers, and the duke's bourgeois sweetheart now declares herself free to follow the princess's example. In this work, Salten attacks both the tyranny of those rulers who abuse their power and the hypocrisy of a society that demands virtue of its women while winking at the seductive feats of its men. Richard Beer-Hofmann declared of this novella, "More than all your other works, this one has the tone that people will probably call 'Saltenish.' One does not often say such naughty things about rulers and subjects with such agreeable ease and such freedom from pathos."[29]

Salten was in need of more income than he was receiving at the *Wiener Allgemeine Zeitung*, where he had no fixed salary and was being paid only by the line. He now sought a position with *Die Zeit*, Hermann Bahr's old weekly, which was about to make the transition to a daily newspaper. In the highly competitive world of journalism, Salten had acquired enemies, and one of these, Jakob Julius David, warned the publisher, Heinrich Kanner, that Salten was "a hollow-headed schemer" who lacked any real talent. Kanner ordered Salten to write under a different name for the paper, and Sal-

ten adopted the pen name "Martin Finder." He then had the satisfaction of learning that David had told Kanner he didn't need Salten at the paper, since "you have a really great talent in Martin
Finder."[30] By the fall of 1902, Salten was allowed to sign his articles
"Felix Salten," although he continued to use "Martin Finder" for
occasional reviews and "Sascha" for satire of the contemporary
political scene.[31]

Despite the debts that had mounted because of the failure of
his theater, Salten trusted that, with Otti Metzl's income at the
Raimundtheater, his authorship of plays and stories, and his full-
time position with *Die Zeit,* they now had a substantial enough income to marry. They were wed on April 13, 1902. Arthur
Schnitzler and Siegfried Trebitsch served as witnesses.

Chapter 7: Consorting with Royalty

Towards the end of his life, when Salten was asked to contribute an autobiographical essay to an American literary dictionary, he wrote, "As interesting episodes of my life, I may mention the friendship which bound me to the archdukes of Tuscany, and ... the freeing of Princess Louise of Coburg from the insane asylum and the rehabilitation of her lover."[1] Politically, Salten was anti-monarchal, although, as a Jew, he welcomed the emperor's firm stand against anti-Semitism. He therefore qualified his views by balancing his arguments against the autocratic, conservative rule of Emperor Franz Josef with praise for the continuity and sense of nation inherent in his person. On the occasion of Franz Josef's sixtieth jubilee, for example, he wrote, "In their day our fathers knew no other imperial face in Austria, and when we were little boys, this face looked at us when we sat in the schoolroom for the first time. Now our children are growing up and going to school, and this same face looks at them too from its ornate frame."[2] This face, he said, represented "not just an emperor but rather a type in Austria: a figure born and rooted in this country."[3]

In truth, Salten took pride in his personal relations with the nobility. He boasted of his friendship with Princess Pauline von Metternich, praising her charitable works and her patronage of the arts and noting that she had asked him to keep her company as an anxious city awaited news of the emperor's death. Salten had known, of course, of Crown Prince Rudolf's frustrated desires to modernize the empire; he was nineteen when Rudolf committed suicide at Mayerling. He, like most of his fellow citizens, sympathized with Empress Elisabeth's obvious unhappiness as empress and her long sojourns abroad. Salten was too good an Austrian citizen, however, not to respect the imperial office and to appreciate the emperor's dedication to duty and to the nation.

As for socializing with the royal family, it is reasonable that Salten might want to compensate for lingering feelings of being an outsider in Viennese society by linking his name with members of the royal house, even though most of these linkages were with individuals who would fail as royalty and be cast out from the House of Habsburg. In a more sober and critical vein, Salten referred to them as the "backside of imperial and royal splendor," calling them "pathetic, ignorant, hapless, naive, and frivolous."[4] Nevertheless, the fact remains that these relationships played an important role in his life, not only on a personal level but also as source material for numerous newspaper articles, three novels, a short story, a film script, and two plays.[5]

Salten's autobiographical writings suggest that his friendships with the archdukes of Tuscany, while flattering, were also trying in the extreme. Salten opened an essay about this friendship, "Suffering, Wanderings, Comraderies," with the statement, "I was a servant. My lack of knowledge, which, to be sure, I tried to improve by means of a complex personality, my financial plight, and my eager enthusiasm for others put me into this position. But I served gladly and cheerfully...."[6]

Of these archdukes, he became intimate only with Leopold Ferdinand, a man whose character was a curious blend of arrogance, intellect, naiveté, and charm. Leopold appears to have been in great need of a confidant. He first approached Salten at an outdoor luncheon in 1897,[7] and it was through him that Salten became acquainted with his two younger brothers, the Archdukes Joseph and Heinrich. Salten and Leopold soon spent a good deal of time together, hunting, dining, and lounging at Café Pucher, where Leopold confided in Salten about his frustrations and humiliations at court. Salten saw how, "along with revolutionary ideas, along with atheistic beliefs, Leopold possessed a rigid feudal pride, a high opinion of his lofty rank, and burning ambition, even though he bled from many wounds caused by the humiliations he had sustained" at court.[8] "With the emperor," Leopold told Salten, "the rule is to stand at attention and keep one's mouth shut."[9] Salten was often shocked by the three brothers' insensitivity to the feelings of others. Despite their high royal status, all had low positions in the military, and the brothers delighted in provoking their military superiors through deliberate acts of negligence and then, when they were called to task, watching these same officers stammer and apologize upon learning their identity. Although Salten's resources were extremely limited, Leopold sometimes asked him to lend him money. On at least one occasion, Salten arranged a loan of eight thousand crowns for him through a cousin.[10]

In spite of the brothers' thoughtlessness, Salten enjoyed hunting with them; he also enjoyed their gossipy stories and the access they provided to the imperial court. His closeness to the archdukes provided him with fascinating material that he used in entertaining his friends, as Schnitzler noted more than once in his diaries. At one point, Salten, annoyed about the assumptions being made by Paul Schlenther at the Burgtheater, asked Schnitzler to make sure that the director of the theater knew that Otti Metzl's lover was Salten himself and *not* Archduke Leopold.[11] This rumor was based on Otti's close personal relationship with the archduke some seven years previously.

At Easter 1898, after Leopold's mother had the emperor take him resoundingly to task for his open display of impiety, Leopold considered freeing himself from the constraints of the court and giving up his rank. Salten managed to persuade him that he could keep his rank and restore harmony simply by expressing remorse and promising to go to confession. For a time, tensions between Leopold and the emperor eased, and he seemed able to view his hypocritical situation with ironic detachment.

When Leopold was transferred to a regiment in Iglau, however, Salten saw less of him. Leopold told Salten nothing about his relationship with the commoner Wilhelmine Adomovic or his plans to flee the empire with her and with his sister, Princess Luisa of Saxony. When Salten heard the news, at Christmas 1902, he said, "the news affected me like a bombshell."[12] He immediately made arrangements to meet Leopold and Luisa at their Swiss hideaway in Montreux. Leopold welcomed the visit and wrote Otti, "I am glad that Felix has come; he is the only one who has not thrown me on the garbage heap the way even my own brothers have done."[13] Salten not only got a journalistic scoop for his efforts; he even advised Leopold successfully on how he might get a sizable payment from the Court for relinquishing his title.[14] Salten, too, benefited monetarily from his visit to Montreux. When he returned to Vienna, he was able to use his exclusive interviews as a bargaining chip for a quadruple raise in salary at *Die Zeit*.

In addition to newspaper articles, Salten made use of his adventures with the archdukes in his autobiographical work *Der Hund von Florenz* (The Hound of Florence), 1923. Salten said of this novel that he carried the material for it around with him for twenty-five years before he "dared to write it," which thereby places it squarely during the period of his first acquaintanceship with the archdukes.

It was, he said, "an expression of my own youth, which I became aware of only later."[15] The work is set in the early eighteenth century, and the hero, Lucas Grassi, is an aspiring young artist who cannot afford the luxury of studying and practicing his art. Through a magical ring, he is transformed every other day into a dog named Cambyses and experiences all the humiliations, fears, and pleasures of that species. Cambyses is the property of an arrogant archduke of Tuscany; he accompanies the duke on his trip to Florence, where, as Lucas Grassi, he is allowed the pleasure, every other day, of working with a school of Florentine artists. Grassi leads a double life in this novel, as a young artist among equals and as royalty's pet dog, a clear parallel to Salten's own life as a member of the Young Vienna circle and as servant to the archdukes.

The archduke portrayed here is considerably older than those with whom Salten cavorted, but he is similar in that he does not brook any challenge to his authority. When Cambyses is invited into the royal coach, it is by command, "Come along, jump up!"[16] Able at last to take a close look at his master, the dog notes "with eager curiosity" that "the listless face, with its expression of imperious and unquestioned authority, filled him with astonishment and fascinated him as an altogether new phenomenon."[17] The archduke quickly makes it clear that he is the master, and when he beats the dog, he works himself into an orgy of frenzy and rage.

Salten had a major falling out with Archduke Leopold when he was unable to share Leopold's glee in a story about the Archduke Peter:

> His brother Peter had climbed up into the music gallery of the great hall of the Salzburg residence, let a cat into this hall, as well as a pack of dogs, and watched from above as the poor kitty was hounded to death and torn to pieces. I was enraged and cried out, "What a stupid prank!" Leopold said very stiffly, "You are speaking about my brother!"[18]

Salten incorporated this episode into *Der Hund von Florenz* by having Cambyses locked in a room with a cat. Cambyses, however, is more humane than the Tuscan archduke: "No matter how near he got to her ..., he never snapped at her, not even once, but held his head up high, as though pity or disgust prevented him from touching her."[19] At the end of the novel, the archduke and Grassi compete for the affections of the same young woman, a reflection, perhaps, of Salten's and Leopold's interests in Otti Metzl. In life, Salten won the woman. In the novel, the hero is stabbed to death.[20]

Because Leopold chafed under the tyranny Franz Josef exercised over the royal family, he gave Salten "valuable, revealing insight into the dynastic family, into its inner conflicts and – the word is not too hard – into its decay, into Franz Josef's psyche, [and] into the bigoted, vengeful, brutal character of the throne's successor, Franz Ferdinand."[21] Franz Ferdinand was Leopold's personal worst bugaboo, and, if Leopold's accounts are to be believed, he and the Emperor took an almost fiendish delight in thwarting Leopold's every ambition and desire.[22]

In spite of this, when Leopold took advantage of his sister Luisa's unhappiness as wife of the Crown Prince of Saxony to flee the land with her, Salten was skeptical as to the wisdom of their actions. "Both of them," Salten wrote, "brother and sister, want nothing except to *live*, to live freely, to live without constraint, to be able to forge their own fortunes. Childlike, inexperienced, trusting, and ignorant of the world, both are heading towards an uncertain, perhaps a terrible future." Their real flight, he felt, was from the harsh control and outdated demands of the Court. "Whether the crown princess and her brother are headed for a dark or a kind fate," he concluded, "they remain memorable to us through their flight from the gray middle ages into the present, from the sixteenth into the twentieth century."[23]

Salten stayed in touch with Leopold during the years that followed. He visited him in Munich in 1916, and when Leopold made his first return to Vienna in 1921, Salten met him at the train station and put him up in his home. In addition, he helped him out financially and presented him with a warm winter coat. He wrote that Leopold continued to make "an inestimable" and "admirable impression" on him, even after he had "stopped being an archduke and the misfortune of his wasted life brought his weaknesses, but also his predominant, numerous virtues to light," adding that his own study of history had caused him to recognize "what a wealth of talented, even brilliant personalities the House of Habsburg had produced."[24]

Salten's 1927 novel *Martin Overbeck* may be considered both a paean to the city's working classes and a parable of Leopold's redemption in civilian life. Salten made a clever twist on politics here, in that the revolutionary act of the novel comes from its rich, rebellious hero and not from the proletariat workers. In the novel, Martin renounces his rigidly exacting father and his wealth to prove himself by living and working among the proletariat. He has a number of misfortunes, although he always redeems himself through his own efforts. He retains his upper-class contempt for the proletariat, however, until a poor family takes him in and he is forced to accept its unquestioning kindness. A comparison of this work with Leopold's autobiography suggests that Leopold had to go through a similar period of hard work and misfortune before being selflessly nursed through a case of malaria by a young working-class girl and settling in to live with her and her husband in a Vienna suburb. In his own memoirs, Leopold concluded, "My more recent years have been clouded by poverty and want. Yet, on balance, I am happier now that I am a working man than I was at any period of my life as a royal personage."[25]

Salten did not meet Leopold's sister Luisa until after she and Leopold had fled Austria and were in hiding in Switzerland. Although Luisa had been married to the Crown Prince of Saxony for eleven years, had five children, and was expecting a sixth, Salten was stunned by her naiveté. "There was a great deal of freedom and spirit, a great deal of wit, and a great deal of will in her words," Salten wrote, but she was an "innocent." "Peace, I want nothing but peace! So spoke the woman who came from a king's castle, who was young and beautiful, and bursting with energy. And she said it so devoutly, with such naive conviction, as honorably and gullibly convinced of her intent as a child who says something like 'I want to be good, always.'" Salten already foresaw her unhappy fate at their first meeting: "This princess possessed energy and imagination, passion of heart and of spirit. ... This woman is not a strong person, however; she simply has strong instincts."[26] He was certain that the bond between herself and her lover could not hold since she had attempted flight from court before, with other lovers.[27] He urged her to return to Dresden while there was still time to regain her station and repair the damage caused by her disappearance.[28] She refused and instead summoned her lover to her side. Less than two months later she dismissed him and, through this action, fulfilled Salten's prophecy. As long as people had believed that Luisa had fled for love, they had sympathized with her. Now, however, "[h]er bankrupt passion robs her of the appearance of greatness." Still, Salten wrote, "this woman was never more in need of general compassion than now, as she ..., alone and disappointed, awaits a new and painful motherhood."[29]

Luisa fascinated Salten as a woman who was "delightfully charming, thoroughly and naively devoted to her instincts,"[30] and he decided to write her story, fleshing it out with his insider's knowledge of the politics and pressures of the Habsburg court. He wrote it as the diary of a Princess Anastasia, and published it anonymously as *Die Bekenntnisse einer Prinzessin* (The Confessions of a Princess) in 1905.

The work may be read on many levels, but it is clearly a sympathetic portrayal of a naive young princess who cannot accept the fact that her spontaneous acts can have serious repercussions for the court. She is thwarted in her desire to learn and grow; she feels neglected by the royal family, resents the king's spies who report her slightest transgressions, and reads royal jealousy into the fact that, among the populace, she is the best loved of the royal personages. She wants the benefits of the court without its burdens, wants to be unconventional and free to seek out her own friends and pursue her own interests. Salten underscores her naiveté when she misidentifies one of Goethe's most famous quotes ("Two souls dwell deep within my breast"[31]) as having been written "by Schiller, I think."[32] He does not fault her for her limited education; instead, he blames the court for banning all reading materials that are not religious in nature or do not support the institution of royalty. Leopold had told Salten how Luisa's copy of Nietzsche had been "confiscated and torn to pieces."[33] In Salten's novel, the king discovers Heine's *Atta Troll* and Nietzsche's *Thus Spoke Zarathustra* in her room, throws them down at Anastasia's feet, and calls them "disgraceful books."[34] Later the fictional king condemns her reading of Hauptmann, Balzac, Zola, and Taine.[35] This reading material had been given to Anastasia by her rebellious brother and by her first lover.

When the ex-Princess of Saxony published her own memoirs

in 1911, she wrote in her foreword, "I want ... to protest ... against the rumor that I am the author of the 'Confessions of a Princess.' I neither wrote the work nor supplied any material for it, either directly or indirectly. And it is incomprehensible to me how any woman can be viewed as author of such a report of her love affairs."[36] Luisa denied having taken her children's tutor as her lover, and so far history has been unable either to confirm or to deny that the relationship extended beyond deep friendship. Salten's sources were, of course, confidences made to him by Luisa's brother Leopold. Salten had also seen the royal miseries caused by an autocratic and unyielding monarch at home – in the suicide of the Crown Prince Rudolf, in the restless self-exile of the Empress Elisabeth, in the banishment of troublesome royals to distant garrisons and isolated residences – and could empathize with Luisa's struggles against her despotic father-in-law, King George of Saxony. As Salten portrayed them in the novel and as Leopold described them in his memoirs, arrangements were being made in secret to rid the court of Luisa's troublesome presence by declaring her insane and confining her to an asylum. "She was," Leopold declared, "to be made another victim of the strange unreasoning despotism wielded by kings and emperors in Central Europe at this period."[37]

It is this despotism that is the focus of Salten's work. Again and again, royal personages are banished to the country, stationed at remote military outposts, or confined to mental institutions when they dare to challenge the arbitrary authority of the king. In this novel, Anastasia is convinced that her father-in-law resents her because she, not he, is greeted jubilantly by the public. The king rebukes her, Anastasia writes, because she is "too relaxed, too lively, too cheerful, and in my public appearances call too much attention to myself."[38] Instead of making herself less visible, Anastasia decides to gratify herself even more by going to the theater, reading uncensored newspapers, and eventually making friends with congenial men who then become her secret lovers.

These lovers introduce her to the revolutionary currents spreading throughout Europe, currents which at first appall her. When, for example, the crown prince dies and the court both banishes his common-law widow from the residence and removes her children to the poor house, Anastasia pleads for clemency – until the socialist newspapers take up the widow's cause. She then writes, "I am deeply outraged at the tone that this rabble takes against us. For I must say that this story about the widow Schneider is a family matter, and Jews have no right to interfere in family affairs." She is so outraged that she withdraws her plea for clemency and remarks, "now dear Mrs. Schneider has only herself to blame in this matter."[39] A later lover brusquely informs Princess Anastasia that the common folk do not cheer her out of love, as she had always thought, but primarily because "they know that they annoy the king by doing so." She also learns, to her horror, that the public believes that she has had many more lovers than is the case, "men I have never thought about, as well as some whom I don't even know."[40]

As the years pass, Anastasia learns that there is no proper way to defend oneself against the tyranny of the king; placation brings only temporary relief. "Being a hypocrite is the only way to protect oneself against this system," she says, but determines nonetheless, to remain true to herself: "I am as I am, and penance is a feeling I have never known."[41]

Salten is critical of the princess, of her self-absorption and her inability to gauge the effects her actions will have on others. Her struggle for autonomy becomes a war against the king and the spies he has planted in her household, and she describes the outcome of each "battle" as a "triumph" or "defeat." She lives for the day when *she* will be queen, not because she wants to help initiate reform within the country but only because she will then be free to pursue her own interests.

Despite Anastasia's shallowness, however, Salten is empathetic to her in her harsh environment and recognizes her devotion to her children. In his novel, Anastasia abandons her children only when she realizes that she will lose them in any case since, if she remains, the king will have her confined.

In spite of the novel's outspoken revolutionary undertones, Salten's main concern was to portray the rarified environment of royalty, and to show how its liveliest and most sympathetic members are often destroyed by a despotic and outdated system. As in *Josefine Mutzenbacher* and in *Bambi*, works that appeared after this novel, Salten portrays here an environment unfamiliar to many of his readers and presents it from the point of view of a vulnerable protagonist who is driven by instinct. By doing this, he provides an inside picture of what life really is like for those forced to live within the confines of this foreign world.

Although Salten was personally acquainted with the younger members of the House of Tuscany, he reserved his greatest sympathy for yet another member of the royal family, for the princess of Belgium, Louise of Coburg, who, unlike Luisa of Saxony, had been forced into marriage with a rough and insensitive spouse fourteen years her senior. Rather than fictionalize her tragic story, Salten became a player in her fight for love and freedom.

Louise had wed Prince Philipp of Saxe-Coburg-Gotha when she was seventeen; she had endured a loveless marriage for over twenty years when she met and fell deeply in love with Géza Mettachich, a handsome Croatian nobleman and first lieutenant in the cavalry who, at age thirty-five, was five years her junior. Before meeting Mettachich, Louise had struggled to maintain the public fiction that her marriage was a solid one, and her greatest offense appeared to be her extravagant expenditures on clothes. Now she threw discretion to the wind, made Mettachich her equerry, and publicly displayed her love for him. Emperor Franz Josef was outraged and forced Prince Philipp to fight a duel with Mettachich, which the prince lost. Philipp then tried to regain some semblance of dignity by ridding himself of both his wife and her lover. He had the two captured in their retreat in Croatia, and, with the approval of the king of Belgium, had Louise pronounced insane and committed to an asylum and Mettachich accused of forging signatures on some banknotes. After four years imprisonment, Mettachich was pardoned, and he immediately wrote a pamphlet in which he declared Louise to be sane and pled for her immediate release from the asylum.

It was at this point that Salten became involved in the effort to rescue the princess. According to Salten's memoirs, Mettachich made a secret midnight call on Salten, and Salten was won over to the cause by Mettachich's apparent selflessness and by his complete dedication to winning the princess's release. Salten wrote a newspaper article declaring that he was convinced of Mettachich's honor and Louise's sanity and that they had been imprisoned simply for loving one another. "Even if the offended sense of spousal honor was bent on retribution," he wrote, "then one must say, with four years in prison for the lover, six years in a madhouse for the adulteress, that the revenge is complete, yes, that it is outrageous."[42] After Mettachich rushed to the Saxon town where Louise was imprisoned and won nothing for his trouble but a brief glimpse of the princess and an even tighter guard set to watch her, Salten helped devise a plan for her rescue. At his behest, Mettachich returned to Vienna and resumed an apparently normal life while waiting for the princess's watchmen to lower their guard. In the late summer of 1904, that moment came; Louise had been allowed a two-week visit to a health resort in Bad Elster, Bavaria, where she would be staying in a well-guarded hotel. It was then that Salten's plan came into play.

First, a Viennese restaurateur named Waitzer signed in to the Bad Elster hotel as a guest and took a room on the ground floor, with an exit into the hotel gardens. Waitzer knew the owner of the hotel and managed to get the message to Louise that Mettachich would be there to rescue her on the final night of her stay. On the night in question, Mettachich stole to the second floor of the hotel, bribed one guard, evaded the others, and got Louise safely to a carriage. To avoid detection, the lovers again followed Salten's advice by traveling first to Berlin, where they stayed with agents of Dr. Albert Suedekum, a socialist member of the Reichstag who had become interested in their case, until things quieted down and the two lovers could more safely leave German territory. They then took a train to Paris, where expert psychiatrists examined the princess and declared her completely sane. At this point, the Habsburg court capitulated. Prince Philipp granted Louise a divorce, and Mettachich's rank and privileges were restored to him.

The story was a happy one in that Louise and Mettachich spent the remainder of their lives together, albeit in poverty. It was less than happy because Louise was told she could get her share of her father's inheritance only if she renounced Mettachich and returned to Belgium. This she refused to do. Although Louise was not as charming or as spirited as Luisa of Tuscany, Salten had more respect for her position, for, unlike Luisa, "Louise of Coburg was in no way in love with love but rather, with the intensity of her dry personality, in love with only this one man." He remarked:

> This woman was strange, filled with a strong,

proud sense of her heritage and her position, extremely wise and at the same time completely naive. In all human matters, she revealed a sharp,
merciless gift of observation, [but] in practical
matters, especially those regarding money, she remained totally ignorant. She was cool and yet passionate, possessed enormous will power in dis-
sembling and holding back until a moment came
when she seemed to lose all inhibitions and was
carried away in abrupt outbursts without thought
of the consequences.[43]

When the two refugees arrived in Paris, Salten was waiting. He
saw at a glance that Louise was worn and aged by her six-year in-
carceration. Still, she maintained all the ceremonial behavior of a
royal princess. Since Salten was the only Viennese reporter who
knew of the princess's location, he created great excitement in the
press with the publication of her first interviews. At the same time,
Die Zeit printed a reproduction of a handwritten letter from the
princess in which she thanked the paper, through Salten, for taking
up her cause.

In spite of Salten's coups in the press, it is doubtful that the
princess was ever enlightened as to the full extent of Salten's assistance in her successful rescue. Her memoirs[44] make no mention of
him, and Salten remained silent about his role in the affair until
long after both she and Mettachich were dead. Then he wrote a
play entitled *Louise von Koburg*, in which he told the whole story of
the lovers' imprisonment and rescue.[45]

The play is composed of fifteen scenes and is set in Vienna, in
the Saxon insane asylum Lindenhof, in the military prison of
Möllersdorf, in Bad Elster, and in Paris. Except for Louise, Philipp
of Coburg, and Mettachich, the names of all figures have been
changed, and some tightening has occurred, as when, for example,
Louise and Mettachich are captured at a hidden resort in the Vienna Woods rather than in Croatia. The events of the Coburg affair
create a natural dramatic structure, with Salten's entrance into the
story being the turning point of the drama. In this play Salten is
transformed into the young, blond author and publicist Herbert
Iffinger, who, through his pen and his brain, is instrumental in or-

chestrating the princess's escape. In a slightly comic turn, Salten reveals the attitude that the aristocracy had toward the press in Louise's reaction to Mettachich when he asks her to meet with Iffinger: "Such a situation! Good heavens – such a difficult situation. Never in my entire life have I spoken with a journalist. Is he very repulsive?"[46] Salten knew from experience that the aristocracy paid little heed to journalists and their writings, but he also knew that the real power of journalism lay in its sway over broad public opinion. He made this point more strongly in his memoir fragment, where he wrote about the effect his newspaper articles had had in the Coburg affair:

> A fundamental principle was applied in Austria at that time: one should pay no heed to a man of the pen, let alone concede that he is right. This lack of effect was taken for granted. But another, equally expected effect quickly set in – the effect on broad layers of the public. Its [prior] acceptance of the decision of the military court was destroyed, its trust in the illustrious court marshal was eradicated, its indignation over the double injustice was widespread.[47]

Although Salten was at the peak of his power as a journalist at the time of Louise of Coburg's escape, he knew his limitations. While it was true that he could speak directly to the public and create outrage over an injustice, this was not enough to bring about actual change. Indeed, as he revealed in *Die Bekenntnisse einer Prinzessin*, the aristocracy held the liberal press in such low regard that its members almost instinctively rejected any arguments made in its pages. The pen could create sympathy and understanding for a victim of injustice, but change could be brought about only by those willing to get actively involved. And in the case of Géza Mettachich and Princess Louise, Salten did just that.

Chapter 8: Building His Reputation

Otti Metzl did not go into marriage with Salten with closed eyes; she knew very well about his constant monetary difficulties, his extravagant lifestyle, and his affairs with women. They had been living together in his two-room apartment in the eighth district[1] but now began looking for larger quarters. After a honeymoon in Italy, they moved in August 1902 into a spacious apartment in Porzellangasse, in the ninth district,[2] in a building bordering the park of the Liechtenstein Palace. Despite Salten's new position with *Die Zeit*, finances were extremely tight, and Otti was unable to wean Salten from his profligate spending. One telling episode occurred soon after their move: while Otti was worrying over the household bills, Salten showed up at the apartment with an elegant new walking stick and a bottle of expensive perfume that he gave to his wife.

Salten had described his move from the *Wiener Allgemeine Zeitung* to *Die Zeit* as a move from "fifth wheel" to "seventh wheel" at his new employer's.[3] This lasted, however, only until he had proven his abilities under the pseudonym "Martin Finder." As an unknown, Salten got the attention of Paul Goldmann, who praised this rise of "new blood"[4] in journalism. Schnitzler reported hearing that even Karl Kraus was "delighted" by Finder's writings and that he was convinced that he was a Christian "or even an anti-Semite." "Against my will, I find this objectivity amusing enough to report it to you," Schnitzler added.[5]

Years later Hermann Bahr would declare that it was a piece about Zola that propelled Salten into the top ranks of Viennese feuilletonists. Bahr wrote, "Emile Zola died on September 29, 1902. The news came to Vienna that afternoon, and word came from all the editorial offices to prepare obituaries quickly for the morning papers. One obituary with brilliant power of characterization appeared in a paper that was otherwise little read …: overnight Felix Salten was famous."[6] Bahr's memory may have exaggerated the importance of a single newspaper column – more likely Salten's fame came about because of his exclusive interviews with the Habsburg family's failed royals – but Salten made, without question, a powerful statement about the man whose novels had rocked

Europe:

> This much-hated man, who was never re-
> strained, has been compared to a volcano that
> suddenly turns the morality of a world into ashes,
> spewing out glowing filth through which the vir-
> tue round about is set in flames. To quench it, the
> heavenly-blue aestheticists of Europe have for
> years poured the waters of their criticism over him
> .... They all declared: a monster has crawled out
> of the sewers of the city. Later, however, the next
> generation came to a proper understanding: a poet
> had descended into the depths of existence.[7]

The very fact that Bahr would remember this newspaper column as the basis for Salten's fame indicates the prominent position
of the feuilleton in Viennese society. These pieces, whether
sketches, reviews, commentary, satire, or personal tributes, were
published daily on the lower half of the first page of the city newspapers and were often the first items that the public read. Scholars
have noted that in Vienna the feuilleton filled a need similar to that
of the operetta and the coffeehouse, "bridging classes and differences of opinion by providing music in words to lull a people who
feared moral issues."[8] This was precisely the reason why Karl
Kraus hated feuilletons and the men who wrote them. The pieces
were often light and extemporaneous in nature. In Vienna they
"developed into a chatty essay on any topic, written to match the
verve and sparkle of conversation," serving as "a model of wit and
good taste, catering to a demand both for novelty and nostalgia."[9]
A glance at Salten's output during the first three months of 1903
demonstrates his breadth of topics: he provided behavioral descriptions of a government gathering and of a court ball, reviewed plays
by Maeterlinck and Shaw and novels by Heinrich Mann and Pietro
Aretino, described a visit to a varieté theater, reflected on the fate
of Louise von Coburg, painted a sympathetic portrait of an old
piano teacher, and provided a nostalgic look back at the old Danube shores then being paved for flood protection. Salten had written a good many feuilletons for the *Wiener Allgemeine Zeitung*. After
he was promoted to literary editor at *Die Zeit* in November, he also

helped in the solicitation and selections of the other columns that appeared in its pages. He generally authored the most important Sunday feuilletons himself. He became so widely read that the aspiring young novelist Walter von Molo and his friends "asked each other after every public event: What does Salten say about that?"[10]

Salten's route to the coveted first page of *Die Zeit* was typical of many of his competitors, who, like him, had begun by writing brief theater or book reviews and had gradually gained enough name recognition to attract readers and branch out into other fields. Feuilletonists had a great deal of freedom, be it in approach (subjective, objective), in style (scholarly, satiric, analytic) or form (essay, glossary, drama, poetry). The only forbidden topic was editorializing on Austrian politics. Most pieces were characterized by the grace of their writing and a striking *pointe* at the end, but, as Salten demonstrated in his tribute to Zola, he could also write impassioned prose when he was moved to do so. Bahr had already made his name as a feuilletonist, and Hofmannsthal frequently wrote guest pieces for the Vienna papers. It was, Schnitzler acknowledged, a talent he lacked, and he, like Kraus, tended to speak disparagingly of the feuilleton as an inferior, improvisatory art form.

Schnitzler was, by this time, acknowledged as a master playwright and prose artist. As Salten's reputation for journalism flourished, his relationship with Schnitzler faltered. One day he confronted Schnitzler, saying that he had the impression from his remarks that Schnitzler looked down on him. He complained that Schnitzler failed to defend him the way that Salten always did for him. Schnitzler admitted that this was "very true" and wrote a defensive analysis of the situation in his diary, commenting that Salten's "oversensitivity" and "occasional irritability" probably arose from the fact that people often spoke of his own literary influence on Salten and that this made Salten appear to be dependent on him. He then addressed Salten's complaint that he was not "appreciated enough" by Schnitzler:

> In reality, I believe that no one thinks more highly of his talent than I do, but [I also believe] that his *distinctiveness* in an artistic sense is not significant, which does not exclude the fact that I be-

lieve him capable of works of brilliance, maybe even of power (not just journalistically, in which area he is absolutely first class, but also "literarily"); intelligence, force of will, artistic understanding and insight into human relationships are often worth more than this vague "distinctiveness," which actually makes up only the atmosphere, not the intensity of works of art.[11]

Salten did have a literary breakthrough of sorts when his novella *Die kleine Veronika* (Little Veronica) was accepted for publication by Samuel Fischer's publishing house in Berlin. Salten had read the work to Hofmannsthal, Schnitzler, and Beer-Hofmann in September 1902, and Schnitzler noted in his diary that it was "a superb new novella."[12] Schnitzler passed the work on to Samuel Fischer with his recommendation, and Fischer, although he had "some objections," acknowledged that it had "Zolaesque power, especially in the last third."[13] It appeared in the December issue of Fischer's *Moderne Rundschau* and in book form the following year.

In this work, Salten's Veronica is a pious, innocent young girl from the country who comes to Vienna for her confirmation when she is thirteen. She stays there with her aunt, who hides from her the fact that her elegant boarding house is actually a bordello. Veronica and her aunt follow the Viennese tradition on confirmation day by going from the church to the Prater Park to continue the day's celebration. As the evening progresses, Veronica is left alone with a man who seduces her. She innocently believes the man loves and will marry her; when he rejects her and her beloved aunt first harshly condemns her for her profligate behavior, then laughs over her naiveté, Veronica commits suicide.

The irony of the tale lies not in the corruption of innocence but in the fact that a corrupt society assumes corruption everywhere. The plot's melodramatic and sentimental overtones are subverted by careful structuring of parallels and contrasts throughout the work: between Veronica's unloving mother and her seemingly carefree aunt, between the all-embracing centrality of the village church and the urbanites' indifference to church services in Vienna, between the coarse life of toil in the country and the decadent entertainments of the city. All of this is filtered through the eyes of the innocent Veronica, who is herself on the cusp of adulthood and does not know whether to behave like a child or woman.[14] *Die kleine Veronica* was a strong work with which to make an entry into the Berlin market and confirmed Otti's conviction that Salten should focus on writing fiction and drama – that this would bring him greater critical recognition and ease the financial situation at home. It was doubtless also with her encouragement that he published another work that year under the title *Gustav Klimt: Gelegentliche Anmerkungen* (Occasional Comments). This slim volume was inspired by the furor over Klimt's *Beethoven Frieze* in the Secession exhibition of 1902 and recalled for Salten the furor created over his own short-lived cabaret project. One can see that Klimt is Viennese, Salten wrote, "because he is praised by the whole world and insulted only in Vienna."[15] Salten describes Klimt's sovereign and bemused reaction to an incensed patron of the arts who, when he first viewed the *Frieze* as a work in progress, shouted out "Revolting!" and fled the hall.[16] Tellingly, Salten added an aside to his depiction of Klimt's equilibrium in the face of such criticism:

> To be sure there are some artists … for whom the thoughtless word whistles down into their breast like a whetted knife so that the heart bleeds. It is a bit of good fortune for these men when they find comfort and consolation, recognition and encouragement in the circle of their fellow artists. Comrades … rescue his talent from the lynching critics, support the faltering man, restore him who has become uncertain about his talents to his old self.[17]

Clearly, Salten, in praising the support that the Secessionist artists provided to one other, was thinking of his own situation and especially of the loyal support Hermann Bahr, Siegfried Löwy, Siegfried Trebitsch, and Otti and Richard Metzl had given him following his cabaret fiasco.

Salten then went on to answer the various charges that had been leveled against Klimt. He argued that Klimt's nudes should not be viewed as prurient since art was – and always had been – sensualist. He expressed admiration for the manner in which Klimt envisioned old themes in new ways and had especial praise for Klimt's 1901 depiction of Judith, in which the traditionally pious matron of Biblical history is transformed into a modern-day femme fatale. It was, Salten stated, his favorite work of Klimt's precisely because he takes the Jewish women of contemporary Vienna, "slips their fashionable clothes from their bodies, takes one of them and places her, clothed in her timeless nudity in front of us and – *ecce* Judith – the heroic women of a previous age rise up before our gaze, come to life and stroll among us." "The creation of this contact between past and present objects, this demonstration of the eternally human, eternally enduring, this emphasis of a continuity which otherwise escapes our grasp, this is modernity,"[18] he declared. He noted that Klimt's controversial paintings for the Aula of the university were similarly radical rethinkings of old allegorical ideas, and he condemned a Viennese public that passed instant judgment on something new and strange to it.

Despite his marriage, new job, book publications, and involvements with Archduke Leopold and his sister, Salten allowed himself in November 1902 to get entangled in a difficult love liaison with Mirjam Horwitz, a young Berlin actress who was thirteen years his junior. The liaison had come about during Salten's visit to Berlin to attend the premiere of his play *Der Gemeine*; it had been a rash and impulsive act that led to a confrontation with Horwitz's father and Salten's promise to end the affair. Salten confessed to Schnitzler, "I would probably not have given her father any promise if I had cared very much for [her]."[19] Still, he worried about scandal if, as Mirjam suggested, she were to make the affair public or, worse, commit suicide. At Salten's request, Schnitzler sounded her out when he was visiting Berlin; he found Mirjam more angry than despairing and assured Salten that he had nothing to fear from her. Nevertheless, the affair dragged on for several more months, and Mirjam even moved to Vienna to be nearby. Finally, in September 1903, she was persuaded by Salten and by Schnitzler's wife, Olga, to return to her parents in Berlin. Salten never again got involved with someone who could compromise him so publicly.

In the meantime, Otti had become pregnant and in May 1903 retired from the Raimund Theater to await the birth of her first child. On August 11, she gave birth to a son, whom she and Salten named Paul. When Paul was two months old, a ten-year-old girl joined the household, the offspring of a liaison Salten had had with one of his parents' serving girls. Salten was willing to give the girl whatever support she needed, but she was discontented and soon returned to her mother.

Schnitzler now had a son, too, and the two families socialized frequently, despite a minor falling out over a review that Salten wrote of Schnitzler's *Reigen* (The Round Dance). After an exchange of letters over the subject, Schnitzler wrote to Salten: "I think we are both a little bit more sensitive than is absolutely necessary ... and would be less so, if the thought of one of us losing the other were not painful."[20] Salten had taken up photography as a hobby, and some of his pictures from this period show Schnitzler, Hofmannsthl and his wife Gerty, and Otti and her siblings. Salten had also become an avid hunter, and Schnitzler noted disapprovingly that he kept "unloaded shotguns" in the corner of his study.[21]

Otti kept urging her husband to write books, and in October he read an early version of a long Renaissance prose piece entitled *Der Schrei der Liebe* (The Cry of Love) to Schnitzler, Hofmannsthal, and Beer-Hofmann. Schnitzler described it as a "failed novella,"[22] an opinion that he did not alter when he read the revised version a year later. This was not a view shared by everyone; a quarter century later, Rudolf Krentz declared, "'Die Gedenktafel der Prinzessin Anna' and 'Der Schrei der Liebe' will always be counted among the best pieces of amorous literature."[23]

The basic premise and *pointe* of the novella – that real love is to be found in a true marriage partnership and not in casual erotic couplings – is presented in a novel manner. The women of the island kingdom of Ravellaska cry out when they climax during lovemaking; this "cry of love" is not just a sign of passion but a revelation of the women's essence, a sign of her giving herself completely to her lover, body *and* soul. When the young king of Ravellaska weds a beautiful princess from another land, the country waits in vain to hear her cry of love when she is bedded. When she remains silent, the islanders assume that the virtue of the princess has triumphed over the passion of the young king, and the women honor her for her strength of character. The next time she is bedded by the king, she bites him in passion, and *he* cries out; the tables have turned, as the king gives himself to his wife, body and soul.

There are striking parallels here between King Pescaro and Salten, between Princess Lianora and Otti; even their appearances are comparable. Pescaro is "not very tall but slim like a boy." He is "young and handsome," smiles "proudly and shyly,"[24] and has "chestnut brown hair." His mouth is "like a woman's mouth, red, full, and tender." "But the king sometimes had a habit of compressing his lips, drawing down the upper lip, so that an expression of determined, impudent grandeur appeared on this fresh, youthful face."[25] Lianora is characterized by her "calm, constantly questioning eyes," "the flicker of an imminent smile,"[26] and the unusual timbre of her "strangely dark, resounding voice."[27] Pescaro's break with his last mistress echoes Salten's break with Mirjam Horwitz, and one can even compare Pescaro's desire to level his love nest with Salten's determination to renounce any further love liaisons. Although it seems unusual to place a love story for one's wife in a Renaissance setting, this "contact between past and present objects, this demonstration of the eternally human, eternally enduring," conforms with Salten's notion of modernity.[28]

Salten made *Der Schrei der Liebe* a parallel work to *Die Gedenktafel der Prinzessin Anna* by showing how the actions of princes take an ironic turn in influencing the lives of the masses. In *Die Gedenktafel* the prince's action freed the masses from its sexual double standard and helped to create a more even match of the sexes; in *Der Schrei der Liebe*, the prince ushers in a new age of monogamy, with wives now asserting the privilege of denying marital rights to their husband until their second night of matrimony. Hofmannsthal declared that he found the work in print made "a much lighter, sensually happier, and more unified impression" than it had when he had first heard it read aloud.[29] It was published, as *Die Gedenktafel der Prinzessin Anna* had been, by Fritz Freund's Wiener Verlag.

During 1903 Salten wrote a more contemporary short story, "Erhebungen über Barbara Liebhardt" (Inquiries about Barbara Liebhardt), which he published the following year as a feuilleton in *Die Zeit*. It is a story critical of the hypocrisy of politicians; in it, a mayor who first intends to honor an ancient, 104-year-old woman, withdraws this offer when he learns that she, as a young girl, had been engaged – but not married – to a soldier who fell in the Napoleonic wars. He cannot, he says, honor "a fallen woman." The story is an ironic take on the false morality of Vienna's populist mayor, Karl Lueger. It would have to wait four years before appearing in book form in the collection *Die Geliebte Friedrichs des Schönen* (The Sweetheart of Friedrich the Handsome). During 1904 and 1905 Salten poured out columns under three names: Felix Salten, Martin Finder, and Sascha. "Finder" now became a pseudonym to conceal the true extent of Salten's literary production and was most often assumed for shorter book reviews and occasional feuilletons about topics Salten felt could be more effectively treated under a lesser-known pseudonym. "Sascha" became a satiric alter ego, a successor to Salten's *Wurstel-Theater* voice of 1899, and Salten used this name most frequently when he covered internal parliamentary gatherings and the foibles of foreign kings. At this time he was writing a series of articles, as "Felix Salten," about the threatening situation in Russia – the Russo-Japanese War of 1904-05, the Bloody Sunday massacre of Russian civilians at the Tsar's winter palace in January 1905, and the strategic errors of the tsar's relatives and advisors. It is striking to see how differently "Salten" treated Russian affairs and how "Sascha" – of necessity – covered political events at home: "Salten's" essays were thoughtful, critical, and put his remarks into historical context; "Sascha" produced verbal caricatures of the people he treated, spoofing rather than critiquing Austria's parliamentary figures.

Still, like political cartoons, the Sascha pieces reveal a good deal about Salten's attitude towards his subjects through his selective emphasis on aspects of body build, gestures, and facial appearance. Although Salten often used internal monologue in his works of fiction in order to reflect the psychology of his figures, he was also an adherent of the pseudoscience of physiognomy and incorporated detailed descriptions of facial features and posturings into both his essays and his works of prose fiction. Salten always downplayed his intellect, claiming, "I must confess that, besides my excessively bold nature, I am rather stupid, although some people erroneously consider me wise."[30] He could, however, lay claim to remarkable observational skills and defended his use of physiognomic descriptions by stating, "Let us not underestimate external traits. A man who has his hair cut short or lets it get long, who parts his hair on the right or left, brushes it smooth or simply strokes it back, wants to say something by doing so. In the end we want to make of ourselves what we consider especially beautiful. And then each one betrays how he thinks about what is most beautiful."[31] Salten rather prided himself on his ability to read faces. His study of Tsar Nicholas II is typical, even though "Sascha" at first seems to mock the very idea of physiognomy by saying of the young tsar's facial features: "There is nothing one can say about his nose except to say that it is just a nose." But he goes on to describe a slender young man who holds his head "down a little bit, like people who step into full sunlight or expect a blow" and whose "soft, obligingly blinking eyes" "wander about frightened and restless." He returns to the tsar's coloring later in his essay; what he first describes as "indoor coloring, the pallor of office, perhaps," is, at the end, the pallor of fear of the outbreak of open revolution.[32]

In 1905 Salten published the Sascha portraits of kings under his own name in a volume illustrated by Leo Kober. The cover art reveals the satiric bent of the work by showing a court jester gazing through a microscope at a tiny figure with crown and scepter who huddles beneath the lens.

Karl Kraus, who continuously mocked Salten's much-vaunted friendships with royalty and his rising fame as the author of naughty Renaissance tales, now added Salten's repetitions of physiognomic description to his list of Salten's failings, writing:

> The fact that the German Kaiser who comes
> so frequently to Vienna has something thundering
> about him, and that he shares this quality with …
> so many of the personalities whom one is forced
> to write about on Sundays, is understandable. But
> is it really unavoidable that a usurer looks exactly
> like a vice admiral and that all of these remarkably
> lifelike portraits are remarkably similar? In particu-
> lar, I would like to be excused from having a fluffy
> little white mustache *ride* again on a voluptuous
> upper lip under the sharp nose which pokes gently
> forwards from a round face. We have taken part in
> that all too often.[33]

After the birth of her son Paul, Otti returned briefly to the stage before retiring, once again, at the end of the spring season of 1904. On August 18, she gave birth to a daughter, whom she and Salten named Anna Katharina. Salten was now at the top of his

profession. Instead of dying in March 1905, as he had once predicted, he had achieved a reputation as one of Vienna's premier
feuilletonists. That year he was able to publish four books: *Das Buch
der Könige* (The Book of Kings), *Der Schrei der Liebe,* the anonymously written *Bekenntnisse einer Prinzessin,* and *Wiener Adel* (Vienna
Nobility), a book of essays about the Viennese aristocracy that was
culled, in large part, from previously published newspaper pieces.
That year Schnitzler noted in his diaries that Salten's one-act play
"Schöne Seelen" was also being performed to great acclaim at the
Lustpieltheater in the Prater.

Indeed, Salten's success was marred only by an annoying affair
of honor that would plague him for many months to come. This
time the conflict was with his former editor at the *Wiener Allgemeine
Zeitung,* Julius von Gans-Ludassy. The affair started off innocently
enough. The Concordia organization of journalists had gathered to
protest Heinrich Kanner's behavior toward his editors at *Die Zeit,*
claiming that he intimidated them by yelling at them. Salten spoke
up in Kanner's defense by saying that the yelling meant nothing,
then added, jocularly, "My friend Ludassy is sitting here next to me;
he was my first chief editor and he yelled too. That's why we are
still friends!" According to Salten, Ludassy backed away from Salten, muttering, "I was your friend, and you will regret these
words."[34] As Salten related it, Ludassy began to circulate rumors
about him, saying that he "knew things" about Salten that demonstrated that he was harming the profession. One claim was Salten's
supposed blackmailing of Ludassy, by asking him for a loan of
eight thousand crowns just before the premiere of a play by
Ludassy back in 1900.[35] After Stefan Grossmann printed these rumors in the *Arbeiterzeitung,* writing that Salten had the "inherited
instincts of a junk dealer,"[36] Salten succeeded in bringing claims
against Ludassy and refuting all the charges that had been brought
against him. In May 1907, two and a half years after the initial confrontation, Concordia declared that "no act had been proven
through which Herr Salten had had a negative impact upon the
honor, the dignity, and the reputation of the profession."[37] Ludassy
was censured and forbidden to hold an honorary position in Concordia for a year. Grossmann tried to effect a reconciliation with
Salten, but Salten was too proud to accept it.

In spite of or because of these angry attacks at home, Salten decided to try his luck in Berlin. It was an auspicious time to make the move since he was now known there through the publication of *Die kleine Veronika* by Samuel Fischer's publishing house and through productions of *Der Gemeine* and "Schöne Seelen" in the city theaters. Although *Die Zeit* negotiated to keep him in Vienna, Salten accepted the position of editor-in-chief of the *Berliner Morgenpost* and the *Berliner Zeitung*, and in January 1906 he moved his family to Berlin.

Berlin was, in many ways, the mirror image of Vienna. Whereas the Austrian emperor, Franz Josef, reflected Austria's bankrupt Biedermeier past, Germany's Wilhelm II was of a younger generation – charismatic, bombastic, and the leader of the largest army and strongest economy on the Continent. While the most influential artists of Austria turned away from politics to espouse the tenets of impressionism and symbolism, those of Germany were more inclined to embrace social causes. Vienna was awash in old-world nostalgia and in a state of denial about the approaching apocalypse, but Berlin was a bustling metropolis that looked to the future with confidence and pride.

The two newspapers that Salten was to manage were products of the Ullstein brothers' rapidly expanding empire, one that was moving into book publication just as Salten joined the family team. Inspired by their example, Salten began to come up with his own dreams, writing jokingly to Schnitzler, "When I have founded the great newspaper, *Neue Freie Presse* in Berlin, a weekly in the style of *Zukunft*, and am directing four papers instead of two …, then I will certainly buy the automobile I have long wanted."[38] He claimed that he found little to distract him: "That is what is good about Berlin, that one finds pleasure only in working, in nothing else. Not in walking, not in trips to the country and pleasant chatter, and not in any other friendly, time-consuming activities. One has to work all the time, work all day, if one wants to feel good."[39]

During this period of extreme productivity, Salten appears to have been putting the finishing touches on a novel that would make him forever the center of controversial debate: the notoriously pornographic *Josefine Mutzenbacher*.

Chapter 9: *Josefine Mutzenbacher*

Although it is generally acknowledged that Salten is the author of the anonymous erotic masterpiece *Josefine Mutzenbacher oder die Geschichte einer Wienerischen Dirne von ihr selbst erzählt* (Josefine Mutzenbacher or the Story of a Viennese Whore as Told by Herself), the authorship has never been definitively proven. Nearly all references to the Mutzenbacher volume now name Salten as its probable author, but there are still some scholars who maintain that the memoirs are too indelicate to have been written by Salten[1] or else too well written for his journalistic style.[2] One critic has recently gone so far as to claim that the first journalist to write a review of the novel, Ernst Klein, was actually its author.[3] Certainly Salten's family never benefited from his supposed authorship of this enduring work; a court case determined in 1988 that it was ineligible for the 10% royalty normally paid to authors' families. Tellingly, however, the court never disputed Salten's authorship of the novel; its decision was based solely on the fact that the claim of rights to the work fell outside the statute of limitations.

Since its 1906 publication in limited edition with the Wiener Verlag, the work has been widely reprinted, translated, edited, filmed, and followed up with two anonymous sequels: *Meine 365 Liebhaber von Josefine Mutzenbacher* (My 365 Lovers), ca. 1930,[4] and *Peperl Mutzenbacher, die Tochter der berühmten Josefine Mutzenbacher* (Peperl the Daughter), 1967, neither of which approaches the earlier work in originality or style. The original *Mutzenbacher* has achieved the ranks of world literature,[5] and all agree that a man of considerable literary skill gave shape and style to these charmingly naughty memoirs. At first scholars named two main suspects as their author: Salten's friend Schnitzler and Salten himself.[6] There were good reasons for suspecting each of writing this work. Schnitzler, after all, had a reputation for writing about men's erotic escapades with *süße Mädel*, and in 1902 he had published *Reigen* (The Round Dance), a cycle of sexual romps through all classes of society that confirmed his reputation as the author of scandalous works of erotic fiction. Salten, too, was authoring fiction of questionable bourgeois taste: *Die Gedenktafel der Prinzessin Anna*, 1902, about a town's emancipated reaction to news of a princess's deflowering; *Die kleine Veronika*, 1903, about the seduction, deflowering, and suicide of a pious young girl from the country; and *Der Schrei der Liebe*, 1905, about the public attention afforded a prince's apparent inability to bring his bride to climax. Within a few years of *Josefine Mutzenbacher*'s publication, Schnitzler was effectively eliminated as its author. Both in public letters and in his private diaries, Schnitzler vigorously denied any involvement in the work, and he even confided to his diaries that the author was "probably Salten."[7] Salten, too, denied authorship of the scandalous volume, although his denial was much less vehement and he made no effort to correct his entry as the suspected, then definitive author of *Mutzenbacher* in the *Deutsches Anonymen-Lexikon* (German Index of Anonymous Works).[8] Some have offered as proof of Salten's authorship the fact that he wrote to Hofmannsthal in May 1892 that he was working on a longer work entitled *Mutza*, since the resemblance in names suggests that this was an early draft of the novel.[9] Its plot bears no resemblance to *Mutzenbacher*, however; in July of that year, Salten described *Mutza* as the tale of a woman who partakes in an adulterous relationship, then commits suicide out of guilt.[10] Also, if the foreword to *Mutzenbacher* is to be believed,[11] the actual source of the story did not die until 1904, and it was shortly before this woman's death that she entrusted her autobiographical notes to her doctor. All one can say about the coincidence in names, then, is that *if* Salten were the author of Josefine Mutzenbacher's lusty memoirs, he had already invented her pseudonym when he took up her story.

Two reports of people who asked Salten directly whether or not he had authored *Mutzenbacher* leave the question open. Salten reportedly shrugged when he responded to the writer Stefan Zweig, saying, "If I deny it, you won't believe me, and if I admit it, you'll think I am teasing you. So..."[12] The critic and essayist Robert Neumann reported that in 1931 Salten answered his question by simply "smiling enigmatically."[13] Egon Friedell has been quoted as saying wittily, "this book (a) can only have been written by a real writer and (b) this writer is named Felix Salten," adding, however, that he had never thought Salten capable of such an achievement.[14] More persuasively, forty years after Salten's death, his secretary Gertrud Schattner declared under oath that Salten had told her, sometime during his exile years, that he was, in fact, the author of the memoirs,[15] and Schnitzler's daughter-in-law Lilly Schnitzler stated in a deposition that at no time in her memory did Schnitzler or anyone in the Schnitzler household ever express doubt as to Salten's having been the author.[16]

During his lifetime, the most adamant declarations of Salten's authorship of the *Mutzenbacher* memoirs came, in fact, from his political enemies, who used this assumed authorship as proof of Salten's hypocrisy. Anton Kuh, for example, wrote, "Mr. Salten, about whom one cannot say often and forcefully enough that he is the author of the pornographic prostitute novel *Josefine Mutzenbacher* (he's hard of hearing, you see), functions at his newspaper as the Sunday specialist for morality."[17] Karl Kraus, writing satirically about the fact that Felix Salten never got the Nobel Prize for literature, mused, "[T]he prize committee cannot agree for which of his works he has earned it. ... One group is more for the rabbits speaking Jewish dialect [Kraus's satirical name for *Fünfzehn Hasen* (Fifteen Rabbits), 1929], the other group thinks that there is nothing to top *Josephine* [sic] *Mutzenbacher*."[18]

Some critics have argued that Salten's refusal to answer his attackers is proof of his authorship and cite as evidence his earlier attacks, both physical and legal, on his enemies in the press. Of course, during the 1920s, when Kraus's and Kuh's attacks were the most virulent, Salten had good reason not to draw public attention to his authorship, either by admission or denial, since any speculation linking his name to *Mutzenbacher* might in fact have caused the public to question his position as lead journalist for Vienna's most influential newspaper.

However, on at least two occasions, Salten actually did deny authorship of the work. Klaus Pinkus reports asking Salten straight out in 1932 whether or not he had authored *Josefine Mutzenbacher*; Salten replied, "I have neither written Mutzenbacher myself nor have I ever read it. People have approached me so often about it that I would be deeply grateful to you if you could get me a copy of this book."[19] Such a remark – especially the comment that he had never read *Mutzenbacher* and would like Pinkus to find him a copy – suggests that Salten was pulling Pinkus's leg. Certainly in the twenty-five years since the book's publication, Salten would have read it, especially since so many were naming him as its author. The testimony of the German literary scholar Willy Haas is far more credible. He reported that Salten responded to his inquiry with a sigh. "I wish I were the author," he replied. "But unfortunately I am not."[20] For Haas, at least, this was the definitive answer that finally laid the matter to rest.

We, too, might let the matter rest if, some time after Salten's death, Salten's coworker at the *Neue Freie Presse*, Adolf David, had not made the credible claim to the publisher Fritz Peter Molden that, in the early part of the century, he had been paid 1000 crowns to type a clean *Mutzenbacher* text from Salten's handwritten copy. According to David, Salten had told him at that time that he "was writing an original pornographic manuscript for a wealthy man and that he had been promised an honorarium of 10,000 crowns for it."[21] If this story is true, and Molden testified to it under oath, Salten must be recognized as the author of the work.

During Salten's lifetime, in fact, both his friends and his enemies believed that he was the *Mutzenbacher* author, while doubts have been raised primarily by scholars who came later or who did not know him well. All agree that the work is a masterpiece, and that is the problem. Was Salten capable of crafting such a work? His literary oeuvre is uneven and often sentimental. Could he – would he – have written a work in which the heroine expresses no self-pity or remorse for her life as a prostitute?

Salten had already published the anonymous first-person novel *Bekenntnisse einer Prinzessin* (The Confessions of a Princess) with the Wiener Verlag just the year before *Mutzenbacher*, and Salten might well have been spurred by its success to follow that work with the ostensible confessions of a prostitute and to publish it with the same firm. On March 4, 1903, he wrote to Schnitzler, "I'm now reading the 'Dialogues of the Heavenly Aretino'[22] and finding in them, to my astonishment, the confessions of a Roman courtesan. You know that I wanted to write such a book."[23] This quotation is certainly proof of Salten's interest in writing a work like *Mutzenbacher*, as with Salten's comments on his *Mutza* work, however, the date of this quotation precedes the death date of the novel's ostensible model.

Was there, in fact, a model for this story, as there was for *Die Bekenntnisse einer Prinzessin*? The foreword to the earliest edition asserts that there was, that she was born in the Viennese suburb of Hernals in February 1852 and died of a sexually transmitted disease in a sanatorium in December 1904 after passing her memoirs over to the safekeeping of her doctor. Her editor goes on to say, "For the most part, not much has been changed [in the book]. Only linguistic and stylistic errors were corrected and the names of known personages ... replaced by others."[24] This is demonstrably not the case. The work is a careful literary construction in two parts. The first half of the novel follows the narrator's childhood sexual encounters from age five up through the death of her mother, when Mutzenbacher is thirteen, and all is told in a straightforward and unpretentious manner, while the second half, which covers only a few months of her fourteenth year and traces her beginnings as a prostitute, is rich in humorous metaphor and gives Mutzenbacher's story a Rabelaisian flavor. The novel is constructed as a *Bildungsroman*, or novel of development. The first part is introduced with a statement of non-repentance, and in that is reminiscent of the introduction to Grimmelshausen's *Lebensbeschreibung der Erzbetrügerin und Landstörzerin Courage* (Life of the Arch-Deceiver and Vagabond Courage), 1670, and of John Cleland's *Fanny Hill, Memoirs of a Woman of Pleasure*, 1748-1749, both works that established a new genre of bawdy female memoir by breaking with the tradition of religious confession. Like these predecessors, Mutzenbacher proclaims that she does *not* repent of her sins, noting, "Coming from poverty and misery as I did, I owe everything to my body. ... I have acquired a good education, which I owe solely to whoring, because it was this which brought me into contact with distinguished and educated men. ... I have seen the world and widened my perspective, and I owe all of that to my lifestyle, which people call 'dissolute.'"[25] Her reason for recounting her childhood, she says, is that "it would perhaps be good if the distinguished and wealthy gentlemen who find enjoyment in us would learn for once how things look to one of those girls whom they embrace so heatedly, where she comes from, what [she] has experienced, and what she thinks."[26]

Several scholars have pointed out that the work appears to be designed to create empathy and understanding for those who are raised in Vienna's poorest suburbs, that, like Salten's later work *Bambi*, *Mutzenbacher* is intended to introduce readers to a side of nature with which they are mostly unacquainted.[27] Both the deer and the prostitute are threatened but manage to flourish in their native habitats. In both works Salten introduces male predators (outsiders) into the world of the young protagonists. Mutzen-bacher, like Bambi, is a creature of instinct, and the two novels trace the development of their title figures from innocence to insight and acquired wisdom.[28] As in *Bambi*, there is a rupture in *Mutzenbacher* created by the death of the protagonist's mother, and the death serves as a marker between childhood and adult self-awareness. In fact, after the publication of *Bambi*, Salten's attackers even referred to him as the "deer sodomite."[29]

There are also many similarities between *Mutzenbacher* and the *Bekenntnisse einer Prinzessin*; that work also introduces readers to a world quite foreign to the general reading public and shows the downside of royalty and the emotional upheavals of a young woman governed primarily by her instincts. Like Josefine, the princess stands up to public censure of her actions, declaring, as she too leaves her home environment for a strange new world, "How far I may sink and fall, how much misery and despair I will experience! And yet ... I am not a bad person, and at this moment in which I am losing everything, I do not feel, and no one can persuade me, that the fault is mine alone."[30]

Unmistakable similarities to the Mutzenbacher figure can also be found in the young female figures introduced in several of Salten's other works of fiction.[31] In *Der Hund von Florenz*, the young hero falls in love with the prostitute Claudia, an apparently conscience-free young woman who has brought many noblemen to ruin. And in this novel, a pimp introduces the artists to a younger version of Claudia – a girl of Mutzenbacher's age who, when undressed, "danced in slow, smooth rhythmic movements, as though she were playing and yet serious as thought. Her frail body, which looked as though it had but then been created, twisting and turning, bending and swaying with graceful pride, seemed, like her closely shut lips, to know more than her eyes. Her eyes, as they gazed calmly in front of her seemed to know more than her soul, and the mild radiance of her soul suffused her sweet childish features."[32] The passage reminds one of Mutzenbacher, who decides not to attract her first clients by smiling coquettishly: "Instead I looked seriously into their eyes, and that was enough."[33]

In *Herr Wenzel auf Rehberg und sein Knecht Kaspar Dinckel* (Lord Wenzel of Rehberg and his Servant Caspar Dinckel), 1907, Salten portrayed an orgy at the court of Emperor Charles V; the protagonist is a voyeur as twenty young girls enter the hall to dance naked before the men of the court:

> The sudden sight of all the naked girls blinded my eyes, and the blood began to throb in my temples. It was as if a heavy fog was sinking before me, but I saw through my veiled senses the gleaming white bodies, the round hips, the full breasts with the red berries on them; I saw the smiles of these prostitutes, their fiery eyes, and much more, and I began to make a racket with the others as the girls now performed their dance to the beat of drums and ringing of cymbals. [34]

As the orgy proceeds and goblets of wine are thrown into the faces and onto the breasts of the young women, one of them "lifted her full breasts with both hands, lowered her head, and with her lips slurped up the sweet drink which moistened her skin, as everyone called to her and laughed."[35] When the orgy is over, the protagonist spends the night with the youngest of the prostitutes.

This orgy scene makes two points. First, it demonstrates that, even without using the specific sexual terminology of *Mutzenbacher*, Salten could be quite graphic in his portrayals of sexual seduction. Second, it is one of Salten's several historical novellas that provide, like *Der Hund von Florenz*, an exaggerated picture of Salten's contemporary society. This becomes evident when one compares the orgy scene of *Herr Wenzel auf Rehberg* with an essay entitled "Nachtvergnügen" (Nighttime Pleasure),[36] a journalistic portrayal of the Viennese clubs where men came between one and four o'clock in the morning to watch young immigrant and country girls dance for their pleasure. In the novel Salten unmasks the men's lust by transforming the scene to another age: where his contemporaries undress the young girls merely with their eyes, the nakedness is literal at the court of Charles V.

Salten frequently portrayed men's lust for young girls in stories set in an earlier age, but he picked up this theme in only one of his acknowledged works of fiction set in the present day, *Die kleine Veronika*, published in 1903 and banned from the bookstores of the German railway stations as unfit reading for the general public.[37] Veronica is thirteen when she is unwittingly made a whore, but her youthfulness is the only similarity between herself and Josefine. Veronica believes in the illusions of love, while Josefine is addicted to sex. Veronica wants a monogamous relationship with her older lover, whereas Josefine has no desire to possess her partners and, in fact, pimps for her mother and brother and enjoys participating in group sex. For Josefine, sex is a joyful act, lightly entered into and easily overcome. Veronica is the pious young girl readers want their daughters to be, while Josefine is the forbidden object that they lust for.

It is notable that, whereas Salten's lustful young women belong to an earlier age, his contemporary works picture them as what his society referred to as fallen women. His female artists belong in this category; some of these are able to benefit economically from their situations, some even settle into monogamous relationships, but in three of his works – *Die kleine Veronika*, *Olga Frohgemuth* (1910), and *Die klingende Schelle* (The Tinkling Cymbal), 1915 – the women die as victims. *Josefine Mutzenbacher*, however, wholeheartedly repudiates the popular view of contemporary society that fallen women suffer consequences for their actions; it is a stirring evocation of women's desires and their right to enjoy uninhibited sex just as men do.

In Salten's novel, the dialogues between the two prostitutes in Aretino's work become dialogues between Mutzenbacher and her more experienced colleague Zenzi, and Salten transposes the sexual adventures of Nanna, a postulant nun, to Mutzenbacher's pleasurable romps with her priestly confessor. Altogether, the second half of *Josefine Mutzenbacher* bears the closest resemblance to Aretino's *Dialogues* since it is here that the young protagonist, having already been thoroughly educated in the art of sex in her poverty-ridden neighborhood, accumulates partners and her first paying customers among the higher classes of society.

It is this contrast between the two halves of the book which has caused critics to note that it is the first half of the work that offers something new, for here Mutzenbacher is a small child of the proletarian ghetto, and her sexual partners are childhood friends, neighbors, overnight borders, family members, and workingclass men – people with rough hands and rougher manners. The environment plays a major role here: there is no hypocrisy, figures simply satisfy their lusts with whatever is available to them. It is a "fairy tale from nature" [*Natur-Märchen*],[38] a "parody" and inverted "utopia,"[39] in which figures, who otherwise have few possessions and fewer pleasures, find their joy in lusty sexual encounters in fields, basements, stairwells, neighboring bedrooms, and even in a tavern toilet. Men and women are equally lustful; there is no competition between sexual partners and no real feeling of exploitation. It is here, and not in the streets of Vienna's inner city, that Mutzenbacher discovers her pleasure in sex; here she does not have to pretend to her partners that she is a sexual victim, nor does she encounter artificial means for achieving sexual climax – masturbation, masochism, pornographic art – until she goes to work among the higher classes. Reverting to deer imagery, one can describe Mutzenbacher's sexual romps in the Viennese slums as her natural state and her business transactions in the city as its corruption. Various scholars have demonstrated how Salten's works [*Die kleine Veronika, Bambi, Die Wurstelprater*] espouse a contemporary world view, one that infantilizes the natural state – whether in the country, the forest, or the Prater Park – as a nostalgic locus of innocence, while portraying urban society as a seat of corruption.[40]

In fact, it is only in the final paragraph of the novel that one is jolted out of Josefine's fond remembrances by what can only be described as a sobering moral lesson. Here, in contrast to everything that has gone before, Mutzenbacher declares: "[A]ll in all, love is foolish. Women resemble an old pipe that has only a couple of holes on which one can play only a few notes. All men do the same thing. They lie on top, we lie beneath them. They do the thrusting and we are the ones they thrust. That is the only difference."[41]

This abrupt, cynical appraisal of love is totally out of keeping with the rest of the novel, where sex, not love, is the central theme. This has led some critics to believe Paul Englisch's claim that Salten composed only the first two thirds of the novel, that part leading up to Mutzenbacher's first day as a prostitute, and that, because his publisher refused to pay Salten the increased stipend that he asked for, he hired the journalist Willi Handl to complete the work.[42] Part of the argument here is the novel's break in time and in tone, an argument that is greatly weakened by the fact that Salten frequently included breaks in his novels, often occasioned by a

death and generally signaling a change in protagonist behavior over
time (*Olga Frohgemuth, Die klingende Schelle, Bambi*).

An undated letter from 1906, which Salten wrote to Fritz
Freund, publisher of the *Mutzenbacher* novel, provides some insight
while also serving as yet another indicator of Salten's authorship
He wrote, "Dear Mr. Freund, Here at last are the long missing
sheets. I would still like to speak with you about the closing [etc.]
....."[43] This letter suggests that Salten and his publisher may have
had some disagreement as to how to conclude the novel. The sober
tone of the final paragraph may well have been the price Salten had
to pay in order to see it published.

Indeed, given this letter and the similar structural components
found in *Mutzenbacher* and in other Salten novels, it is difficult to
believe that anyone other than Salten composed anything but the
final paragraph. The novel does, however, present one striking in-
novation not evident in Salten's other works. In his naughty historical novellas, Salten had presented unspoken, ironic commentar-
ies on present-day society, but here the process is reversed, as Salten demonstrates that the lustful decadence and hypocrisy so often
linked to the distant past were alive and well in the Vienna of his
day, that human passions and misdeeds are not restricted to a given
time period but are eternal. This is a modernist view, since it seeks,
as Gustav Klimt did in his paintings, to establish linkages between
the present and the past and to reveal the eternal qualities of human nature.

To see how well Salten succeeded in this undertaking, one
need only read his review of Aretino's *Dialogues* and simply substitute *Josefine Mutzenbacher* for the work in question and "turn-of-the-
century Vienna" for "Renaissance":

> Nowhere can one find such a moral portrait
> of the [Renaissance], with such satirical flair, with
> such outrageously bold mockery, with such unre-
> strained lack of inhibition, with such magnificent
> colors and with such richness, so alive and so
> witty, so thorough and sweeping and so honest.
> The fact that this portrait comes from a man who
> stood in the midst of it, in the giddiness of his ep-
> och, gives this work of art the additional merit of

being an invaluable document [of its age]. [44]

Did Salten write *Mutzenbacher*? The suspicions of his friends and enemies, the definitive statements by his coworker and his secretary, his stated desire to write a book like Aretino's, the structural and thematic components common to this and other Salten works, his 1906 letter to Fritz Freund: all suggest that he did. Just as Salten took the pampered world of royalty and revealed its stifling restrictions and arbitrarily cruel punishments in *Die Bekenntnisse einer Prinzessin*, and in *Bambi* revealed the "idyllic" Austrian forest to be a place of violent storms, terror, and bloodshed, so the author of *Josefine Mutzenbacher* took the "idyllic" working class districts of Vienna and revealed the dirt, the crowding, the children's lack of supervision, and the incest that were the norm there. None of these three works is sentimental. All, however, reveal their author's complete knowledge of environments quite foreign to the average Viennese urbanite and create reader empathy for the beings who dwell there.

Chapter 10: Flight to the Country

When planning a biographical piece on Salten, Schnitzler made this notation: "His behavior towards his subordinates. Not a pleasant boss."[1] Salten confirms this judgment in his own memoirs when he recalls his first days in Berlin in January 1906 and his efforts not to appear as "the softhearted man from Vienna."[2] He threatened to fire Konrad Alberti, who had been a mainstay at the paper for some twenty years, because Alberti did not show his new superior the proper respect, and it was only because of Franz Ullstein's intervention and Alberti's excellent writing that Salten eventually agreed to let him stay. Because his staff went home regularly at eight o'clock at night Salten referred to them as "journalist clerks" rather than as "journalists";[3] when his German staff said it was impossible to get an interview with Prince von Bülow about the emperor's visit to the Bülow estate, Salten sent a young Viennese reporter, who got the scoop and created a sensation in the papers.

If Salten made demands of his staff, he was equally demanding of himself. He regularly dropped by his office after the theater to check for late-breaking events and, on the evening of April 18, 1906, created his own sensation for the *Morgenpost* by catching the first reports of the San Francisco earthquake. He had the Viennese art reporter Adolf Donas write a fictional account of the panic and looting mentioned in these earliest reports, while he sat down with an encyclopedia to write a description of the city that had just suffered such demolition. By midnight Salten had set the type and created the layout for the front-page coverage. The next day he fired the news editor who had not been available to help cover the story.

In all his Berlin reports, Salten spoke positively only about his Viennese coworkers. Indeed, it was during this period that Salten realized the depth of his love for Vienna and his identification with the city's landscape, intellectual life, and culture. Berlin was for him "the foreign city," with wide boulevards and no hills. "Nowhere outside the city can one rise above the stifling throng," he wrote, "to be an individual among hundreds of thousands of people, to step onto a rise and look down. ... Nowhere is there even a peak from which one can take in the city with a single glance." "Perhaps this city has a face, too," he conceded, "but one cannot see it. One can only perceive things separately, step by step. Streets, houses, churches, squares – everything separately."[4] As for the Berliners, Salten said, "One notices at once, these are really different people. One feels, I don't know them at all. One senses, I scarcely like them, am really unable to like them, because they are indifferent and distant to that which is the deepest part of my being." The very language was foreign to him: "I can't find the rhythm in which they speak. Or, to put it better, I find their rhythm only when I suppress my own."[5] He was horrified whenever he caught himself using a Berlin expression, as if he feared that he might lose his identity in this great metropolis.

Whereas Salten had suffered from feelings of inferiority in Vienna because of his poverty and lack of education, he now was made to feel inferior because of his Viennese heritage. The Berliners acknowledged Austria's cultural contributions in previous centuries, he complained, but they would not accept anything of the last forty years as being of value. Indeed, ever since Prussia had demonstrated its technological superiority over Austria at the decisive battle of Königgrätz on July 3, 1866, with its use of breechloading rifles, steel-rifled cannons, rapid rail transport, and the electric telegraph, most Prussians thought of the old Habsburg empire as dead or dying. Salten wrote a number of newspaper articles, both as "Salten" and as "Sascha," in which he tried to explain the differences between his own deep affection for Vienna and the world's apparent infatuation with Berlin.[6] He blamed the railway through Berlin for consigning Vienna to European backwaters and faulted the Austrians for badmouthing their own country.

As the weeks went by, Salten became so homesick that he even began to miss his feuds with Kraus, Grossmann, and Ludassy. "There is no one here with whom you are angry," he exclaimed. "You do not meet any of those cheesy faces, distorted with envy, in which at home you (often with such revulsion) read so much spite, so much unfounded hatred and so much submissive, shifty meanness." And yet, "Was it really so bad as I often thought? Here, in return, there is no one whom I have loved, no one who has been part of me."[7] Salten missed his easy familiarity with the Viennese scene, the sense of shared history, gossip based on an intimate knowledge of the city's court and theatrical circles, and long walks and bicycle tours with proven friends.

The family had relatives in Berlin, however; Otti's half brother Ludwig was living there with his family, and they socialized frequently. They also managed to make a home in a house Salten rented in Charlottenburg. The two children were happy and enjoyed excursions with their parents to the parks and to the city zoo. The family never lacked for visitors; Salten bemoaned the fact that the socializing sometimes got to be too much: "I want to read instead. Want to read a lot now, a whole lot; learn a little Spanish and go walking with Otti in the Tiergarten."[8] Still, he cemented many contacts and socialized with theater people (directors Otto Brahm and Max Reinhardt and their actors), journalists and critics (Alfred Kerr, Siegfried Jacobsohn, and Maximilian Harden), and, through his half brother-in-law Ludwig Metzl, musicians (Fritz Kreisler, Arthur Nikisch, and Leopold Godowski).

He made the most pleasant social contacts through his Berlin publisher, Samuel Fischer, whose home became a welcome refuge from the tumult of the city. Salten quickly became good friends with Fischer's wife, Hedwig; she was an accomplished pianist and gracious hostess who kept open house for her husband's many German and foreign authors. Salten described the Fischer villa in the Grunewald district of Berlin in idyllic terms. Coming to this house, whether to a candlelight dinner, afternoon tea on the terrace, or an early game of tennis, was "as if someone has been swimming under water until his ears buzz, until his temples throb and a relentless pressure squeezes his breast. But then he surfaces, and the air calmingly brushes his cheek and he has the heavenly delight of drawing deep breaths." The home was tastefully furnished with the finest books, porcelain, etchings, and paintings. "Everything here is young and clean from within," he exclaimed. "Nothing is dusty here, nothing is infiltrated and restricted by the rubble and debris of the past. Here everything is like the resplendent rhododendrons in the Tiergarten, wrested from barren ground. That is why I am inundated here with so much confidence, creative desire, and Sunday joy."[9]

Even as Salten was regretting his move to Berlin, he was thinking of projects that would free him from the pressures of managing two large daily newspapers so that he could devote himself to more creative work. That spring he was putting finishing touches on his novella *Herr Wenzel auf Rehberg und sein Knecht Kaspar Dinckel* and apparently concluding his work on *Josefine Mutzenbacher.* He had hoped to write a biography of Theodor Herzl that summer but never completed this project, in part because of a severe, prolonged attack of kidney stones, in part because of changes in travel and career plans. He also considered establishing a weekly arts journal that he would direct and co-publish with the painter Max Liebermann and the composer/conductor Richard Strauss. The Ullstein brothers were willing to risk a guaranteed run of three years, he wrote Schnitzler, and it would be staffed by "a small, exclusive, constant circle of contributors."[10]

The problem with this project was that by July Salten had decided that he could no longer live in Berlin. He had begun sending articles to his old Vienna paper *Die Zeit* in May, and a cautious enquiry had shown that its editors might be willing to take him back into the fold. Salten tried for a while to justify his return to Vienna as advantageous for the new arts journal: he could, he said, create a broader scope by commuting between the two cities and covering theatrical performances in Vienna as well as in Berlin. This would free him from "the danger of being deported" and the constraints of living "under the thumb of the political police in Prussia, which is more severe than one would think."[11] He argued that he could manage the journal by making ten shorter trips to Berlin each year.

During his seven months in Berlin, Salten had, in fact, grown increasingly critical of Prussian politics, Prussian schools, and Prussian manners. England provided a welcome respite when, in his capacity as editor-in-chief of the *Berliner Zeitung* and the *Morgenpost*, he was invited to visit for two weeks as a participant in a "journey of peace."[12] In the meantime Otti took the two children to the Baltic Sea resort of Bausin to await his return. On his visit to England, Salten met three future prime ministers: Lloyd George, who was at the time President of the Board of Trade; Lord Richard Burdon Haldane, then Minister of War; and Winston Churchill, "a young man with blond curls" who headed the ministry of colonial affairs.[13]

He was much impressed with the English countryside and the way the English interacted with it: at Cambridge, where the university students played games on the spacious lawns or went punting on the River Cam; on a boat trip on the Avon River for a garden tea party at a fine lady's villa; and at an evening gathering at the Earl of London's country estate, where, as special guest, Salten was allowed to assist the lady of the house in feeding bread to the tame carp in the lake on the estate property. Of these and other rural delights, Salten wrote, "At the sight of this cultivated landscape and the people who strolled in it, playing instruments or singing, I said, 'The Elysian Fields.'"[14] The highlight of the trip was an outdoor performance of Shakespeare's *Midsummer Night's Dream*, which was held in the meadow of London's botanical garden on Midsummer Eve, under a full moon.

During this trip Salten made his decision about Berlin; he went straight to Franz Ullstein upon his return and asked to be released immediately from his contract. He collected the ten thousand marks that were due him, then went to join his wife and children at Bausin. Otti was panicked at the idea of her husband's being unemployed, but Salten contacted *Die Zeit*, and after a hurried visit to Vienna, was given his old job as Sunday feuilletonist while his replacement, Ludwig Bauer, retained the duties of editor. Salten was immensely relieved. Now he would be freed of the onerous tasks of reading and editing other people's manuscripts, and he would have more leisure to devote to his own writing. He could even move further out from the center of town, somewhere close to the Vienna woods. He now returned to the family at Bausin, where he thoroughly enjoyed the warm sand and surf. Near the end of their stay, the Saltens joined family members on a short excursion into Denmark and spent a day with Schnitzler and his family at Marienlyst, near Helsingör.

Emil Salzmann had been looking around Vienna for a suitable home for his brother's family and found for them a ramshackle eighteenth-century villa out in Heiligenstadt, in the city's nineteenth district.[15] The Saltens had the villa's overgrown park all to themselves and benefited from the fact that the caretaker of the grounds was a fiacre coachman, with his own carriage and horses. Salten's daughter recalled that "only one wing of the building was habitable; and modest though the rental was, the owner must have been glad to find so romantic a tenant as my father, who was willing to put up with the family of owls in the tower, a horde of rats in the cellar, mice in every room and heaven knows what animals all over the grounds."[16]

It was the family's favorite and happiest home, despite recurring health problems, such as Otti's occasional nervous attacks and Salten's frequent headaches. Salten's daughter Anna would later draw a sketch of the house and park for her father's children's book *Bob und Baby*, in which Salten expanded rapturously about the ancient ivy that "embraced the stairway" and, in the summer, was "thickly hummed over by bees," about "the jungle of a gigantically big garden" that surrounded the house, and a "splendid old birch tree" whose sweet sap the children collected and drank. The children also collected the fruits of the century-old hazelnut trees in the fall.[17] Although the fixtures of the house were rather primitive, the rooms were spacious, and Salten now had a huge study with five windows facing onto a large, shaded terrace. His daughter, Anna, has preserved one particular memory that captures the family's happiness in the new home:

> One of my earliest memories is of father sitting in the sun on the great lawn – a kind of glade enclosed by old trees. I can still see him, with his tanned face, his light-green eyes and blond mustache, wearing a wide, embroidered, Hungarian peasant shirt that hung down over his knickers, a gorgeous Persian cat is lolling on his knees and purring under the gently scratching touch of his fingers. Not far away from him my brother lies on his belly, allowing his special protegé, a tamed magpie, to strut to and fro on his back and amuse itself by pecking at his ears or the nape of his neck. Two young terriers crouch in the bend of his arms – while their mother, a big, strong-limbed schnauzer, is bustling about the lawn. I myself, hardly more than a baby, am sitting on a spread-out blue blanket, and a couple of piebald rabbits hop about me. A lame, old, wise-looking duck waddles from one group to the other, dignified and curious. Near by, my mother is resting in a hammock. Her crochet work has slid down on the ground. Slowly swinging, she looks sidewise

through the meshes of the big net at Father, and smiles.[18]

The family always kept dogs and cats and often harbored other species, including "all sorts of warblers and even some tamed birds of prey." The children "'bred' squirrels and guinea pigs, hedgehogs and turtles, snails and lizards, frogs and mice," had for a time a pet monkey, and "at some other time a doe and a small donkey."[19] Many of these animals would appear in Salten's later animal tales and essays. Salten, who took care to teach his children reverence for all animal life, often read to the children those animal tales by other authors that he found especially appealing. Anna particular remembered "his voice reading to us Marie Ebner-Eschenbach's *Krambambuli* and growing thick − while everybody's eyes moistened − as the tale reached its climax and moving ending."[20]

On December 24, 1906, Salten and Otti organized a delightful Christmas celebration with a large family gathering in their new home. Unbeknownst to the children, Salten had acquired a gramophone that he hid behind a Spanish wall. Then, when the candles on the tree had been lit and the children summoned into the room, Salten began to play an instrumental recording of "Silent Night." "The children, who came out of their room, looked through four open doors upon the lighted tree .... [A]s they entered the room where the tree was, the organ was just beginning to play. Paul and Annerl appeared dazed; everyone there was deeply moved. Even the cat walked around excitedly with its tail bolt upright."[21]

Salten was delighted with his rural home and relieved to be back in Vienna, where he could resume activities with old friends. The spacious home provided many opportunities for entertaining large groups; in February 1907 Salten and his wife hosted a party called "Man and Superman... A Dionysian Costume Party" together with the writer Jakob Wassermann and his wife, Julie. Salten and his brother-in-law Richard Metzl frequently played tennis with Schnitzler, Wassermann, and others. Unfortunately, however, Salten's return to Vienna also reignited his public feud with Ludassy, which dragged on until the summer of 1907.

Salten did make peace, of sorts, with Stefan Grossmann. Grossmann had founded the Freie Wiener Volksbühne, a theater designed to bring the classics to the working classes of Vienna, and he called on the Saltens to ask if Otti might appear as Aline Solness in his May production of Ibsen's *The Master Builder*. Salten could never forgive Grossmann for his slanderous involvement in the Ludassy case, but he was willing to let Otti perform in his theater under the condition that she accept no money. The play debuted on May 5 and, when Josef Jarno of the Theater in der Josefstadt took over direction of the play for a late-summer performance in Graz, the Saltens made a pleasant family vacation out of Otti's engagement there.

In the meantime, Salten's relations with Richard Beer-Hofmann had cooled during his absence from Vienna, and even his relationship with Schnitzler was often on shaky ground. Schnitzler, who, shortly before Salten's move to Berlin, had reflected, "Our relations have often been very strange; my error regarding him in earlier times was often that I showed too little regard for the difficulty of his external circumstances,"[22] now seemed to pay too much heed to negative statements about Salten made to him by others. Salten tried to address the tensions between the two of them directly, as in December 1906, when Schnitzler noted "[In the] afternoon an almost four-hour-long conversation dealing with the deepest aspects of our relations, that on the whole confirmed our absolute, indestructible solidarity and that also ended well on the surface."[23] Nonetheless, new caution had entered the relationship, and despite their continued socializing, Schnitzler believed that "As a 'friend' [Salten] is probably to be given up once and for all for lost."[24] Although they continued to take walks together, play tennis, discuss work projects, and invite each other to dinner parties, Schnitzler did not read to Salten his drafts of *Der Ruf des Lebens* (The Call of Life) nor did Salten share with Schnitzler his trilogy of one-act plays *Vom andern Ufer* (From the Other Shore) until it had been published. In spite of this, each praised the work of the other when it appeared.

While Salten was still in Berlin, however, he had mailed his manuscript of *Herr Wenzel auf Rehberg und sein Knecht Kaspar Dinckel* to Schnitzler and gotten back thoughtful, helpful criticism. Salten apparently chose to ignore it since Schnitzler's suggestions were not incorporated into the work as it appeared with Samuel Fischer in 1907.[25] This tale of corruption at the sixteenth-century court of Emperor Charles V is told by a Bohemian lord who is invited to the imperial court in Augsburg and is intoxicated with the power, arrogance, and debauchery that surround him, until he is recalled to his senses by the emperor's command that Dinckel, a good-natured, hard-working commoner whom the emperor had just freed from a death sentence, have his nose and ears cut off. At Dinckel's request, the Bohemian lord shoots him; he then leaves the emperor's service and returns to his home. The work contains elements of both of Salten's anonymous novels: like *Die Bekenntnisse einer Prinzessin*, it shows the arbitrarily cruel nature of a powerful monarch; like *Josefine Mutzenbacher*, it paints a picture of lustful abandonment. The work is rich in period detail, and Samuel Fischer's son Gerhart reported to Salten that his history teacher related portions of it to the class, citing it as an authoritative portrayal of the emperor and his court.[26] Even Schnitzler called it "an excellent piece."[27]

At the end of the work, the narrator points out that many years after the events described, Charles V gave up the throne and entered a Spanish monastery to become a monk. Reflecting that this too may not have been the right decision, the narrator notes, "[W]hat do I know about the emperor, except that he was angry in that hour of misfortune. ... People speak, and know nothing about one another, and there is no way that one can prove to them that they are doing someone an injustice." Salten may have been thinking about his own situation and the slander spread by Ludassy and Grossmann when he has Wenzel add in protest, "I am not a rogue."[28]

The gaps between appearance and reality, class and morality are also dominant in *Vom andern Ufer*, the cycle of three one-act plays that Salten wrote in the spring of 1907 as he sat by an open window and enjoyed the scent of lilacs and jasmine that wafted in from the park. The first, "Graf Festenberg" (Count Festenberg), shows that a Viennese waiter is more aristocratic in motive and in bearing than many of those born to the blood, while the second, "Der Ernst des Lebens" (Life's Gravity), unmasks a rather pompous, self-righteous doctor to reveal a petty, vengeful man. In the third, "Auferstehung" (Resurrection), a dying bachelor experiences a miraculous cure through which he learns that even those people who are most devoted to him are easily capable of finding happiness and success without him. Seeing that he is no longer needed, he sets off to begin a new life far removed from all who knew him. In the summer of 1907, both Salten's brother Emil and his wife, Otti, were plagued with illness, and Salten spent the month of August with his wife at Marienbad, where she underwent treatment. In this peaceful woodland setting their son, Paul, who had also been ailing, quickly regained his strength, and Salten could note with pleasure, "Annerle is having fabulous social successes, while those with deeper natures hold Pauli in high regard." The family enjoyed long woodland walks, and the two children were thrilled to perform "Little Red Ridinghood" for their parents in "a real forest."[29] For the most part, the Saltens avoided socializing, except on the tennis courts. Salten had plans to write the final manuscript of *Der Hund von Florenz*, which, he told Schnitzler, "was ready for that and much changed" from its original conception.[30] Although Salten complained that the fictional hound kept coming up to him wagging its tail and barking as he worked on other novellas, it would be another fifteen years before he submitted this manuscript for publication. In the meantime his volume of plays appeared with Samuel Fischer, and Otto Brahm accepted the trilogy for production in Berlin's Lessing Theater in October. The Viennese premiere followed a month later.

Because he was not burdened by editorial pressures, Salten was able to devote time to his own literary output. In the spring of 1907, he began publishing a series of fictional sketches in *Die Zeit* that he identified as part of "a cycle of small novels" called *Künstlerfrauen* (artist wives). [31] Salten had by now had ample opportunity to observe the marriages of his writer, painter, and musician friends and could compare the married lives of some with the heady days when they had been bachelors. As in his cycle of one-act plays and his novella *Herr Wenzel auf Rehberg*, Salten portrayed here the often mistaken images that people hold of one another, adding to the complexity of this theme the sometimes ridiculous, sometimes tragic, sometimes ironic situations these create within a marriage setting. These tales appeared in book form in 1909, with the Georg Müller press in Munich.

Although this was a productive period for Salten, he was still unsatisfied with his achievements. "If I could get free of the newspaper, I would be happy and might perhaps be able to achieve something good," he wrote. "Writing for the newspaper is getting drearier and drearier."[32] Otti shared his desire that he should become an independent writer, but she also longed for the day when they could, like so many of their friends, get together enough money to purchase their own home.

Salten had an established writing pattern that bordered on eccentricity – he called it "a laughable pedantry." He felt compelled, he said, always to use "the same size [writing] paper and the same pencil (Koh-i-Noor [brand]), the same, really one and the same, writing pad made of an already worn board cover, the same little antique bronze hand that holds the paper firm, and the same sharpener."[33] These he always carried with him. He also kept "80 to 100" pencils on his desk "always in the foolish fear that I could run out of writing material."[34] He had disciplined himself to become insensitive "to noise of any kind." "People can be in the room chattering loudly, carpets can be beaten outdoors, or guns fired, I hear nothing. ... I have often written for days on end in our cabana in the middle of a beach while other members of my family were enjoying themselves with friends who dropped by."[35] "Nor," he added, "have I ever begun a manuscript, whether a play, a novel, or indeed even the smallest feuilleton, without first having the conclusion firmly in mind. That is why my manuscripts are nearly entirely free of corrections. ... I cross nothing out since I put nothing down without forethought."[36] His work as a theatrical critic had provided him with his training. From the theater he generally went to the Café Landtmann to write his reviews, then dropped them off at the editorial office of the paper before going home.

As for his handwriting, Salten admitted, "[I]t must surely be the result of pure pedantry that in the course of time my handwriting has drawn ever closer to the printed copy. It has become an absolute necessity for me to have the approximate type-area in my manuscript before me. I of course know that in its diminutiveness and tightness my handwriting is a lot more copious than any book page .... I can offer no explanation for how it happens that in the course of my work my handwriting gets smaller and smaller, narrower and narrower, so that even I can read it only with a magnifying glass afterwards."[37]

He said, "the figures in my plays and novels talk, and I follow their dictation. But I always have to wait until these people begin to speak. I must not begin any earlier with the material at hand."[38]

Even though the hound of Florence was "barking" at Salten, it took many years before all the figures of that novel spoke to him. But many others did.

In addition to *Künstlerfrauen*, Salten published a collection of short stories under the name of the longest of these, a novella entitled *Die Geliebte Friedrichs des Schönen* (The Sweetheart of Frederick the Fair). A number of these stories had been written earlier, but others were quite new and the collection was a mixed bag of offerings, including even a dramatic sketch ("Ein Tag" [One Day]) that had been composed in 1896. The tales dealt with the death of a loyal but mistreated old dog ("Die Wege des Herrn" [The Ways of the Lord], 1908), two exemplary tales of the dangers of asserting oneself before royalty ("Mit grossen Herren Kirschen essen" [Eating Cherries with Great Rulers], 1906) and of the secret thoughts that go through the minds of an established singer and a young prince during the singer's command performance ("Der Sänger vor dem König" [The Singer in Front of the King], 1907). In addition there is an Easter piece entitled "Feiertag" (Holiday), 1898, which traces the activities of an infatuated young man and all the neighbors and acquaintances he sees during a one-and-a-half-day period; a 1902 prose version of his play "Der Ernst des Lebens" that shares the play's title but offers quite a different ending; and his 1903 tale, "Erhebungen über Barbara Liebhardt" (Inquiries about Barbara Liebhardt). Samuel Fischer did not publish this collection, doubtless because of its unevenness. It was published instead by Marquardt and Company, another Berlin press.

The most remarkable work in the collection is its title piece; it is also the longest and represents a turn from Salten's usual brevity and use of an ironic *pointe* to a remarkably nuanced and empathetic portrayal of a feeble-minded old woman who is deposited by her brother in the Mauerbach Home for the Aged, where she grows increasingly unstable mentally and dies within days of her arrival. Until now Salten's deepest empathy had been reserved for children and animals; now he looked at one of society's older outcasts and captured her humility, shyness, pride, anger, and despair.

From its descriptive passages, it is clear that Salten had made several visits to the church and grounds of the former Carthusian monastery of Mauerbach, possibly with the idea of placing his mentally disabled brother, Theodor, in this seemingly idyllic rural setting. In this tale, however, Salten shatters Mauerbach's image as a peaceful sanctuary and shows the harshness of abandoning the elderly to an impersonal institution, a conviction he came to share with his sister Rosalie. At this time, however, Theodor was not the family's greatest problem; the siblings' concern was directed to Salten's favorite brother, Emil, who was suffering from an undiagnosed illness that caused him increasingly intense physical pain. This illness cast a shadow over the entire family.

Chapter 11: The World Intrudes

Soon after Salten had moved back to Vienna from Berlin, his brother Emil Salzmann, who was then forty-nine, began suffering from intense fatigue and severe cardiac pain which his doctors diagnosed as neurasthenia; this was an all-inclusive term for chronic fatigue, anxiety, hypochondria, and general lassitude, for which bed rest was prescribed. The pain worsened as the months passed, and by July 1907 Emil's pulse was racing at 125 to140 beats per minute. Salten took his brother to a sanatorium in Semmering, an Alpine resort not far from Vienna, in the hope that the fresh air and change of scene would prove beneficial, but Emil was too exhausted even to leave his bed, and after a few weeks he returned home to his mother and sister. In May 1908, the doctors gave up all hope of recovery and declared that Emil's death was imminent. Salten spent a good deal of time at the end administering morphine to his brother, whose suffering, "with all the agony that can be imagined," lasted for four weeks.[1] He died on June 28 of what the doctors described as "degeneration of the heart muscle."[2] Salten went into deep mourning over the loss of this brother, his favorite sibling and long-time confidant, "a man of incomparable kindness, loyalty, enthusiasm, selflessness, naiveté, charm, and devotion." "Nevertheless," he wrote to his new confidante Hedwig Fischer, "I am working very hard; indeed, I must say that I wouldn't have any idea how to keep going otherwise."[3] He was also going ahead with travel plans since he, his wife, and children all desperately needed a change of scene.

Salten was comforted in part by the new friendships in his life. One was with Samuel and Hedwig Fischer in Berlin, the other with the brilliant, Hungarian-born actor Josef Kainz and his wife, Margarethe. During the previous winter, the Fischers had visited Salten and his family in Semmering, and in July 1908 the Saltens joined the Fischers at the Dutch seaside resort at Noordwijk, where they rode horses on the beach, swam, bicycled around the countryside, and took automobile trips to The Hague, Delft, Antwerp, and Bruges. At the end of the month, Otti and the children went to Marienbad, while Salten went home via Heidelberg, where he and the Kainzes shared a suite of rooms and could enjoy each other's company.

136

Today we have only old photographs to give an idea of Josef Kainz and his remarkable hold on theatergoers and friends. They show a slim, athletic-looking man with dark hair and expressively large brown eyes in the costumes and dramatic poses of Don Carlos, Tasso, Hamlet, Prince Hal, Oswald, and Cyrano de Bergerac. Kainz was the lead actor of the Burgtheater, and the Viennese made a cult of their leading actors and actresses. Kainz shared Salten's hatred of Paul Schlenther's rule at the theater because Schlenther appeared to favor other actors and thwarted Kainz's desire to direct. Like Salten, Kainz had a passion for technological advances and enthusiastically bought such devices as stamp moisteners and altimeters; he also took great interest in Salten's photography. Salten was pleased that Kainz considered him a friend but was never as completely at ease around him as he was with the Fischers. As he confided several times to Hedwig Fischer, he enjoyed socializing with Kainz and his wife, but they also made him a bit nervous.[4]

That summer Salten followed his old habit of going for his annual stay at Berghof, the social watering hole for writers and musicians near Unterach am Attersee, in the mountains near Salzburg. He had first visited this spot when he was young, as a guest of Richard Specht's family; here he had gotten to know the family of the composer and pianist Ignaz Brüll, whose spacious summer enclave drew many musicians and writers. The Saltens had now become a regular part of that community. The Fischers' daughter Brigitte described the Saltens' house as a country home "overgrown with wild grapes," with a "wooden balcony which ran around the second story and was trimmed with Jugendstil wood carvings," and with "a splendid view onto the Attersee and the mountains round about." Where the forest began, "there was the fragrance of pine trees and cyclamen, which blossomed in great profusion on the forest floor."[5]

The fall of 1908 brought new difficulties. Salten, who was still grieving deeply over the loss of his brother, had headaches and intestinal pains, and Otti was nervous, despondent, and irritable. In October she underwent minor surgery that provided only temporary respite. During this time Salten had little contact with his former friends. "I see no one, hear from no one, and it also seems to me as if it is better this way," he wrote Hedwig Fischer. "Many illusions of friendship have vanished this year; I see many relationships that I believed to be on solid ground quite differently now, and it would only be a tremendous effort for me if I should be together now with just these people."[6] His relationship with Jakob Wassermann was foundering; he had sent Schnitzler a copy of his novella *Die Geliebte Friedrichs des Schönen* and not received any reaction or word of thanks. Schnitzler defended himself in his diary: "I didn't like it very much. As for the rest, he avoided company, turned down every possibility."[7]

The fall was a difficult time for the nation as well, as tensions mounted between Austria and Serbia. The crisis began with a revolution in Constantinople and the introduction of a constitutional government in Turkey in July 1908. Austria was fearful that Turkey would now regain power over the Balkan provinces of Bosnia and Herzegovina. These states were still in Turkish possession, although the 1878 Congress of Berlin had given Austro-Hungary the temporary right to occupy and administer them. Austria had vivid memories of the Turkish occupation of Austrian lands; to thwart the possibility of new incursions by the Turks, Austria annexed the two states in October 1908, and then, under its own sovereign power, granted Bosnia and Herzegovina a constitution. Serbia, which had closer ethnic ties to the two annexed states than either Turkey or Austria did, protested and demanded at least a strip of land so that it would have access to the Adriatic Sea. Meanwhile, Russia sought exclusive naval access to the Mediterranean through the Dardenelles, and Austria pledged its support to the Russian foreign minister, as long as that nation did not protest the Austrian annexation. The Russian minister had not foreseen the strength of anti-Austrian sentiment in his homeland, however, and soon a larger international conflict appeared imminent, with Russia and Serbia squaring off against Austria. In mid-March 1909 Austria mobilized for war, and Salten had his bags packed and was taking riding lessons in preparation for being called to the front. War was averted, however, after Germany stepped in firmly in support of the Austrian annexation. Russia backed down and accepted it as well, and an isolated Serbia was forced to do the same.

In October 1908 Salten stated that he regarded the annexation of the two Balkan states as a triumph for the old emperor and for the Austrian people, since it had occurred without fanfare or braggadocio. Privately, however, he expressed his concern that war was still on the horizon, if not immediately, then certainly within the next two years.[8] As if to confirm this, Salten's newspaper *Die Zeit* told him to be prepared to serve as the paper's war correspondent and to hold himself ready for immediate departure with the army's general staff, should that become necessary. Still, Salten had no idea when he attended German/Austrian field maneuvers that September in Groß-Meseritich, seeing there the three sovereigns Franz Josef, Wilhelm II, and Franz Ferdinand, that he was witnessing an anti-Serbian alliance that would, in four years time, propel Austria into a world war. Instead, he marveled at the technological advances that had replaced the old war machinery: machine guns and smokeless cannons and, for relaying messages, telephones instead of trumpets and cars instead of horses.[9] Ever an admirer of modern technology, Salten traveled to Graz in October to witness the flight of the first zeppelin over Austrian soil.

During this period of national insecurity and personal misfortune, Salten found it difficult to do any serious writing. He needed income beyond that provided by his Sunday feuilletons, however, and began work on a new series of sketches and short stories, somewhat along the lines of his collection *Künstlerfrauen*, which had just appeared in book form that year. As he had with that collection, Salten grouped eight new pieces together under the heading *Karriere, Lebensgeschichten* (Careers, Life Stories) and published seven of them in *Die Zeit* from April through December 1909.[10] Salten did not consider these sketches to be great art; he wrote them as he did his weekly columns, keeping them to the length of a column and providing each with an ironic *pointe*. He also began a "Sascha" series of royal portraits of visitors to Emperor Franz Josef's sixtieth jubilee, with the hope of publishing these in a jubilee volume that would resemble his 1905 *Buch der Könige*. Neither of these collections appeared in book form, although six of the *Karriere* pieces were included in a later retrospective collection of Salten's short stories.[11] Samuel Fischer did, however, publish a volume of Salten's essays under the title *Das österreichische Antlitz* (The Face of Austria) in 1909. This volume was broadly conceived and included essays on royalty, the military, popular entertainments such as dance halls and the Schönbrunn zoo, parliamentary gatherings, court entertainments, restaurants and wine gardens, the suburbs, and the theater. Special attention was given to portraits of Emperor Franz

Josef, Empress Elisabeth, Field-Marshall Count Radetzky, author Peter Altenberg, Paderewski's teacher Theodor Leschetitzky, actors Alexander Girardi and Josef Kainz, and Mayor Karl Lueger. Most of these pieces had appeared previously as columns in *Die Zeit*. The essays in this collection reveal once again that Salten was an ardent patriot but that he carefully avoided direct involvement in domestic political debate. Like most of the men in his circle of friends, he eschewed politics as a necessary evil. In his feuilletons he made an effort not to criticize Austria's political leaders, preferring instead to treat parliamentary proceedings as volatile theatrical performances in articles he wrote as "Sascha." There he described each individual's appearance, posturings, and outbursts as one would describe actors on a stage, praising or critiquing their performances rather than their policy statements. Nowhere is this more evident than in his feuilleton pieces on Dr. Karl Lueger, who served as a highly effective mayor of Vienna from 1897 to 1910 and who used anti-Semitism as a tool to win popular support among the lower middle classes. Salten was clearly disturbed by the outrageously anti-Semitic tone of Lueger's speeches, but he chose not to make this the centerpiece of his feuilletons; on the contrary, he performed a fine dance in trying to create a fair, yet critical picture of the city's controversial mayor by emphasizing the performance aspect of his public appearances.

In a feuilleton published in November 1902, for example, 'Sascha" portrays a parliamentary brawl in which Lueger emerges triumphant, then bursts into "the laughter of the victor, gloating, intoxicated with success, cocky in the awareness of power." When, however, Lueger sits down, "the piece of paper that he had seized rustles in his hands, he is trembling so violently." He is "pale as a ghost," realizing that he cannot relax in his struggle, that his opponents will continue to "rip from his body" "the high dignity, long desired and finally achieved, in which he would now like to wrap his tired limbs as in a purple cloak."[12] In another piece, entitled "Lueger," which Salten wrote on the occasion of Lueger's sixtieth birthday, "Sascha" portrays the mayor as a highly talented stage actor. "This is his hold over the people of Vienna," he wrote, "that all types of people speak from his mouth, the fiacre coachman and the committee chair, the cobbler's apprentice and the good lawyer, Mrs. Sopherl of the market place and the father of the poor. And all of Vienna's folk singers, as well." Lueger's voice can turn emotional, he wrote, but when it does, the "thundering organ" of his voice is always accompanied by a "tremolo of light irony." In the "vortex" of his speeches, "astonishing, unbelievable, and seductive thoughts sparkle, spin, and perform somersaults." Salten never mentions what these seductive thoughts are, but he does note that, if one listens closely, one hears "the raging gallop of ambition that leaps over everything with wild hooves, indifferent to everything, ruthlessly mowing everything down." Salten concludes that "the text of his stage role may be repulsive, and the pleasure that the people find in it destructively harmful. That does not diminish his talent if one regards it in the absolute. He plays his role as a true artist among dilettantes."[13]

In the following year, Salten gave Lueger his own stage piece, publishing an unsigned monologue in which he has Lueger searching for an appropriate quote for a speech he is to give to honor the hundredth anniversary of the German poet Friedrich Schiller's death. As he pages through Schiller's works, he remarks, "Everywhere there's freedom.... (Reads:) 'The house of freedom...,' 'Freedom's banner waves...,' 'Freedom ... freedom...'" and he ponders, "On my oath, he is lucky that he's been dead for a hundred years... with communist views like these, I couldn't even hire him as a grade school teacher, this Mr. Schiller..."[14] He also portrayed Lueger's extreme Christian morality in his tale "Die Erhebungen über Barbara Liebknecht" (1908).

Salten was, in fact, fascinated by Lueger, a larger-than-life figure who incorporated the force of the Vienna suburbs, "in all their broad, unswerving audacity, in their ironically disrespectful, terrible lashing out," through whose power "the modestly proper, arrogant inner city is simply overrun, its established tradition finished, torn to shreds like a piece of yesterday's newspaper."[15] He saw Lueger in Shakespearean terms, with ambition the fatal flaw that drove him to appeal to the lowest common denominator in the masses. He continued to view the theatricality of the situation when Lueger lay on his deathbed in March 1910, and he described the "terrible drama" taking place, one that moved the entire city, "no matter whether we honored the man or not."[16] After Lueger's death Salten published a number of "scenes" from his life, highly dramatic vignettes that revealed that Lueger was truly "an incarnation of the

Viennese character."[17]

In his essay on Lueger for *Das österreichische Antlitz*, Salten remarked that years would have to pass before anyone had the proper distance to write Karl Lueger's story. It would have to be written, he wrote, by someone "whose gaze is not veiled by hatred or admiration."[18] Salten felt both: admiration for a man who, like himself, had come from a poor home in the suburbs and, through his own efforts, conquered his arrogant superiors in the inner city, and hatred for his anti-Semitic message, of which he wrote: "Because all his other tricks were unsuccessful, this man comes and slaughters a Jew before the howling mob. On the speaker's platform, he slaughters him with words, stabs him to death with words, tears him to pieces and throws him to the people as sacrifice. It is his first monarchic-clerical act: to point the way for the discontented general public into the streets of the Jews, where it can let out its anger."[19]

Salten would speak out about Lueger again in 1926 when a statue to him was unveiled on the newly named Karl Lueger Square in downtown Vienna. Salten viewed the statue as a memorial to the "transitoriness of all flesh," erected at a time when the Viennese "no longer know all that much about Lueger." Then Salten proceeded to portray the strengths and the weaknesses of the man he considered "the embodiment of the Viennese petit bourgeoisie," adding, "In truth, he probably did not hate doctors and professors and culture and the Jews all that much; ... he was not really a hater, just a good ranter."[20] Sigmund Freud wrote to praise Salten for his essay, saying, "this awkward assignment could hardly have been carried out with more tact, dignity – and truthfulness."[21]

One should not be misled by Salten's nuanced Lueger pieces to believe that Salten sugar-coated actions that he saw taken against the Jews. He never turned to the Jewish faith, as he had seen his father do in the years before his death in 1905, but he had, ever since his misadventure as a boy in the Hernals Gymnasium, been brutally aware of the repressed anti-Semitism that flourished throughout the city, and this awareness had been greatly strengthened through his interactions with Theodor Herzl. Lueger's reign reinforced Salten's self-awareness that he was an outsider on two counts: first, among educated intellectuals and Jews for his impoverishment and lack of a formal education; second, among Vienna's predominantly Catholic population for his Jewish ethnicity. Still, Salten distinguished himself from most of his colleagues by not shying away from the topic of anti-Semitism in his columns. As one scholar has put it, most of the city's Jews were not political Zionists but thought of themselves primarily as "Austrians, as members of the German cultural sphere."[22] In addition, the city's mainstream newspapers strongly discouraged their feuilletonists from dealing critically with any governmental issues. The only way in which Jews could safely criticize the government was to cloak their thoughts in the kind of humor Salten used in his Lueger articles and his "Sascha" pieces. As a later Viennese humorist put it, "There was – and is – for a Jew only one certain method for moving people to listen to him: he has to dress up what he wants to say with humor."[23] From his earliest days as a journalist, Salten did just that, as, for example, in the *Wiener Allgemeine Rundschau*, where he published a comic sketch that treated a rumored attempt by "Jewish doctors, who haven't any patients" to introduce the plague into Vienna by poisoning people's coffee.[24] He published his strongest remarks in that paper under the heading "Parliamentary Question," where, with tongue firmly planted in cheek, he questioned the right of the police to protect the Jewish streets from a mob of six hundred rowdies and the rights of Jewish shopkeepers to put up heavy shutters on their windows to prevent looting during a pogrom in the Moravian town of Holleschau. "Is our prime minister willing to express his regret over the fact that the organs of security are disturbing harmless public entertainments?" he asked.[25]

In his weekly feuilletons for *Die Zeit*, Salten seldom made the Jewish question the focus of his writing, but he made a point of reviewing plays with Jewish themes and protested loudly about the opening of an all-Aryan theater on the occasion of the emperor's sixtieth jubilee. He wrote rapturously about the young Burgtheater actress Lia Rosen, who performed "as if she were stepping out from a race that knows tragic experience to the fullest, as if she is the heir and harbinger of this tragic experience and creator of great destinies." Her origins, he said, were evident in her eyes and facial features: they came from the "proletarian classes of the Jewish people in wretched Russian or Romanian pogrom-towns, where the children detect early on the reflection of bloody censure in the dark eyes of their parents even before their parents can tell them about the hatred lurking round about."[26] In a review of a play by the Russian Eugen Tschirikow entitled *Die Juden*, he wrote that only the Russians, with their "longing for freedom and passionate desire for leadership," were capable of understanding "the misery of mishandled peoples."[27]

To show that he practiced what he believed, in February 1907 he gave a public reading with Beer-Hofmann, Jakob Wassermann, and Schnitzler to benefit Jewish orphans in Russia. And in November 1908, when German pan-nationalist students viciously attacked Jewish students at the University of Vienna, Salten wrote an impassioned exposé that was published along with a call for the funding of an independent Jewish dormitory at the university. A month later Salten received a letter of appreciation from the Jewish labor force in Vienna for a speech he had given to honor the fifth anniversary of Theodor Herzl's death and for other services rendered to Vienna's Jewish population. In recognition of his services, an olive tree was planted in Salten's honor in the Theodor Herzl Park in Jaffa. "The thought that such a Biblical tree is growing in the Holy Land and bearing my name is something very dear to me," he remarked.[28]

Although Salten was forced to be circumspect about making too much of his Jewish affiliations in the Vienna newspapers, he was becoming an increasingly coveted speaker for various Jewish organizations. This differentiated him from Schnitzler and Beer-Hofmann, who, although they readily gave readings from their works to benefit Jewish causes, never gave speeches about the Zionist cause. In January of that year, after they had both declined the invitation, Salten was asked to share the stage with Martin Buber at the first gala evening organized by the Jewish Zionist organization Bar Kochba in Prague. Buber was nervous about appearing with Salten, who, Buber said, was known for being a remarkably lively speaker. Buber's fears were proven accurate. Salten carried the evening, and his lecture, which was entitled "Der Abfall vom Judentum" (The Lapse from Judaism) was printed in its entirety in Prague's Zionist weekly *Selbstwehr*. In this lecture, Salten took on the issue of the assimilated Jews who underwent Christian baptism in order to cement their hard-won positions among Europe's intellectual and financial elite. He called on these Jews to recognize their long history and strong cultural contributions to the

European nations; they should, he said, be proud of these contributions and reject the arguments of anti-Semites who merely tolerated them as "guests" in their countries. A columnist for the paper stated that the selection of Buber and Salten had been a deliberate attempt to show two very different sides of Jewish modernity:

> The two writers ... are strong opposites. Felix Salten, the journalist and feuilletonist, the author of sparkling novellas, the piquant stylist who has been influenced by the best of the Germans and French, who masters such a rich scale of notes, whose works shimmer and sparkle – even with real gold; and Martin Buber, the mystic, the priest, the engrossed one who has awakened a forgotten or, for us, submerged world.

The basis of Salten's writings, he added, was irony, that of Buber's, pathos.[29] It is not surprising, then, that Salten would be perceived as both the more popular and the more superficial speaker. He would be invited back two years later to speak before a packed house on the significance of the Bible for Jews and non-Jews and to introduce a reading of his friend Josef Kainz's drama fragment, "Saul." At that time *Selbstwehr* praised Salten, by noting that "the student association – thanks primarily to the aid of Felix Salten – has breached Jewish indifference, cantankerous assimilationism, and anti-Zionist mistrust."[30] By now Salten had established a strong reputation for himself as a leading voice of Zionism.

On Christmas Eve 1908, Salten was surrounded by family and friends. It was important to maintain a cheerful demeanor in front of his children, he said, since he wanted them to look back on their childhood as "on an experienced delight." He was determined to remain strong "until I have raised my children and provided them with reasonable security."[31]

That spring, however, the family had to leave the idyllic home in Heiligenstadt, for it was purchased by the city and torn down, and an orphanage was erected on the site. Salten found a spacious house for the family in Cottage, not far from Schnitzler's home, at the corner of Cottagegasse and Colloredogasse. Salten insisted that the yard be allowed to grow wild to better accommodate family pets and wildlife and that his wife restrict her love of cultivated plants to a few boxes of flowers. The house was in much better condition than the ramshackle Heiligenstadt property, and the family dreamed of purchasing it as their permanent home. Unfortunately, Salten was still unable to save money. He confessed this fault in a letter, commenting on how his wife and friends accused him of being a spendthrift: "I cannot find that so terrible and am always of the opinion that I still have had too little from life, too few walking sticks, too little tableware, and especially too few nice things."[32] If Salten was going to get enough money to purchase a home, it would not be by curtailing these small luxuries; he would have to find a way to earn a large amount of money quickly. He decided to try doing this by writing operetta librettos.

The first golden age of the Vienna operetta had been reached in the 1870s and 1880s; operetta had flourished even as the city reeled through a stock market crash in 1873. These operettas had contemporary, lighthearted plots, and their music was more accessible to a broad public than the music of opera; in difficult times they served to distract the Viennese populace from its real problems by bridging class differences and featuring the gaiety of masked balls and confused identities. It is not surprising that one of the most popular numbers of Johann Strauss the Younger's *Die Fledermaus* (1874) has as its text: "Glücklich ist, wer vergisst, was doch nicht zu ändern ist" – "Happy is he who forgets that which cannot be changed."

When Strauss died in 1899, it seemed as if the age of operetta had passed away with him, and the operetta sank in popularity and reputation until it was forcefully revived in 1905 by the tremendous success of Franz Lehar's *Die lustige Witwe* – *The Merry Widow*. Two years later, Salten's childhood friend, Felix Dörmann, made the move from poet to operetta librettist, achieving a popular and financial success with *Ein Walzertraum* (A Waltz Dream), which he co-authored with Leopold Jacobsen to music by Oscar Straus. Hoping to replicate Dörmann's success, Salten began in 1908 to write a new text to Johann Strauss the Younger's 1875 operetta *Cagliostro in Wien*, in which he attempted "to make a figure of Cagliostro who is brought closer to our modern understanding and is congenial as a human being."[33] Evidently, he was unable to reach an agreement with Adele Strauss as to its publication and perform-

146

ance, but he was able to get her approval for a new plot and libretto for Strauss's *Die Göttin der Vernunft* (The Goddess of Reason), a comedy about the French Revolution which Strauss had set to music only under the threat of a lawsuit from his publishers. Salten rewrote the work completely and turned it into a farce set it in contemporary Vienna, in which two daughters of a wealthy industrialist and members of the impoverished aristocracy turn to each other in order to set up marriages of mutual self-interest. In this work, Salten has everyone gradually realize that money is not necessarily a blessing, as the wealthy bourgeois father deliberately loses his fortune and moves his family to a happy home far out in the Vienna suburbs, to a setting much like Salten's own former Heiligenstadt dwelling. Salten named this operetta *Reiche Mädchen* (Rich Girls); it premiered as a "new" Strauss work after Christmas 1909 and had the popular stage comic Alexander Girardi singing the role of the father. The production was a popular success, and Salten regretted that he had sold the text to Adele Strauss rather than contracting for a percentage of its profits. He confided in Schnitzler that he hoped to earn 800,000 crowns in the next ten years through operetta writing.[34] He then tried putting together several Strauss tunes to a libretto he entitled *Der blaue Held* (The Drunken Hero). It had its premiere some two years later but was not the success of the former work.

In 1910, in what would be his last work in the field of operetta, Salten collaborated with Oscar Straus on a new work entitled *Mein junger Herr* (My Young Lord).[35] Unfortunately for Salten, the success of an operetta often depended more on the catchiness of its tunes than the quality of its libretto, and this, like his former works, did not enjoy lasting stage success. Otti had been worried the entire time that Salten's operetta libretti would damage his reputation as a serious writer, but, just as Salten compartmentalized different aspects of his feuilleton writing by using the pseudonym "Sascha" for his humoristic portrayals of parliamentary proceedings and aristocratic social gatherings, he had been careful to create a name that he used only for his work with operettas: Ferdinand Stollberg.

1909 had been a difficult year for Salten. He did not achieve the wealth he had hoped for, and Ottilie was diagnosed with an inoperable heart condition. He dropped two book projects that had long been on his mind: one a book called *Aus einem Wiener Kreis*

(From a Viennese Circle), begun during his Griensteidl days, about his fellow writers; the other a book about Paul Schlenther's tenure at the Burgtheater. Actually, there was a reconciliation of sorts in June of that year when the actress Wilhelmine Mitterwurzer died, and Otti, to whom the actress had acted as a mother figure, was one of the few people who showed up for her burial service. Paul Schlenther was also in attendance, and he "suddenly" offered Otti his hand. "Thus old differences and hurts are wiped away at the edge of life through a gesture," Salten noted.[36] That summer Salten took his family to Grado, Italy, to recover their health, then joined the Fischers for a vacation at Landro. On December third, Salten's mother died, of "the weakness of old age."[37]

Salten hoped that 1910 would be a better year, beginning as it did with the successful premiere of his operetta *Reiche Mädchen*. That year Paul Schlenther was fired from his position as director of the Burgtheater. The position was given to Baron Alfred von Berger, a former university professor in Vienna who had spent the ten years prior to this engagement as the first director of the newly founded *Deutsches Schauspielhaus* in Hamburg. But Salten's joy over Schlenther's departure was soon muted by Josef Kainz's sudden death of intestinal cancer in September. Salten was made literary executor of Kainz's estate.

In addition to his operetta work, Salten translated a play by André Rivoire, entitled *Le bon Roi Dagobert* (Good King Dagobert) into German for production in Berlin. However, Salten's most lucrative independent income during 1910 came from Samuel Fischer, who, in addition to publishing a new edition of *Das österreichische Antlitz*, made Salten's new novella, *Olga Frohgemuth*, part of his popular second series of contemporary novels; this series of "yellow" books was designed to reach a broad audience through the use of less expensive production techniques. In this long novella, Salten shows the conflicting views of the Viennese public towards its popular operetta singers. On the one hand, Olga is adored by her fans, winning the hearts of both men and women for her unaffected singing and natural stage presence. On the other, she is condemned by her very choice of profession to the popular view that operetta singers are immoral women who cannot be accepted into high-class society.[38] It was the theme he had treated once before in his drama *Der Gemeine*.

The Saltens and the Fischers were now fast friends, visiting each other's homes with frequency, and spending several weeks each summer together, usually in the Alps, most often at Berghof, in Unterach am Attersee. Because Samuel Fischer had an automobile, they were able to make many daylong trips, visiting sites of interest and friends living in the area. The Fischers' daughter Brigitte ("Tutti") was just one year younger than the Saltens' daughter Anna, and she recalled, "'Uncle and Aunt Salten' were ... like my second parents. When we went to Vienna, which we generally did once each year, I usually stayed with the Saltens in their house in Cottage and was very spoiled by them. Uncle Salten was always cheerful and friendly; I admired him very much and found him handsome to look at, especially when he was in the country and wore his lederhosen, green hunting jacket, and a colorful neck scarf. He urged us children to behave but without being stern, and I never saw him angry."[39]

The poet Rainer Maria Rilke was likewise flattering in his assessment of Salten, following a couple of days the two spent together in Italy: "I enjoy his company, in which all the Austrian traits are gathered, shining and well preserved as if in a soft case. And in his view on life there is so much charm and polite flexibility without his selling himself cheaply. His temperament works quietly like a scale, displays everything and positions itself with graceful vacillation back into a natural equilibrium."[40] When he was at home, Salten delighted in showing visitors special, hidden places in Vienna's inner city and in its rural suburbs. Many of these guests found Salten to be the very personification of the Viennese spirit: elegant, congenial, witty, and charming, and, like the city itself, clinging to a dying culture and struggling on the edge of bankruptcy.

Chapter 12: Prelude to War

In 1911 university professor and theatrical scholar Alexander von Weilen published an article surveying Salten's development as a prose artist and dramatist. It was a fair but critical piece that took into account Salten's determined path from reviewer to feuilletonist to "one step away from poet." In his first journal pieces, von Weilen noted, Salten "constructed strangely twisted sentences, was uncertain in word forms and linguistic usage," and "had ideas without the training to express them." But, because of "his restless, tough and ruthless ambition and tireless pursuit of greater development," he had become "a stylist." "Not even his enemies can [now] dispute the praise given to the careful polishing and effortless formation of his sentences," von Weilen added.

Von Weilen traced two aspects of Salten's development as a prose fiction author. One was his training as journalist, which gave him "the most assured concentration and condensation of sharply observed miniatures." This special ability to focus on small detail had its downside, however, since Salten's precise writing lacked "breadth and fullness." Another aspect of his development was the amazing ability to reproduce the style and substance of other writers. Salten "can write like Schnitzler, like Bahr, like Maupassant, like Turgenjev," he noted, clarifying that Salten was not "a mimic" and that he did "not use obvious models" in his work. The fatal flaw that von Weilen found in Salten's writing was, in fact, something quite different: "His temperament, which can suddenly burst into flame, is one of understanding, one of the senses, but never one of the heart." When Salten describes a place, a person, an animal, "he doesn't go into raptures …: he [just] looks and looks." He is, von Weilen states, like a surgeon performing "psychological anatomical studies" on his subjects, be they insects, dogs, princes, or young girls, and this makes his studies "almost cruel." He found Salten's depictions of suffering and dying clinical rather than empathetic because the author did not let his own voice intrude to mediate, modify, or alleviate. For this reason von Weilen found the sensuality in his tales similarly "cruel" and "torturous," although quite in keeping with the main theme of all Salten's works, that "people speak and know nothing about one another."

Von Weilen had special praise for "Die Erhebungen über

Barbara Liebrecht," *Herr Wenzel auf Rehberg, Olga Frohgemuth*, and the collection *Künstlerfrauen*. Up to now, he added, Salten had not reached similar heights in his dramas, but he did not doubt "that with his energy he will be able to prevail there as well."[1]

It must have been flattering to Salten to have a man of von Weilen's stature write a long retrospective of his creative work and especially satisfying to have him rebut the criticisms of his enemies. Von Weilen asserted that Salten no longer made the stylistic blunders of which Kraus had accused him in the past and that, in Salten's remarkable ability to adapt his pen to the style and substance of the theme at hand, he was not aping his betters, as Kraus had suggested on more than one occasion. Nevertheless, the variety of Salten's themes and stylistic treatments, along with the unevenness of his work, continued to baffle even well-intentioned critics; as they saw it, Salten simply attempted too much and therefore could not be placed in the forefront of any one category of fiction. As Kraus put it, "The aesthetes had divided things up. Dying belonged to Doctor Arthur [Schnitzler], living to Richard [Beer-Hofmann], the Votive Church with the evening sky to Hugo [von Hofmannsthal], the Ambraser Collection [of medieval works] to Poldi [Leopold von Andrian-Werburg], and to Felix all of that and much more and the Renaissance as well."[2] Even Salten's friend Hofmannsthal criticized his subjective, variable approaches to literature and criticism, commenting, "He disavows and promotes [literary trends], rejects and endorses [them], each time veering around everything. The final word: his thinking is not healthy."[3]

Ever since the Griensteidl days some twenty years before, Salten had been known to friends and foes alike as "Felix Salten." It was now time, he decided, to make the name change from Sigmund Salzmann to Felix Salten official in order to avoid bureaucratic confusion for himself and his family.[4] Accordingly, he went to Budapest in May and, with little difficulty, legally changed his name and the family name of his wife and children to Salten.

1911 was altogether a good year for the publication of Salten's books. First, he had a retrospective of sorts published in a volume by the Deutsch-Oesterreichische press entitled *Die Wege des Herrn*. The only new works in this volume were six of the eight stories Salten had published in *Die Zeit* as part of his series called *Karriere* (Careers) in 1909. The book also included four tales from Salten's first volume of short stories, *Der Hinterbliebene* (1901), and seven from *Die Geliebte Friedrichs des Schönen* (1908). There was no mention of their having appeared previously.

A more interesting revival occurred when Salten took the pieces he had written for the *Wiener Allgemeine Zeitung* in June 1895 under the title "Quer durch den Wurstelprater" and issued them in book form with some seventy-five photographs by Emil Mayer. As an ardent amateur photographer himself, Salten was especially interested in film as an art medium, and Mayer was a remarkably talented man who was equally innovative in photographic techniques and in his choice of subject matter. He eschewed formal portraiture, preferring unposed pictures of unsuspecting subjects taken on the streets of Vienna with a hand-held camera. One remarkable factor in these pictures is the lack of interest that Mayer showed in portraying the wonders of modern technology and architecture. Instead, his pictures show common people interacting in the streets, buying from a vendor, sitting at an outdoor café, gathering around a fallen horse. Around 1908 he turned his attention to Vienna's popular park and published a postcard series of photographs entitled *Volksleben Prater* (People's lives, Prater) that showed the people who attended its attractions and bought from its vendors. Salten's early essays reflect a similar interest in the park, although his interest focused more on the park's performers: its barkers, artists, freaks, and musicians. The collaboration of photographer and writer therefore required a little give and take. Mayer added pictures of those performers who were still active in the park, while Salten added text that treated the park's visitors.[5]

This collaboration, *Wurstelprater*, is a remarkable achievement, for it captures perfectly the spirit of the old Prater, when rides were no more breathtaking than those on carved carousel horses, children were still enchanted by hand puppets, and soldiers and young working men and girls escaped the oppressive heat of the city to gawk at freak shows, hear musicians perform popular and ethnic folk songs, drink, dance, and seek escape through flirtations and sexual encounters.[6] Neither Salten nor Mayer chose, either in picture or in text, to mention the giant Ferris wheel that had been erected in 1897 at the park entrance and become an important Prater symbol.

1911 was not solely a year of retrospection, however. Later that year three new novellas appeared in a volume published in Leipzig: *Das Schicksal der Agathe* (Agathe's Fate), *Heimkehr* (Homecoming), and *König Dietrichs Befreiung* (King Dietrich's Release). All three stories concern figures in crisis who must free themselves from the veil of self-delusion that separates them from their real selves. The first, *Das Schicksal der Agathe*, treats a young camp follower at the turn of the fourteenth century of whom it was prophesied that the head of the emperor would one day rest in her lap. The second is a contemporary tale about a man who falls in love with a woman only to have her demand of him that he kill her husband. The third, another historical tale set in late medieval times, treats a tyrant king who is suddenly overcome by the futility and impermanence of his bloody rule. When Schnitzler received his copy of this volume, he expressed admiration for Salten's artistry but not for his analytic insights. As he noted in his diary, "[I] read "Heimkehr," which unknown to me. Excellent – and yet: nothing! Then his best piece, already known to me: 'König Dietrichs Befreiung.' And here too, in the highest sense, only the 'gesture' is portrayed. Brilliant feuillitonism."[7]

At this point in their writing careers, Salten and Schnitzler had begun to part ways. Salten had never taken more than a passing interest in Freudian psychology, despite the fact that he and Freud had once been neighbors.[8] More and more, Salten was convinced that it was time for writers to move on from the narrow confines of "literature hazy with the smoke of little coffeehouses"[9] and to confront the problems of the contemporary world. "We have now passed through a long period in which the subtlest and strangest problems of eroticism have been treated," Salten would write a couple of years later. "Endlessly and in countless variations, people have tracked down and solved, or tried to solve, the most hidden mysteries of psychology, have explored the deepest recesses of the female soul." Now, Salten felt, "people would like to believe it almost possible that the wide world with its shocks, catastrophes, destinies, and national tragedies is also in a position to offer artists what they long for so much and speak of constantly: an inner experience."[10] He felt literature could – and should – cover topics like finance, technology, and war. In *Der blaue Held* he had, as critics noted, "made the attempt to conquer a place in operetta for politics and ethics, poetry and satire."[11] Salten admired writers who traveled broadly and incorporated their insights from these travels into their writings: Johannes V. Jensen in America, for example, or Hermann Hesse in India. During this same period of rich literary output, Salten had become even more prolific as a newspaper journalist. Even as he was growing more dissatisfied with his work at *Die Zeit.*, he had begun writing feuilletons in 1910 for Hungary's German-language daily, *Pester Lloyd*, and in 1912 he became a regular contributer to the *Berliner Tageblatt*. One reason for this burst of activity may have been the need for funds to cover the construction work he was having done on his house. He did abandon the field of operetta, however, since his libretti had not brought in the income he had hoped for.[12] In December 1911 his translation of André Rivoire's *Le bon Roi Dagobert*, completed two years earlier for production in Berlin, was performed at the Volkstheater.

The following year, in February, Salten was awarded the Bauernfeld literary prize; this carried a stipend but did not otherwise give Salten the recognition he desired, since he had to share the prize with Jakob Wassermann, Siegfried Trebitsch, Paul Apel, and Friedrich Adler. Nevertheless, in the spring of 1912, Salten was hard at work on a new three-act play entitled *Das stärkere Band* (The Stronger Bond). Much to his disappointment, Otto Brahm turned it down for his Lessing Theater, but it was accepted immediately for the Volkstheater and premiered there on March 16. For his plot Salten turned once again to his rich store of knowledge of unhappy royalty asked to choose duty over love. The play ended with a happy compromise: the young duke is allowed to keep his mistress and children and still rule the land.[13]

Paul Schlenther's predecessor at the Burgtheater, Max Burckhard, was now theater critic at the *Fremden-Blatt*, the official organ of the Austrian Foreign Office and the emperor's favorite source of news. In preparation for the premiere of Salten's play, Burckhard read the text and wrote his reactions to it, but he died just hours before he could attend its premiere performance. In an ironic turn of fate, Salten was then asked to take over Burckhard's position at the *Fremden-Blatt*. Salten jumped at the opportunity to break ties with *Die Zeit* and move to what he regarded as a more stable and lucrative position. A few months later, he also signed on with the *Neue Freie Presse* as an independent feuilletonist. This was even more prestigious than the *Fremden-Blatt* position since the *Neue Freie Presse* was the most widely circulated and highly regarded newspaper in Austria, and Salten was permitted to write about topics of his own choosing. Salten's last feuilleton for *Die Zeit* was published on March 29; it was a review of Bernard Shaw's *Caesar and Cleopatra*, as translated by his friend Siegfried Trebitsch. Ludwig Bauer, who had served as Salten's replacement as Burgtheater critic for *Die Zeit* while Salten had been in Berlin, now returned to that post.

The Saltens spent the summer at the Berghof in Unterach, with Julius Ferdinand Wollf and his wife and Samuel and Hedwig Fischer, although Otti again had health problems and had to return briefly to Vienna for a minor operation. Summers at Berghof had become a necessity for Salten. Here he could escape the constant pressures of the city while still having friends with whom he could socialize. He enjoyed hunting, hiking, and fishing, and could engage in his passion for spending early morning hours alone in the mountain forests, studying animals and birds in their natural habitats. This year especially, Salten dreaded his return to Vienna to face difficulties with his builders and landlord and the bills that were all coming due. Still, his new positions with two important Vienna newspapers seemed to promise hope of improvement in his household finances. When Gerhart Hauptmann came to Vienna in November to be feted at a banquet given by the Concordia Press Club of Austrian writers and journalists, Salten was chosen to give the main address.[14]

Salten's new position as main theater critic at the *Fremden-Blatt* led, however, to a falling out with Siegfried Trebitsch, who was irked at the fact that Salten did not like his play *Das Haus am Abhang* (The House on the Slope) and had asked another critic to review its performance. The review was a negative one, and Trebitsch now had his lawyer demand that Salten repay his premarital debts to him at once. Salten was taken by surprise, since Trebitsch had, when he served as witness at Salten's wedding some nine years previously, told Salten that he was releasing him from these financial obligations.[15] Now Trebitsch went around telling everyone about his own largesse and Salten's failure to repay him. Salten saw this as the beginning of a campaign against him, but on Schnitzler's advice kept silent and immediately repaid the full amount of the loan.

Salten's financial situation was now dire. Having given up on operettas as a source of rich income, Salten now turned to the new medium of film.[16] He was always interested in technological advances, and, unlike some aficionados in the theater, regarded film as complementary to the stage rather than as a substitute for it. Films focused on movement and gestures, he wrote, while the stage relied on speech and words. The film was a renewal of the pantomime as art form; it concentrated on portraying events, while the stage dedicated itself to "the drama of the soul."[17] To those who would argue that films lowered the tastes of the masses, he responded that "before the development of the movie theaters the leisure activities and entertainments of the masses were much more squalid, much more debased than afterwards."[18] He pointed out that documentary films, in particular, let people from even the lowest classes learn about foreign lands by seeing the lives of the people there and the marvels of strange cities and countrysides. It was certainly no accident that the people's park, the Wurstelprater, was the location of Vienna's first five movie theaters and that the park became the center of the city's film industry.

As with his cabaret experiment in 1901, Salten now hoped to improve the culture of the masses – and his own finances – by working with this new medium. His first film script, *Der Shylock von Krakau* (Shylock of Krakow), which he penned for a Berlin film company,[19] took up a subplot of Shakespeare's *Merchant of Venice* and developed it along lines similar to those found in his operetta *Reiche Mädchen* and his novella *Olga Frohgemuth*.[20] In this film a corrupt but impoverished aristocrat seduces the daughter of a wealthy Jewish usurer; he gets her to steal money from her father, then abandons her. The film revolves around the elderly father, who first suffers agony and rage over the loss of his money and his child, then stubbornly refuses to take in his repentant daughter when she tries to return to him, and finally, after her death, bitterly mourns his own hardness of heart. In keeping with Salten's view that films could provide cultural lessons to the masses, this film was a rich portrayal of life in Krakow's Jewish ghetto, of services in the synagogue and religious rituals in the home. In his first film role, Rudolf Schildkraut played the Jewish usurer to perfection; as one critic put it, his performance captured "the powerlessness and horror" of a persecuted race: "He tugs at the heart, he whines as he goes out into the ugliness of the world — we know this incomparable face from the real Shylock, the Shylock of the Deutsches Theater."[21] The Jew's two daughters were played by Beate Ehren and the incomparable Lia Rosen; Carl Wilhelm both directed the film and played the villainous aristocrat.

Otti was skeptical about the riches Salten anticipated acquiring through script writing, saying worriedly to Schnitzler, "If only this plan doesn't misfire the way the operettas did."[22] She had good cause for worry. Salten boasted to Schnitzler that he had already received 14,000 marks for the screenplay, although Schnitzler knew that the true sum was closer to 3,000. In October Otti came to Schnitzler in tears, saying that Salten was "emaciated, depressed, and spending a lot of money unecessarily" in spite of their financial worries. She asked Schnitzler to intervene.[23] Schnitzler went immediately to the Salten house:

> Felix does not want to be treated like an invalid. He complains about the failure of his endeavors, the waste of his time on little things, his hurt pride — he is still classified as a "feuilletonist"; he has a rich supply of material and no time, no rest. [He has] no [financial] cares — even though he has nothing, he has earned 56,000 crowns so far this year (shows his book) — I advise him finally to tackle a work of a grander sort, he tells me a plot [for a play] — with splendid comedic elements (The Prisoner[24]) — we speak about the crisis in a writer's production between 40 and 50; everything [is] cordial; even amicable; und still he lacks the last bit (and next-to-last bit) of real sincerity — as, admittedly, I myself do.[25]

It is rather touching that Salten tried so desperately to hide his true financial situation from Schnitzler. In a feuilleton from November of that year, Salten portrayed a couple, like himself and Otti, who try to hide from their friends the fact that they cannot afford a taxi and need to leave parties early in order to catch the

last tram home.[26] It was clearly a matter of pride for Salten always
to give the appearance of financial ease; the ironic *pointe* of his article was the revelation that others in his circle were playing similar
games out of fear that they would otherwise lose their social position and be relegated to the lower middle classes.

Salten had three books published that year, each by a different
firm; one was a volume containing his two earlier novellas *Die
Gedenktafel der Prinzessin Anna* and *Der Schrei der Liebe* that was put
out by Georg Müller in Munich. His second book, *Kaiser Max der
letzte Ritter* (Emperor Max, the Last Knight), respresented a new
direction for the author, in that it was written for a series of works
for young people published by Ullstein. This series featured fairy
tale and adventure stories, with an emphasis on the heroes of German mythology. Salten chose, however, to write a biography of a
man who was "the lastborn son of the Middle Ages and ... at the
same time the firstborn offspring of a new age."[27] Salten portrayed
Maximilian I as a man of immense youthful energy – as an avid
hunter, the author of twenty-two books, a man who had difficulty
handling money, a man who was extremely interested in modern
technology and the arts and who was constantly under attack by his
domestic and foreign enemies. Salten clearly identified with his
subject, whom he portrayed as also possessing traits characteristic
of the House of Habsburg. The work is quite remarkable for its
natural, conversational style, one that reveals Salten's ability to give
a rich portrait of this controversial Habsburg ruler without writing
down to his youthful readership. One can imagine that he used his
own children, nine-year-old Anna and ten–year-old Paul, as critics
of his work-in-progress.

Samuel Fischer published the third Salten volume to appear in
1913, a volume of essays entitled *Gestalten und Erscheinungen* (Figures
and Appearances). This book took a nostalgic look at some of the
people who had played an important role in Salten's life. It was
divided into three parts. The first was devoted primarily to literary
figures whom Salten especially admired, from Boccaccio to Frank
Wedekind, Hans Christian Andersen to Keyserling and Schnitzler.
In addition he included essays on Gustav Mahler, Theodor Herzl,
and the recently deceased director of the Burgtheater, Alfred Freiherr von Berger. Part two treated stage and concert performers
such as Josef Kainz, Adolf von Sonnenthal, Lia Rosen, and Enrico

Caruso, while part three portrayed leaders, from Metternich to Roosevelt to zoo founder Karl Hagenbeck. The work closed with a lovely memory that the Saltens and Fischers shared of Marie Brüll, widow of the composer and pianist Ignaz Brüll, and her habit of playing the piano and singing at her open window at Berghof in Unterach on warm summer evenings.

The essays in this volume had all appeared in newspapers prior to the book's publication; many were tributes written upon the death of their subjects and provide excellent overviews of the subjects' lives and achievements. Salten's tribute to Schnitzler is particularly warm and not a little nostalgic when he writes about Schnitzler's effect on his generation of readers: "This generation's feeling for love was influenced by his way of viewing love; its thoughts of transience were colored by his way of thinking about death; its desire to live was exalted and fueled by his reverence for life."[28]

In *Gestalten und Erscheinungen* Salten looked back on the formative figures of his life, past and present, who exemplified Vienna's "gay apocalypse";[29] it was an appropriate companion piece to his earlier collection *Das österreichische Antlitz* and was, like this earlier volume, colored by nostalgia for the past. Salten was well aware that this world was changing, that the violence in Russia, the unrest in Serbia, the pogroms in Romania, the German and French rivalries in Africa, and the recent Turkish-Italian war were all ominously indicative of a catastrophic rupture of the old world order.

The rumbles of revolution were audible even in Salten's beloved Austria. By 1911 the situation of members of the underclasses and recent ethnic immigrants in Vienna's industrial suburbs had become especially dire; there was not enough housing, speculation had driven up the rents of the few rooms that were available, and, in September of that year, there was a sudden sharp rise in food prices. At the call of the Social Democrats, 100,000 people came in from the suburbs to gather in front of the town hall for a hunger demonstration. The military and police were out in force, and, at the end of what had been a peaceful gathering, just as the crowds were beginning to disperse, violence broke out as several teenagers in the crowd threw stones in the direction of the town hall. The police fired their guns, and mounted cavalrymen drove the demonstrators back out of the city. Before all was over, all the lower windows of the town hall had been smashed, stores were plundered, and streetlights broken. A longer revolt continued in the Ottakring district when demonstrators were joined by women and children in erecting barricades against the forces of capitalist order.[30]

This was an uprising by the victims of bourgeois capitalism, the forgotten underclasses that Salten had portrayed in *Josefine Mutzenbacher* and *Der Wurstelprater*. In one of his rare political pieces, Salten responded to the short-lived violence by pleading for understanding. He pointed out that Vienna had a class still lower than the working classes, one "that starves and suffers privations and freezes and seeks refuge in fornication and alcohol." "With all our humanity, with all our social endeavors, we have not yet penetrated down to this class," he argued, "we have not yet come so far that these pariahs have been saved, taken up into our society, allowed to share in our efforts, our joys, our struggles, and our peace." "If we do not want these poorest of the poor to raise their balled fists against us, we must climb down to them" to help, he added. "If we do not want them to behave like criminals, we must help them to live like human beings."[31]

As someone who had lived among the underclasses in his youth and known first-hand the pangs of hunger and the overcrowding of the city's *Mietskasernen* (rental barracks), Salten was able to empathize with the demonstrators without, however, having the slightest desire to associate with them. In one of his earliest columns for the *Fremden-Blatt*, in fact, he wrote of the noise and dust that "outsiders" were bringing in to his quiet villa neighborhood of Cottage.[32] Salten had struggled all his life so that he might rub shoulders with successful bourgeois professionals, not with the underclasses of Währing's more impoverished neighborhoods.

By 1913, however, even the inner city was experiencing difficulties. Salten noted that 1912-1913 was the year of "Balkan turmoil [the Balkans wars, in which Serbia took the provinces Macedonia and Kosovo away from the Ottoman Empire and Bulgaria], the threat of war [Serbia with Austria], a sharp fall in prices, a general economic depression, a notoriously bad business course and the equally notorious slack attendance under which all the Viennese theaters had to suffer."[33] When Alfred Freiherr von Berger died suddenly, Salten briefly harbored hopes of being named the next director of the Burgtheater, but Hugo Thimig, long-time actor at the theater and patriarch of one of Europe's great acting dynasties, was given this position instead. Salten had to content himself with having his one-act play "Auferstehung" (Resurrection) performed there instead, in March 1914, one month after *Das lockende Licht* (The Enticing Light), a pantomime (sung ballet) he had written for music composed by Wladimir Metzl, son of Otti's half-brother Ludwig, had its premiere at the Royal Opera House in Dresden. He and the actor Rudolf Schildkraut also gave a program before a large audience in Prague's Central Hotel. The program was sponsored once again by Bar Kochba, and an announcement of the program proclaimed that Salten would, "in his penetrating and convincing manner, in his elegant and yet never superficial style of speaking," discuss the state of contemporary Jewish letters, while Schildkraut would read examples from several of these works.[34] At least one of these Jewish writers, Franz Kafka, made a point of attending the evening program.[35]

Felix Salten with his hunting dog "Hex," ca. 1890.
Photograph by Karoly Zureich, Miscolcz. (DLA Marbach)

With two "sweet girls" in the Prater, ca. 1892: Front: Richard Beer-Hofmann and Felix Salten; Rear: Hugo von Hofmannsthal and Arthur Schnitzler. (DLA Marbach)

Archduke Leopold Ferdinand of Tuscany, 1898. (FSE/LWA)

Ottilie and Felix Salten, ca. 1910. (FSE/LWA)

Paul and Anna Salten, 1906. (FSE/LWA)

Felix Salten, 1911. Photograph by d'Ora, Vienna. (FSE/LWA)

Karl Lueger, Mayor of Vienna 1897-1910. (ÖNB)

Felix Salten and Arthur Schnitzler in the Salzkammergut, ca. 1912.
(FSE/LWA)

viii

Felix Salten with daughter Anna at his Cottagegasse home, ca. 1935.
(FSE/LWA)

Felix Salten with Max Reinhardt (right) at *Faust* rehearsal in Salzburg,
1935. (FSE/LWA)

Felix Salten with son Paul, ca. 1934. (FSE/LWA)

Hugo von Hofmannsthal, 1904, photographed by Salten. (FSE/LWA)

Felix and Ottilie Salten in Zurich, ca. 1941. (FSE/LWA)

Chapter 13: War

In May 1914, Germany launched the world's largest passenger ship, the luxury liner *Vaterland*. As a member of the press, Salten was invited on board for the ship's maiden voyage from Cuxhaven to Southampton. The piece he wrote on this for the *Fremden-Blatt*[1] had nothing but praise for this sea-going wonder – for its spacious two-room cabins, its luxury restaurants, its 2000-volume library, and its large swimming pool. He defended the luxury of the ship against those who maintained that the romance of sea travel had been sacrificed for opulent splendor, pointing out that the ship was intentionally designed as a floating luxury hotel for frequent travelers tired of the normal discomforts associated with sea crossings. In his article about this same voyage for the *Neue Freie Presse*, however, Salten was slightly more critical. From the luxury of the promenade deck, he wondered whether those emigrants housed between decks had comforts at all comparable to those he and Otti were enjoying. And he regretted the fact that the ship's musicians performed the Austrian national anthem to its German text, "Deutschland, Deutschland über alles."[2] At the end of their journey, he and his wife spent several days in London and Paris, little dreaming how soon such visits would become impossible.

A month later Salten recorded in his memoirs that he was a witness to a seemingly inconsequential event[3] that attained significance only after the fact:

> I was in Triest, making a film. One morning I was standing on my balcony when I saw the car of Franz Ferdinand and his wife drive to the pier. A large crowd had gathered, but no one removed his hat and no one greeted him. Franz Ferdinand climbed into the motorboat with his wife, rode out to the warship that was lying at the ready and immediately steamed away. The two of them came back to this shore as mere corpses.[4]

Franz Ferdinand, the heir presumptive to the Habsburg throne, and his wife Sophie Chotek, Duchess of Hohenberg, had gone to attend military maneuvers in Bosnia, and on June 28 they

162

were assassinated by a Serbian nationalist in Sarajevo. Few people had any love for the Archduke; in addition to being a rather crude man with a violent temper, he had alienated the ruling elite by aiming to modernize the structure of the Austrian State. He had further alienated Emperor Franz Josef by marrying a woman below his station; the emperor disliked him so intensely that he stayed away from the Archduke's funeral, and, contrary to tradition, Franz Ferdinand was interred in the crypt of his home chapel at Artstetten rather than in the imperial vault of the Capuchin church in Vienna. Salten recalled his own close association with the archdukes of Tuscany and their many stories of the Archduke's mean-spiritedness. In addition to the Archduke's "greed, stinginess, and malice,"[5] Salten had always been especially repulsed by the Archduke's brutal slaughter of game. Still, Salten's own early memories of social humiliation at school caused him to feel some degree of sympathy for a man snubbed at court for the simple act of wedding beneath his class.

In spite of the nearly universal dislike of the Archduke, his assassination, which everyone referred to as "the outrage," served as a catalyst for the nationalistic rivalries that had been gathering strength in Europe during the previous decade. Austria saw this as a chance to crush Serbian nationalism once and for all and issued a formidable ultimatum in the expectation that Serbia would reject it and Austria could then enter into a limited war. War was declared on July 28. Russia was bound by treaty to Serbia and immediately began mobilizing its army, whereupon Germany declared war on Russia on August 1. The chips fell quickly. In early August France and Britain entered into war against the German-Austro-Hungarian alliance and the Great War had begun. Salten wrote Schnitzler from Berghof, "When one realizes what is happening now, and why it is happening – I could despair. I can actually envy those who believe that this is all because of Serbia, for they have something to feed their sense of justice." "Perhaps it is good that this war will be fought out now," he added, "good for our sons; that may be an ugly and egoistical thought, but I am thinking it anyway."[6] Both Paul Salten and Heinrich Schnitzler were too young to be called up as soldiers.

Salten was not alone in believing that a great war was inevitable, but he wrote a feuilleton for the July 29 issue of the *Neue Freie*

Presse whose title "Es muß sein" (It Has to Happen) the pacifist Karl Kraus would throw in his face for years to come. The article was a clear propaganda piece, arguing that Austria had, in the face of numerous challenges, kept the peace for fifty years, that even with countless Serbian insults and indignities towards Austria, indignities now crowned by the assassination of its heir presumptive, the country had shown immense restraint before taking the necessary step of going to war. Austrians should not be ashamed of this restraint, he added, "It links us with all those other nations that live within Europe's cultural borders." In this article Salten described the shared rapture of the thousands of people who gathered spontaneously on July 28 in the squares of Vienna and in cities throughout the empire to sing patriotic songs. Because, like so many of his circle, Salten clung to the idea that cultural activity was superior to – and more enduring than – politics, these old songs were proof to him that "life goes on. Even beyond this war, which we believe wants to pull us into an abyss. Life has gone on beyond all wars that have faded away, flourishing, intensified, enhanced, irresistible in its progress, in its development, in its liberating cultural activity. Let us think of this in the solemn days that are now coming."[7]

This was an argument that Salten would make throughout the conflict. In late September, when people were beginning to question whether it was appropriate to go to the theater when their friends and neighbors were suffering and dying on the battlefield, Salten wrote an enthusiastic piece about a production of Paul Heyse's *Colberg* at the Deutsches Volkstheater. Reminding his readers of Schiller's statement that the stage was a "moral establishment," Salten affirmed, "never have we needed moral establishments as much as we do now." Furthermore, the production of Heyse's tale of Colberg's brave resistance to siege by Napoleonic forces was relevant to the situation at hand: "For several moments the present was linked to the past. Reflections flashed from the poetry into reality, illuminating connections between what was and what is, between our forefathers, who once had to risk life and death for their free honor in the world, and us, who today have to risk life and death for honor and freedom." He allowed that theaters should avoid performing facile comedies but argued that "one covers the mirrors only in a house of death"[8] and that, as a mirror, the stage could serve to strengthen and comfort a suffering populace.[9]

As a contributing feuilletonist to the *Berliner Tageblatt*, Salten wrote pieces describing the war mood in Vienna, striving to show how the Austrians were united with the Germans not only in their cause but in their history and their strength of purpose. Where he had written for the Vienna papers of Austria's united front by describing the singing of Austrian patriotic songs on the eve of the war, he wrote for the Germans of the Austrians first singing their own national anthem, then gathering before the German embassy to sing the German one.[10] Some six months later he would even go so far as to call for the unification of Germany and Austria, arguing that Austria's detachment from Germany "no longer makes any sense."[11]

Prior to the summer of 1914, Salten had shown pacifist tendencies and expressed misgivings about war as a patriotic or noble act. In 1899 he had portrayed the senselessness of war in his novella "Sedan," by having a sparrow slain in the throes of battle. He had questioned the concept of heroism in his 1895 novella "Heldentod" (A Hero's Death) and the moral high ground of army officers in his 1901 drama *Der Gemeine* (The Common Soldier) and in his 1907 novella *Herr Wenzel auf Rehberg und sein Knecht Kaspar Dinckel*. As late as 1911, he had published two works even more critical of war as a positive solution to conflict: *König Dietrichs Befreiung* (King Dietrich's Release) had shown the transience of glory achieved through bloodshed, and *Das Schicksal der Agathe* (Agathe's Fate) had portrayed war as a dehumanizing theater of bloodlust, pillage, and rape. Now that war was at hand, however, Salten spoke as a patriot.

In the summer of 1914, Salten was back at Berghof with the family; Richard and Paula Beer-Hofmann were neighbors in Weissenbach. All would have been quite idyllic except for all the heartbreak Salten witnessed among the local population. He wrote a feuilleton entitled "Farewell… Come Back" with the subtitle "Little Pictures of Important Days," in which he described heart-rending scenes of parting, as the normally taciturn, hard-working men of the village said goodbye to their wives and left for the front:

> We people of today know such scenes only
> from books: women who cry and ring their hands,

> children who sob: "Father! Father!" No one could console the woman, no one could placate the children. How would one, anyway? ... These were men marching off to war. Perhaps they'll come back, although this word "perhaps" is enough to make the women ring their hands. And of the two possibilities inherent in the word, the bad one weighs threateningly enough on every heart in this hour of leave-taking.

However necessary or inevitable the coming conflict, Salten felt the injustice of the mass mobilization and the special burdens placed upon the poor, writing of one such soul: "Somewhere in the depths of our nature a desperate shame stirs, with all the jabbing pain that it inflicts. Good God! How much, how very much peaceful, liberating, redeeming work people everywhere might have carried out at home in the country and go off to war instead. And this poor devil goes away without a murmur, away from his wife and child."[12]

Salten was successful in getting at least one soldier released from trench warfare. At Christmas in 1914, Salten used his powers as chief editor of the *Fremden-Blatt* to change the format of the paper and to add a separate photographic section called *Welt-Bild* to the paper's weekend edition. In one of these earliest editions, he printed, at the behest of the art patroness Jenny Mautner, several drawings by Victor Hammer, along with the comment that Hammer had three pictures in the print collections of the Albertina museum and was now serving at the front. Salten recalled that within hours of the appearance of these pictures Archduke Friedrich, who was both commander-in-chief of the army and owner of the Albertina, had gotten Hammer transferred from battlefield duty to a position as war artist.

Salten's literary output in 1914 made no mention of the war since most of his work was well under way before August of that year. He scripted two new films – *Gerettet* (Saved) and *Das Urteil des Arztes* (The Doctor's Judgment). He also completed a new novel entitled *Die klingende Schelle* (The Tinkling Cymbal),[13] in which he condemned the idle aestheticism and cold egotism that had characterized so many in the Young Vienna circle. It related the tale of an independently wealthy protagonist who weds the impoverished girl he has gotten pregnant under the condition that she not interfere in any way with the conduct of his life. He continues to socialize, attend the theater, dine at fine restaurants, and court beautiful women, while completely ignoring his wife and child. But when both die, he is suddenly overcome with remorse and regret. A heartbroken admirer of the dead woman challenges the protagonist to a duel; he accepts, hoping that he can end his life in this manner. Instead, the challenger sees the protagonist's remorse, embraces him, and offers him the healing power of his friendship.

Salten had already used the theme of regret following the death of a rejected loved one in *Olga Frohgemuth* and *Der Shylock von Krakau*. It made for dramatic effect but was less successful here than in his earlier works since Salten gave no indication in his novel that the protagonist had ever felt any love for either wife or child. Schnitzler found the work both exaggerated and dishonest and condemned it thoroughly for its psychological blunders and sentimental ending.[14]

In January 1915 Salten completed his first piece of fiction dealing with the World War. It was entitled *Abschied im Sturm* (Departure in the Storm), and Schnitzler considered it "quite a nice novella."[15] In this work Salten showed how the seriousness of war took precedence over one's own personal situation at home, whether breaking off a casual affair or leaving behind a beloved wife and child. As one of the experienced soldiers notes at the close of the novella, "So much trails behind them now, I tell you … they are really more here … than there … they can't yet imagine it … can they? … But that will all change … change entirely, my friend! When they are finally out there … you know … when they see the first people fall … that will change!"[16] The novella was published by Albert Langen of Munich as one of Langen's War Books, a series of stories about Germany's battles (*Kämpfen*) in 1914/1915. Salten included in this volume a story of fate entitled *Die Gewalt der Dinge* (The Power of Things) about a wounded but vigorous veteran of the sixteenth-century battle of Pavia who returns to his hometown and marries a widow, only to be murdered by the widow's weak but angry son. Both *Die Gewalt der Dinge* and *Abschied im Sturm* deal with personal conflicts at home rather than on the battlefield; in both, the battlefield is a world quite apart from domestic existence, a place where the individual is a mere cog in an abstract war machine governed by powers vastly superior to the will of any one person. The soldiers in *Abschied im Sturm* sing as they ride off into battle; they are united in their cause, a cause that, however necessary and inevitable, Salten continued to regard with ambivalence. Salten put into this novella an insight he had had the previous fall on a train ride to his summer home on the Attersee: that the Austrian landscape was oblivious to the doings of men:

> High in the air a cormorant was moving off; the warblers sang in the brush; the blackbirds came out, sat in the treetops and whistled. The sun sparkled in the waves [of the Danube] and laid wide beams on the backs of the mountains. Here one could detect nothing of the events that people were calling "great," the present was not stormy here; here everything remained the same, whether the youth of this country danced in the inns, plowed in the fields, or went out to fight and die. Eduard turned away. The sight or this peaceful and resplendent landscape oppressed him; the sublime indifference that it seemed to be full of excited him and drove him almost to despair.[17]

For his part, Salten relished the fact that "in the forest one is able to forget the events and the noise of the world." Here one could be "truly alone with oneself, alone with nature."[18] More and more frequently, Salten fled to the woodlands to hunt. Most of his older friends could not share this passion; Leo Van-Jung, for one, argued that he could not understand how anyone could ever raise a gun to kill a stag or roebuck, until, that is, Salten took him along with him one day and Van-Jung excitedly asked for a gun and experienced the delight of making a kill. In May Schnitzler noted rather laconically in his diary that Salten had just returned from a three-day hunt of wood grouse, and, in November, that Salten insisted on showing him his hunting trophies. Salten never regretted a clean kill; from his regular visits to a friend's hunting preserve near Stockerau, Salten knew the necessity of thinning herds and killing off weaker, aging, and overaggressive game. "To the hunter," Salten wrote, "wild game is by no means a 'sacrifice' and he alone has a deep feeling of responsibility towards all living creatures. He kills, to be sure, but he is in fact the only one whose killing is like a mild form of fate." Salten believed that hunting had to be carefully regulated; he did not believe, however, that people could keep from killing animals completely, feeling that "[i]t is still impossible to become so ... Indian."[19] Schnitzler could not understand Salten's love both for animals and for the hunt: "Certainly his joy in the hunt [and] in nature is genuine," he reflected, "and [yet] through extreme nuance and reflection of self, it somehow becomes untruthful."[20]

One important lesson that Salten learned through his many hours alone in the forest was that, while nature was dispassionate and unchanging, the animals that inhabited field and forest were not. Many hunted and killed the smaller and weaker species, while those that did not kill lived in continual fear of being preyed upon by others. In times of great hardship, animals fell upon one another the same way the nations of Europe were now attacking each other at the front. As he would express it some years later in *Bambi*, "The terrible hardship that seemed to have no end spread bitterness and brutality. It destroyed all their memories of the past, their faith in each other, and ruined every good custom they had. There was no longer either peace or mercy in the forest."[21]

Similarly, among men the cultural unity that had once sustained Europe crumbled soon after the declaration of war. First, the Nobel prize-winning Belgian poet and playwright Maurice von Maeterlinck had declared the conflict a war between the civilized world (England, France, Russia) and barbarianism (Germany and Austro-Hungary). Salten responded angrily that the Germans and Austrians had always praised the cultures of their enemies but that these countries were making no effort to get to know them in return. He exclaimed at the incongruity of republican France and democratic England uniting with despotic Russia in this war.[22] He reacted with equal vehemence when French novelist Anatole France and Irish playwright George Bernard Shaw declared that they were not opposed to the great figures of German culture such as Beethoven or Goethe but only to the "spirit of Potsdam." Salten replied that Potsdam was a quiet little town, a center for hard work and discipline – qualities epitomized by King Frederick the Great [Friedrich II of Prussia], the man who had made his court there in the 18ᵗʰ century. These qualities were not appreciated by Germany's enemies, Salten remarked, adding that it almost seemed as if the enemy nations were calling for a pogrom against Germany.[23]

Meanwhile, thousands of refugees poured into Vienna as Galicia was overrun by Russia in the first months of the war. In addition to putting severe strains on the food supply, this influx unleashed a new wave of anti-Semitism in Vienna. Salten visited the tearoom in the Tabor-Strasse where many of these refugees gathered to seek news about friends and family members. He wrote about the attempts to feed and clothe them, visited a kindergarten that was set up for Galician orphans in the Prater, and called on the people of Vienna to contribute to the support of these first innocent casualties of war.[24]

He now wrote a new biography for Ullstein's series of books for youth, this time on *Prinz Eugen der edle Ritter* (Prince Eugene, the Noble Knight), Austria's great military leader in Austria's wars against the Turks and the war of the Spanish secession. The title of the work comes from a famous Austrian folk song, one of those spontaneously sung by the Viennese populace when Austria declared war on Serbia in 1914. The Prince, like Kaiser Maximilian in Salten's earlier volume, was both a warrior and a scholar; he established a zoological garden on his Belvedere property and his large collection of books became the foundation of the Austrian National Library. In this book, however, Salten was writing for a nation at war, and there is very little mention of the prince's peacetime activities. Instead, Salten focuses on the contrast between the superficial and flamboyant French and the sober Austrians, portraying the prince as a brilliant, daring, and incorruptible leader in wars where his troops were nearly always outnumbered by French and Turkish armies. As Salten described the battle at Petrovaradin, "Sixty-five thousand imperial forces fought against two hundred thousand Turks. But here again the size and power of the body that fought did not matter, but rather the heads that set these gigantic bodies in motion. It was, after all, Prince Eugene, the greatest field commander of his age, fighting against the grand vizier Ali."[25]

As for the present war, Salten continued to mourn the loss of young soldiers. He wrote of one burial he attended:

At this grave, into which clods of earth are
falling, above this grave everyone senses the terrible doom that now infests the world, friends and
enemies, all of them people, people who suffer
and feel pain the way one has not suffered and felt
pain for centuries upon this earth. And at the coffin of this young man who is being buried here,
the people are weeping for all those young men
who have fallen, mourn in the loss of this one all
the flourishing youth that have been carried off,
the twenty-year-olds, the sons who are born in
pain and lost in pain.[26]

In the summer of 1915, Salten was back in the Salzkammergut,
and he wrote a column for the *Neue Freie Presse* describing the
changes that had occurred there in the first year of war. In the resort town of Ischl, the streets seemed empty because the young
people were missing. Many of the shops were closed. The tennis
courts were empty, and visitors to the town were subdued. There
were no British or American tourists, but soldiers – Croatians and
Hungarians – were here to recuperate from their wounds. Commenting on the beauty of the surroundings and of Ischl's history as
the Emperor's favorite hunting spot and a meeting place for kings
Salten declared that the town was the embodiment of "the Austrian
character, that can be felt and understood only with the heart and
with the senses."[27]

It was just such a sentimental flight into Austria's romanticized
past that inspired Salten's film script *Der Schuß im Traum* (The Shot
in a Dream).[28] It premiered that summer in Berlin and Schnitzler
described it as "fabulously posh, with hunting and counts and cas-
tles."[29] That same year Salten's one-act play "Auferstehung" was
filmed by the Nordisk Films Kompagni under the Danish title *En
Opstandelse*.[30]

At the end of his summer holidays Salten went to Budapest to
inquire about the regulations regarding volunteer duty. He was now
forty-five and knew that his work as a chief editor at the *Fremden-
Blatt* legally relieved him from active military service. It therefore
came as a surprise when his inquiries were apparently misinter-

preted and he was called up to duty early in 1916. After taking a physical and being declared *felddiensttauglich* (fit for field service), he was ordered to report to the Ullöer barracks in Budapest. His friend, the poet Georg von Terramare, accompanied him there; when they met with the commanding general, the situation was quickly cleared up and Salten was allowed to return home. He then volunteered to do whatever journalistic work was needed for the Austrian War Ministry. He was placed on call for projects as they arose at the War Archives, but little real use was made of his talents. As he recalled it, he would frequently be "summoned" to the archives and then made to wait most of the morning before being given petty, insignificant assignments. It was enough, however, to keep him from doing as much of his own literary work as he would have liked. Instead, most of his attention was taken up with his work at the *Fremden-Blatt* and in writing columns for the *Neue Freie Presse, Pester Lloyd*, and *Berliner Tageblatt.*

Salten was now saddened even by the apparent triumphs of the Central Powers in the Balkans. In January he was invited to take the first train to run since the beginning of the war from the North Sea through the reconquered Balkans to Constantinople. Salten noticed the devastation of the land and "a poor, quiet populace living in unending squalid huts …, an unhappy populace that must be helped." "How much there was to do in Serbia (and elsewhere in the world), better things, more important things than making war," he exclaimed.³¹ He clung to the idea that art was the hope of the future: "For the time must come again – soon! – when works of art possess the same importance for us as they once did, more, in fact: an exalted importance that is felt with renewed fervor. Otherwise, this war will have alienated us from the highest goals of humanity, and our grandchildren will call us to account for all the precious legacy of countless centuries that we have allowed to be destroyed."³²

He wrote three one-act plays that year that he grouped together under the title *Kinder der Freude* (Children of Joy). The "children," in all three cases, are actors and actresses who are susceptible to flattery and value this above the devotion they might find closer to home. One, "Lebensgefährten" (Life Companions) is a dramatized version of the short story "Katharina Krons Liebhaber" (Katharina Kron's Lover), which he had written in

1907 and published in the series *Künstlerfrauen*; it tells of the long-suffering wife of a fifty-two-year-old actor who is still playing lovers both on the stage and in the bedroom with younger actresses. "Von ewiger Liebe" (Eternal Love) is, in a manner of speaking, another treatment of the theme of his one-acter "Auferstehung." Here a young admirer of an actress attempts suicide because of her; when he is saved from death, he tells the besotted actress, who has just broken with her fiancé, that he has learned from his experience to value life and that he does not love her any more. The play "Auf der Brücke" tells the story of an actress who, like the hero of "Lebensgefährten," has enjoyed great triumphs but is facing the inevitability of having to move on to matronly roles. Her ego is nourished by a young admirer until she learns, to her horror, that the young man is the son of one of her former classmates. This play is the most complex and Ibsen-esque of the three plays. In an ironic gesture of self-mockery, Salten introduced a poem he had written to Berta Karlsburg in his own youth[33] as the immature outpouring of the actress's young admirer.

Salten also had four films come out in the spring of 1916. Three of them featured Rudolf Schildkraut in the lead; two of these – *Die Glücksschmiede* and *Der Glücksschneider* (The Forge of Fortune and The Lucky Tailor) are probably two versions of the same basic tale,[34] a social satire about a tailor who wins the lottery but still lacks the manners and bearing to be accepted by the wealthy class to which he has always aspired. Salten both wrote and directed Schildkraut's third film, *Der Narr des Schicksals* (The Fool of Fate),[35] while the great Jewish comic Heinrich Eisenbach played in a Salten film with the title *Moritz Wasserstrahl als Stratege* (Moritz Wasserstrahl as a Strategist).[36] Although only a portion of one of these films – *Der Glückschneider* – has been preserved, it appears that all four films were Jewish comedies designed to entertain and distract a nation suffering under the privations of war.[37] Salten continued to hope for a speedy conclusion to the hostilities. Instead, Austria was struck by another blow when, on November 21, 1916, its emperor died.

The whole town kept watch in the hours leading up to Franz Josef's death, with many coming to the imperial castle gardens of Schönbrunn to hold a silent vigil. Salten spent these hours in the third district, in the apartments of Princess Pauline von Metternich;

173

she, who was much admired in Vienna both for her salon and her many charitable activities, talked to Salten about the emperor in his younger years, telling him how "she had spent her youth with Franz Josef, had danced through the night with the young emperor, then had, like him, mounted on horseback and ridden to the Prater."[38]

Franz Josef had aroused a good deal of controversy in his younger years and in 1853 had narrowly escaped an assassination attempt by a Hungarian nationalist. His life had been difficult; raised to a life of responsibility and diligence, he became estranged early on from his beloved wife Elisabeth. His first daughter died as an infant, and his son Rudolf died as an apparent suicide at his hunting lodge at Mayerling. Elisabeth had retired from the court and taken up a restless life of travel; in 1898 she had died at an assassin's hand. The Austrians had lived through these tragedies with their emperor and admired the stoicism with which he had survived these calamities. He was now widely regarded as a kindly old man, a vestige of a simpler past, and the nation's grandfather. When news came of the emperor's final passing, Salten accompanied the Princess to Schönbrunn and was allowed to view the emperor in his coffin. "I am incapable of describing the sensations that moved me, nor do I want to," he wrote many years later. "Suffice it to say that I became conscious of the fact that a new, a different, and not a better age was now beginning."[39]

Chapter 14: Days of Hardship

Emperor Franz Josef's death marked the end of an era. Nowhere was this symbolized more clearly than in the decision of Karl I to substitute a fleet of motorcars for the imperial horse-drawn coaches. Salten was worried about the change in emperors on a more personal level. Franz Josef had been a friend to Vienna's assimilated Jews, but Salten had heard that Karl intended to "destroy the Jewish press."[1] As a consequence, Salten told Schnitzler that he was pulling back from the duties of chief editor at the *Fremden-Blatt* to serve the paper merely as critic, even though this would mean a drop in salary.[2] When Karl gave his first address before parliament, Salten did his patriotic duty by speaking approvingly of the appearance of the emperor and his wife, saying of the empress that "her being exudes vigor and assurance." He praised Karl for his youthfulness, the musicality of his voice, and his smile, calling him the embodiment of "an officer's youth, princely earnestness and free, inner cheerfulness."[3]

Editorial policy required that columnists avoid open criticism of the regime and of the war effort in their columns, a situation that makes it often difficult to determine exactly what Salten's political stance was. Salten's friends noted that in private conversation he expressed views that were more pessimistic and far more critical than anything he said publicly or wrote in the newspapers. As Schnitzler noted in his diary, Salten "said many intelligent things, but he will never write or publish them (even when it becomes less dangerous to do so than it is now)."[4] He toed the party line by writing some purely nationalist propaganda, criticizing the British for their "villainy," the French for their "hysteria," the Russians for their "brutality," and the Serbs for their "insidiousness,"[5] but he also objected to the purely propagandistic plays being performed in the theaters:

> In the one play the Russians are scoffed at, in the other the French and English are. And now and then, one of the actors steps forward and declares that we will "chop up the vermin like boiled pig's belly" … "finish them off" … "mow them to the ground" etc. Out there shrapnel is flying above our soldiers; out there our young men are

lying in trenches, jumping up, storming enemy batteries, collapsing with blown-off limbs, and paying for our triumph with their youth, their blood, and their lives. And here, far away from the shooting, a made-up comedian opens his mouth to utter made-up boasts that a pathetic hack who is speculating on the gallery's applause has pieced together at his peaceful desk. It is shameful.[6]

Salten disliked all works that preached hatred, he wrote, even though he could understand the conditions under which they were produced. For this reason, much as he admired Kleist's war play *Der Prinz von Homburg*, published in 1821, he hated Kleist's *Die Hermannschlacht* (Arminius's Battle), 1809.[7]

Although Salten himself railed against the English and the French, especially in the early years of the war, and wrote patriotic pieces about his visits to a soldiers' hospital[8] and to the Skoda arms factory,[9] he more frequently presented touching portrayals of the war's victims. In the summer of 1916, he issued a new appeal for assistance in caring for the orphaned refugees from Galicia.[10] He wrote a number of telling vignettes: about the nineteen-year-old peasant boy who cannot adjust to the war's bloody bayonet attacks and asks his mother to pray for him,[11] about the one-armed war veteran mesmerized by a shop window full of spring flowers.[12] He contrasted the joy of past holidays – Easter, Christmas, Carnival – with the muted pleasures of the present. In the first summer of the war he wrote, for example: "Do you remember Whitsunday last year? We will never again be as carefree as we were then."[13] His ability to express both love for his country and regret for the war made him an excellent representative of all that was good in Austria. This was surely one reason why the Ministry of War sent him as a cultural representative to Switzerland in December 1916. Although Switzerland was officially neutral in the European war, its French-speaking and German-speaking citizens were divided by their loyalties. The War Ministry hoped to shore up support for the war effort in the German-speaking cities of Switzerland; Salten was the first man they sent there, followed a couple of months later by the theater director Max Reinhardt. Karl Kraus mocked the idea of these two men creating a "bridge" between warring nations, writing, "The enemies of today will be reconciled tomorrow on the bridge of Messieurs Salten and Reinhardt, and the first threads are being tied in Zurich."[14] In addition to lecturing in Zurich on the dramatist Franz Grillparzer, Salten attended a performance of *Kinder der Freude* at the Zurich city theater.[15] In Zurich, Bern, and Lucerne, Salten saw many nationalities on holiday: English, Germans, French, and Italians, including many soldiers who were there on leave. In Switzerland one could enjoy a semblance of peace, Salten wrote, as well as a plentiful supply of butter and eggs. What struck him the most, however, was a new awareness of the suffering endured by *all* participants in the Great War.[16]

Back home, Salten served as a guide to those Swiss journalists who came to see for themselves what life was like in a nation at war. Although Salten carefully avoided any critical mention of the regime or the handling of the war in his columns for the *Neue Freie Presse*, he urged Moritz Benedikt, the owner of the paper, to adopt a more forceful tone. He toyed briefly with the idea of starting his own publishing firm but quickly dropped it and concentrated instead on his journalism and independent writings. His only original fiction to appear in print in 1916 was an inspirational piece that he wrote for the Christmas Eve issue of the *Fremden-Blatt* entitled "Gute Botschaft: Ein Brief aus fernen Tagen" (Good News: A Letter from a Faraway Time). It was composed as a letter fragment from an unknown Austrian woman who had just gotten the news that the Napoleonic wars were over. It is an occasion for crowds to gather in the streets, lock arms, and sing patriotic songs, just as they had when the war began. The woman reflects, "Many of those who sang back then are no longer alive. But in the singing that was roaring around me, life seemed to be jumping for joy, life eternally renewing itself, eternally young, unconquerable." Thinking back, she reflects, "Uncounted personal tragedies are interwoven in this war. … But the children who rejoice here, in these children the war that is over has already begun to fade away. We ourselves are not very important. For our children, though, and the generations that grow up after us, a free fatherland has been attained and a peaceful existence on an unthreatened plot of earth."[17] At this point, after so much privation and hardship, Salten apparently still harbored a vision of the Great War ending in jubilation, with a triumphant Austria promising all its citizens freedom and peace.

In 1917 Salten continued writing about the situation in Austria – from meat rationing[18] to the closing of the Dehmel confectionery shop.[19] He wrote very little about the shortages at home in textiles and foodstuffs, except to note that things would be better after the war and to express the hope that some fashion changes occasioned by the war, such as the soft collar on men's shirts, would be made permanent.[20] He lauded the schoolboys who had, on their own, taken over the task of clearing the city streets of snow.[21] He had special praise for the charitable work being done by some of Vienna's most admirable women, Anitta Müller, for example, a lively young Jewish woman who had established food centers, birthing centers, kindergartens, and training programs for the thousands of Galician refugees who had overrun the city. He also asked the people of Vienna to support Nelly Wahliss, who was raising funds in order to place war orphans in residential homes in the country. He compared the plight of the city's war orphans with that of the helpless young of deer and game fowl killed by poachers. "Should we plaintively lament the young animal and be less sensitive towards orphaned human children?" he asked, adding:

> We who were enmeshed in this war have no other claim on existence than to serve those who will be here tomorrow. ... If the youth that grows up after us is not given the opportunity to prosper in safety, then there is little purpose in running our factories again. ... If we do not expend all our efforts on the children, who have already been horribly neglected during the war, if we allow, as we do now, thousands of children whom the war has thrown out into the street, to be poor, orphaned, languishing, starving, and helpless, then no one can hope that culture and art will ever again regain their worth and importance.[22]

For his own part, Salten contributed his Christmas Eve story about the end of the Napoleonic wars to a collection of legends and fairytales that were published as part of a fund-raising campaign for daycare centers for the children and orphans of Austrian soldiers.[23]

That summer Samuel Fischer published Salten's three one-act plays, *Kinder der Freude*.[24] Schnitzler, who read them for the first time, found them "sloppy works, in part moderately clever theatrically, emotionally crude, some of it quite ridiculously influenced by me."[25] Schnitzler saw similarities between these plays and his own *Komödie der Worte* (Comedy of Words), which had received less than sterling reviews two years before. He was therefore particularly annoyed at the "unanimous delight" with which Salten's plays were greeted by the critics when they premiered under Salten's direction at the Volkstheater in December.[26] Salten also co-wrote a screenplay with the Berlin stage actress Else Bassermann, who had adopted the pen name Hans Hennings for her film scripts. The film, entitled *Der eiserne Wille* (The Iron Will), premiered in Berlin in January 1918.

By early 1918 many Viennese were disenchanted with their new emperor. Salten recalled the Prime Minister saying of him, "He is thirty, looks like he's twenty, and has the understanding of a ten-year-old boy!" It was widely believed that Karl's mother-in-law had undue influence over foreign policy. When Salten was asked to write some newspaper columns that might improve the image of the new emperor and his wife, a princess of Parma, Salten responded that journalism would not help, that only the couple could improve their image by moving from the suburban town of Baden to the Vienna Hofburg (city palace). In addition, he said, "The Empress Zita must stop doing as she now does, distributing cigarettes to Italian prisoners while passing by the Austrian soldiers." In addition, she should not "show her piety in such a way that it looks like bigotry." "A bit of imperial splendor, frequent appearances among the populace, these are the devices that will help them achieve popularity," he argued.[27] Privately, Salten was now expressing his own strong displeasure with the young Austrian emperor, while calling President Woodrow Wilson "a decent person."[28] Publicly, he continued to avoid taking any stand and sought daily refuge in the theater and at the Stockerau hunting preserve.

Ever since the United States entered into the war in 1917, the Central Powers had suffered stunning losses, and it became clear in the spring of 1918 that the situation within the Empire was rapidly disintegrating. Salten was concerned on a number of fronts. As a Jew, he worried about the rising anti-Semitism, caused by the thou-

sands of refugees still flooding into Austria and the fear among the
Catholic population that these refugees from Eastern Europe were
not only straining the city resources but also bringing with them
the seeds of Bolshevism. A degree of paranoia swept Salten's circle.
In July, for example, Leo Van-Jung reported that the popular Jesuit
priest Heinrich Abel, known for his opposition to the liberals
through his work with the Christian Social party and for his founding of the Catholic student fraternity Austria, was calling for a pogrom against the Jews. Salten responded sardonically, "Pogrom, ...
that's how it starts, then the revolution... Wasn't it always so? One
cannot, should not even do anything to prevent this."[29]

Salten was starting to develop his own theory of revolution,
based in part on his observation of the collapse of the Russian empire and the triumph there of Bolshevism. He now began to view
revolution as a fundamentally Jewish revolt against persecution.
This theory, he believed, explained not only many of the political
upheavals in history but also the rise of radical Jewish philosophers,
such as Spinoza and Voltaire. For his own part, Salten abhorred
violence, but he admired the great Jews able to survive it and to
make the inner transformation from victim to revolutionary. He
himself was now a prominent spokesperson for both the Austrian
and Jewish cultures. When an Austrian Congress Committee was
formed to unite the conflicting Jewish groups under a single umbrella organization, the Jewish leaders Leo Hermann and Siegmund
Kaznelson came to Salten to persuade him of the value of the idea
and to ask him to promote their cause among Jewish and non-
Jewish writers and journalists.[30] For his own part, Salten warned
the Austrian Prime Minister about the rising tide of anti-Semitism
and railed against the so-called "Esoi" Jews[31] – such as the critics
Alfred Polgar, Karl Kraus, and David Josef Bach – who, he felt,
not only denied their Jewish ethnicity but showed Jewish artists a
lack of respect while fawning upon every third-rate Christian talent.
Salten was always the most sincere, Schnitzler wrote, when he
spoke about Jewish issues.[32]

Despite his intellectual understanding of revolution, Salten had
a profound fear of mob violence. As the war drew to its disastrous
close, refugees fleeing into the city were joined by large numbers of
deserting soldiers and members of the Red Guard. Rumors were
rampant: that the mass revolution of workers, soldiers, and stu-

dents in Budapest would spread to Vienna; that twelve thousand Italian prisoners of war had broken out of their camps and were marching on the city. In November, Salten got wind of an attack that had been planned on his home district of Cottage. He warned his neighbors of the danger that faced them if they remained in their homes; then he, Otti, and the two children moved into a hotel in the inner city for the duration of the greatest unrest. There were street fights and shootings, and the offices of the *Neue Freie Presse* were occupied for several hours, but Cottage remained unscathed. By the time the Saltens returned to their home, Austria had capitulated to the Allied forces, the emperor had abdicated, and Austria had been reduced from a large multinational empire to a small parliamentary democracy.

Salten wrote no film scripts that year, although his friend Else Bassermann took one of Salten's film outlines in order to pen the film *Dr. Schotte.* His book production was minimal: only one volume of previously published short stories appeared in an inexpensive edition by Rudolf Mosse in Berlin. It was called *Der alte Narr* and was essentially a reprint of the 1911 anthology *Die Wege des Herrn*, minus five stories in that earlier collection.[33] Salten was already planning a collection of essays, however, intended as a physiognomic study of contemporary musicians that would appear in book form, probably with caricature drawings along the lines of his successful 1905 volume on European kings. He called the sketches *Bilder aus dem Konzertsaal* (Pictures from the Concert Hall) and published three of them in the *Neue Freie Presse* in 1918, two in 1919, and one in 1921. Eventually, this series numbered sixteen. Like other collections that he had published in the newspapers: his second series on royalty, his short story collection entitled *Karriere*, these ironically telling portraits never found a publisher willing to put them into a single volume. This is a shame because they provide insight into performers who are now legendary: Richard Strauss, for example, who conducted with small gestures, an "unchanging" expression of "monumental composure" on his face, a vision of the musician as priest, as one "who has shaken off the proximity of crowds";[34] or Arthur Nikisch, whose "constantly shrouded dreamy gaze" and "slightly cocked head" gave the impression "of a man who unrelentingly listens to his innermost being" and belongs "to a vanished age."[35]

Salten had hoped that the conclusion of the war would bring about a positive era of rebuilding. Instead, as the legal successors of the large empire that had declared war on Serbia, Austria and a now independent Hungary were required to pay full war reparations even as thousands of German nationals from other parts of the old empire crowded into their territories. In Vienna human suffering not only continued but intensified. Already in August 1918 Salten had expressed distress over the fact that the war had shoved aside the concerns of the individual – "love, loyalty, sensual pleasure, personal tragedy" – for "national struggle, world dominance, heroism, [and] mass death." People had, he said, gotten into the habit of comforting people for their personal tragedies by saying "So many people are dying today!" as if that could be of real consolation to anyone. He asked for more understanding for the individual, for the nineteen-year-old boy, for example, who had forged bread rationing cards so that he could, for once, eat his fill.[36] He begged his countrymen to be more tolerant of their neighbors: "We are comrades in suffering, not adversaries."[37]

In February 1919, Salten published a remarkable article, "Letter to an American Friend," in the *Neue Freie Presse*, in which he answered the suggestion that the artists and intellectuals of the world should unite in order to reestablish cultural ties between the former enemies of the Great War. This suggestion, Salten replied, is "very tempting" and had, in fact, already been made in 1917 and in 1918 without anything coming of it. "Since then," he wrote, "many kind words and many enticing thoughts have come through to us." But he reminded the Americans that "we were not conquered by the sword, as Mr. Clemenceau would assert, but instead were fascinated by the Fourteen Points and surrendered with full confidence in the promises that came out of Washington." These promises were not being fulfilled. Instead, "the most frightful weapon was taken up again, the blockade, more effective then any tanks and any barrage of military fire, for three months, against women, invalids, and children." Saying, "there are moments in which all hope is lost," Salten warned that "much is permitted to the victor, but he must, if he is wise, guard against sowing hatred against himself for future ages." There was "no practical value in planning cultural congresses at a moment when this entire old culture is perishing," he added, since the only hope of reconciliation lay not with a nation's "statesmen" but with its "masses."[38]

That same month Salten published *Das engere Leben* (Life Close at Hand),[39] three sketches of present-day circumstances in Vienna. The first tells how a man walked by a certain clockmaker's shop every morning. The large clock in the window had always shown the correct hour until, one day, the shop was closed and the clockmaker gone. The big clock stopped and remained silent for years. Then one day the shop was reopened, the clock was again running correctly, and a new clockmaker sat behind the workbench. The man reflects that the old era is gone, that he has lived through a number of wasted years, and a new age is now beginning. He then shrugs at the idea of attaching so much importance to his observations.

The second episode tells of an old farmer who went to the January auction of the former horses of the Vienna court and paid an exorbitant fee for two fine Lipizzan horses. The farmer's son had been a court coachman and loved these two horses, but he had died in the war.[40] In the third, a man embittered by the loss of so many young people in the war goes to a school to do business with the school director. When he hears the voices of schoolgirls united in a song of spring and rebirth, he feels as if the voices of all those who had ever attended this school have joined in song, and he leaves the school humming.

These three vignettes, all so different in mood, show once again Salten's fine eye for detail. For Salten the "masses" were made up of individuals, and each had his own unique story; one could best capture the truth of these stories through a precise rendition of the subject's actions and behavior. And although Salten believed that one could never fully understand the motivations of another individual, he thought that one could discover larger truths about humanity through close observation of its members. For example, he cited a specific court case where the twelve jury members had requested that the defense attorney shorten his closing remarks so that they might catch the last streetcar home. This example, he said, demonstrated the current population's regrettable devaluation of powerful speech-making in an age of tumult and anti-intellectualism.[41]

During the war Salten had taken up a new cause: the rights of school children to have kind and enlightened teachers. He still recalled with vivid clarity his own unhappy schooldays when teachers had branded him a liar and a cheat.[42] Now he defended the rights of secondary school students to rebel against a hopelessly authoritarian, outdated system. Three thousand of these students had organized a demonstration and been brutally beaten to submission by the police. Salten reminded his readers that some of these young demonstrators had been soldiers at the front not long ago and that all of "these children" had "endured more, seen and experienced more than many generations of adults in peaceful times." "It is shameful," he cried, "that the children are stepping forward to remind us not to fritter their precious time away with foolish demagoguery and hypocritical guidelines." These young people were simply demonstrating for "the removal of an old system of punishments, prohibitions, rewards and threats"; they wanted to "remove the distance between themselves and their teachers." Put simply, they longed "to be better educated." Recalling that the old emperor had been an enemy of education, Salten called on the new government to pay its teachers better wages, and to make the proper education of the young one of its top priorities.[43] Several months later, however, when these same students wanted to do away with the examinations given at the end of secondary school,[44] Salten spoke out in disapproval, saying that reform must come before these examinations could be challenged. He repeated his proposals that teachers receive more pay and schools be opened to poor as well as wealthy children.

The situation in Vienna continued to worsen. In June Salten noted in his column[45] that the blockade had now endured for eight months beyond the end of the war and that people were starving. In December he bemoaned the fact that people were now cutting down his beloved Vienna Woods for fuel: "They are felling the trees out there, they are destroying the forest, and things have become so base, that they don't even know how ridiculously little they are gaining and how immeasurably much they are losing." "Now," he said, "the entire Vienna Woods are just a tub of wood for a freezing city."[46]

Professionally, Salten's year had been mixed. On the positive side, he had the satisfaction in May of staging his own play *Der Gemeine* at the Volkstheater. Because the play had been banned by the censors for eighteen years on the grounds that it defamed the mili-

184

tary, this was its Vienna premiere. Schnitzler noted that the play had held up well over the years and found it "lively" and "amusing."[47] Public and critics alike praised Salten for his achievements as the play's director. Then, in December, Salten's three one-act plays, *Kinder der Freude*, saw a new Viennese production at the Burgtheater. They were praised for language "that has the sharpness and suppleness, brilliance and elegance of polished steel" and for the manner in which "form and content correspond so felicitously."[48] Even Schnitzler, who attended the dress rehearsal, admitted that the trilogy "pleased me more today in some respects."[49]

A greater professional upheaval came in March of that year when the *Fremden-Blatt*, as the official newspaper of the old Habsburg empire, suspended operations and was replaced by a paper called *Der neue Tag*. Salten put a couple of mini-dialogues between a man and a woman into the *Fremden-Blatt*'s last issue. Although they go back twenty years to the days when Salten edited the *Wiener Allgemeine Rundschau*, they acquired new relevancy in the difficult days that followed the war. One read:

> He: Why do you despise me? I only did what anybody else would have done in my situation...
> She: That's the reason... because you did what anybody else would have done... That is why I despise you![50]

Salten had only one piece of new prose fiction published in 1919; it was entitled *Im Namen des Kaisers* (In the Emperor's Name) and was based on an actual event from 1490: the proxy marriage of Emperor Maximilian I and Anna of Brittany. This marriage was never consummated, and Anna was wed instead to Charles VIII of France. The story is told as the reminiscence of the melancholy knight who had, in his youth, served as Maximilian's proxy at the wedding ceremony. The book was a novelty in that it was part of a series of inexpensive works that were printed in such a manner that the book's jacket served as its mailing envelope.[51]

In November 1919 Schnitzler noted that his old friend had become "anti-revolutionary, almost reactionary."[52] They had spoken about the conditions in Vienna and about their own expenses; the situation was "grotesque." Salten had "already spent 100,000 [crowns] this year, I probably double that amount."[53] It had, in fact, been a difficult year for the entire country. The Austrian aristocracy was given the choice of giving up all claim to their titles and staying in the country as private citizens or choosing to live in exile abroad. Emperor Karl was one of the many who left. Political parties and special interest groups were jockeying for position and influence over a chaotic and despairing nation. Jewish nationals, who had sought a role in the new democratic government, saw their success in the May elections quickly dashed and lost their influence four months later. The Austrian people could not adjust to having their empire of fifty-three million suddenly reduced to one eighth its former size, with a population of only a little over eight million. They had hoped to have their reduced borders defined at the very least by the inclusion of all the German-speaking portions of the old empire, but the Treaty of Saint Germain-en-Laye dashed even these hopes, as well as the desire of Austria to seek protection by merging with Germany in a German-Austrian Republic. Because of this treaty Austria was burdened with enormous war payments even as it was deprived of the land and resources necessary to sustain itself. The treaty was signed four days after Salten's fiftieth birthday.

Chapter 15: Days of Recovery

Because the dual monarchy of Hungary and Austria ended with the formation of two separate nations in 1919, Salten took advantage of Article 80 in the Treaty of Saint Germain-en-Laye to opt for Austrian rather than Hungarian citizenship for himself and his family.[1] He was determined, through the power of his pen, to play his part in restoring Vienna to its prewar position as a major European cultural center. He was particularly eager to see the former court theaters – the Burgtheater and the Court Opera – regain the prestige they had enjoyed before the war.

During the last months of the war, the situation of these two institutions had in fact become critical. In March 1919 Salten had written about how they were deeply in the red and needed generous donors to rescue them since neither the state nor the city could afford to. Tickets to the Burgtheater now cost so much that the faithful middle classes could no longer afford to attend its performances. Salten felt that both houses needed the security that would allow them to experiment and do exciting things as they had in the past.[2]

The last years of the Burgtheater had been especially difficult. Following Hugo Thimig's retirement in 1917, after his five-year reign as its director, the Burgtheater had floundered under the brief and somewhat contentious directorships of Max von Millenkovich (April 1917-July 1918) and a triumverate of Hermann Bahr, Max Devrient, and Robert Michel working under the general oversight of Leopold Andrian-Werburg (September-October 1918). Finally, at the war's end, the Austrian national assembly determined that the theater should come under the supervision of the new state government, and Albert Heine took over its reins in November 1918.

As for the old court opera, Salten was outraged when, in the spring of 1919, its members protested against having Richard Strauss take over their direction because they objected to his plans to fire some of the opera house's lesser talents and to introduce opera concerts that would compete with those of the Vienna Philharmonic. "Has the public no rights, no defense, no say over Vienna's growth and reputation?" Salten fumed. "Does Vienna have to turn Richard Strauss down because he stands in the way of a few special interests and because dictatorship by the members of the opera does not allow him to come to us?"[3] He joined many distinguished names in Viennese arts and letters in signing a successful petition[4] asking that Strauss be hired over the objections of those self-interested parties.

With the discontinuation of the *Fremden-Blatt*, Salten had lost his position as Burgtheater critic. He continued as lead feuilleton writer at the *Neue Freie Presse*, but Hugo Wittmann retained the position of premier theater critic. Salten's loss of voice as Burgtheater critic did not diminish his reputation as a major voice on affairs of the theater, however. In fact, Salten now asserted his authority over theatrical matters in Vienna by publishing two volumes of his theatrical essays under the title *Schauen und Spielen: Studien zur Kritik des Modernen Theaters* (Watching and Performing: Studies in the Criticism of the Modern Theater). Although most of the essays had appeared previously in the newspapers, the collection served to provide a remarkably comprehensive and cohesive survey of contemporary trends in the Vienna theater. As a foreword, Salten opened the first volume with a dialogue between a painter and his friends in which the painter opines that only a person who has himself worked as a creative artist has the right to criticize publicly the work of others, the reason being, "With him I can find the explanation as to why his nature withdraws from mine in his work, in his body of material, in his technique." Salten's painter claims that there is a sense of brotherhood with critics who are themselves artists: "A common destiny links me even to the artist who condemns me so much. He too struggles with himself and with his work, struggles with his material and with his technique, and somewhere in his and my heart there is a region in which we understand one another like brothers."[5]

By forcefully making the case for the supremacy of artistic experience over scholarship in the field of drama criticism, Salten effectively established his own credibility as a major voice. In the first section of the first volume, entitled *Ergebnisse* (Conclusions), Salten writes about the unique nature of the theater, declaring that the real world must not intrude on art. He demonstrates how acting styles and stage settings differ from the gestures and settings of real life and therefore can and should never be confused. On the other hand, he points out that the personality traits of an actor, even his weaknesses, create the totality of his craft. He offers a poet's interpretation of Hebbel's Biblical play *Judith*, reflects on the reasons why women had not succeeded as dramatists, and defends film as a new medium that does not threaten theater but instead augments it.

In the second section, entitled *Erlebnisse* (Experiences), Salten republished his critiques of specific works by some of his favorite writers.[6] This section shows a bias in favor of Shaw, Hauptmann, and Schnitzler, each with five reviews; Ibsen with four; and Strindberg, Tolstoy, and Wedekind with three. Other critiques cover one or two works by Karl Schönherr, Arnold Zweig, Fritz von Unruh, and Björnstjerne Björnson. He closed the volume with a rebuttal of Tolstoy's critique of Shakespeare, in which he drew a sharp distinction between Tolstoy the "poet and Tolstoy the windbag."[7]

The second volume contains many more reviews in sections entitled *Abende* (Evenings) and *Franzosen* (Frenchmen). In the first, he looks primarily at German-language writers, showing which of the new works meet his criteria of beauty, humanity, and relevance to the human condition and which take the easier path of character manipulation and artificial, hackneyed plots. Many of these reviews are mixed: of Carl Sternheim's *Der Snob* (The Snob), for example, he writes that, while the playwright has created true comedy, "one experiences like a jolt the enormous indifference with which he discounts everything affecting the emotions."[8] Even though he affirms the extraordinary talent of his friends Hugo von Hofmannsthal and Hermann Bahr, he finds fault with their latest works, writing, for example, of Bahr's *Der Querulant* (The Grouch), "Again and again one has the feeling with Hermann Bahr, that sometime he must succeed at achieving the ultimate and the very best. And he always seems to miss by just a hair's breadth."[9] He shows that he can be completely enthusiastic about some works as well, as when he writes of Franz Molnar's *Liliom*: "In this play he has great atmospheric artistry, he has social sensibilities, and: talent, talent, talent."[10] On the other hand, he can be completely dismissive, as when he writes of the childish morality in Ludwig Fulda's *Der Dummkopf* and calls Fulda's *Herr und Diener* (Master and Servant) kitsch. He devotes four essays to the weaknesses and vanity of Hermann Sudermann. Salten admits that the critics have treated Sudermann badly but says that Sudermann brings this on himself by creating true and lifelike characters whom he then bends to his plotline by forcibly "converting" them: "Their inner character does not determine the plot with its necessary emotions, but instead the … maudlin plot of the piece determines the maudlin, forced course the characters take."[11]

Still, Salten allows that Sudermann is superior to the French playwrights currently being performed in Vienna's theaters, and he devotes an entire section of this volume to the French, where, in addition to single performances of works by French playwrights, he includes essays on French comedy and Louvet de Couvray's four-volume work *Les amours du chevalier de Faublas*. In one essay he proclaims that he is "stalking" French dramatists because "in these cool autumn days, they are beginning to roar [in the theaters] again, just as the elk out in the forests are now bellowing and roaring. Rutting season," adding, "But if they were only capable of a single natural sound, these French dramatists, just one single accent that breaks out of the depths of the blood genuinely, truthfully, and harrowingly, like the cry of the panting elk, then I would certainly not set out to hunt them."[12] Salten decries the plethora of bad French drama on the Vienna stages, where the same trite plot lines play out again and again and characters have no grounding in reality but serve instead as "templates,"[13] exclaiming, "Everything that preoccupies our generation, the question of the modern woman, the problem of child rearing, the relations between man and woman, a thousand serious things of general and individual existence, all this is not French."[14]

In the last two sections of Salten's work, *Puppenspiel* (Puppet Play) and *Aus der Ferne* (From Afar), Salten includes studies of single stage performances, such as Alexander Moissi in *Hamlet* and Max Pallenberg's comic turn in the Kadelburg comedy *Die Familie Schimek*, and offers career portraits of artists like Eleonora Duse and Helene Odilon. Salten closes the volume with a tribute to Gustav Freytag, a writer from a bygone bourgeois age and the only playwright ever to portray newspaper writers on stage in his 1854 comedy *Die Journalisten*. This man, Salten declared, should not be forgotten, "because he believed in the middle classes as the source of all intellectual riches, as the womb of all fruitful development of scholarship, insight, and freedom."[15]

Upon reading Salten's *Schauen und Spielen*, Hugo Wittmann

praised it as "a Viennese dramaturgy" and urged the owner of the *Neue Freie Presse* to give the position of Burgtheater critic to Salten upon his own retirement. When that time came, however, Salten learned that Theodor Herzl's nephew Raoul Auernheimer also had his eye on the position and was ready to raise a "ruckus" if it was not given to him. Salten claimed that he voluntarily withdrew himself as a contender for the position.[16] He was named critic for the Theater in der Josefstadt instead.

These assignments did not diminish Salten's authority on matters relating to the Burgtheater, however, especially when, in 1922, Salten followed up his two volumes of theater essays with a little book entitled *Das Burgtheater: Naturgeschichte eines alten Hauses* (Natural History of an Old House). In this work he expressed his concerns for the future of the Burgtheater. He declared that unlike most of Europe's theaters, the Burgtheater was not dependent on directors and actors alone since "the political fate of Austria," "the soul of the country," "court, society, and common folk" all had shaped its traditions and had a share in its development and continuity.[17] He noted that, ever since those days when Maria Theresia's enlightened son Joseph II had had the foresight to make the Burgtheater a national theater devoted to quality productions, it had existed "as a living being, following internal laws,"[18] like "a tree, sprung from the earth, towering up in storm and sun, ... like a human being in sickness and in growth."[19]

With the collapse of the empire, however, Salten felt that the Burgtheater was in crisis. Having lost its court sponsorship, it was threatened by multiple, often conflicting, political interests. The American star policy had weakened the theater's strong collective of ensemble players, and low wages forced many of the Burgtheater's actors to take on second and third jobs in films, vaudeville, and variété shows. The audience, too, was a new one, made up largely of immigrants from the new Eastern European nations who were not attuned to the traditions of the theater. There was a temptation to lower performance standards since the audience could not discriminate as well as earlier generations had. Salten called for a strong director who could resist the temptations of the star system, of following every new trend in drama, and of mounting easy (mediocre) productions.

The release of Salten's book was timed to influence the choice of a new director of the Burgtheater. Albert Heine had resigned as director to return to acting and directing. Heine was replaced first by the writer Anton Wildgans, then, in 1922, by Max Paulsen, a member of the theater ensemble. Salten personally longed to have director Max Reinhardt come to Vienna and help the city reclaim world status for its theatrical work. For years Salten had been an intense admirer, calling Reinhardt "the greatest stage artist of today," "the most fruitful, most imaginative stimulator and innovator of the modern theater."[20] He had enthusiastically followed Reinhardt's career from his early days as an assistant to Otto Brahm, then as founder of the Berlin cabaret *Schall und Rauch*, soon renamed *Das kleine Theater* and transformed into a venue for the performance of smaller chamber plays.[21] Salten was particularly impressed, however, by Reinhardt's larger endeavors, staging spectacular productions in amphitheaters and indoor circuses, creating larger-than-life epic productions of total theater that incorporated multitiered stage designs, revolving sets, stark use of color, vivid lighting, dramatic music, and huge mob scenes in his re-imaginings of Shakespeare and the other classics. Of Reinhardt's production of *Oedipus* in the Busch Circus in 1911, Salten exclaimed, "For the first time the theater as we know it has been blown up and for the first time thrown away, discarded, set aside, with all its problems, with its own laws of light and space, perspective, and technique of word and gesture, with all its struggle for illusion or deception. And we have a new stage, and new possibilities of light, of space, of language, of gesture."[22] Salten continued to defend even Reinhardt's failures, and in July 1921 wrote an article about Vienna's need to have Max Reinhardt as a resident director in the city, just as Richard Strauss was now resident director of the State Opera.[23] This wish came true when Josef Jarno retired as director of the Theater in der Josefstadt in 1923; Reinhardt acquired the theater, had it thoroughly renovated, and served as its director from 1924 to 1938. Because it was only one of a large chain of theaters Reinhardt owned, he began sharing its directorship after his first two years there: first, with Emil Geyer (1926-1933), then with Otto Preminger (1933-1935), and finally with Ernst Lothar (1935-1938).

In the meantime, another Reinhardt venue had been established in Salzburg, when Salten's old friend Hugo von Hofmannsthal joined in partnership with Reinhardt, Richard Strauss, Franz Schalk (Strauss's co-director of the Vienna State Opera), and Alfred Roller (a founding member of the Vienna Secession and revolutionary stage designer for Gustav Mahler at the Court Opera) in founding the *Salzburger Festspiele*. The festival opened in August 1920 with Reinhardt's production of Hofmannthal's reworking of the old morality play *Jedermann* (Everyman).[24] It was performed outdoors, using the Salzburg cathedral as a backdrop and incorporating the ringing of church bells and organ music from deep inside the cathedral as part of a truly haunting production. Salten did not care for Hofmannsthal's text; he considered it to be merely a reworking of the old morality play, without any real relevance to modern audiences, especially when he compared it with the passion and vitality of Hofmannsthal's earlier treatment of this theme in his youthful drama *Der Tor und der Tod* (The Fool and Death), 1893.[25] Still, he applauded the partnership and began to report each summer on the Reinhardt productions staged in and around Salzburg.

Salten remained extremely productive during this period of national recovery. In addition to his theatrical pieces, he gathered together a collection of essays that was published by Ullstein in 1920 under the title *Die Dame im Spiegel* (The Lady in the Mirror). Most of these pieces had appeared as feuilletons in *Die Zeit* between 1903 and 1912; many were lighthearted studies of women: elegant lady, young woman, little girl, child. Still, the title is misleading, as is the inclusion of Countess Christine von Kalckreuth's illustrations of society women, since the volume contains a number of pieces that do not relate to women at all. Two of these are particularly noteworthy in that they are early treatments of themes that Salten took up in later works: "In Schönbrunn" (At the Schönbrunn Zoo),[26] which introduces the imprisoned animals that would reappear in *Freunde aus aller Welt* (The City Jungle) in 1931, and "Verwickelte Geschichte" (Complicated Story),[27] which treats Salten's views of childrearing, expanded upon in the 1925 novel *Bob und Baby*.

More significantly, Salten began work on a new novel, to which he gave the working title *Apoll und der Kardinal* (Apollo and the Cardinal).[28] As in so many of his historical works, Salten sought to illuminate the present by setting his work in an earlier age. The basic conceit of the novel is that, during the bloody turmoil that followed the investiture controversy of the 11th and 12th centuries − a period similar to the present in that a once powerful and unified German empire had disintegrated and civil war was rampant throughout the countryside – the joyously natural beauty of classical art had been suppressed by the Church and replaced by stiff Byzantine forms more acceptable to the Catholic hierarchy. Into this setting steps the pagan god Apollo, who finds a world devoid of joy. He assumes the name "Benvenuto Solari" since he "will bring light, warmth, charm [and] music" into cheerless Rome.[29] Under the protection of a sympathetic Cardinal, Apollo introduces graceful classical influences into forms of Christian art and thereby ushers the Renaissance age into Italy.

The message of this work was clear: great art could be momentarily silenced but never defeated either by the ravages of revolution and warfare or by the dictates of a dominant Christian culture. Increasingly, Salten made it his mission to praise the contributions of Jewish artists to the cultures of the old German and Austrian empires. In May 1920 he traveled to Amsterdam to participate in a Mahler festival held in honor of that great Jewish conductor and composer. His speech was a paean to Vienna as the fertile soil not only of Mahler, but of Haydn, Mozart, Beethoven, Bruckner, und Brahms. He noted that the destruction of the Biblical Tower of Babel had broken peoples into many factions and many languages but that music had the power to bridge these differences. He praised Vienna as the crossroads of East and West, North and South, a gathering place for peoples of many cultures and ethnicities who found in Vienna the perfect climate for their musical work. "In this city, in which all kinds of people live near one another and mix with one another, music develops as the result of a hundred blendings of thought, a hundred mixtures of longing," he proclaimed.[30] Despite the current episodes of violence, anti-Semitism, and revolution in the city, Salten continued to regard Vienna as a potential utopia for all the ethnic minorities who lived there and enriched the nation's culture.

From Holland, Salten traveled to Berlin, where he had preserved an idealized image of the home of Samuel and Hedwig Fischer. To Salten, the Fischer home had always been an island of peace in a raucously loud city, a place of refined enlightenment where artists of all nationalities came to mingle and feel welcome. During this visit he was bitterly disappointed to hear disparaging remarks made at one of the Fischers' soirées about the Mahler festival and about Mahler's Jewishness. Ever over-sensitive, Salten told Schnitzler that he now felt that a "renegade position against Austrians – and Judaism" was at work in the Fischer firm.[31] He would continue to remain personal friends with the Fischers, even though he felt that Fischer no longer represented his professional interests. Despite Fischer's interest in reprinting *Herr Wenzel auf Rehberg* and in publishing a revised version of Salten's new novel *Der Hund von Florenz* (The Hound of Florence),[32] Salten had no new works published by Fischer after the war's end.

Back in Vienna, Salten was involved in various actions to raise money for child victims of the war. In January 1920 Salten hosted a reception to honor the ladies of the Swedish Red Cross Society, who had cooperated with the Swedish organization *Rådda Barnen* (Save the Children) in bringing food to starving German and Austrian children harmed by the postwar blockade. That year a number of organizations concerned with the welfare of children in war-ravaged Europe merged into an International Save the Children Union under the leadership of Eglantyne Jebb, the British founder of the Fight the Famine Council and the first European to raise funds for people hurt by the Allied blockade. Salten was much impressed with the idea of an international charity working beyond political and nationalist interests. When he attended a meeting of about twenty people who were invited by the Austrian State Office for Education to discuss ideas for raising money for children's charities at home, and Schnitzler suggested that the Austrian writers should donate their royalties from the fiftieth printing of their literary works and the fiftieth performance of their staged plays directly into this fund, Salten urged that such donations should become part of the larger international movement and draw in writers from around the world.[33] Schnitzler agreed, and the two friends worked on an appeal published in the Viennese newspapers. In 1923 they collaborated again when Schnitzler's "Comtesse Mizzi" and Salten's "Schöne Seelen" were performed at the Kammerspiele in an action to raise money for German charities.

After the war was over, Salten briefly renewed his acquaintance with Leopold Wölfling, the former Archduke of Tuscany, who was now able to return to Vienna for the first time since his banishment. Since the collapse of the empire, Wölfling had been cut off from his small Habsburg stipend, and he was scrambling desperately to earn a living. Salten realized just how desperate Wölfling's position had become when he asked him how he could stoop to portraying an archduke at a rather seedy Berlin variété, and Wölfling replied, "My friend, hunger is very painful."[34] This reunion with the former Tuscan archduke may have been the motive for Salten taking out his Tuscan manuscript, *Der Hund von Florenz*, and resuming work on it after a break of many years. It is the only work that Salten referred to as overtly autobiographical.[35] While admitting that all fiction is to some extent "one part autobiography and one part confession," Salten insisted that *Der Hund von Florenz* contained "much autobiographical material" and "much confession."[36]

Salten dedicated the novel to his wife and placed a quote ascribed to "The Hermit of Amiata" both before and within his story: "If so be thou art poor on this earth, thou must be a dog for one half of thy life; then mayest thou spend the other half as a man among men."[37] Salten often stated that he became conscious of the many similarities between himself and the hero of the novel only as he grew older, which would suggest that the work probes more deeply into his character than indicated by the humorous interplay of human and canine behavior and that he now saw both admirable and less than desirable doglike tendencies within himself at a period when he had tried desperately to play the role of gentleman.[38] His words also suggest that it took Salten many years to realize that his "dog" life of labor had always kept him from being a fully accepted member of the Young Vienna circle – that in the minds of his friends he was merely a working journalist and not an artist of their caliber. This suggestion is supported by Salten's statement late in life that, as a member of Young Vienna, he had "served" the other writers "gladly and cheerfully, [and] had only little, and rarely, occasion to regret it."[39] In the many years that had transpired since those heady days at the Griensteidl, Salten had come to view himself as someone who had furthered the careers of his friends through his work as a newspaper critic without getting the complete support from them that he felt was his due.

The strength of Salten's story lies in the portrayal of the dog Cambyses. Here, as in his very first published tale "Der Vagabund," we see Salten's brilliant portrayal of a dog's character, this time with the consciousness of a man under a magic spell. It would be only a few months before Salten began work on *Bambi*, a work in which animals are portrayed with numerous human characteristics. In *Der Hund von Florenz*, this anthropomorphism is reversed, in that a human being is portrayed as a dog. The conflict between human artistic aspiration and lowly animal instinct reaches a climax when Grassi reaches Florence and, in the form of Cambyses, lays eyes on Michelangelo's marble statue of David:

> The dog was struggling to raise his eyes to the statue, though some invisible power was drawing his nose to the ground. Twice, thrice he tried to gaze up at the marble monument, but each time the irresistible force exercised by all manner of scents drew his nose down to the plinth. Obliged at last to yield to the impulse, he sniffed quickly and uneasily round the sides of the base, turned in anguish this way and that, but could not tear himself away. At last, cocking his leg up against the statue, he gazed in front of him with bowed head and clouded eyes, full of dumb agony.[40]

It is in passages like these, where human aspirations come into conflict with animal drives, that Salten reaches his greatest achievement and demonstrates a richness of canine character unmatched by any of the work's human figures.

After the war's end, Salten had the satisfaction of seeing three of his literary works transformed into films: *Herztrumpf* (Heart Trump), 1920, based on his 1911 story *Tini Holms Aufstieg*; *Olga Frohgemuth*, 1922, from his 1910 story of the same name; and *Graf Festenberg* or *Der Kellnergraf*, 1922, from Salten's one-act play of 1908. In addition, Salten wrote a screenplay in 1923 for a film entitled *Der Türmer von St. Stephan* or *Der Jude von Granada* (The Bell-Ringer of St. Stephan's or The Jew of Granada), a melodrama about two Jewish brothers, the treachery of the one, and his ultimate punishments by the Catholic church.[41] Salten was once again in top form. He took full advantage of his ability to travel again: in 1921 he went on a reading tour to nine cities in Czechoslovakia, and in 1922 he returned to Italy for a tour of Venice, Rome, and Naples.

Chapter 16: *Bambi* and the Other Talking Animals

Bambi, with the subtitle *Eine Lebensgeschichte aus dem Walde* (A Life Story From the Forest), is an unassuming tale about a baby deer whose very name, a corruption of the Italian word *bambino*, serves to emphasize his vulnerability.[1] Schnitzler noted in November 1921 that Salten had spoken to him about "the novella he is working on now – hero a roebuck."[2] The following year, *Bambi* appeared in serialized version in the *Neue Freie Presse* from August 15 through October 21, and two months later Salten gave a bound copy of the work to Schnitzler as a Christmas present.

It has often been mentioned that Salten was inspired to write *Bambi* on his annual summer vacation in the Salzkammergut[3] and that he did so quickly and easily. Certainly, the period between the work's conception and final composition was a short one when compared, for example, with *Der Hund von Florenz*, which he carried around with him for some twenty-five years. Salten has noted that the ideas for all his works came swiftly, noting, "The subject matter for my fictional and dramatic works always occurs to me in a single moment. In this short moment it stands before me completely finished, completely alive, and in a form of perfection that I try to achieve later during its implementation," adding that this perfection is something "that I of course am never able to achieve." The moment of envisioning the material is one "of the happiest, that one can experience,"[4] whereas the process of writing it down is associated with "inhibitions," "shame," "fear," and "difficulties."[5] *Bambi*, apparently, flowed rather easily.

One motivation for writing *Bambi* was Salten's desire to disabuse readers of the idea of nature as a sunny paradise. As early as 1906, he had noted people's tendency to enjoy nature only when the weather was perfect and to return quickly to the city as soon as rainy, cold weather ushered in the fall.[6] He hoped with this book to show nature lovers, who traveled by daylight on established trails through the forest, something of the true nature of the forest animals they only fleetingly observed. At the same time, he wished to share with his readers his own awe of nature and to show it both in good times and in bad. He had acquired his knowledge through his hunting forays into the Austrian forests. Only the hunter, he remarked, goes alone into the deep woods in all kinds of weather, moving as noiselessly as he can through rugged terrain and concentrating intently on the sounds and the sights around him: "Where the hunter goes there is, in the entire region of the preserve, no human being, no one who meets us, no one who can cross our path. There is no street here that joins cities or villages, no promenade walkway for sightseers. Nowhere is one so close to the original state of nature as in the immense, mysteriously bustling silence of such a forest."[7]

As a hunter Salten was attuned to all signs of animal life; he saw the trees deer had damaged as they rubbed against them to remove the skin from their new antlers, the mangled bodies of small animals killed by martens and picked at by crows, the abandoned hiding places of pheasants, the tracks and droppings of elk and fox. He frequently arose early and went out into the hunting preserve long before sunrise in pursuit of game. For him this was a time of wonder as shapes slowly emerged from the darkness of the night and the sounds of woodpeckers and songbirds gradually replaced the calls of owls. He frequently described this period of transition in his works, as he does, for example, in this piece about a chance, pre-dawn meeting a with a deer:

> There is a soft movement among the young trees and hazel bushes – so quiet, it is rather to be felt than observed. I stand still and turn my glance that way, searching.
>
> It is a roebuck. The head thrown back is a faint outline in the gray of dawn; slowly I make out the crown between the ears. Both of us remain motionless, the buck and I. We look at each other for a few moments, a little eternity. At last the animal turns away, disappears, and I am free again. I wait a bit, and then I go on.[8]

In this passage, Salten makes the decision not to kill the game he is after. He emphatically noted that he was "not a shooter," that he went into the hunting preserve many times "just to look and without carrying my weapon,"[9] and that he used his hunting of the royal stag "just as a stimulus, as an excuse, as the means ... for being close to nature and free creatures."[10]

Still, there is no denying the fact that Salten was an active and committed hunter. After one case of killing a fine royal stag with a clean shot, Salten wrote, "As I do every time, I stand by the slain animal, moved with painful remorse and at the same time ... fierce joy."[11] He got quite defensive when others referred to hunting as a cruel blood sport. His main argument in such cases was that instantaneous death in the wild is far more merciful than death in a slaughterhouse and much more humane than that caused by other animals. His most convincing argument, however, was that, in an age when many were preaching the "back to nature" movement, its most vocal adherents were actually ignorant of the real violence and blood-letting that occurred on a daily basis among the animals in the forest. Salten noted that those who purported to be a great "friend of nature" were actually "strangers to nature," "familiar only with the lifeless forest, the forest without animals,"[12] adding "that Bambi would never have come into being if I had never aimed my bullet at the head of a roebuck or an elk."[13]

When Salten took up hunting he spent "whole days and half the night in the forest," where he "got to know the forest in a new way, got to know the game for the first time, its pathways, its favorite places, got to know, little by little, all animals, not just deer, elk, pheasants, or hares, but all animals."[14] Salten's daughter described the hunting preserve in Stockerau as "Father's most beloved place" and his "home":

> It was situated in the Danube lowland, and any number of streamlets ran through it. Conifers and leafy shade trees abounded. There were junglelike thickets, swamps, flower-strewn meadows, even patches of farm land teeming with a great variety of animals – from the proud deer to the lithe marten, from the aristocratic pheasant to the preying buzzard. The immortal *Bambi* owes its existence to my father's thorough familiarity with and his great love of that woodland, as do all of Bambi's companions, big and small, which have come to life in Felix Salten's stories.[15]

Although he always defended the sport, Salten consistently

emphasized the importance of responsible hunting. He admitted to having killed over two hundred "Bambis" in his lifetime, but noted that there were only three cases when he did not make a clean kill with his first shot.[16] Salten remained an ardent opponent of the irresponsible slaughter of game animals. Writing, for example, of Archduke Franz Ferdinand, a man who once boasted of killing more than five thousand deer, Salten noted: "When his brother Otto died, he telephoned right away to his forest preserve Schönau and asked how many bucks were available to be shot. At the answer one hundred and ten, he went out, had the bucks driven past him on a constrained pathway, and killed them all." Furthermore, when invited to a hunt and being told that "a tame buck with a red collar went around near the castle, the first thing the Archduke killed from his window was this buck." And, on a third occasion when the Archduke was invited on a hunt, "he shot down all the game, including the female elk and deer."[17] No doubt Salten had the Archduke in mind when he wrote in *Bambi* about how the tame buck Gobo is killed even though he is wearing a collar.

Salten included a version of himself as keeper of a hunting preserve in his novels *Bambis Kinder* (Bambi's Children) and *Kleine Welt für sich* (translated as *A Forest World*). In *Bambis Kinder* he portrayed both aspects of his life in nature: as one who rescues and heals hurt animals and provides food for them in winter, and as one who pursues and kills them during hunting season. In *Kleine Welt für sich*, which was written after Salten had been forced to leave Vienna and live as an exile in Switzerland, only the old forester Heinrich does the necessary killing, while the humpbacked hermit Martin spends hours of each day on a hunter's stand, in quiet contemplation of the animals and birds on the preserve. More than *Bambi* does, these works emphasize the importance of responsible hunting; Salten showed no sympathy for poachers, trappers, or reckless gunmen.

In fact, in all of Salten's animal books, hunters are only one threat to animal life. The forest is a place of constant danger — from hunters, of course, but also from other animals, violent storms, and prolonged periods of drought or freezing temperatures. As carnivorous animals, the fox and the marten are a constant threat to the squirrels, rabbits, and even to young deer, but, as Salten makes clear, these animals have to kill if they wish to survive. Owls and hawks feed on small rodents; ospreys and herons feed on fish; swallows and bats feed on insects. This is the unsentimental view of the forest that Salten wanted to show his readers, and the reason why the British novelist John Galsworthy wrote that he would "particularly recommend" Salten's book "to sportsmen." Galsworthy was less pleased with a "method which places human words in the mouths of dumb creatures," stating that it is "the triumph of this book that, behind the conversation, one feels the real sensations of the creatures who speak."[18] William Rose Benet was less tolerant in his review of *Bambi*, noting: "Mating, even among wild animals may well be accompanied by tenderness. But when the words 'I love you' are put into the mouth even of an ordinarily gentle deer, it seems to us a blunder. The gentler side of mating might have been more convincingly rendered."[19] Many critics accepted the animal conversations as part of a deeper allegory, little realizing that Salten was firmly convinced that animals actually did communicate with one another in nuanced conversations. "People explain everything a deer does, an elk, a falcon, a magpie, an owl, a weasel or polecat – to say nothing of the fox or the work of hunting dogs – with the arrogant and meaningless expression 'instinct,'" he wrote. "It now became my firm conviction that animals think and they even speak with one another!" He claimed that he could bring "proofs" of this, but that that would be "too boring." Nevertheless, he declared, "Bambi was born of this insight, of this conviction."[20]

Instead of suppressing animal speech in his future novels, Salten would continue to have domestic and forest animals carry on sometimes lengthy conversations about weather, relationships, dangers, and adventures. Such conversation is particularly stressed in *Bambis Kinder*, where the young deer find great delight in hearing about the narrow escapes of others and where Faline's children ask her, again and again, to repeat the story of her brother Gobo. As the fawn Gurri explains, "I can always listen to this story, always! It gives me such a nice fright."[21] The animals converse across species boundaries: the heron speaks with the fox, the owl and the squirrel with the deer, the magpies with the thrushes. Not only do they speak, in Salten's novels their speech is appropriate to the species: the squirrel has "a rapid, wayward chatter," the butterfly "an affected idiom," while the screech owl is "noisy and assertive."[22] Salten's old nemesis Karl Kraus mockingly referred to the rabbits of

Salten's novel *Fünfzehn Hasen* (Fifteen Rabbits) as *jüdelnde Hasen* (Rabbits with a Jewish dialect).[23] Certainly Salten seemed to support this connection between Jews and rabbits when he described one of his rabbits as looking like "some timid, worried, humble little shopkeeper whose naivete and limited experience have accustomed him to suffer much hardship, to endure much mistreatment – while it has never entered his head to defend himself."[24] Passages like these support the consensus of many readers that his works are allegories for activities then going on in the human sphere: with the hunting down of innocent animals reflecting the pogroms conducted against the Jews in Eastern Europe and the massive killings of game representing the carnage of World War One.

One could also make the argument that Salten used animal speech as a way to comment ironically on various aspects of human nature, as when an overly talkative magpie, ignored by Bambi's mother, retains its sense of self-esteem by remarking to itself that the doe is "very nice, but stupid"[25] or when the young stag Ronno, who is losing a battle with Bambi, whines, "I was only joking. ... Can't you take a joke?"[26] Even insects converse with one another in Salten's novels. In the last chapter of *Bambi*, for example, a swarm of midges, with a life expectancy of one to two days, talk about the thirty-to-forty-day life expectancy of a May beetle, which makes it "as old as the hills, as old as the hills. He's seen more and been through more in this world than we can even imagine."[27] But Salten goes even further, by having vegetation speak. One of the most poetically moving conversations in *Bambi* occurs in late autumn when two of the last leaves on an oak tree speculate about what will happen when they fall to their deaths, with one asking, "Do we feel anything, do we know anything about ourselves when we're down there?" and the other responding, "Who knows? Not one of all those down there has ever come back to tell us about it."[28] Scenes such as this led one contemporary critic to exclaim, "In *Bambi* the author has, while writing wholly of animals, somehow transcended his subject. He has given us the life story of a forest deer, and Felix Salten's comprehension of the entire universe as well. Here is a rationale of life ... that is delightfully implicit in a charming story. Throw away your Spinozan tomes on pantheism and read *Bambi*."[29]

Although Salten gave all living objects the power to communicate, to philosophize, gossip, and banter, he bemoaned the speech barriers that exist between man and animal, animal and plant. In *Kleine Welt für sich*, when the forester and veterinarian are unable to determine the cause of the donkey Manni's sudden decline, the cow mourns, "All our misfortune comes from their not understanding us and our not understanding them .... All we can do is guess a tiny bit, no more. And what do they understand about us? Almost nothing."[30] Even Salten's alter ego, Martin, who has spent a lifetime studying and loving all the creatures of the farm and forest, is forced to admit:

> We always remain strange to them. They don't understand us. They don't know what an endless measure of inspiration they are, what a font of mystery and magic. No. We fill them only with fear and enmity. It's been in their blood since the oldest times, and has become their sharpest instinct. It is sad. And the worst of it is that I suppose we human beings are responsible for it.[31]

Only by actually becoming a dog, as Lukas Grassi does in *Der Hund von Florenz*, is a Salten hero truly able to understand life as an animal and to experience not only its good nature and loyalty but also its uncontrollable animal drives. Tellingly, however, the dog Cambyses does not converse with other animals, and the hero is deprived of those insights that might have come through communication with others of the dog species.

By the time he wrote his animal novels, Salten was fusing Freudian concepts of the pre-conscious and conscious selves with the Biblical story of man's fall in order to explain the speech barriers that exist between man and animal.[32] At the beginning of his novel *Perri,* the animals and birds visit little Annerle (Salten's own daughter Anna as a young child), when she is still at an age when she "did not know the language of men" and "only babbled it clumsily." At this early stage of life, Salten wrote, children were blessed with the gift of being able to understand "the speech of all innocent creatures." It was Salten's conviction that, during this brief, pre-conscious period of childhood, when children "enjoy the infinite blessing of having no fate," they "live in natural innocence, like Adam and Eve before they ate the apple from the tree of knowledge." Perhaps the animals "half-consciously or quite unconsciously, have an inexplicable hope and longing for the old original harmony between man and beast," Salten continued, adding, "If only human children could grow up with the memory of all the gentleness, all the patience and devotion, which they have had from living creatures!" "But when they grow out of the dawning of their lives, they forget everything" and "animals become to them what they are to everyone else – arbitrarily exploited victims, callously misused creatures, in the best case: dumb friends."[33]

Salten not only viewed the loss of understanding between man and beast as a tragic sign of man's fall from grace and his expulsion from the Garden of Eden, in *Der Hund von Florenz* he rounded out his theories of non-communication by explaining the loss of understanding between different ethnic groups and nations as an example of another Biblical fall from grace, this time as recorded in the story of the Tower of Babel:

> "In those days mankind was still an actuality... men still understood one another... and they tried to produce a great work together... a piece of idiocy.... They might have thought of something better.... But they were at least united. Ever since that day, however, they have never been united... they can never be united again.... Yes, and ever since that day there have been only men, but no mankind...."[34]

Salten put his own interpretation on these stories when he has one of his characters remark, "Perhaps [God] may be over-hasty when we make Him angry."[35]

For Salten the man, "God" is no more comprehensible than He was when the child Salten said his nightly prayers without any idea of the god he was addressing. One of the charms of *Bambi* is that the animals' (and oak leaves') naive speculations about God, suffering, and death reflect mankind's deepest concerns. Throughout most of the novel, the animals regard man as an angry and incomprehensible god; they refer to him as "He" and give "Him" magical powers, as when He hurls "thunder" "from His hands"[36]

or topples trees with a "gigantic flashing tooth."[37] After Gobo has
been rescued by a hunter and cared for in his home, the young deer
returns to the forest to contradict this view, exclaiming, "Why
should I have been afraid? You all believe that He's wicked. But He
isn't wicked. If He loves anybody or if anybody serves Him, He is
good to him. Wonderfully good! Nobody in the world can be as
kind as He can."[38] This introduction into the *Bambi* story of a merciful (Christian) god is short-lived, however.[39] Gobo is killed by
"Him" and the dream the deer harbor of a peaceable kingdom for
man and animal is abruptly extinguished by an onslaught of exces-
sive violence among the animals and a bloody roundup by the
hunters, who kill Bambi's gentle mother.

Bambi's father, the old stag, now becomes Bambi's mentor,
teaching him the secrets of moving silently through the forest and
the wisdom of learning to live alone. The final lesson that he im-
parts to Bambi is the most important one: he teaches Bambi that
man is not the omnipotent force the animals think he is. He shows
Bambi a dead poacher and says, "Do you see, Bambi? ... He isn't
all-powerful as they say he is. Everything that lives and grows
doesn't come from Him. He isn't above us. He's just the same as
we are. He has the same fears, the same needs, and suffers in the
same way. He can be killed like us, and then He lies helpless on the
ground like all the rest of us, as you see Him now."[40] Bambi is inspired by the sight and exlaims: "There is Another who is over us
all, over us and over Him."[41] He sees now that man and animal are
equally vulnerable to forces larger than themselves, and both have
reason to be fearful.

This attempt at reconciling man and nature gets to the heart of
Salten's animal tales. For Salten, animals are not soulless creatures
of instinct, any more than man is. Although only man has eaten
from the Tree of Knowledge, this has not given him the right to
kill indiscriminately; he has, in fact, a responsibility toward all living
beings. Salten was horrified by royalty's mass killings of game, by
the brutality of the World War, the murderous turn taken by the
Russian Revolution, and the bloody pogroms against the Jews in
Eastern Europe.[42] He did not find a mitigating deity who intervened when mankind went on these bloody rampages; in fact, these
cruelties convinced him that all living creatures were subject to the
whims of a distant and arbitrary God. He developed this idea in an

essay he entitled "Winzige Begebenheit" (translated as "Brother Ant"[43]) in which he described the rushed movements and abrupt turns of "a very small reddish-brown ant"[44] who finds himself momentarily trapped on a man's sheet of writing paper, "far from its home, from earth and food and from the life it knew." Upon examining the animal attentively, the man sees "a small animal, strong and trim, confident and unsuspecting." "Are we any different?" he reflects. "Confidence and trust – these are the two worthiest attributes of a living being. These are the ones that count!" The man is aware of his power: "This ant is so small … that I could squash it with the tip of my finger. But there is a still higher power that can squash me in turn with a fingertip. I comprehend this higher power as little as this ant comprehends me. The difference between me and this insect may not at bottom be so considerable."[45] He releases the ant, wondering, "Did the ant understand its great adventure? … Would it now feel something akin to thankfulness for the miracle of its salvation? Or … would it attribute everything to its own cleverness and grow boastful about it?"[46]

It is this sense of the unity – and fragility – of all life that gives *Bambi* its poetic impact. After it sold in the thousands on the European market, Simon and Schuster bought the rights for publication in America, and the newly formed "Book of the Month Club" ordered 50,000 copies of the first trade edition prior to its appearance in July 1928. *Bambi* was translated by Whittaker Chambers, illustrated by Kurt Wiese, and marketed to an adult audience. Critics praised it as being "as profoundly pertinent to modern experience as [Thomas Mann's] *The Magic Mountain* or [Theodore Dreiser's] *An American Tragedy.*"[47] Unfortunately, the subtle ambiguities of Salten's little masterpiece would fade with the 1942 release of Walt Disney's animated film version of *Bambi*. By turning the forest into a happy animal playground and by eliminating the old stag's lessons about the vulnerability of man, Disney erased from public consciousness Salten's central idea that, in their vulnerability, humans and animals are not so different after all.

Chapter 17: Taking Stock

Although *Bambi* was to gain world recognition and be translated into multiple languages, its 1923 publication did not assure Salten a comfortable income. The monetary situation in Austria had stabilized, but outrageously high inflation peaked in Germany that year, and German book publishers were struggling to stay afloat. Authors used to receiving 20-25% of sales were now receiving only 15-18%,[1] and these reduced percentages had little purchasing power. In frustration, Salten and his friends criticized the German publishers for their loss in income. Many, like Salten, published with multiple firms in an effort to attain the best terms for each new book; by the time *Bambi* appeared, Salten had had books published with a dozen presses. With *Bambi*, he went to Ullstein, who had published Salten's two books for youth as well as *Die Dame im Spiegel*. *Bambi* appeared in a limited edition and apparently was a moderate success.[2] Salten, however, derived little benefit from it.

Wherever authors gathered, they complained about their financial arrangements with the German publishing firms. One evening, at a social gathering near Bratislava at the family estate of Adolph and Amanda Zsolnay, the topic came up again. The Zsolnay sons were present; one of them, Paul, ran a successful garden nursery. Their guests were the writer and founder of the Pan-European Union, Richard Coudenhove-Kalergi; his wife, actress Ida Roland; author Franz Werfel; and Gustav Mahler's widow, Alma. When the writers began their usual complaints about finances, Coudenhove's wife suddenly spoke up and suggested that Paul Zsolnay start a press, since he was "a good organizer" who understood "something about literature." Werfel immediately promised him his first long novel, *Verdi*, and Paul Zsolnay, who loved literature but knew nothing about the book business, made up his mind "from one day to the next, so to speak, to found a publishing company."[3]

Zsolnay had the strong financial support of his father, a well-to-do industrialist, importer of tobacco, and consul general; Coudenhove described Paul as "an idealist with politically leftist leanings" whose wealth was such that "in his founding of a publishing house the hope for profit plays no role at all."[4] Both Zsolnay's independent wealth and his idealism made it possible for him to provide his writers with extremely favorable conditions, since he was willing to assume substantial financial risks. He was also greatly aided by his mother, Amanda Zsolnay. As a long-time admirer of the arts, she had established ties of friendship with Gerhart Hauptmann, Richard Strauss, Felix von Weingartner, Franz Werfel, and Richard Coudenhove-Kalergi, as well as with Hofmannsthal, Schnitzler, and Salten.[5] These contacts immediately drew important authors into the Zsolnay fold. Paul Zsolnay was especially fortunate in finding a partner who would prove invaluable in getting his new business venture off the ground. This man was Felix Kostia-Costa; he had been a co-founder of the ILF-Press, served as its business manager, and continued to work there when it was taken over in 1921 by the banker Richard Kola and renamed the Rikola Press. Costa's experience gave Zsolnay's new venture the credibility needed in wooing world-class authors into its fold, for, although Zsolnay had the social connections helpful for bringing in Austrian writers, Zsolnay's aim from the very first was to publish an international roster of noted authors. Costa served as literary director of the Paul Zsolnay Press and its sole authorized signatory until the press became a limited liability company, and Stefan Halasz came on board in October 1925.

Salten was enthusiastic about Zsolnay's venture from the very beginning. He had been publishing either with German firms, where inflation had eaten into any profits he might have hoped for, or with Austrian firms which did not last long. Zsolnay promised to build an Austrian press that would, for the first time, compete favorably with the prestigious German firms of Fischer, Ullstein, Langen, and Georg Müller. One of Zsolnay's goals was to publish the collected works of his authors in single editions. On November 25 Salten and Schnitzler went to dinner at the Zsolnays, again with the group that had first raised the issue of a press there, and discussed Zsolnay's plans for his new firm. Four days later Salten brought Paul Zsolnay to Schnitzler's home, and the three men had an "animated conversation" that lasted "over two hours."[6] Schnitzler eventually decided to publish his novella *Fräulein Else* with Zsolnay as a single work but never broke his long-standing ties with Fischer. Salten, on the other hand, transferred his loyalties to Zsolnay and never went back either to Fischer or to Ullstein.

In 1924 and 1925, the first years of the Zsolnay publishing

house's full operation, Heinrich Mann and John Galsworthy were fully on board, and ten of Mann's works and eight by Galsworthy were published. Salten had three works published during this period: a volume of essays entitled *Geister der Zeit* (Spirits of the Age), the travel book *Neue Menschen auf alter Erde* (New People on Ancient Soil), and a children's book entitled *Bob und Baby*. He would continue to publish with Zsolnay until this was made impossible by Germany's annexation of Austria.

Salten's first work for Zsolnay, *Geister der Zeit*, was a collection of essays culled from his newspaper columns. Quite a number of them had appeared previously in the volume *Gestalten und Erscheinungen*, which Samuel Fischer had published in 1913. The book bore the subtitle *Erlebnisse* (Experiences), echoing the title of the first section of his more recent *Schauen und Spielen*. The essays selected for this work had a broader perspective than those theater pieces, however, for, in addition to a large number of actor studies, Salten now included writers, painters, musicians, and even Vienna's former mayor Karl Lueger among his subjects. Most of the pieces were necrologies; indeed, it seems that Zsolnay was interested in having the older Salten preserve in this collection his prewar memories of Vienna's cultural scene before the city's collective memory of these individuals faded. Hofmannsthal wrote an appreciation of this volume, noting that the heart of all the essays was "the live encounter" with their subjects. "Nothing in [these essays] is contemplative, nothing is analytical," he stated. "Everything is sympathy and split-second empathy; these would be accurate physiognomic feats, if they were not true physiognomic works of art."[7]

With the publication of this volume, Salten proclaimed his transfer of allegiance to Zsolnay's fledgling press, especially when he included in it an essay on Hans Kaltneker, an expressionist poet and playwright who had died in 1919 at the tender age of twenty-four. Salten aided Zsolnay in getting the rights to Kaltneker's plays, and Zsolnay reprinted the Kaltneker essay as a foreword to the collection of Kaltneker's poetic and dramatic works that he edited and published in 1925. Salten provided an even more valuable service to the young publisher in his position as chief editor for the *Neue Freie Presse*, by seeing to it that the Zsolnay authors were reviewed in its columns.

Then, in the spring of 1924, Salten turned to an entirely new project: he traveled to Palestine to see for himself the achievements of the fledgling Jewish state and to write a book about his findings. It was a well-timed project since it had been twenty years since the death of Theodor Herzl. Salten had always admired Herzl not only for his commitment to the Zionist cause but also as a superb journalist and stylist; he could identify with the man who, like himself, had been born in Budapest, then moved to Vienna and made a name for himself as one of the city's leading feuilletonists. When Herzl died in 1904, Salten had been one of the graveside speakers, and for a long time he had played around with the idea of writing a biography of Herzl. It was Herzl who had first awakened Salten to the fact that the liberal age into which he had been born had given away to "hateful strife." In the years since Herzl's death, the situation in Vienna had grown much worse. "What would the Jewish students who spilled their blood on the pavements of Vienna and Berlin for the cause of freedom say," Salten asked, "when today at the universities in Germany and Austria they would find the narrow-minded brutality of aggressive, German national attitudes instead of the humanity of 1848?"[8] Indeed, Salten was growing more and more disturbed by the anti-Semitism that was spreading throughout Europe. When Eugen Tschirikow's play *Die Juden* (The Jews) returned to the Vienna stage for perfomance at the Raimund Theater, Salten noted its new relevance. It had originally been written about the situation in Russia, about "pogroms and assassination by bombs," he noted. "When Eugen Tschirikow wrote this play twenty years ago, when we saw it in the theater then, everything was still very far away. It was just theater, a play of strange, barbaric conditions that one watched with horror from the safe seating of European culture, but still with a feeling of security." Now, however, this culture "was smashed to pieces, security has waned. Now all this has moved quite near, the chaos of barbaric conditions, assassination as a political tool, perhaps even the lovely custom of pogroms."[9]

He was concerned enough about the contemporary situation in Vienna to suggest that German Jews should form their own universities where they could study without the constant threat of physical violence. In August 1923 Salten attended the Zionist Congress in Karlsbad and wrote admiringly of the work being done in

Palestine. It was, he noted, a country for young people, "different from those who come to blows with anti-Semitic scum at German or Hungarian or Romanian universities. ... It is disciplined, austere, soberly enthusiastic young people who want to go to Palestine," where "they no longer know anything about pogroms, about rabble-rousing and persecution, about all those actions aggravated by mid-European venom."[10] Salten did not believe that Palestine was the answer for everyone. It certainly was not an option for his generation of Austrians, "not for us, who sit here in solid communities, inseparably grown together with a country and committed to its destiny"; it was only an option "for all the homeless, for the wistful, for the refugees, for those among our youth who are tired of Europe."[11]

It was in this frame of mind that Salten set out, via Egypt, for a tour of Palestine, where he was eager to see for himself to what degree Herzl's dream had been realized. For Salten, Herzl's achievement had particular significance because "it can never be forgotten that it was a poet who undertook the task of freeing the Jewish people."[12] Salten's journey coincided with the time envisioned in Herzl's utopian novel *Altneuland* [Ancient New Earth, 1902]. Herzl had died before his dream could become reality; now Salten was making the journey for him in order to inform the world of the young country's promise and achievements. Paul Zsolnay put up money for Salten's journey, while the Central Zionist Office in London provided letters of recommendation and suggestions for his travel agenda.

The resulting book, *Neue Menschen auf alter Erde* (New People on Ancient Soil), 1925, is a paean to Herzl's Zionist dream.[13] In Palestine, Salten wrote, "a figure always walks beside me, floats before me on the streets, beckons to me in so many images from so many walls and lives in my thoughts. I remember him and recall our discussions when I am out in the settlements that he was not destined to see. And whenever I walk through the Jaffa Gate in Jerusalem, his tall and noble apparition rises before my eyes."[14] Salten rhapsodized about the cheerful, healthy young Jews who had come to this land of promise, learned Hebrew, and were busily turning arid ground into gardens. He visited frontier settlements, communal camps, cities, and Biblical sites; toured governmental buildings, museums, and social clubs; interviewed students, work-

213

men, and government officials. When he saw young men constructing the initial building of what was to become the Hebrew University in Jerusalem, he remarked, "Perhaps they are thinking about the fact that later they will be students again, here at this university …. Perhaps … they find satisfaction in the fact that a university is rising that is erected completely through the work of Jewish hands, an alma mater … that will truly become a kindly mother for all who come to her."[15]

Salten was not a thoughtless admirer of all that he saw. He criticized the Bulgarian director of the Jerusalem art academy for "balkanizing" the arts; he argued with a fanatical young commune member that the family unit is part of the natural order and could not be discarded at will; and, although he recognized the threat posed by militant Arabs, he expressed the hope that Jews, Christians, and Muslims could all live together in peace. He was disturbed at seeing young Jewish men carrying rifles and wrote:

> The Jews must not tread here on the soil of their original homeland like Europeans lusty for conquest …. They are now sowing the seed in the earth and in human hearts for eternal cohabitation with the Arabs, and if they now sow hate or vengeance, they will never harvest love or even tolerance. They must approach the Semitic Arab peoples, who are their brothers, in brotherly fashion.[16]

A "policy of peace and reconciliation is the only correct one that the Jews can follow," he concluded. "This conforms to the Jewish heart and the Jewish spirit, conforms to the true commandments of humanity."[17]

Salten's journey had become for him a true pilgrimage, in which he not only traced Herzl's footsteps but felt reconnected with his own Jewish heritage. Although he had made the journey alone, he had been "surrounded and accompanied by people and memories," "bombarded by the past," "fired up by the present." "My father has been with me here and my mother," he declared, "all my ancestors have surrounded me."[18] Wherever he had traveled in Palestine, he was tangibly aware of the ancient history of his race.

> There the old ancestors arose to life and
> strolled about and were not distant, not sanctified,
> but were people, real people, understandable, vig-
> orously hard working and yet weak people who
> had bright days and dark days; all of them, begin-
> ning with Jacob, Samson, the jovial strong man
> Saul, who became melancholy, despairing and
> petty because he could not bear … the triumph of
> youth, and then the greater man, the royal poet
> David, and all, all the others.[19]

In spite of his enthusiastic Zionism, Salten was not a practicing Jew, and his work makes clear that he regarded the books of the Old Testament primarily as "a collection of unsurpassed allegories of human life and human suffering."[20] Salten identified himself proudly with an ancient people but believed that Palestine should serve as a model utopian community for Europe as much as it should serve as a refuge for persecuted Jews. He urged all Euro-pean Jews, especially those living in comfortable circumstances, to support the project. Salten showed courage in writing this book at a time when pogroms and anti-Semitic rhetoric were at an all-time high. It remains a superb piece of travel literature, one that presents a rich and multi-faceted portrait of the fledgling Jewish State.[21] As Hermann Bahr noted, the work possesses "a fervor, a joyous opti-mism, [and] a noble pride that is unparalleled."[22]

During these years Salten took considerable pride in his chil-dren. Paul and Anna were now young adults: Paul was studying art history and showing interest in working in the film industry; Anna was also interested in the arts and studied at the city's drawing academy. Salten now began to collaborate with his daughter on a book called *Bob und Baby*, about Paul's and Anna's childhood nearly twenty years earlier when the family had lived in the old Heiligen-stadt villa. Anna drew the book's colored illustrations for Salten's text. In this work Salten demonstrated his ability to enter into a child's world and recreate both the language and the fragile mindset of his subjects. As he had already done in "Die verwickelte Geschichte" (Complicated Story, composed in 1913[23] and pub-

lished in 1920 in the essay volume *Die Dame im Spiegel*), Salten portrayed the children's father as a wise and kindly teacher who allows
his children to speak openly and to use the informal form of address even with adults and strangers. This idealized father treats his
children's fears and fancies with respect. He encourages a child's
reasoning, knowing that it has its own logic, "For he remembered:
I thought something like that, too, as a small boy. I just didn't dare
to say it."[24]

Bob und Baby served two purposes. One was to recapture the
golden age of innocent childhood; the other was to demonstrate
proper forms of adult interaction with children's eager, but fragile
egos. The work is episodic in that each of the interior chapters is
interchangeable and represents a closed adventure or experience in
the young lives of the two protagonists. However, it is also a work
of development in that the work ends when the children, having
had a number of confrontations with helpless animals, beggars, a
chimney sweep, and a cripple, begin their schooling and are forced
to assume their first duties and responsibilities. As Salten put it at
the opening of his work, "For children the whole world is full of
the blossoms of splendid surprises and amazing wonders. Every
day brings something new, brings an experience that was never
there before, until the day comes when the young child stops being
a child and becomes a 'reasonable,' grown person."[25] Once the por-
tals of childhood close, "only a breath of innocence continues to
gleam on the brow and in the eyes, a lingering sound as of heavenly
music remains for a little while in the soul, growing softer and
softer."[26] At the close of the work, the children's toys and garden
flowers call to them, "Where are you, Bob? Where do you linger,
Baby?" but the children no longer can hear them. Although they
sometimes play with their toys and go frequently into the garden,
"A separation is taking place. Gently, but inexorably. Bob and Baby
do not notice it, so softly, so slowly the golden door of their earliest childhood closes behind them."[27]

In the spring of 1925, Salten went on a reading tour to nine cities in what had been part of the old Habsburg empire and were
now in Poland and Romania. He continued to be interested in the
film industry; in 1924 he wrote the screenplay for the film *Das ver-
botene Land* (The Forbidden Country, also called *The Life of the Dalai
Lama*) for the Vita Film Company in Vienna, where he also served

as consultant on scripts. He continued to watch over developments at the Burgtheater. He had called in the newspapers for Max Paulsen's dismissal as director of the Burgtheater and, when Franz Herterich was appointed to the post, Salten, who now served as mediator between the Burgtheater and the Ministry of Education, advised the director on hirings and firings.[28]

However, as Salten's influence in the publishing business, theater, and film studios expanded, he found himself frequently at odds with old acquaintances. He was feared by some and hated by others. Salten's enormous output in domestic and foreign newspapers, his many contributions to anthologies, his appreciations as forewords and afterwords in the works of others, all contributed to the impression that Salten was not "genuine" in his writing. Karl Kraus, whose critical journal *Die Fackel* was now a quarter of a century old, was tireless in his mockery of Salten. He delighted in referring to him as a Zionist who was, nevertheless, hard at work trying to restore the Habsburg monarchy, as the anonymous author of *Josefine Mutzenbacher*, and as a Hungarian immigrant named Zsiga Salzmann. Kraus delighted in Salten's defeats, and there were few issues of *Die Fackel* which did not make mention of Salten and his weaknesses, particularly of his tendency to make feuilletons out of the most trivial of matters. One typical Kraus tirade of the period speaks of Salten's defense of the actress Else Wohlgemuth in a contractual conflict with Max Paulsen. Kraus mocked:

> The spiritless zeal with which he protests in a matter that couldn't interest anyone, even if it were not known to everyone, the endless unwinding of a thesis that is too empty for anyone to have any inclination to contradict it, the unanswerable insignificance, the apodictic boredom, ... the abysmal ability to delve into the contractual problem and personal background of the busy but not always animated Miss Wohlgemuth, and all in all the art of making so much noise, of getting up in arms about the matter and by doing this showing that he would like to make the omelet himself, but is not able to ....[29]

In Kraus's attacks, Salten became the personification of all that he hated in journalism, especially the journalist's desire to please an audience and bring in money. As Kraus had already noted in 1909:

> The best journalist in Vienna knows at any moment what is worth knowing and saying, whether about the career of a countess or the ascent of an air balloon, a session of parliament or a court ball. In western Hungary one can lay bets at night that the gypsy band leader will be on the spot with his whole orchestra within half an hour; you send someone to wake him up, he gropes for his fiddle, wakes the cymbal player, they all leap out of bed and into the carriage, and in half an hour the show is on, gay, melancholic, uninhibited, demonic, or whatever mood you care for.[30]

Because Salten had vowed, early on in his career, never to read anything written by Kraus, he rarely replied to Kraus's attacks except to make occasional mention of the bitter enmity directed at him by "the man who was born in Jicin."[31] One of the rare occasions when he covered Kraus in the papers was when he reviewed a performance of "Last Night" (Letzte Nacht), the epilogue to Kraus's masterpiece *Die letzten Tage der Menschheit* (The Last Days of Mankind), when it was performed at the Neue Freie Bühne. Kraus professed surprise that Salten would condescend to cover his work but rejected Salten's critique that it was composed of "the content of newspaper articles, set to verse and placed in the mouths of caricatured types. … In short: journalism"[32] and that the work was "not an artistic act of creation, but a publicist's attack of rage, instead."[33]

Kraus responded by asking:

> What does Mr. Felix Salten have [a heart] for? For … everything that lets itself be made into a feuilleton faster than the page is made from the tree? For nothing except for the opportunity, as one more nimbly and uninhibitedly moved than anyone else, to make the man [i.e. Kraus] pay for

his [Salten's] decades-old resentment at having been identified in his deepest triviality, and to prefer compromising his reputation for adroitness to allowing this opportunity to escape.[34]

Even Salten's friends Richard Beer-Hofmann and Arthur Schnitzler[35] occasionally accused Salten behind his back of showing jealous resentment of their successes by sometimes giving them less than stellar reviews in the papers. As a critic, Salten tried conscientiously to separate a work from its author; he looked for humanity, universality and poetic truth in the literature that he read rather than critiquing works according to their philosophical integrity or their abstract aesthetic values. In this respect he was the very opposite of the analytical Karl Kraus, and it is not surprising that two men were at odds throughout their lives as to what comprised good art. Kraus never was able to appreciate the Young Vienna authors, while Salten had little understanding for Robert Musil and Hermann Broch. Kraus might have found comfort in the fact that Salten never pandered in his criticism and was always careful to draw a distinction between an author, however talented he might be, and the particular work he was examining. A good example of this is a review that Salten wrote of the play *Die Maschinenstürmer* (The Machine Breakers), 1922, by the socialist pacifist Ernst Toller, a work written and produced while Toller, who was in prison for treason, was being honored as a cause célèbre among intellectuals throughout the German-speaking world. Salten denounced the play as a weak imitation of Hauptmann's 1893 play *Die Weber* (The Weavers) and declared, "This play is simply not strong and simply not significant. Without the emotional illumination that it receives through Ernst Toller's person and experience, it would hardly, in and of itself, have such intense, uncritical admiration … bestowed upon it."[36]

One of the nastier attacks on Salten during this period came from Franz Blei, editor of the magazine *Die Insel*, a translator and, like Salten, a critic, essayist, and author of erotic literature. In his work *Das grosse Bestiarium der Literatur* (The Great Bestiary of Literature),[37] Blei caricatured the major writers of his day as animals, birds, or insects. Of Salten he wrote:

> There is a type of fly that, under the name of
> Salten, one knows only in its state as larva. As this
> larva Salten unprepossessingly but tenaciously
> lives in and from newsprint of every color and
> every consistency. When hatched, the Salten-larva
> leads a life of one day in diverse forms. It crawls
> out as a green, as a blue, or as a black and yellow
> fly, according to the sewage on which it has lived
> out its day.[38]

Salten was critiqued by a number of his colleagues as a facile writer who spread himself too broadly, writing of anything and everything without real conviction behind his words. Occasionally, he even turned pieces of literary criticism into sentimental word pictures. Heinrich Mann may have credited Salten with having discovered him as a writer,[39] but he must have cringed when he read the epilog that Salten wrote for two Mann novellas published in the 1920s:

> Reflection rises on its own from the turmoil
> of his figures like the dust that swirls up from the
> stamping feet of dancers. It lies like a heavy vapor
> above the banquet of life that he arranges, above
> the tragedies and comedies of the eroticism that
> he reveals. And this reflection quickly pales again
> when a fresh draft of air pours in.[40]

In his satirical journal, Kraus "left it open" as to whether two works by Salten did, in fact, possess true artistry: *Josefine Mutzenbacher*, "a work unjustly fallen into oblivion," and *Bambi*.[41] Ironically, these are still the two works for which Salten is best known. In 1926 Paul Zsolnay acquired *Bambi* from Ullstein and published it in an edition of five thousand. Many printings would follow, and, in terms of sales, *Bambi* was the most successful of Salten's works that Zsolnay published.

Shortly before Christmas 1926, Salten's brother Theodor died. Salten wrote a touching tribute to this feeble-minded brother who had always shown so much innocence and spontaneity:

220

> He was shut out from life, sometimes he even
> knew for several moments that he was shut out,
> and he still enjoyed living. I miss him terribly,
> good, little delicate Theodor, with his naïve, child-
> like eyes, great white mustache, and innocently
> bright, joyous laugh. I miss him, not just because
> he was my brother but because of all the feeble-
> minded people that I know, he was one of the
> cleverest and one of the most honest; because
> among the unfortunate people that I have seen, he
> was one of the happiest, and because he lived be-
> side me like a permanent piece of my own child-
> hood.[42]

Salten's workload of these years had taken a heavy toll on his health and infringed on old friendships, and Theodor's death served as a reminder that time was passing. In 1927 he spent several weeks in a sanatorium in Dresden-Loschwitz and wrote to Schnitzler, "Dear friend, where are you? How are you? We are so distant from one another in Cottage, as if the way were too far. You can see from the place I am writing from how I am doing – in case you are still concerned about that. ... When I am back in Vienna, I'll come by. The time is so short!"[43] Schnitzler sent a warm reply, telling him, "Do not believe, that I think less and differently about you than in earlier times." He assured him that he had kept informed about Salten's activities, including "the broad resonance" achieved by Salten's "lovely Bambi book," and the fact that Salten was working on a novel. He told Salten that he had been deeply moved by his newspaper tribute to his brother Theodor and had learned "with delight" that Salten's daughter had been developing her acting skills and was now touring with Helene Thimig.[44]

When Salten returned to Vienna in late February, he did indeed stop by to see Schnitzler, who noted in his diary that his old friend was "not looking well."[45] Schnitzler resumed the careful, slightly distrustful relationship he had had with Salten for many years. When the Saltens celebrated their twenty-fifth wedding anniversary in April 1927, Schnitzler sent over a tasteful arrangement of lilies of the valley in a vase from the Wiener Werkstätte. He and Sigfried Trebitsch were especially welcome guests at the dinner held to honor this occasion, since they had been the two witnesses at the Salten wedding. Other guests included Hofmannsthal and his wife Gerty, Paul Zsolnay, journalist Bertha Zuckerkandl, writer and journalist Julius Bauer, playwright Karl Schönherr and his wife Malwine, the industrialist Siegfried von Strakosch-Feldringen and his wife Wally, actress Else Wohlgemuth and her husband Count Emmerich von Thun-Hohenstein, and actress Lilli Marberg and her architect husband Karl Hans Jaray. There were many toasts and speeches given to honor the couple, and it was a gratifying occasion for both of them.

Chapter 18: Years of Achievement

In the spring of 1927 Salten came out with a new novel, *Martin Overbeck*, that carried the subtitle *Der Roman eines reichen jungen Mannes* (The Novel of a Rich Young Man). Like *Die kleine Veronika*, *Olga Frohgemuth*, and *Die klingende Schelle*, this work was set in present-day Vienna. As in *Die klingende Schelle*, the hero is a self-centered young man whose family wealth precludes the necessity of working for a living. Just as the hero of *Die klingende Schelle* had to go through a painful process in order to learn the values of familial devotion, Martin Overbeck has to go through a harrowing ordeal before he can declare his solidarity with the proletariat and acknowledge the difficult life and the selflessness of its members. On a challenge by his father and his would-be lover, Martin leaves the family home to earn his living through hard work. He is admired by his fellow workers for his diligence, but Martin has nothing but contempt for the lower classes until he suffers an accident and is taken into the crowded quarters that one worker – a jovial former alcoholic – shares with his wife and his hunchbacked sister. While Martin heals, the tuberculosis that afflicts the worker reaches a crisis. Martin has now come to appreciate the sufferings and the simple virtues of the proletariat and takes desperate measures to help his new friends. The work ends happily with the reconciliation of all parties.

Schnitzler liked this novel no more than he had *Die klingende Schelle*, a work he had condemned not only for mimicking his own work in style and content, but also because he found its "moralizing ending false and lamely glib."[1] He reacted similarly to *Martin Overbeck*, calling it "hypocritical, stupid and badly written."[2] Richard Specht had rich praise for the characterization and moral lesson of the work but found himself wondering how the reconciliation between father, son, and girlfriend could possibly hold beyond the happy reunion that closed the work, since the hero had been through so much that it would be nearly impossible for him to return to his former life.[3] Ironically, neither of these two friends commented on Salten's realistic portrayal of the situation of the proletariat, its harsh living and working conditions, and its need to unionize.

It took a German film company to pick up on the sociopolitical aspects of the Salten novel. Almost immediately after the release of the book, the prolific cinema director Carl Boese began making a film at Berlin's Ufa studios that was advertised as an "adaptation of motifs from Felix Salten's novel 'Martin Overbeck.'" It debuted in Berlin in November, where it was proclaimed "a cheery Zille-film."[4] The German artist Heinrich Zille (1858-1929) was known for drawings and cartoons that provided both an affectionate and a critical view of Berlin's proletarian classes, leavening the tragic circumstances of their lives with humorous commentary. Zille was revered by Berlin's working poor and, especially through his frequent contributions to the satiric journals *Jugend* and *Simplicissimus*, became widely popular throughout Germany. The decision to move Salten's characters from Vienna's working class districts to the Berlin *Milljöh* recreated by Zille guaranteed the film's success by wrapping Salten's message in an already familiar, warmly sentimental story line.

That summer Salten took a break from his own writing to translate Anne Nichols's comic play *Abie's Irish Rose* into German. He translated it, he said, because, (a) two friends had begged him to,[5] (b) because he, as a Jew, was intrigued by the play's theme of Judeo-Christian strife and reconciliation, and (c) because he found the task to be a relaxing break from his newspaper work. Nichols's play tells the amusing story of how an Irish Catholic girl falls in love with a young Jewish man and how the two get married in spite of the stereotypical cultural and religious objections of the fathers of both families. Salten was used to writing film scripts in which one makes calculated adjustments of the literary works that serve as their inspiration. He took similar liberties with the Nichols play, moving the setting from New York City to Vienna and adapting the characters and their situations to suit an Austrian audience. He therefore changed the characters' names from Rose Marie to Rose Christine and from Abie to Sami to conform better to stereotypical Christian and Jewish names in his home country. In Salten's adaptation of the work, the heroine is deemed doubly "unsuitable" to the urbane Jewish father, not because she is Irish − she isn't, in the Salten version −, but because she comes from a rural farm family. Salten gave his translation/adaptation the title *Dreimal Hochzeit* (Three Marriages). Shortly before the work was to be performed on the Vienna stage, he published an apology of sorts in the *Neue Freie Presse*, asking the public not "to take this occasion more seriously then I did then or do now." His adaptation was merely a product of leisure, he noted, much like his pursuits in photography, in nature study, and in collecting old drawings and prints.[6] The play was performed by the Max Reinhardt ensemble at the Johann Strauss Theater and praised by one critic as "an excellent jargon play, one that possesss all the advantages, all the impact of this genre." Salten had "very tastefully translated" the Nichols work, and had "certainly given to it much that is effective on the German stage." The critic's only reservation was that "to understand and appreciate it fully, one must be acquainted with the pleasures of the words 'mazel tov.'"[7]

Salten was encouraged by this success to translate playwright Ashley Duke's *The Man with a Load of Mischief* into German for a production at the Burgtheater. Dukes declared that Salten's "cuts and additions to the text pleased me greatly" and that the "English character of the comedy ... readily became European."[8]

In the eight years since the war, Salten had become convinced of two things: one was the necessity of an independent Jewish state where the oppressed members of his race could live in dignity, the other was the necessity for the European states to work together in an effort to promote international understanding and prevent the outbreak of another world war. He was convinced that both these goals could best be accomplished by the younger generation. He had seen the work accomplished by young people in Palestine on his 1924 tour. At home, he was convinced that the young Richard Coudenhove-Kalergi presented the best hope for Europe's future since he promoted transcending national self-interests through participation in a European union. When Salten read Coudenhove's ground-breaking work *Pan Europa* in 1923, he had proclaimed Coudenhove "a young leader" who, unlike the men of Salten's generation who "all see out of clouded eyes, are poisoned by some hatred, [and] paralyzed by the epidemic of political parties that now rages so fiercely," "is free from any hatred, is immune against the infection of the party spirit [and] has complete equilibrium of the soul." In Salten's view, Coudenhove's mixed heritage (his father was an Austro-Hungarian diplomat, his mother was Japanese) gave him the benefit of uniting in his person "the intellectual and spiri-

tual mysteries of two great worlds." Salten applauded Coudenhove's call to replace the traditional religions with a union of technology and ethics that would bring about the establishment of the
Kantian ideal and lead to the "Europization" of the earth.[9] Like
many intellectuals of his day: Albert Einstein, Sigmund Freud, Rainer Maria Rilke, and Thomas Mann, Salten joined the Pan-Europa
movement and participated in its first Congress, that was held in
Vienna in 1926.

Soon, however, another international organization occupied
most of Salten's attention and efforts. This was the new international P.E.N.[10] movement, headquartered in England, which promoted friendship and cooperation among writers in Europe and
the United States in the belief that the universality of literature
could – and must – prevail over narrow nationalist interests. This
organization was founded in 1921 by Catharine Amy Dawson-
Scott, a prolific English writer and spiritualist, in collaboration with
the internationally renowned novelist and playwright John Galsworthy, who served as the club's first president. Just as Dawson-
Scott was the organizational force and energy behind the movement in England, an Austrian woman, novelist and journalist Grete
von Urbanitzky, was the driving force behind the establishment of
the Vienna P.E.N. Club in 1923. Arthur Schnitzler, Galsworthy's
Austrian counterpart, was heavily involved in its organization and
served as its first honorary president. Salten's co-worker at the *Neue
Freie Presse*, Raoul Auernheimer, became the first active president of
the organization and Richard Coudenhove-Kalergi its first vice-
president.[11] Salten appears to have joined its executive board in
1925.

By 1926 the Vienna P.E.N. Club was torn by various conflicting self-interests. Auernheimer felt overburdened by the demands
of the presidency and was tired of constantly standing in
Schnitzler's shadow. The club's general secretary, Grete von Urbanitzky, was actively campaigning for Salten to assume the position in his stead, but Schnitzler was aware of the partisan rivalries
that might erupt if Salten replaced Auernheimer and asked Anton
Wildgans to consider accepting the presidency instead. Wildgans
refused, and in October 1927 Salten was elected to the position by
a vote of 4-2.[12]

Salten had the energy to revitalize the organization. Whereas

Auernheimer spent hours and even days preparing every introductory speech he had to give to welcome the club's international guests, Salten was a natural speaker who could polish off speeches with the same graceful ease with which he wrote his feuilletons. Furthermore, he was able to work in harmony with Grete von Urbanitzky. Urbanitzky was a complex figure, a sympathizer with the German nationalist movement and yet a figure bound in friendship to some of Vienna's most prestigious Jewish writers. She and Salten successfully raised funds to support the club's endeavors and sharpened its profile abroad.

Salten took the initiative in expanding the Vienna P.E.N. Club's activities beyond mere social exchanges and honorary dinners. In December 1927 the Hungarian arts patron, novelist, and journalist Lajos Hatvany returned to his homeland to face charges that he had, in his writings, vilified the fascist regime of Milós Horthy. When, in February 1928, Hatvany was sentenced to pay an excessively high fine and to be confined to the penitentiary for seven years, Salten drafted a letter, cosigned by Arthur Schnitzler, that was sent to P.E.N.'s international headquarters with the request that the various national P.E.N. clubs take action to try to reduce Hatvany's sentence. "We should consider it a shame for Europe, if such an act of brutality were possible to occur without all representatives of the liberty of speech interceding in behalf of their colleagues," Salten wrote in his faulty English. Because "raising a mere protest" would bring no result, Salten declared that "a petition for mercy addressed to the Hungarian government in suitable form and coming before the whole worlds [sic] eyes from so authoritative a part were likely to have success."[13]

By asking for intercession on Hatvany's behalf, Salten was calling on P.E.N. to defend the rights of free speech. He was careful, however, not to make the issue a political one. He agreed with Galsworthy that P.E.N. should work for "healthier and more peaceful relations between nations" but at the same time not get involved "in [any] direct sense with politics."[14] Salten strongly believed that protest could only antagonize politicians, while a plea for clemency might be heeded if it came from an organization of Europe's leading intellectuals. And in truth, the plea was partially, if not entirely, successful. Hatvany's fine and sentence were reduced, and in April 1930 he was granted a pardon.

In 1928 Salten seemed to have fulfilled many of his life's ambitions and was relishing his acceptance as one of Vienna's most influential voices. In addition to the presidency of the Vienna P.E.N. Club, he was now an active member of the Rotary Club. His Sunday feuilletons in the *Neue Freie Presse* gave him the prestige of being Vienna's premier journalist. Zsolnay now began releasing Salten's collected works in anticipation of his sixtieth birthday the following year. The first volume, a collection of Salten's short stories that bore the title *Der Schrei der Liebe*, was published in June; it reprinted four of Salten's novellas.[15] And, in July, Salten reached an even more prestigious milestone when *Bambi* was simultaneously published in England and in America, where it had an initial run of 75,000 copies.

In September Paul Zsolnay published the second volume of Salten's collected works, this time a new Biblical novel entitled *Simson, das Schicksal eines Erwählten* (Samson: the Fate of a Chosen One).[16] As he had for *Der Hund von Florenz*, Salten prefaced the work with a quote from the "Hermit of Amiata." This one read: "Do not, in reading the Bible, set store by the letter, or you will go astray. Rather set store by men and the beam of light which their souls diffuse."[17] Salten began his novel midway through Samson's story, at the point where Samson tied together the tails of jackals and foxes and set them loose with burning firebrands into the Philistines' cornfields as punishment for the loss of his Philistine bride (Judges 15:4). By opening his novel with this scene, he portrays Samson as a vengeful strongman who gives little thought to the consequences of his actions. In addition, Samson makes frequent visits to the Philistine prostitutes of Gaza instead of seeking a wife among his own kind. In time, Samson's Hebrew neighbors come to view him not as a chosen one but as a mere "bully" and "a hero with the women."[18] He is, like the heroes of *Die klingende Schelle* and *Martin Overbeck*, a self-absorbed hedonist, and, like them, he suffers a change of heart only after being struck by misfortune, when he learns to appreciate the devotion of a loving partner and a faithful (dog) friend. Salten changed the Biblical tale by making Delilah a truly devoted lover who stands by Samson when he is captured and blinded, endures his captivity with him, and encourages him in his final act of bringing the temple of the Philistines down upon their enemies and themselves.

Salten was a deist, who saw God as the creator of the world but also as a force indifferent to its tragedies. At the same time, he marveled at the mysterious bond that had existed throughout the centuries between the Jews' "invisible God" and the great figures of their history; he had felt this linkage quite strongly in his 1924 visit to Palestine and his tour of its Biblical sites. *Samson* appears to reflect Salten's efforts to reconcile these two conflicting views of the deity. Samson rarely prays in the novel and never calls on his God for guidance. Yet, in one of Salten's strongest passages, the hero reflects on God both as creator and as personal companion of his people:

> He saw his God in the exquisite beauty of the landscape, in the rising and the setting sun, in the splendor of the overarching starry skies. He heard Him in the roaring of the tempest as in the low soughing of the tree-tops and the soft whispering of the wind-stirred grass on the meadows. He felt His omnipresent power in those profound laws, fixed for all eternity, which govern all life; flowering, ripening, withering, birth and death, decay and renewal succeeded one another. ... [W]henever he recalled the many destinies, the adventures, sacrifices, and mysteries that bound his people, bound himself from birth onward, to God, his heart was consumed with so fierce a flame that all else faded away, became as nothing. Even the name of Delilah.[19]

This double aspect of the deity: as an abstract creative force and as a personal, partisan God, creates ambivalences in the novel. Early in the work, when Samson cries out that "the time is gone when God sent His angels. He reveals Himself no longer in burning bushes," [20] his mother asks, "Who was with you when you destroyed our enemy's fields? ... Who guided the living torches, the jackals and foxes, so that they ran into our enemy's fields, and not into ours? ... The Lord is with Samson."[21]

After Samson has been captured and blinded, however, he repents of his earlier actions. When a stray dog befriends him, Samson recalls with anguish the pain and terror of the jackals and foxes that he had once captured and used as living firebrands. Delilah tries to comfort him by saying God had willed this act, but Samson cries out "No, it is not His will! ... It is we men, we are as cruel to animals as if no God existed."[22] Salten took a calculated risk in fleshing out the scanty report of Samson's deeds, betrayals, and acts of vengeance, and critics were divided in their opinions of the novel. Zsolnay announced the book as "a novel in which the rich colors of the Orient are united in the finest manner with European psychology and strictness of form."[23] Salten does indeed capture the psychology behind a rich variety of figures – many of whom play little or no part in the Biblical account – such as Ehi, the Philistine prisoner who rages against Samson and bides his time until he can exact his revenge on him; Zemeah, the ruler of the Philistines, who is powerless to capture Samson and suffers the taunts of his beautiful wife, Ganna; and Ganna herself, who is both attracted and repulsed by Samson's manly strength. One of Salten's critics purported to find a hidden message behind the work and wrote: "It would be false to attribute a particular slant to the book. But between the lines, rather to be felt than seen, it is written: Whoever wants to annihilate this people will himself be buried."[24]

Despite his heavy workload, Salten felt that he was leading an ideal life, one that rotated between the social and cultural events of the city and the quiet refreshing solitude of the forest. This was a schedule he tried to maintain whether he was fleeing from his Vienna home to the hunting grounds of Stockerau or from his summer vacation home at Berghof in Unterach am Attersee to concert and play performances in Salzburg. "I've experienced the charm of this kind of change for many years," he wrote. "Away from the city and into the forest, from the forest back to the city. How often a single day encompasses morning hunt and evening premiere! And it is the especially rich, splendidly vital, splendidly exhilarating days that bring forest and theater back-to-back."[25] The young poet Victor Wittner described Salten during his summers in Salzburg, wearing a Styrian loden suit with a green hat with boars' bristles and sporting a russet tan; a man "who always kept his dignity but who also understood how to smile charmingly," "of average height, upright posture, at all hours of the day fresh, groomed, elegant, always leisurely and serene in his movements, never hasty, never erratic," more a "gentleman who writes" than an "author." "What wasn't he, this tireless and always calm and dignified, also tolerant, nevertheless very vivacious and occasionally angry and vengeful man? ... He was not smug, but instead susceptible to enthusiasm, right to the end. ... And he also had humor and heart, even though he occasionally might appear haughty."[26]

Zsolnay published two more volumes of Salten's collected works in 1929: a volume reprising six of Salten's novellas appeared in May under the title *Die Geliebte des Kaisers*,[27] and a new animal book entitled *Fünfzehn Hasen – Schicksale in Wald und Feld* (Fifteen Rabbits – Fortunes in Forest and Field) that appeared in time for the Christmas market.

With *Fünfzehn Hasen* Zsolnay was eager to recapture both the sales magic of *Bambi* and Salten's unique ability to portray the brutal life of the forest through the eyes of its animal inhabitants. *Fünfzehn Hasen* is, in fact, bloodier than *Bambi*; the descriptions of the dead and dying are starker, and at one point in the novel, the birds and animals are all forced to admit that nearly all of them, at least on occasion, feed off other living creatures. In the very first chapter, in fact, a mother rabbit must explain to her son that he must not try to meet his father until he is fully grown because his father would surely kill him. The work makes references to *Bambi* throughout; Bambi and Faline both appear in the course of the story, and the rabbit Plana is a witness to Gobo's death. The work was serialized in the *Neue Freie Presse* from August 20 to October 10 of that year, to coincide with Salten's sixtieth birthday. Salten's intent was expressed in an epigraph to the work: "If you would keep men from becoming as animals, strive ever to see animals as men."[28] In his review of the work, written as an open letter to Salten, the German novelist Walter von Molo explicated this admonishment: "I believe I read your motto correctly when I found its sarcastic undertone: all too easily man becomes an animal the way he imagines an animal to be, in other words, he easily becomes bestial"; while animals are "in reality much closer to that which we so seldom are able to call human." Molo noted, for example, that, because animals never make "ethical excuses," "one immediately longs to live with them."[29]

In her review of the novel for the *Saturday Review of Literature*,

Gladys Graham instructed readers not to pay overmuch attention to the motto that introduced the work:

> [W]hile so kindly a plea for understanding comes most appropriately from the creator of Bambi and Hops, the fact remains that his distinctive achievement lies not in picturing deer and rabbits as men on four legs but in giving some essential wild quality to his animals that marks them off sharply from the domesticated human race. There is relaxation and refreshment in putting aside humanness for a time and meeting the moment with only the moment, memory too slight to be of much use, and foresight and calculation almost unknown; that is what one feels in reading the Salten animal stories.[30]

Karl Kraus, however, mocked the creatures as Salten's "rabbits with Jewish dialect." "[I]t is amazing how they [have] assimilated the enemy's speech," Kraus mocked. "Perhaps mimicry as a defense against persecution? One easily gets used to Jewish dialect being used in time of danger; when they are among themselves, they know how to talk German."[31] It is precisely the conversations of the animals that support an allegorical interpretation of the tale. When, for example, Hops suggests a union of "us rabbits, all the deer, all who are oppressed and persecuted," one inevitably thinks of Pan Europa, P.E.N., and other European organizations committed to countering war through supranational, humanistic collaboration.

1929 was, in fact, a high point for Salten and the Vienna P.E.N. Club, when, in June, the club hosted its first international P.E.N. meeting. By now the Vienna Club had greatly increased its membership, and Michael Hainisch, the first elected president of the Austrian Republic, had been offered and accepted an honorary position as club sponsor. Salten led the club in trying to reach across national and ideological lines by establishing contact with writers in Soviet Russia – and not just those honorary Russian members of International P.E.N. in England. One hundred and sixty writers from fifty different countries came to the grand opening of the international P.E.N. meeting on June 24.[32] Salten and his organizers took this meeting as an opportunity to showcase Vienna to the world. In his opening speech, Salten told the guests that their welcome to Vienna should not be taken "as the offer of a defeated people," that the welcoming smile of their hosts arose "from the intuitive notion that Austria's old power, the power of Vienna, that sole power that we intellectuals recognize, cannot be destroyed."[33] The purpose of the meeting, he said, was "to bring all of us and with us the world one step closer to that goal that unfortunately still eludes us: the detoxification of hatred and distrust between nations."[34] Salten pursued his first aim by arranging for official receptions, a performance of *The Marriage of Figaro* at the State Opera, a trip down the Danube from the abbey town of Melk through the Waldau valley to Krems, an excursion to a Viennese wine garden in Grinzing, and a closing banquet at the Hotel Panhans in the Semmering mountains. At the meetings held during the congress, the members agreed to form an executive committee to meet several times during the year in order to promote the P.E.N. program, sent a resolution to all governments that would extend writers' copyrights from thirty to fifty years, and resolved to abolish all forms of censorship. A French participant at these meetings called it "one of the most successful P.E.N. congresses ... that has ever occurred."[35] Salten was particularly gratified to see the reaction to a speech Sholem Asch made on the last day of the meeting, when he read a resolution for the protection of national minorities. "He was quite pale and the manuscript trembled in his hand," Salten recalled. "Everyone in the hall understood what Sholem Asch did not say in words: he spoke for the heart of his people, for the Russian and Polish Jews." The resolution was greeted with a spontaneous and enthusiastic standing ovation. It "marked the personal success of the congress," Salten stated, and made, "next to John Galsworthy, the strongest impression."[36]

In July Salten lost the first of his close friends from the Griensteidl days, when Hugo von Hofmannsthal, the youngest of the circle, died of a stroke just two days after the suicide of his son Franz. Since the heady days of their youth, Hofmannsthal had, through his close collaborations with Richard Strauss and Max Reinhardt, grown somewhat apart from his old friends, although he always retained a strong interest in their work and kept up the reading circle for many years. Salten noted that it was hard to establish a close relationship with Hofmannsthal, that his aristocratic, impersonal style prevented true intimacy, and yet, he wrote, Hofmannsthal "remained the only one among all the writers I have ever known who really took an active and challenging interest in the work of others." Salten mourned the loss of this great talent, whose verses he could recite by the hour. He mourned particularly the fact that "such a full life, in spite of all its fullness, remained only a torso" and that Hofmannsthal "had not yet reached his true potential."[37]

One of Hofmannsthal's last pieces of writing was a tribute that he wrote for Salten's sixtieth birthday. It was a warm appreciation that addressed all facets of Salten's writing. Salten, Hofmannsthal wrote, was a "model" writer. "He was that as a young lad and his early assurance was just as amazing as his temperament, and he is that today, and his temperament is just as amazing as his mature assurance."[38] He called Salten "passionately and from his very roots" an artist, a "tireless" critic who was "one of the most famous and most influential" of his day.[39] One of his greatest assets was his "spontaneity"; he had "the least abstract brain that one can visualize" and "the most immediate sensitivity that one can imagine."[40] Because of these qualities, his "ability to identify vicariously with young people, with old people, with illness, with health; to identify vicariously with pride, power, misery, and with being an animal" was unequaled.[41]

Paul Zsolnay had solicited statements from Hofmannsthal and other friends for his 1930 *Jahrbuch*. Max Brod, Gerhart Hauptmann, Richard Beer-Hofmann, Sigmund Freud, John Galsworthy, Paul Géraldy, Arno Holz, H. R. Lenormand, Heinrich and Thomas Mann, Franz Molnar, Fritz von Unruh, Franz Werfel, Walter von Molo, and, of course, Arthur Schnitzler sent in their appreciations, noting Salten's youthful nature, his honest critiques, his humanity, openness, and enthusiasm. Molnar paid special tribute to "Salten, the passionate hunter, [who] with the years has become the deeply sensitive friend of the forest and its inhabitants" and "Salten, the passionate critic, [who] through the years has become the affectionate friend of the theater and its people."[42] "As a young man, he set forth in these two preserves to kill," Molnar added, "and in both he acquired love."[43]

Schnitzler wrote of his old friend that Salten was "filled with the most fruitful curiosity and with the most appreciative receptivity." He was "motivated from all directions, motivating near and far, a reader of feelings and thoughts in the best sense, and at the same time self-willed and independent like few others." It was natural, he wrote, that such a man would acquire enemies as well as admirers. "What satisfaction it must be," he added, that over the years Salten's "rich, manifold, and lively talent" prevailed "to an ever greater degree" against misunderstandings that were "not always unintentional."[44]

Salten's birthday coincided with the opening of the theater season, and in both Berlin[45] and Vienna, his trilogy of one-acters, *Vom andern Ufer*, was presented in his honor. In Vienna, Leopold Kramer, who had played the three leads in these plays at their premiere some twenty years before, now reprised these roles at the Deutsches Volkstheater on September 6 in a theater filled with Salten's friends and admirers. One critic, after commenting on the graceful language of the plays and the positive, constructive tone Salten always used, even in his negative newspaper reviews, remarked on the genuine warmth shown to Salten by all who were present at this performance. "What [other] critic of high reputation and standing can still enjoy this kind of wide popularity today?" he asked.[46] During the fall several official banquets were held in Salten's honor both in Vienna and in Budapest. The Austrian *Tierschutzverein* (Animal Welfare Society) paid tribute to his animal writings by making him an honorary member and presenting him with a medal, and he made a number of reading and lecture appearances in Germany and Hungary as well as in Vienna.

Salten offered his own self-assessment:

> One speaks about the threshold of old age. [How] antiquated and ridiculous! I am not at all worn out, I play tennis, have made a dozen Alpine climbs, swim like a fish, and I like pretty young girls more than ever.... I am a passionate amateur of this lovely world. I do not want to be a dilettante of life.[47]

In November, his play *Der Gemeine* was performed at the Josefstadt Theater in a production by Max Kalbeck, with Paula Wessely in the leading role. Critics noted that the play had held up extremely well since its composition in 1901 because the characters presented "destinies" rather than "just types." One critic noted that in this work Salten, as a product of the "classical soil of the folksong," had created "the comedy or tragedy of the Viennese petit bourgeoisie in social decline"[48] and showed the new thinking of the young people who were, at the same time, its victims. Author and actors were repeatedly called to the stage at its November 22 premiere. Within the Salten family, however, these festivities were overshadowed by a more momentous occasion, the marriage of Salten's daughter Anna to the Swiss stage and film actor Hans Rehmann on November 30. At Anna's request, Arthur Schnitzler and Siegfried Trebitsch served as witnesses as they had for her parents twenty-seven years before. The wedding was followed by a family dinner in the Salten home. Salten gave a deeply moving toast to his daughter, thanking her for all that she meant to him and the joy she had brought into his life. Schnitzler, whose own daughter had committed suicide the year before, gave Salten a heartfelt embrace at his departure.[49]

Although Salten continued to be plagued with bronchial troubles and sleeplessness, he remained fit in body and in spirit. In the spring of 1930, he was given the *Wiener Bürgerrecht* (the rights of a Viennese citizen) in recognition of his sixtieth birthday and his contributions to the city as author and journalist. This honor was somewhat lower on the scale than that of "honorary citizen"; Freud, a recipient of the *Wiener Bürgerrecht* in 1924, jokingly referred to it as "essentially a ritual performance, just enough for one Sabbath."[50]

Salten remarked modestly that his aging was nothing particularly noteworthy. "For the artist, the moment when one turns sixty signifies a short pause in one's work, nothing more, a second's rest, in which one draws a breath in order to take up his workload immediately again, encouraged, refreshed and strengthened by new hopes, by new plans, and by newly opened perspectives."[51]

Chapter 19: Struggling to Maintain Optimism

Salten acquired several interesting new perspectives on the world when he was invited in the spring of 1930 to participate in an all-expense-paid three-month tour of the United States under a grant from the Carnegie Foundation. Fourteen journalists were selected for this tour. They were "bourgeois and socialists, progressives and conservatives" and came from a wide range of European nations, all of them "without distinction of nationality or world view, beneficiaries of Andrew Carnegie for the duration of this journey."[1] Salten was not blind to the fact that many Europeans had visited the country and even written about their travels there; at the same time, he believed that a visit to the United States, "the second large lobe of the lung from which the white race breathes," was essential for anybody inclined to visit more exotic climates since only there could one "sense in advance … the coming liberation of all colored peoples" and comprehend the debate occurring "between the black, brown, yellow, and white race" that was "already in progress."[2]

Salten did not share the usual visitor's awe for the Statue of Liberty that guarded the entry into New York Harbor. It was, he wrote, no longer an imposing monument to "freedom," "equality," and "brotherliness" in America, but rather a sorry symbol of "the pathos of the past." "The fact that there is no equality among people, no more than among the animals or plants, is something they know best in America," he commented.[3] Salten had trouble identifying with the black race and found it difficult even to imagine a true integration of whites and blacks in America, but he struggled to keep an open mind.[4] He deplored the restrictive laws against blacks in the South and made a point of visiting an all-black college and talking to its teachers and administrators. He saw that the blacks still were denied many of their basic rights, despite the fact that they were making such a mark on American culture through their jazz bands, gospel music, and dance steps. America's ambivalence, he said, reflected a guilty conscience over its earlier practice of slavery, which Salten referred to as America's "original sin."[5]

When he got to the southwest, Salten found the pathetic sight of Indians even more lamentable than that of the blacks. The few that he saw were "fat and seedy" and wore their feathers "like plucked turkeys" as they danced for visiting tourists in what Salten called "a deplorable comedy, a squalid parody of their own past."[6] The closest thing Salten found to true integration in America was the situation of the Chinese living in San Francisco, for there "[t]he buildings are American, the lights, the shops, the women and children are Chinese, while the men show mostly in their clothing this wonderful blend of China and America."[7] In San Francisco, he wrote, "one promenades on the final, outermost edge of the world inhabited by the white race. Europe disappears here completely."[8]

On his journey, most of it by train, Salten visited many American cities, including smaller ones like Denver and Cincinnati, admired such natural wonders as the Grand Canyon and Niagara Falls, and met individuals as varied as President Herbert Hoover and a Chicago truck driver. He visited a Hollywood film studio, a penitentiary, the Ford car factory, and Henry Ford's museum at Greenfield Village. He looked up Wilhelm Engelbrecht, a former German marine officer and American prisoner of war, who had established a farm, brought his German fiancée to the United States, and raised a family in Georgia. He conversed with film stars, society women, businessmen, young socialites, and fellow writers.

Salten found it impossible to classify the Americans. He found most of them likable and was intrigued by their ability to work and play hard. It seemed to him that the Americans "enjoy without reflection."[9] He was baffled but intrigued by the way a Cincinnati audience used the two intermissions of an outdoor performance of Verdi's *Rigoletto* to take to the dance floor and to view an ice show. In many ways he considered Henry Ford an embodiment of America, filled as he was with "so many blatant contradictions": "bold, smart, tough, unerring in every undertaking" but "clueless, full of disdain and yet full of craving in all areas of culture and of art."[10] He was amazed at how the Puritan spirit contradicted the very freedoms of which the Americans boasted. Salten regarded prohibition as a vastly ill-conceived law; it was being blatantly disregarded by all branches of society, and he was glad to learn that it would soon be revoked. He found America's "sexual prohibition" even more dangerous; it assumed that all women were virtuous and noble, thereby making men the only guilty party in matters of seduction and divorce. "The ridiculously privileged position of the woman, that barbed wire-like privilege that protects the young girl, sets horrible traps and snares for the men at every turn, intercepts and throttles them at every all-too-hasty word," he declared,[11] adding, "No publicist dares to raise his voice against the guilt-ridden woman on behalf of the innocent man."[12]

Salten was always alert to human interaction with animals. He commented on the man he saw feeding squirrels in a Washington D.C. park and a loving confrontation between a small child and a doe on the railroad tracks in the southwest. When Salten and his journalist companions were invited to see the slaughterhouses in Omaha, he alone stayed behind to spend five hours watching the complete process by which sheep, pigs, and cattle were put to death, gutted, and butchered. To him it was "hell,"[13] filled as it was with the cries of terrified animals, the stench of blood, and the lack of feeling with which the workers slit animal throats or struck them on the head with heavy mallets. Always on the lookout for particulars, he was especially haunted by the death of one single pig among the hundreds he saw slaughtered that day: "Now it has been dead for just four hours. A young, thin animal, it stood in the crowd of the others and suddenly looked up at me, with amber-colored eyes, with sorrowful, pleading, imploring eyes. Our gazes became immersed in each other's, until … until I lowered mine because I could not endure the cry for help in those eyes."[14]

In the crowded ramps that led to the slaughter, Salten saw a metaphor for war, with men taking the place of the animals. Men "are driven into war this way, into every battle; like them, they are the unsuspecting sacrifices of changing powers. Like them, single individuals want to break out and seek deliverance or escape where neither the one nor the other exists."[15] The parallels Salten saw between men and animals should, he felt, help weaken the godlike arrogance with which mankind tended to view domestic animals. He went even further when he stated, "In order not to be completely overcome by pity, it can even act as a comfort when, in looking at these wretched creatures, one reflects that, strictly speaking, we human beings endure not less but much more than they."[16]

Salten sent his travel reports to Vienna for publication in the *Neue Freie Presse*. After his return to Vienna, Zsolnay collected them in book form, and they appeared in 1931 under the deliberately ironic title *Fünf Minuten Amerika* (America in Five Minutes). In the meantime, Zsolnay published a new volume of Salten's collected works in the fall of 1930, this time a volume of animal essays with the title *Gute Gesellschaft: Erlebnisse mit Tieren* (Good Company: Experiences with Animals). In many respects this was a companion volume to his 1924 volume chronicling his "Experiences" with the great men of his age. As in that volume, most of Salten's essays had previously appeared in the newspapers, and several had been included in earlier collections of his works.[17]

In this new volume Salten expresses his joy in both wild and domesticated animals, addresses the problem of trying to keep wild animals as pets, writes of the natural affection that often exists between dogs and cats, and portrays the sufferings of animals in zoos and cages. He tells of favorite family pets and of pleasurable days spent roaming the forests and meadows in search of game. In one essay he attests to his own soft heart when confronted with captive animals of all species: "In Padua I have bought mice from children and freed them in order to save them from being tormented, in Venice a turtle in order to protect it from cruelty, and in Aquileja a young falcon because the nice street youths would otherwise have tortured it to death."[18] Salten proclaimed in this work again and again that "only when a person is no longer capable of tormenting an animal will he no longer tolerate it that small children suffer, and no one will bear it any longer that another person suffers an injustice," adding, a little sadly, "But perhaps I am ... a fool in these matters."[19]

Salten had returned from America in time to relax at his Berghof retreat in Unterach and to take in the Salzburg productions of Mozart's *Marriage of Figaro* and Maugham's *Victoria* in a staging by Max Reinhardt. That fall he also wrote and published an unusual work entitled *Teppiche* (Carpets). The work was remarkable in that it was neither a travel piece nor a work of fiction or drama, although Salten claimed that he was writing about his visit to the carpet factory in Maffersdorf, Czechoslovakia, "the way one reports about a trip or some other experience."[20]

Salten disingenuously declared that the book came to be written because (a) he happened to travel to Maffersdorf to give a reading, (b) he was naturally curious and eager to increase his basic knowledge of carpets and carpet-making, and (c) he was inspired by Fedor Mamroth's 1877 booklet about Ignaz Ginzkey and his rise from being a worker with a single loom to founding a carpet factory of world renown. As Karl Kraus delighted in pointing out, the publisher of *Teppiche*, Professor Emanuel Fischer, was "the owner of an advertisement agency that works only for first-class firms and employs only first-class writers."[21] The colored illustrations proclaiming the glories of carpets and the black-and-white photographs of the factory itself, all supplied by "Prof. Emanuel Fischer's studio," support Kraus's claim. On the other hand, the assignment reflected Salten's optimistic view of technological development, one that he had held throughout his life, whether it was developments in cars, cameras, the telephone, airplanes, or typewriters. Salten put it this way: "Whatever may be said against technology and against civilization, the same thing is being implemented in large-scale industry as is being done in film or in radio. Bit by bit the broadest layers of society will benefit qualitatively, will be nurtured to culture and to cultured needs, to cultured habits. Motion pictures and the radio contribute to this effect just as the affordability of good carpets does."[22]

Indeed, Salten had taken a particularly strong stand on technology five years earlier, when he and Stefan Zweig had gotten into a journalistic debate about whether the rapid technological developments of the day were ultimately beneficial or detrimental to European culture. The argument had begun when Salten published an essay entitled "Moderne Wunder," in which he first addressed the triumphs of science and medicine:

> If in years to come world history is written not according to the bloody battles but rather according to the intellectual achievements of nations, then one will have to praise as great triumphs not the battle of the Marne or the battle of Tannenberg, but instead Freud's teachings, Einstein's theory, the results of Steinach's research, and the discovery of insulin. ... Then one can confidently call the first quarter of the twentieth century a great time period, or will at the very least be able to say it was the interesting prelude to a new and splendid age.

The fate of the world, he claimed, belonged "to its technicians and medical researchers" while, in comparison, "politics appears to be only an ugly, and not very clean, entanglement." The train, the telephone, and the radio had brought the nations of the world closer together, and Salten even claimed that if the radio had been perfected earlier everyone might have been spared "the horrifying world war with all its consequences" since timely communications "between Berlin and London, Vienna and Belgrade, Petersburg and Paris" would have prevailed over the confusion, ambiguity, and delay of the wire services. "How much one would give to see the world in fifty or a hundred years," he exulted, concluding, "It is delightful to look down the road to the future that lies shimmering in the dawn of a new age."[23]

Zweig responded in an article that blasted the technological advances of the age as forces that eroded European culture. He condemned the "monotonizing of the world" through which "everything becomes more uniform in external forms of life, everything is reduced to the same level in a unified cultural pattern. The individual customs of nations are sanded down, clothing becomes uniform, traditions become universal." The regrettable move to uniformity, he wrote, came from the United States. "In reality we are becoming colonies of their … lifestyle," he wrote, a lifestyle that is "erratic, nervous, and aggressive." Fashions were dictated from abroad and thoughtlessly adopted by everyone. The colorful individuality of the European nations was being lost to drab conformity to American values. Since "a tremendous power lies in all these new means of mechanizing mankind," since "movies enthrall the illiterate and do not require an ounce of learning," the nations of western Europe were losing their cultural distinctions and intellectual edge. Zweig felt that the narcotic power of American entertainments was matched only by communist Russia's drive "to uniformity of world view." The nations of western Europe were threatened by "this technological uniformity" into losing their free will and hence going "without resistance into the hands of every agitator, every warmonger, every political gambler"; technology had made it impossible for Europe's intellectuals to fight the universal pull towards "pleasure … without effort." "We can do nothing, prevent nothing and change nothing," he concluded sadly, "one can only defend his own individuality."[24]

Salten responded almost immediately. He pointed out that

fashion had been dictated throughout the ages and had always swept quickly across the European continent. Similarly, there had been many dance crazes in the past, but they had not destroyed Europe's native folk dances. Salten, for one, was delighted to see how trucks were replacing the overworked horses that had once been forced to pull heavy loads up hillsides. As for the effects of radio and film on the broader public, "How can one regret that the horizons of the masses grow infinitely broader, infinitely richer?" Salten reminded Zweig that the path from the United States to Europe was not a one-way street; through the medium of radio and film, "America … will become interlaced, suffused, and imbued with European culture more thoroughly than ever before."[25]

Salten was torn between his enthusiasm for the rapid technological developments of the age, which permitted people to fly through the sky and travel beneath the surface of the ocean, and worries about the ethnic and class hatreds that appeared to be rampant both in the United States and in Europe, fueled, in large part, by the crushing, worldwide depression that hit Europe with particular force in 1931. His columns appeared to alternate between descriptions of technological achievement and descriptions of misery, hunger, and homelessness in the Vienna streets. "We live in a time of poverty," he wrote, "of the most horrible hunger that tens of thousands must endure, and of hopelessness that drives a great many old people to despair and that oppresses our young people. … Nevertheless, I will risk praising the splendors of this present time." These were recordings, which preserved the voices of great artists like Enrico Caruso; radios, which brought comfort to the sad and lonely; and the weekly newsreels, which enabled people to witness great events in the world. These three developments alone had made it possible for the proletariat to achieve "forms of existence fit for a human being."[26]

Salten could not resist being optimistic, even though he could see the devastating effects of the depression on those cultural institutions that he held most dear. The Neue Wiener Bühne, the Carl-Theater, the Bürgertheater, the Schauspielhaus, and the Renaissancebühne had all been forced to close; Josef Jarno, the director of the Renaissancebühne, had struggled for years to raise the cultural level of his audiences and to champion the works of August Strindberg, but he was now without work. Still, Salten reasoned, one must examine the theaters that had closed and compare them with the two that had opened: the new Kleine Kömodie under the direction of Rolf Jahn and the reopening of the Kammerspiele with the performance of a farce. Both of these theaters were concentrating on performing comic pieces that drew good-sized crowds and cheered a populace desperately in need of comic diversion. Salten joked that, given the circumstances, the theater critic would soon become an endangered species.[27]

Fortunately, there were still serious theaters left in Vienna, such as the Burgtheater, the Raimundtheater, and the Theater in der Josefstadt. And Salten relished his summers in Unterach am Attersee, when he could travel to Salzburg to see the Reinhardt productions at the summer festival. In the summer of 1931, however, he was somewhat hesitant about making the trip. "How ... will it look this summer with the total collapse of central Europe and with the economic crisis in the rest of the world?" he wondered, adding that it was "the memory of Hofmannsthal" that drove him to make the trip to Salzburg, since Hofmannsthal had devoted his "fabulous energy" to getting the festival firmly established there. Once in Salzburg, Salten was glad he had made the journey. Despite the harsh economic situation, there was an enthusiastic, international crowd in attendance at the festival. Salten found the theater "filled completely with Hofmannsthal's spirit." "Not just the writings of Hofmannsthal live and will remain," he concluded, "his creative idea of the Salzburg festival has also taken root, and will grow and blossom into the future."[28]

When Salten returned to Vienna, one of the first things he did was call Arthur Schnitzler and have a long telephone conversation with him about family, friends, and the world economy. Although they had now been friends for over forty years, most of this period had been marked by Schnitzler's pronounced distrust of Salten's sincerity and reliability. Salten had always been the active party in keeping up the relationship, by calling or writing to Schnitzler when they had not seen each other in some time. They were generally in accord on matters of literature and in their work with P.E.N. Still, Salten annoyed his friend when he acted on his behalf without consulting Schnitzler first; most recently, Salten had decided to hold up an author's entry into P.E.N. because his "indecent reviews" would be an "insult" to Schnitzler as the organization's honorary president.[29] In spite of these disagreements, Schnitzler had always retained an interest in Salten's activities, and whenever they spent some time alone together, Schnitzler was struck anew by Salten's charm and genuine warmth. Some days after Salten's phone call they met on the street, and Schnitzler joked about his upcoming seventieth birthday. This was, Salten would note, one of the few things Schnitzler was unable to achieve. On October 21, Schnitzler died of a cerebral hemorrhage.

Richard Beer-Hofmann and his wife Paula came to the Salten home to grieve with them; this was one of the last occasions when the two men came together as friends, since their relationship had been held together primarily through their common friendship with Schnitzler. Salten kept to his schedule of articles, reviews, and creative writing but did not talk about Schnitzler publicly except to write of his many accomplishments as a writer, saying of him that he had given the world an understanding of "the true Vienna, heartily buoyant, melancholic yet thoughtful, overflowing in spirit, in soul, and in music." Schnitzler was, Salten affirmed, a "true … and unique poet" and "one of the noblest and most uncorrupted human beings" he had known.[30] When Anton Wildgans, their mutual friend who was once again director of the Burgtheater, asked Salten to speak at the memorial service he was planning for Schnitzler, Salten declined, saying, "My dismay and my broken-heartedness over Schnitzler's loss make me incapable of speaking publicly about him. I am unable to be the author or the performer of my pain."[31] Many of Salten's generation were dying, and many of his feuilletons were now necrologies; in the coming months, he would write about the deaths of actor-director Josef Jarno, journalist Maximilian Harden's widow Selma Aaron, novelist Edgar Wallace, the founder of the Eastman Kodak company George Eastman, former Austrian foreign minister Count Ottokar Czernin, and, with genuine distress, of poet and Burgtheater director Anton Wildgans.

There was a tinge of melancholy in much of Salten's writing of this period; many of his activities now recalled memories of the past. When he went to Berlin to watch Reinhardt rehearse a Hauptmann play, he recalled earlier Reinhardt rehearsals with Hofmannsthal and "how Hofmannsthal had sat here, both excited and restrained, diffident and superior, charming and momentarily tart. How he leapt up and stomped nervously back and forth out in the corridor, and how he became more and more enchanted, captivated and inflamed by Reinhardt."[32] He published a long account of Louise von Coburg's 1904 escape from the insane asylum in the Christmas edition of the *Neue Freie Presse*[33] and then, almost immediately, turned that account into a play. Finally, he continued to publish a series of articles about his boyhood under the title *Die Währinger Erinnerungen* (Memories from Währing).

Even Salten's new novel of 1931, *Freunde aus aller Welt, Roman eines zoologischen Gartens* (Friends from All Over the World, a Novel of a Zoo[34]) was constructed in large part out of memories of specific animals from different zoos that Salten had visited over the years: of a tame and gentle wolf in the Schönbrunn zoo tormented and badly mauled by the wild she-wolf with which it was placed,[35] and of an elephant in the Dresden zoo that had a white goat as its closest companion.[36] The book was augmented with photographs from zoos in Stellingen (Hamburg), Dresden, Munich, and Schönbrunn (Vienna), which illustrated, wherever possible, the very animals Salten described.

Salten had once written admiringly of Karl Hagenbeck, animal supplier to zoos all over the world, praising him for his "humanity." "When he began, the showing of animals was a miserable industry of show-booths," Salten had noted. "Now it is a multibranched, large-scale resource for science and for general education."[37] In *Freunde aus aller Welt* Salten portrays zoo workers as individuals, with some of them rough and callous and some loving and kind. The zoo's director is a well-intentioned man who has fought for funding to create ample space and a natural habitat for his birds of prey. He dreams of the improvements he would make for all his animals if he only had the funding to do so: "What a zoo he would open then! On a huge terrain, that would include whole forest areas, wide stretches of grasslands, rocks and large bodies of water."[38] Visitors would be able to see how the animals lived "in the fashion intended for them by nature." The problem, as Salten now presents it, is that the director doesn't think about the fact "that one should not catch the wild creatures at all, that one should not haul the children of the tropics to the raw climate of the north, … that mankind had, for millennia, inflicted too much cruelty on animals and that it was finally time to stop."[39]

Salten made it a point of visiting – and revisiting – the great zoos of Europe. In some respects these visits had the masochistic aspect of his childhood visits to the dissection rooms in the Allgemeines Krankenhaus and his daylong tour of the Omaha, Nebraska, slaughterhouses, since he saw the misery in the eyes of the captive creatures and studied the various ways in which they had lost their fear of mankind to become beggars or performers for the public. Even in Dresden, "one of the best and most merciful zoos that one can find," where the animals are "cared for with understanding and with love," the animals are "all sentenced to life imprisonment and are all innocent," he noted. "The whole world knows that these imprisoned creatures are innocent, but most people stroll indifferently past the dreadful, distressful tragedies that are played out behind iron bars."[40]

Although the animal models for Salten's novel come from several zoos, it is the Dresden zoo with its progressive director[41] that is represented in the work, to show the depth of suffering endured by captive animals in even the best of circumstances. Salten gives all the caged animals names, just as he did for the deer and rabbits in his previous works dealing with animals; here, too, the animals converse with one another. A mouse named Vasta witnesses many of the tragedies of the zoo and serves as message bearer from cage to cage. Salten describes several visitors to the zoo, emphasizing those who are sympathetic to the animals: the director's friend Dr. Wollet (probably a self-portrait), the little boy Bob (probably Salten's son, Paul), a former prisoner, and an overly sensitive young man so overcome with a sense of the wrong done to the caged animals that he seeks his own death in the elephant's cage. The father of the young suicide states the basic idea behind Salten's novel: "Many people assert that [the zoo] is useful and instructive, a cultural necessity, and a joy for children and adults! ... I don't, I really don't! ... [T]here will be a true culture only when people no longer have any joy in imprisoned animals; ... there will be a true culture only when they experience such a zoo no longer as a delight but as a place of horror."[42]

More interesting are the musings of a young man who has been unjustly imprisoned and only recently released by the authorities; he identifies with the caged animals since they, too, are innocent of any crime and yet must live out their lives in the confines of this outdoor prison. "Proletarian childhood," he muses, as he sees two young lion clubs being carried away from their mother for sale to another zoo, and he makes the prediction: "One day, it will break out in them. Against constraint! Against injustice!" ... [T]here won't be any joshing when the beast of prey awakens in the proletariat."[43] Salten seldom spoke politically, except on issues that directly affected the Jewish populace, but he retained strong memories of the proletarian neighbors of his childhood and on occasion spoke out on their behalf.[44] He was aware of the impotent rage that filled the hearts of oppressed individuals and could relate it to the emotions of a raging fox, the lion cubs' grief-stricken mother, and the elephant deprived of its goat companion.

Still, Salten continued to eschew political activity as something base. He saw politics as a divisive force and lauded instead works of art and social movements that promoted "the true relationships of one human being to another," something that was made possible only "when they are not poisoned and indoctrinated by politics."[45] He continued to believe that Hitler represented a transient anomaly and that memory of the horrors of the World War would work as a preventative among European nations. "It is undeniable," he wrote, "that things are not at all good, neither in Austria nor anywhere else in Europe. ... But the madness of war, thank God, has past. Whatever one says, it can hardly happen again, at least not as long as we and our children are alive."[46]

Still, when Salten was invited to participate in a "discussion" about Hitler's allegations that "the Jew" was guilty of Germany's economic disaster, Salten weighed in: "Today we are much too aware of the parasites of the economy to be able to designate the Jews in general as the sole guilty parties," he declared, noting that "heavy industry is not in their hands nor do they possess the immense wealth of forests, fields, and feudal estates."[47] Salten presented his own theory that the Jews embodied "two elements of great power" and that these elements were shaped by the environments in which they lived. He called the first "Mosaic"; this was the element that "is directed again and again against the Pharaoh and most passionately desires again and again: out from servitude! The other element, which reached its high point with King David and his son, is that similarly inherent passionate drive to conservatism: singers of psalms, builders of palaces and temples, pillars of the establishment, preservers of tradition. According to the environment in which the Jews live, the Mosaic or the royal Davidic element emerges."[48] For this reason, he declared, conditions in Russia fostered the success of Trotsky while conditions in England brought forth Benjamin Disraeli and Isaac Rufus.

When Salten looked for positive signs that confirmed his optimistic view that a new and better future loomed ahead, he found it in the international crowds that came to the Salzburg festival: "One remembers, once again, that there are other countries beyond the barricaded German borders. One feels, once again, the presence of a big, wide world in which there are more important worries than haggling over a winning two-vote majority, of more powerful, brighter horizons than the German heaven, that is nailed shut and boarded up by Hitler and his opponents." Salten called on the festival planners to expand their scope and invite artists from all over Europe to perform in Salzburg. "The English, the French, the Italians, the Czechs should come. If all the music-makers from Spain to Scandinavia gathered in Salzburg, a meeting place would be created that would be truly unique." It would, he said, be a "musical-spiritual Olympics."[49]

Salten reacted in a similarly optimistic manner when he attended the International P.E.N. Congress held in Budapest in May 1932. He noted that "intellectuals of completely different attitudes" gathered there, "those oriented completely to the right, those emphatically all the way to the left, and, in between, completely impartial men (like myself)." Political extremists such as the socialist-pacifist German playwright Ernst Toller and the fascist-oriented Italian futurist poet Filippo Tommaso Marinetti took to the floor to present passionately opposing views, but, Salten noted, they did so without coming into open conflict: "One needed only to open the valves a little bit and the longing of everyone burst forth: the demand for activity, for active resistance against the indoctrination of peoples, against trigger-happy party terror, against every undertaking that prevents peace and understanding." Salten found the debates refreshing: "The representatives of the most different schools of thought [began] to sense that the human being is more important than the party man, that contrasting views are by no means a reason for hostility. That is the purpose and the goal of the P.E.N. Club." Perhaps Salten's impartiality blinded him to the passions of many of his fellow members when he declared that, since men of all political persuasions were welcome at these P.E.N. meetings, any unified action taken by its P.E.N. must be taken slowly and with great care: "We are agreed that the path that the International P.E.N. Club now takes is steep, cumbersome, and passable only one step at a time, but that this pathway must finally take us, however slowly, to our goal."[50]

Salten's personal goal was to assist in the creation of an exemplary world community of artists, writers, and musicians that would help further the fulfillment of Richard Coudenhove-Kalergi's dream of a true United States of Europe. In this respect, he was in full agreement with Stefan Zweig's idea of the primacy of culture over politics and the need to preserve that culture at all costs. Unfortunately, Salten would soon learn that it was impossible to maintain a united cultural front against the rising tide of nationalist fascism now sweeping across central Europe.

Chapter 20: A Turning Point

Over the years Salten had watched the cinema develop from silent, flickering images to slick, sound-filled entertainment for the masses. Although he was the first to admit that it had not yet achieved a high cultural status, he remained intensely interested in the progress of the medium and insisted that "film has in fact contributed more to civilizing the world and broadening the public's horizons than any other entertainment or educational factor." He continued to be optimistic about film's artistic potential, despite the fact that, "for the time being, the broad masses force and require kitsch."[1] As long as times were bad, film audiences wanted nothing more than "a quick high" that would probably cause "no lasting harm." "And so the dance of a humanity that never was, that is even less likely today, flickers on the screen: young girls who achieve riches, young lads who are true princes of fortune and are coddled by their successes." The filmgoer "lets himself be seduced for two hours by these fantasies" and "finds the relaxation for the moment that is so necessary."[2] Salten understood the film producers' demand for happy endings since it was "born of the instinct that, after the war as well as during the war, people did not have the nerves to bear unhappy endings." Salten felt that the eternally happy ending was dangerous, however, since it had "almost completely destroyed a sense for tragedy, especially in the youth."[3] Still, he was certain that when better times came, audiences would again become more selective in their entertainments and film would "change for the better."[4]

In New York Salten had been overwhelmed by the Paramount Theater on Broadway, a combination of "gigantic cathedral" and "colossal opera house," which he described as "cinema's triumphant cry."[5] At this time the cinema was enjoying unprecedented popularity all over the world, and Vienna alone had 178 movie houses. When Salten returned home, he found the Sascha film studio of Vienna rebuilding its own film palace, the Eos-Lichtspiele, into an enlarged theater for sound with seating for fourteen hundred. As one of the most modern sound theaters on the continent, it boasted special devices for the hard of hearing, several smoking salons, and a promenade terrace.[6] It opened on March 13, 1931, with a gala evening for invited guests only, which was arranged by the city's Concordia organization of writers and journalists. The highlight of the evening was the premiere of the Sascha film *Sturm im Wasserglas* (Tempest in a Teapot), that featured Hansi Niese in the leading role. Salten wrote the film dialogue[7] from what had originally been a theatrical piece by Bruno Frank; the film recounted a journalist's intervention when an elderly woman's beloved dog was seized and scheduled for execution because she could not pay the town's new, arbitrarily high dog taxes. The happy ending united the dog owner with the man who had been in charge of the dog during its captivity, and the journalist with the wife of the philandering bureaucrat who had initiated the cruel tax. The papers reported that the Sascha studios had, with this film, "brilliantly proven Austria's competencies in the field of the sound film industry."[8]

Salten's second film venture of 1931 was for the Richard Oswald production company, a Berlin firm. Once again the film was based on a play, this time from the pen of Ladislaus Fodor, entitled *A templom, egere* and translated into German as *Arm wie eine Kirchenmaus* (As Poor as a Church Mouse). This had a characteristic plot of the period about a poor plain Jane who is a highly skilled secretary and who not only replaces the beautiful but lackadaisical secretary at a large Vienna bank but wins the heart of the bank director as well. Salten co-authored the script with Heinz Goldberg, with Salten supplying "the pretty conceits that were effortlessly fused with the original plot."[9]

The following year Salten worked on his last film script, this time based on a play by Dario Niccodemi entitled *Scampolo*.[10] Salten wrote the original screenplay with assistance from the writers Max Kolpé and Billy Wilder. This Sascha film transposed the Roman setting of the play to Vienna; Scampolo is a lovable waif who lives in a telephone booth and ekes out a living by delivering laundry. She falls in love with a once-wealthy man who is down on his luck. At the close of the film, his wealth is restored and he carries her off with him to London. The plot is complicated by a banker's attempted seduction of the innocent Scampolo. When the hero confronts the banker to scold him for his action, he uses a Salten-like metaphor, accusing the banker of acting like a rich "Rockefeller" who entices a poor man's much-loved "dog" away from him.[11] The Franz Waxmann songs, such as "Ach wie ist das Leben schön"

(Oh, How Lovely Life Is), reflect Salten's stubborn optimism in those bleak times.

Despite this optimism, however, Salten was becoming increasingly aware that he was part of the old generation; he was, after all, over thirty-five years older than his two collaborators on *Scampolo*, and a good many of his P.E.N. colleagues were younger and more politicized than he. Worse, friends from his generation were dying off. In March 1932 he lost one of his oldest friends when Richard Specht died; it was Specht who had introduced Salten to the Berghof near Unterach am Attersee where for decades Salten had spent a good portion of every summer.

Then in June Salten's family suffered the first of several tragedies that put Salten under increased stress. His son Paul had gotten involved in film-making, occasionally as an extra, more frequently as a film editor. He, like his father, traveled between Berlin, Budapest, and Vienna to work with various film studios, and on one of his trips from Berlin to Vienna he suffered a serious automobile accident. Although he appeared to recover from this accident and was able to continue his film work, he began to suffer pain and serious nervous disorders in the fall of 1933, and these only increased with time.

In 1932 Zsolnay printed his last volume of Salten's collected fiction, this time a collection of previously published short stories with the title *Mizzi*. But Salten was also working on a new novel, one that Zsolnay would publish in 1933. *Florian* told the life story of a royal Lipizzan stallion, setting the horse's story against the background of the dying Habsburg empire. It is a skillful blending of meticulously observed animal life and knowledgeable history of the Austrian royal court during its decline and fall. The life, triumphs, and sufferings of an exemplary horse play out against the intrigues, changing fashions, and politics of the court. As Salten put it, "the life story of this white Lipizzan horse blossomed as a dream and, inextricably linked to it, all the splendor of the Habsburg court, together with the misery that followed the demise of the Habsburgs."[12]

The animals in *Florian* do not converse with one another, although, at several points in the novel, Salten suggests a dialogue through his interpretation of the animals' movements and attitudes, especially in the interactions between Florian and a fox terrier named Bosco, who form a deep, co-dependent relationship with one another. Conversation is unnecessary to describe Florian's emotions when he is separated from the dog or when he feels the touch of a whip for the first time in his life; his feelings are portrayed through Salten's readings of the horse's body movements. When, for example, Florian first performs in public, "His heart beat a violent tattoo, but he had himself under control. He concentrated and gradually submerged everything but his curiosity and his instinctive willingness to respond to the master. His beautiful dark eyes shone. His ears showed listening expectancy. His whole body listened, waited." Despite his impulse to neigh, he "thought better of it. He would have liked to snort but his instinct commanded him not to disturb the fluid seconds of waiting. His nostrils opened wide, exposed their rosy interiors, contracted and opened again."[13] Salten summarizes the moment by noting that "Age-old tradition, spanning many centuries, struggled forth in Florian as something akin to genius, making it easy for him to fulfill his destiny."[14]

The portrayals of royalty are as compelling as those of the animals. Franz Josef's strict sense of duty and tradition, Franz Ferdinand's brutal coarseness and his impatience to ascend to the throne and modernize the empire, Prince Edward VII of England's relaxed loftiness of character, Karl I's unobtrusive modernity – all are portrayed through their relationship to and appreciation of the Lipizzan stallions. Under Franz Josef's reign, Florian rises to the position of lead horse at the Spanish Riding School, then becomes one of the horses chosen to pull the imperial coach, until the tragedies of the royal heir's murder and the First World War intervene to end the secure and loving world of the imperial horses. Even before Florian's own future is directly affected, the deaths of the fox terrier Bosco and of the stable boy Anton cast a pall over Florian's life. After the war he is auctioned off. After being misused by a city coachman, he is sold to a former stable boy from the Spanish Riding School, is housed with cows, and used to pull a milk wagon before he is finally released from his labor and allowed to spend his remaining years in a suburban meadow.[15]

The novel spans the years 1901 to 1921; at the close of the novel, Neustift, a former aristocrat who had first become acquainted with Florian as a newborn foal, happens to meet the horse in his meadow retreat and reflects on the hard times that the horse

254

and he have survived. As he caresses the horse, Florian "sniffs at Neustift" and "remembers, not clearly yet unerringly, that this is a man from the strangely vanished past for which he is forever longing. In misty pictures the past rises before him." Neustift reflects: "we two ... what have we been? Once upon a time. Once! Now we are through, we two. Nobody needs us any longer. And we mean nothing. We are through, you and I...." Florian, however, "is incapable of sentimentalities. Gently he disengages himself from the man's embrace and stands for another few moments beside him, as if in deep thought. Then he slowly moves away. Slowly he strides across the meadow, is distinct, is a pale luminous shadow in the falling mantle of the night."

Florian is Salten's most perfect blending of animal and human existences and a compelling portrayal of the "secret door" that forever separates the two, "no matter how longingly they beat against it."[16] The work quickly went into a second printing at Zsolnay's and came out in an American edition in 1934. One American critic declared that *Florian* was a "revelation, comparable to the revelation of 'Nijinsky' to those who thought the ballet a triviality,"[17] while another one enthusiastically wrote, "If there are enough people in the world to appreciate this book and make it a success, we shall not despair of humanity, though kings are killed, and great lords die, and evil flourishes in high places. There is still the fineness of breeding in man and horse and dog, still an understanding of the value of beauty, in the clean-run up-lands of high-thinking and fine-living."[18]

Florian was one of Salten's few triumphs of 1933 in a year that can best be characterized as the start of Salten's own decline. The year began auspiciously enough with the January premiere of Salten's latest play, *Louise von Koburg*, at the Deutsches Volkstheater. The production was directed by Schnitzler's son, Heinrich, while Salten's son-in-law, Hans Rehmann, played the role of Géza Mettachich. Salten's friend Ernst Lothar praised the play, noting, "It is high time that one unequivocally show people – at least on the stage – what these [pre-war years] were like: how beautiful and how dreadful."[19] With his book and his play, Salten had created two remarkable documents of that age – an age already being overly romanticized in the films of that period.[20]

Salten's final involvement in film work took place in late 1932, when he had provided the story line for one film and served as special consultant for another; both premiered in Berlin in late February 1933, some three weeks after Adolf Hitler had been named Chancellor of Germany. The first, *Ich und die Kaiserin* (The Empress and I) is typical of the period, a light work of mistaken identity in which a marquis and the empress's pretty young hairdresser are united. The second film was Max Ophüls's treatment of Schnitzler's *Liebelei* (Flirtation), his breakthrough play of 1894. For Salten it was a labor of love to serve as adaptor and consultant on the film, particularly since his son, Paul, was also involved in the production as an assistant director and film editor. It was the last film in which Salten would play an active role. Three days after its Berlin premiere, the German *Reichstag* burned.

Hitler used the Reichstag fire as an excuse for declaring a state of emergency and consolidating his own dictatorial powers. The Nazis rounded up communists, Jews, and socialists, and many writers and artists fled the country. Then, on May 10, Joseph Goebbels, propaganda minister of the National Socialist Party, orchestrated book burnings at thirty-four German universities, demonstratively ridding the nation of the "intellectual garbage of the past."[21] Schnitzler's *Liebelei* was burned there, along with the books of Albert Einstein and Sigmund Freud, and the works of many of Salten's other friends, such as Franz Werfel, Stefan Zweig, Jakob Wassermann, Max Brod, Heinrich Mann, and Sholem Asch. Salten himself was temporarily spared, but, in fact, the situation in Germany itself was chaotic. Books by Jewish authors were still sold in a number of cities, while they were banned in some and burned in others. Many Jewish writers were less than eager to speak up, hoping that if they lay low, things would blow over and they could regain their German markets. The timing of these burnings was especially critical, for the annual meeting of the International P.E.N. Club was scheduled to begin on May 25 in Ragusa [Dubrovnik], in what is now Croatia. Salten was now Honorary President of the Vienna P.E.N. Club, having succeeded Arthur Schnitzler in this position in an effort to provide stability to the organization, and he was well aware of the critical nature of the meetings. He had two weeks to come up with a plan for what was certain to be a contentious meeting.

One of the first things he did was to ask Stefan Zweig to join the Austrian delegation to Ragusa as one who, because of his international standing and his pacifism, might serve as a voice of reason, but Zweig was on his own flight from Vienna and declined the invitation, stating, "At this time I consider every public appearance and action of Jewish-German writers at congresses to be a false move. *Others* must take up our cause, because it is a matter of the freedom and honor of the [written] word."[22] Zweig, who, by his own admission, was a man whose "natural attitutude to all dangerous situations has always been to evade them,"[23] suggested instead that he and several of the most distinguished German-Jewish writers -- Salten, Franz Werfel, Richard Beer-Hofmann, Josef Roth, Jakob Wassermann, and Alfred Döblin -- write a manifesto that would make no demands of the Germans but would instead serve "as a masterpiece of German prose, as a document for the ages" to remind the Germans of the Jewish contributions to German culture. Salten questioned the feasibility of such an undertaking, noting that he had not laid eyes on either Beer-Hofmann or Werfel in the past weeks, even though he knew that both were in Vienna. Rather than gathering together to cooperate on a manifesto, it seemed to him at the present time "as if the Jews were, of their own accord, avoiding one another" out of fear of being reproached for their Jewishness.

Salten told Zweig, however, that he was not to be dissuaded from attending the Ragusa conference:

> I cannot share your view that we Jewish-German writers should avoid appearing and speaking at congresses. I now consider it my duty to go to Ragusa and to look people like Hinkels [sic],[24] Johst,[25] *e tutti quanti* in the eye. After all, I was unanimously elected to the position of honorary president of the Vienna P.E.N. Club by Catholics, Aryans, and people of all party affiliations. If I were to stay away from Ragusa, it would give rise to all kinds of misinterpretation. One could say I lacked the courage to face up to the Nazi gentlemen, one could say I was submitting to the programmatic cleansing of the brutal German forces. One could and would say everything imaginable

that one cannot say if I appear in accordance with my duty, my rights, and my conviction.[26]

Zweig quickly assured Salten, "you have never been more necessary," adding, "You proved in Budapest that you personally proceed in such cases in the most tactful and sure manner. I am afraid only of those who are pushy, who like to hear themselves bark, and for whom noise is their favorite element of existence."[27]

Salten told Zweig that he had discussed the matter with all of Vienna P.E.N.'s executive committee members and all had approved his determination to address the issue of the book burnings, should it become necessary, and say "that the attack by any one nation against the internal affairs of another nation contradicted the aims of the International P.E.N. Club, that the Vienna P.E.N. Club could not permit an attack against the Germans, and that the Austrian delegation would, if a debate of that nature was nevertheless introduced, lodge a protest and leave the hall."[28]

Salten's argument that the International P.E.N. should not get involved in the internal party politics of any member country was in full accord with the policy that had been propagated by P.E.N.'s first international president, John Galsworthy. Salten not only ascribed to this policy, he was convinced that this international organization of writers and editors must hold together on international soil if the aim of a peaceful, unified Europe should ever be realized. He believed further that isolating Germany could serve no useful purpose. As he had already shown when he spoke out at the P.E.N. meeting of 1928 on behalf of the imprisoned Hungarian writer Lajos Hatvany, and in 1931 when he pled for clemency for the German pacificist Carl von Ossietzky,[29] Salten believed that the P.E.N. organization was well within its charter when it pled for leniency but that it violated the statutes of the international organization when it expressly condemned the actions of any nation or political party.

This stance united him with the Vienna P.E.N. Club secretary, Grete von Urbanitzky, although their reasoning was very different. At a meeting of the executive committee, Urbanitzky betrayed her own National Socialist leanings by declaring that she had spent several months in Germany and that "the Vienna newspapers included untrue reports about affairs in Germany." Salten did not dispute the reports in the Vienna newspapers but argued instead that the members of the Vienna P.E.N. Club "live in a German-speaking area," which made them "to a high degree one family." For this reason they must not "behave as hostile brothers" in an international forum.[30] "We must remember that we are an international club," he continued; "The most fervent effort of all intellectuals strives for international unity." As a Jew he considered himself "a member of the German living space," especially since "there isn't any international Jewry." For this reason it was impossible "to exclude Jewish people from the living space of a nation." Nevertheless, he said, as a Jew, he "would like to avoid our saying unfriendly words against Germany." He closed his speech by declaring, with astonishing political naiveté, "I refuse to attack Germany because of a temporary situation."[31]

On May 22 Salten held a meeting at his home in Cottagegasse to share the executive committee's decision to remain neutral with the members of the Vienna P.E.N. board and to ask for the board's concurrence that all delegates to the Ragusa meetings submit to this policy. Salten defended the policy by noting once again the thousand years of a unified German/Austrian culture, declaring, "no German government may reproach us for joining the battle against the German nation."[32] Robert Neumann, for one, protested that the executive committee had made the unilateral decision for neutrality without first consulting the board members, but by the end of the evening, he and the other board members, save one, supported the committee decision, once Salten agreed to delete the phrase that stated that the Austrian delegates must leave the hall in the event of an anti-German debate. The single dissenting vote came from Hugo Sonnenschein, a communist writer better known as "Sonka," who went to Ragusa as a representative of Austria's socialist writers.

The official German delegation to the meetings was made up of Hanns Martin Elster, Fritz Otto Busch, and Edgar von Schmidt-Pauli.[33] Of these delegates, the banned authors most respected Elster, since, in his edited collections of contemporary literature, he had included such writers as Thomas Mann, Stefan Zweig, Jakob Wassermann, and Alfred Döblin and in 1931 had been active in promoting an international Heinrich Heine Society. Salten was doubtless hoping that Elster might help forestall a confrontation between liberal and nationalist forces in Ragusa and serve as a mediator between the two camps. However, this hope had already been rendered unpromising by the German P.E.N. Club's deliberate breach of the international P.E.N. charter when, one month prior to the meeting, it had taken the action of removing all communists, liberals, and Jews from its membership rolls. Distinguished literary figures such as Heinrich and Thomas Mann, Jakob Wassermann, Else Lasker-Schüler, Erich Maria Remarque, and Alfred Döblin were stripped of their P.E.N. membership without a word of protest from those German writers not affected by the cleansing. Because the German P.E.N. Club was now subject to the cultural politics of the National Socialist party, its censorship by the international organization appeared inevitable.

Salten was doubtless naive in his belief that the Vienna P.E.N. Club should – and could – avoid being drawn into active debate at the Ragusa meeting. Because of the close cultural ties between Germany and Austria, because many of the burned books were penned by Austrian writers, it was nearly impossible to expect the membership of the Vienna P.E.N. Club to remain silent at the meeting. It counted communists and German nationalists, Catholics and Jews among its membership, and Salten was in the unenviable position of trying to represent them all. He apparently was hoping that the spirit of tolerance that had characterized the 1932 meeting in Budapest might again prevail and prevent an open rift at Ragusa, despite the deep passions that threatened to break the group into two hostile camps. He still believed that, by taking a neutral stance, he could maintain peace among all members of the Vienna P.E.N. Club while avoiding a direct confrontation with the Germans.

It is unlikely, even had his friends and colleagues Arthur Schnitzler and John Galsworthy been heading the Austrian and international delegations, that a confrontation could have been avoided.[34] Salten could only hope that the situation could be diffused by the German P.E.N.'s joining in the disavowal of the Nazi book burnings. And, in fact, in meetings prior to the official opening of the congress, the new international president, H. G. Wells, worked frantically behind the scenes to try to avoid a public rift. A member of the American delegation, Henry Seidel Canby, cofounder and editor of the *Saturday Review of Literature*, set forth a moderately worded protest against any actions by a member nation that persecuted writers or restricted their access to P.E.N. Wells sat down with the American delegation, with the Germans, and with members of the French and Belgian delegations to hammer out a somewhat stronger statement that would clearly affirm the P.E.N. charter's policy of the necessity of free speech and of membership not defined or constrained by race, religion or party politics. The Germans finally agreed to allow either the American resolution or the Franco-Belgian one to be put forth and voted on without discussion; after its passage, individual members might speak directly and more forcibly to the specific situation in Germany. Unfortunately, however, things did not go according to plan.

On the first day of the official meetings, after the American resolution was presented, the English general secretary, Hermon Ould, took to his feet and directly asked the German delegates whether they had "protested against the ill-treatment of German intellectuals and the burning of books" and whether it was true that the Berlin club had sent a notice to its members "depriving those of communist or 'similar' views of their rights of membership."[35] As various delegates insisted that a discussion of the German issue must precede passage of the resolution, the Germans threatened to withdraw their support of it and to walk out of the meetings. Wells insisted that Ould's questions were legitimate and said that he was now willing to give the floor to Ernst Toller, the German expatriate dramatist who had been expelled from the German P.E.N. Club and who was scheduled to speak the next day.[36] At this point the German delegation left the hall, as did some of the Swiss and Dutch delegates. Grete von Urbanitzky also left the hall with a number of the Austrians.[37] Except for the Germans, most returned to their seats once they had made their point through this protest.

Salten remained in the hall. He felt that the P.E.N. leadership had, "on impulse," prevented the international organization from passing its resolution while Germany was still in the hall. He would declare later that the German delegates had appreciated Ernst Toller's tact when Toller had agreed to speak only after passage of the resolution, and that they had further agreed to respond to charges made against them at that time by Sholem Asch. It was Salten's belief that "the fate of hundreds of intellectuals in Germany" could well have been alleviated had the Germans been present to accept the resolution and carry it back with them to their homeland. For these reasons, Salten rose to give the speech he had prepared in the event of such a crisis. He had always identified himself, he said, as a "German Jew" and had always had "friendly association with German poets and writers, without people asking one another about their 'origin.'" The delegates could therefore imagine, he said, "with what emotions I regard the present situation in Germany. Nevertheless, I have tried to make it possible to keep the German delegates in the congress, out of loyalty to the goals of the P.E.N. Club, which are now threatened!"[38]

After Ernst Toller's eloquent and impassioned speech, however, the majority of delegates regarded the German exodus as a positive event. On behalf of the Union of Socialist Writers of Austria, Salten's P.E.N. opponent Sonka presented a resolution expressing solidarity with the persecuted German writers, but this resolution never came to a vote. The French-Belgian resolution – the resolution the German delegates had agreed to prior to the general meeting – passed with twelve votes in favor of the motion, two against, and fourteen abstentions.[39] Salten was one of those voting in its favor.

When Salten returned home, he was horrified to see how the leftist newspapers had twisted his words to make him a traitor to his craft and the patsy of the new German government. Even before he had left for Ragusa, somebody had leaked Salten's intentions to the press, misinterpreted his motives, and asked in outrage, "How is it that the most significant writers and poets of Germany have been expelled, imprisoned, and tortured – but that doesn't affect the writers of other countries?" The article, which appeared under the headline "Felix Salten for the Nazis," closed with the question, "Does Mr. Felix Salten believe that the Nazis will not notice that he is a Jew and that his name is actually Salzmann?"[40] The socialist *Arbeiter-Zeitung* called Salten a "Jew of the Third Reich"[41] and declared that he had, in his speech at Ragusa, pandered to the Nazis.[42] Friedrich Torberg published a piece in *Die neue Weltbühne* in which he declared that Salten had, to be sure, protested against the treatment of the Germans but that it was "not the Jews deprived of rights, martyred, and killed that made his blood boil but rather a petty administrative trifle that disadvantaged the Nazi delegation" at Ragusa. He added, however, that Salten was, "after all, just the designated executor of this [committee] decision" and that "whatever Felix Salten may have done and said in Ragusa is no worse than what the exiled literary prize holders and expelled academicians do not do and do not say."[43] Salten tried to defend himself. Declaring that "the acoustics are strange that are bestowed upon individuals in such a heated assembly,"[44] he gave his account of the Ragusa meetings to the *Neue Freie Presse* and insisted that the *Arbeiter-Zeitung* publish his response to its attack upon him. "I have never aligned myself with Hitler," he wrote. "I never declared or indicated with a single word my solidarity, or that of the Austrian delegation which I led, with the barbarism of Hitler. Furthermore, I have done nothing that could be construed as a wish to 'make up for my ancestry.'" He pointed out, "I am still a Jew and have committed myself to my Jewishness in Ragusa, just as I always have everywhere," adding, "Your conclusions, drawn from an untrue report, are therefore groundless, also in the point in which you maintain that I was competing for the respect of the Nazis."[45]

The furor of the Ragusa meetings did not die with a few newspaper articles. Even though the Vienna P.E.N. executive committee approved the actions of the Austrian delegation at its June 9 meeting, the general assembly meeting of Vienna P.E.N. members that Salten convened on June 27 at Vienna's Hotel Imperial did not run so smoothly. There a resolution was presented condemning the Nazi persecution of German writers; in its original form, it included a passage expressing disapproval of the actions of the two official Austrian delegates, but that was eliminated before it was presented for passage, in large part out of respect for Salten, who declared that he had been motivated primarily by a desire to protect his "Austrian colleagues, who still make their living in the Reich and whose livelihood could have been destroyed."[46] When members raised the question as to why Salten and Grete von Urbanitzky were presenting two separate reports about the Ragusa meetings to the larger P.E.N. membership, Salten replied that he was "not solidly united" with Urbanitzky, whose pro-Nazi partisanship was becoming increasingly apparent. After passage of the anti-Nazi resolution, Urbanitzky and the German nationals withdrew from P.E.N. in protest.

The discussion continued for several hours. Many members

complained that the executive committee had taken too much authority upon itself and that such important decisions regarding the stance to be taken by the Austrian delegation at the international P.E.N. meetings should be first voted on by the full membership. In order to prevent any personal conflict from impeding progress towards these ends, Salten announced that he would give up his honorary presidency of P.E.N. at the end of the year. During the months ahead, he would take the lead in drafting new statutes for the Vienna P.E.N. Club, in keeping with the will of the general assembly and the ideals of democratization. These new statutes would be brought before a special meeting of the general assembly in November.

The assembly elected Salten, Friedrich Schreyvogel, Hans Nüchtern, Josef Hupka, Oskar Jellinek, and Robert Neumann to the committee assigned to write the new club rules. Even though the six-and-a-half hour meeting ended peacefully, forty-six of the Vienna P.E.N.'s 182 members withdrew from P.E.N. between June and October of that year. Since this number included three members of the eight-member executive committee and since six votes were required to validate any resolution, the Vienna P.E.N. Club could no longer function. On July 23 Salten called a second special meeting of the general assembly to deal with the issue. The remaining members of the executive committee resigned their positions, and P.E.N. was put under a temporary trusteeship administered by Salten, Hans Nüchtern, Rudolf List, Oskar Maurus Fontana, Julius Bauer, and Felix Costa. This committee was to serve until a new executive committee could be elected in the fall. Since part of the complaint of the membership against its leadership was the excessively long terms of its officers, such an arrangement could not last long. By late September all the trustees save Julius Bauer laid down their mandate, and all but Bauer and Fontana withdrew from P.E.N.

Salten had suffered a tremendous loss of prestige through the Ragusa affair. He had tried to prevent a rift in the international P.E.N., but his actions had contributed instead to a rift in the Austrian club. The kindest views of him were that he had allowed himself to be used by Urbanitzky; Robert Neumann, for one, included Salten among a small number of "cautious" former P.E.N. members whom he described as "excellent men."[47] Others, however, were less willing to differentiate between liberals and German nationalists among those who had resigned from P.E.N., and put them all into the same pro-German nationalist camp. Leon Schalit, John Galsworthy's translator, was especially vitriolic in the report he wrote to the English P.E.N. following an October 3 meeting of selected members of the Vienna P.E.N. Club:

> …[W]e are very much alive, and by no means dead, as our opponents try to allege. An astonishing number of intrigues by S. [Salten] and U. [Urbanitzky] were brought to light, showing once again that those two are simply possessed by the burning desire to smash us up for sheer personal and political reasons … Under the corrupted regime of U. and S., who did not accept important persons, because they did not suit them personally, quite a number felt so annoyed that they no longer wanted to join the club … We have tried everything in our power to bring about reconciliation; and U. and S. did everything in their power to prevent reconciliation.[48]

The group continued its operation under collective leadership, although after December only Raoul Auernheimer, Julius Bauer, Ernst Decsey, and Leon Schalit were authorized to sign official letters. Auernheimer served as the group's chief public representative[49] while Salten took over Auernheimer's position as Burgtheater critic for the *Neue Freie Presse*.

Chapter 21: Mounting Losses

It may well have been a matter of timing, coming as it did on the heels of the P.E.N. attacks on his leadership and his son's serious automobile accident, that in December 1933 Salten's old friendship with Richard Beer-Hofmann suffered irreparable damage. Salten had always praised his friend for his exquisite critical tastes, his meticulously crafted works of literature, and his work as script editor and theater director. That December, Salten wrote a review of Beer-Hofmann's latest literary endeavor, *Der junge David*, the first part of an ambitious dramatic trilogy on the life of the Biblical King David. In his review Salten pointed out that it had been fifteen years since Beer-Hofmann had composed the prologue to this drama, commenting, "He is, in spite of the sparkle of his intellect, the fire of his temperament, the wings of his fantasy, not of a gushing nature, this Richard Beer-Hofmann. The ability to pour forth is denied him. The richness of his being solidifies slowly, just as crystals are formed slowly and according to strict rules in the earth's depths." But, Salten added, it was because of this long gestation period that "the verses sparkle and shine, the figures stand complete and fully grown" and the drama "radiates the brilliance of fine gems."[1]

Beer-Hofmann was not pleased with the review. It was characteristic of Salten to trace the evolution of writers and actors, bringing in their earlier writings or their earlier roles in a discussion of their latest endeavors. In doing this, Salten had nothing but praise for Beer-Hofmann's breakthrough poem, "Schlaflied für Miriam" (Lullaby for Miriam); however, he also wrote about Beer-Hofmann's unfinished projects, especially his failure as a young artist to complete a painting of King Solomon, noting, "he only played with this picture just as he played with other schemes." Beer-Hofmann was particularly incensed that Salten implied that *Der junge David* could not be performed in Vienna's current political climate. As Salten put it, "He [Beer-Hofmann] simply doesn't know … whether his life's work will ever appear on the living stage. The present age seems not exactly friendly towards biblical dramas from the Old Testament. But, like all of us, he too hopes for a time when humanity will again be viewed in a purely humane way, and poetry will again be valued as poetry."[2]

When Schnitzler had been upset by one of Salten's reviews, he had confronted him directly. Beer-Hofmann, however, took his complaint to Salten's publisher. When Salten heard of this, he refused to retract anything that he had said. To Beer-Hofmann's complaint that Salten had "blocked his way to the Burgtheater," he responded that, if he had written that the play must be performed in these politically sensitive times, Austria's anti-Semitic newspapers, such as the *Reichspost*, would have called it a "Jewish plot" and ignited the kind of polemic that would truly have kept the play out of the theaters. But Salten was also enraged that Beer-Hofmann had gone behind his back to complain about him to his superiors. He now recalled every hurt he had suffered at Beer-Hofmann's hands and the many times Otti had had to smooth things over between them. This time there was no forgiveness; Salten declared, "I regret every good word that I have written about him."[3]

The political situation in Germany and Austria and the P.E.N. rift had taken their toll on Salten, and he was tired of tiptoeing on eggs to appease the egos of his fellow writers, be they communists, German nationalists, Catholics, or Jews. In July of that year, he had written a telling feuilleton for the *Neue Freie Presse* entitled "Wohin soll ich mich wenden?" (Where Shall I Turn?). Its title was taken from the text of Schubert's German Mass, and Salten wrote, "Ever since I was small, the Schubert Mass has been permanently embossed in my memory. ... Constantly, in sad as in the rare happy hours, the melodies of Schubert reverberate in the man's heart with the clear childish voices from long ago." As to the question posed in the text,

> "Where shall I turn when pain and suffering oppress me?" Yes, where? This present with its poisonous politics, with its hatred of everybody by everybody, with the pain of getting one's daily bread, with the despair among the young, this present is unbearable and could scarcely be borne if there weren't so many ways to escape it for hours, for days, for weeks at a time.[4]

Salten suggested three modes of escape: listening to classical music, reading good works of literature, and rambling in field and forest.

More and more frequently in his columns, Salten waxed ecstatic on the wonders of nature. He delighted in going to an abandoned spot to fish as dusk was falling and in rising before dawn to watch the courtship rituals of wood grouse and to encounter grazing elk and deer. After one of these outings, he wrote, "I gladly direct my step homewards, am now sociable again and refreshed as if I had been recuperating for weeks." He found it necessary to "get away from people and from oneself for a few hours, to the simple and eternal things. Then one can bear people and bear oneself much more easily. Then one is milder and more patient towards the foolishness of others and to one's own foolishness as well."[5]

When his old friend Herman Bahr turned seventy, Salten wrote a heartfelt tribute to the man who had ruled the cultural scene in Austria for twenty years, leading the fight for modernity, writing plays that had a tumultuous reception, and making a name as one of Vienna's great journalists. Bahr had long since left Vienna; as Salten put it, Bahr had always been searching for God "on all the streets of this earth, in every gathering, in all directions of the intellect. ... Now ... he has found God, his God, and worships him with the boundless devotion that has always filled [his] deepest being, longingly, expectantly."[6] Despite the fact that Bahr was now a devout Catholic living in Bavaria and "probably a Nazi,"[7] Salten always retained warm feelings for him, recalling how, as recently as 1932, Bahr had spoken out publicly – and emphatically – against anti-Semitism in the European press.[8] Bahr died in January 1934, six months after the appearance of Salten's tribute.

Salten had reverted to the antipolitical stance of many writers of his generation; especially after the P.E.N. debacle, he seldom spoke out publicly about affairs in Austria, despite the frightening turn events were taking. Indeed, during this bleak period of Austrian history, relations between the political parties were as violent and chaotic as those within the P.E.N. Club.

Engelbert Dollfuss, from the conservative Christian Social Party, had become chancellor of Austria in May 1932 as head of a coalition government. Since he had a single-vote majority in Parliament, his power was limited and, in his efforts to curb the country's inflation, he antagonized the Social Democratic (workers') Party, which was his major opposition. The conservatives had their support among the Catholic clergy and among the upper-class and rural populations, while the socialists' strength was in the working-class districts of the cities. Each of these parties had its own paramilitary force. A governmental crisis arose in March 1933 when the president and two vice presidents of the lower house of parliament resigned over a procedural issue, and Dollfuss took advantage of the situation by having parliament adjourned indefinitely. He then took on emergency dictatorial powers and ruled by emergency decree. In June he banned the Austrian National Socialist and Communist parties; he then attempted to secure Austrian independence from Germany through an agreement with fascist Italy. He merged the paramilitary troops of the nation's conservative parties in an umbrella group to support his government and outlawed the Social Democrats' armed forces. More and more, in his attempts to secure an independent, Catholic Austria, he had become a fascist dictator. In February 1934 matters came to a head when Dollfuss's conservative government arrested a number of opposition leaders and conducted house searches for weapons. In response, the Social Democrats called for armed resistance and a civil war broke out. There was brutal fighting in the Vienna suburbs where, in the early 1920s, the Social Democrats had erected improved housing for the working classes. A number of their leaders hid out in the impressive, fortress-like Karl Marx housing complex in the city's nineteenth district. Dollfuss ordered artillery to shell the building, thereby destroying many of the apartments and putting civilian lives at danger. The fighting in Vienna was over within twenty-four hours; in other spots in Styria, fighting continued another three days.

Under these circumstances, Salten found it impossible to escape bitter reality by withdrawing into the arts or escaping to the countryside with good friends: "The days we have just lived through weigh down our nerves too heavily. Whatever one tries, it is impossible to think of anything else, to speak about anything else other than the events of these days." During the Great War, he wrote, Vienna had been spared the sounds of gunfire; now, however, the populace could hear "the dull booming of cannon in the middle of highly populated districts, the deadly prattle of machine guns, Austrians against Austrians." He was oppressed by "all the dead, all the bloody victims, all of them Austrians." All that the people of Vienna wanted, he declared, was "peace and a secure existence." Salten's hope was that, "one day, which we hope is soon, the feeling of security that we long for so very much will come again." "When clemency and reconciliation rule again, ... when the existences that are now broken are set right again and won anew for the community, when we know that the widows and orphans are protected from want, then we will begin to breathe again in wary relief."[9]

Salten was essentially a monarchist at heart. Despite the excesses of the Habsburg empire, he had experienced this much-desired "peace" and "security" during Franz Josef's reign. However, he neither would nor could condemn Dollfuss since the chancellor was fighting to preserve an independent Austria, free of Nazi rule. Josef Roth, another Jewish writer one generation younger than Salten, wrote from Paris "in sincere fellowship" to tell Salten that he was wrong to express support for Dollfuss's "heroic" military forces in a newspaper piece since it was, in fact, the desperate workers who had acted heroically in the February revolution. Roth found fault with Salten's using the term "outside agitators" to describe the leaders of the unrest, pointing out that this was frequently a code phrase that anti-Semites used for Jews. "I write all this to you," he added, "because I am convinced that you, as a writer of international standing, must be extremely careful about your public comments."[10]

And, indeed, Salten did still want to be a part of the international community. In March 1934 he wrote to Hermon Ould to inquire whether he might become an honorary member of the London P.E.N. Club so that he could attend the annual international P.E.N. meeting scheduled for Edinburgh. Such honorary memberships were not without precedent since they had been given to Ernst Toller and a number of other authors expelled by the Berlin P.E.N. Club. Salten's request, however, was denied, since he had not been expelled by the Vienna Club but had quit voluntarily. Perhaps, Ould told Salten in a letter indicating that he had no knowledge of the extent of hostilities among the various political parties in Vienna, the discord that had led to his resignation could be smoothed over, and he could see his way to rejoining the Vienna P.E.N.[11] Salten remarked sadly that "in the midst of ever increasing unruliness, the impartial man of culture recalls, not without wistfulness, a condition of robust culture, civilized decency, a solidly constructed sense of justice, and mutual tolerance." He now saw that "as long as the spirit of the party rages, one cannot hope for anything that is truly spiritual. The spirit of the party is, after all, the incapacity to experience a purely human matter in a pure and humane way or even to grasp things spiritually."[12]

Salten's literary outlets were shrinking. He was no longer published in any German newspapers, and his German book sales were seriously diminished. In 1934 Paul Zsolnay published the last of the volumes that would comprise Salten's collected works, this time a volume of his plays with the title *Vom andern Ufer. Ernste und heitere Theaterstücke*.[13] Besides the trilogy of one-act plays that form the title work, the volume includes Salten's more recent *Louise von Koburg*. It is likely that Zsolnay planned to publish a second volume of Salten's dramatic works, but by 1935 all of Salten's writings were put on Germany's list of forbidden writings and in the following year even copies of *Bambi* were confiscated and destroyed.

One outlet remained open to Salten: the United States. He had firmly established himself there with the 1928 success of *Bambi*; since then, he had seen *The Hound of Florence*, *Fifteen Rabbits*, *Samson and Delilah*, and *The City Jungle* published by Simon and Schuster of New York and *Florian: the Emperor's Stallion* published by Bobbs-Merrill of Indianapolis. Salten sent an American agent, Sanford Greenburger, thirty-three essays and short stories, including a number of his *Bilder aus dem Konzertsaal* (Pictures from the Concert Hall). Greenburger could not be optimistic. Translators of short stories and essays in the United States were paid only when a piece was actually sold to a magazine or journal, and this was a risk few translators were willing to assume. Nevertheless, Greenburger sent out the musical pieces, essays, and short stories to various publishing venues. His success was limited; *Esquire* did publish one of Salten's short stories, "A Shot in the Forest," in 1933, but Greenburger was able to place only one story in 1934 and one more in 1936.

Meanwhile, Salten's situation at home had only gotten worse. In June 1934 the nerve damage his son Paul had suffered in his 1932 automobile accident had so intensified that he was forced to stop his film work in Paris and Rome and come home for extensive treatment. Sometime earlier Salten had assisted his son in taking out a loan of 60,000 Schillings from Paul Zsolnay's father; when the elder Zsolnay died, the Zsolnay press took over that loan, along with an advance payment of some 30,000 Schillings from Salten's future earnings in order to help him through this difficult period. As a direct result of these loans, Salten's payments for book sales were greatly reduced at just the time when he was cut off from his market in Germany.

At the same time, Salten was worried about the health of his son-in-law, Hans Rehmann. A successful stage actor, Rehmann had launched a burgeoning film career in 1929, starring opposite Pola Negri in the Paul Czinner film *The Woman He Scorned*. As recently as 1933, he had starred in films with Lil Dagover and Asta Nielsen. But in 1934 the severe shoulder pain that Rehmann had been suffering for some five years rendered it impossible for him to continue working. He and Salten's daughter, Anna, moved into the Cottagegasse home, where Anna and Otti could help care for him, and Rehmann began a series of experimental treatments to try to alleviate his pain.

Affairs in Vienna also reached a critical stage. After the revolt by the Social Democrats in February 1933, the Social Democratic party was outlawed, and in May the Christian Socialists, whose ties to Italian fascism soon gave their form of governance the name "Austro-Fascism," introduced a new constitution that reinforced Engelbert Dollfuss's power as dictator. At the same time, the National Socialists in Austria were increasing their acts of terrorism. On July 25, 1934, they attempted a putsch, and Dollfuss was assassinated by Nazi agents. The putsch was quelled, but it seemed as if it were only a matter of time before Austria would be absorbed by Nazi Germany. Dollfuss was succeeded by Kurt Schuschnigg, a young man of thirty-six who had served under Dollfuss as minister of education.

At this chaotic time, an American foundation headed by an idealistic – and wealthy – welfare worker in Seattle, Washington, announced that it would be awarding the 1935 Eichelberger Humane Award, given for work on behalf of the welfare of animals, to Salten for his novel *The City Jungle* because of its "plea against the cruelty of zoo captivity of animals."[14] This award had been established in 1931 and had honored several distinguished recipients, including film actor George Arliss, Mrs. Calvin (Grace) Coolidge, and George Bernard Shaw. Ironically, Adolf Hitler had also received this award in 1932 "for progressive humane legislation and anti-vivisection,"[15] which only confirmed for Salten the fact that "one of the strange contradictions of our era is the cruelty of people amongst themselves and their gentle understanding of animals, their disregard for human life and their scrupulously compassionate protection of dumb animals."[16]

Salten had, however, retained his popularity in Vienna. He was invited in January 1935 to give a reading at the Urania center for public education, astronomy, and film, and in April the Akademietheater presented the premiere of Salten's play *Mädchenhände* (A Girl's Hands). This drama, which bore the alternate title *Dieses kleine Mädchen* (This Little Girl),[17] resembles Salten's novel *Martin Overbeck* in that the young hero rebels against his father's wealth. Here the father hires a poor young girl to pretend to fall in love with his son; contrary to his plan, the two young people actually do fall in love, and the work closes with the son's reconciliation with his father and the lovers' projected marriage. In the reviews of this work, Salten was praised for the manner in which the problem of conflicting values between fathers and sons and between fathers and daughters was resolved "with passionate affirmation of the young generation's right to self-determination."[18] At its premiere, Salten was called several times to the stage and greeted with warm applause for this "genuine success."[19]

It seemed, however, that for every "genuine success" of Salten's, there was an irritation. For the first time in nearly twenty years, Salten reverted to writing occasionally under his old pseudonyms "Sascha" and "Martin Finder." Salten was reacting to anti-Jewish sentiment, one reason perhaps why, although he remained active in Vienna's Rotary Club, he cancelled his membership in the Masonic Lodge at this time.

He was now finding it difficult to remain optimistic about the future. Fame, he noted in an admonitory letter addressed "to a young man," is often something that "rises and fades as quickly as dandelions in May," with the result that "living in the midst of one's posterity brings little pleasure." Fame's transitory nature was increasingly on his mind. "Who among us living today can seriously say that the work of this one or that one will live on gloriously through the coming centuries?" he asked. "In truth, we do not know what future generations will read, whose pictures they will want to see, and whose compositions they will want to hear."[20] As he went through the exhibit of Emperor Franz Josef memorabilia now on display at Schönbrunn, he remarked again on how the persistence of these royal items "makes one feel the all too rapid transitoriness of life with double cruelty."[21]

Still, he moved on. In 1935 Paul Zsolnay published a new collection of animal tales entitled *Kleine Brüder*. Most of these recounted Salten's own hunting adventures or experiences with animals in his Cottagegasse garden and had appeared previously as feuilletons in the *Neue Freie Presse*. The volume also included an earlier piece of fiction entitled "Mako, der junge Bär" (Mako, the Little Bear) about an animal captured, brutally mistreated, and trained to perform circus acts by a gypsy family. At the end of the tale, the bear manages to escape back into the forest. "Perhaps at some future time the bullet of a huntsman may reach him," Salten wrote, "but this will be no easy task for anyone. For now Mako knows men. And he will be wary of them."[22]

He gave more direct expression to his cynical view of the times in his report about a pet rabbit that had disappeared one day from his yard. After speculating that a hungry man had probably captured the trusting animal, eaten it, and sold its skin, Salten remarked: "The good rabbit simply fell victim to these times in which an opulent lifestyle has a provocative effect, in which acts of violence are so normal. It really doesn't matter if interesting individuals are annihilated at the same time."[23]

Salten was aware of the difficulties the once well-to-do Viennese were facing in keeping their villas and small palaces intact and in maintaining the lavish collections that they held. Many upper-middle-class women were now holding down jobs, and families were forced to rent out rooms in their homes in order to make ends meet. Salten remarked about how many of these people were striving desperately to maintain an illusion of grandeur, even in these difficult times. He could, in fact, identify with them. Although he had never known the comfort of wealth, Salten had acquired a fine library of leather-bound volumes, antique vases, busts and statuary, paintings and prints, and expensive furniture, and he was as eager as anyone to preserve his collections. After all, he commented, "One clings with tenacious loyalty to these mute companions of carefree days."[24]

Salten's son, Paul, blamed his father for at least part of their troubled financial state. In shades reminiscent of Salten's own concern for his father Philipp's too trusting attitude towards his business partners, Paul wrote to his parents: "One can't simply enter into a contract when he is not informed about its conditions. Why does Papa continually let himself be represented by the publisher and not take a lawyer to a contract signing (look at Schnitzler)[?] Up until now Papa has *always* been cheated."[25] Throughout their marriage Otti had had to cope not only with Salten's bad business habits but also with his penchant for buying expensive items when they could least afford them. As she wrote to her brother, "My husband and I are accustomed (with the exception of a few good years) to take a hard life with relative ease (levity), and today one cannot get through life without a large portion of levity," adding, however, "We are no longer young and feel that most during the night, for sleep is disloyal to us and that is very bad; this is also connected to the great worry that oppresses us all."[26]

In 1936 Salten took on a number of longer writing projects. One was a play – and novel – entitled *Sträfling Nummer 33* (Prisoner Number 33). The plot was suggested by an early episode in Richard Beer-Hofmann's life when he had accidentally wandered into a political demonstration and been briefly arrested for being a participant. In Salten's work, the citizen of a small, bankrupt nation wanders into a crowd of demonstrators and is falsely accused of the attempted murder of a police officer. He is sentenced to an unusually harsh prison term of twenty years and held there until news comes that he has inherited an enormous fortune from a deceased uncle's farms, shipping company, and diamond mines in South Africa. At this point the state officials intervene in the prisoner's case, in hopes that the hero will show his gratitude for his release from prison by donating a large portion of his inheritance to his homeland. This the hero does, under the condition that the state carry out a thorough program of prison reform. He then goes to South Africa to sell off his uncle's holdings so that he can return to his homeland to live. The hero states Salten's own view regarding his feelings for Vienna when, despite the injustices and brutal mistreatment that he has suffered at the hands of the state, he declares rapturously, "to be at home where one has his roots, where he belongs ... like the tree growing out of the earth ... the earth of his homeland ... the soil of the homeland ... nothing, nothing surpasses it."[27]

Salten's feuilletons were being published only in Vienna and in Budapest, but he continued to put in long working hours and spent many sleepless nights worrying about his professional situation, about perceived injustices he might have committed, and especially about finances. "It appears that his memories are just as sleepless as he is, only that the nice memories slumber sweetly while the unpleasant ones, the gloomy ones, awaken one after the other and become terribly lively," he wrote of himself in one of his newspaper columns. "He charges himself with blind confidence, a lack of business sense, and an inability to budget money; he surveys the common economic distress, is deeply contrite over how irresponsibly he manages his household affairs, how heedlessly he has allowed himself to be exploited and cheated on all sides."[28]

In the summer of 1936, before going to Berghof to hunt, relax, and take in the Salzburg festival, Salten and his wife went to Switzerland to visit Anna and her husband. The couple had moved there to be close to Hans Rehmann's family. Unfortunately, Hans's condition had not improved; he had been diagnosed with tuberculosis of the bone and was in constant pain. While they were there, the Saltens made several visits to Thomas Mann at his home in Küsnacht and went on an excursion to Lugano.

Salten also wrote a new play, *Kaisertochter* (Imperial Daughter), which had its premiere at Vienna's Deutsches Volkstheater in October of that year.[29] Salten said the play was based "freely" on history; it related the story of the Austrian princess Marie Louise, who was wed to Napoleon and had borne him a son. The play covers the period between Napoleon's capture and imprisonment on Elba through his escape, his renewed war against a coalition of European forces, and his final exile to St. Helena. During this fifteen-month period, Marie Louise had been taken back to Austria with her son; she fell in love with her escort, Adam von Neipperg, and the two moved to Parma, enjoying what was by all accounts a real love match.

Traditionally, the princess had been regarded as a rather colorless pawn of history, but Salten humanized her figure, giving her passion and stamina. In a confrontation with her father, Emperor

Franz, who is opposed to her love for Neipperg and threatens to send her to a nunnery, Marie Louise replies that she prefers death to separation from Neipperg, that her father had already abused her once by pairing her off with a lawyer's son and allowing a union that was not recognized by the Church. This imagined scene is the dramatic highpoint of the drama. There are obvious parallels between the love story of Marie Louise and that of Princess Louise of Coburg, and, since "the public followed along in great sympathy and granted the play, the actors, and the author a very strong success,"[30] it appears that *Kaisertochter* was as successful on the Viennese stage as the Louise-Mettachich love story had been, nearly three years previously.

Unfortunately, Salten's enjoyment of this professional success was dampened once more by matters at home. Contrary to all hopes and expectations, his son Paul's condition had not improved. He began to have epileptic-like seizures in January 1937 and was in despair about this relapse and about the doctor's uncertain prognosis. Attempted hypnotic treatments led to panic attacks, and he was bitter that he could not work; at one point, he even flirted briefly with the idea of going to fight in the Spanish Civil War to give his life some final purpose.

At the same time, Paul Zsolnay was pressing Salten for repayment of his loans. Zsolnay was feeling a severe economic pinch because so many of his authors were now banned in Germany.[31] Hollywood appeared to offer the best opportunities for Salten to acquire quick funding. Acting on Salten's behalf, the Hungarian-born scriptwriter Géza Herczeg sold the film rights to *Florian* to Winfield R. Sheehan, a successful Hollywood producer who, not coincidentally, owned the first Lipizzan horses in America. At the same time, playwright Carl Zuckmayer spoke with Alexander Korda about making a British film of the novel. Salten had already sold the film rights to *Bambi* to American film director and producer Sidney Franklin for one thousand dollars in 1933. Franklin had hoped to make the novel into a live nature film, but he now felt that it was impossible to capture the poetic beauty of the novel in this manner and passed these rights on to Walt Disney. Salten's agents and his American publisher were now trying to gain for Salten some guarantee of payment from this major studio. Eventually, Disney agreed to pay Salten an additional four thousand dollars for the film rights plus a small percentage on any *Bambi*-related books that Disney might produce. Unfortunately, while this money was a help to Salten in staving off his debts, it could not help Salten's son. Paul was losing interest in life and was hospitalized several times to monitor his attacks. It was during one of these hospital stays, in the night of May 7, 1937, that Paul suddenly lost consciousness. Otti rushed to his bedside, but Paul could not be revived. He died on the evening of May 8. Salten described his reaction to this news as "despair alternating with stupor," adding that Otti, despite her fragile heart condition, was managing to remain "strong."[32] Against Salten's wishes, an autopsy was performed, and it was determined that Paul had died of a brain tumor. His parents announced the death in the papers, giving the time and place of burial but asking their friends "to refrain from visits of condolence."[33] Otti did not attend the burial; instead, family friend Wally Strakosch accompanied Salten to the cemetery and helped him receive the condolences of the many friends from literary and theatrical circles who attended the service. After the crowds had left, Salten took Otti to the gravesite, where she was "close to breaking down" but was soon "once again in control."[34] Neither Salten nor his wife ever fully recovered from this tragic loss of their thirty-three-year-old son; in September 1937 Salten confided his anguish to his diary when he wrote simply: "Pauli! Pauli!! Pauli!!!"[35] Years later he would note that, with Paul's death, "my ability ever to be truly happy again vanished."[36]

Salten plunged onward, continuing to put long hours in at his writing desk. His contributions to the *Neue Freie Presse* were mostly book reviews, hunting pieces, occasional theatrical reviews, and personal tributes. Only rarely did these pieces appear under his full name. Most identified their author as "f.s."; many others were signed "Martin Finder" or "m.f.," with single pieces attributed to "Sebastian Merker" and "Lanzelot." He also began work on a new animal novel about Bambi's child, Gurri. Gurri was the name of Paul's pet dog.

Salten had already finished work on an animal novel entitled *Die Jugend des Eichhörnchens Perri* (The Youth of the Squirrel Perri), a work undoubtedly inspired by the two squirrels in Salten's garden that had spent much of the previous winter in the attic of his home. In the novel, Salten reverts to a time when his daughter

Anna was small, a time of innocence when his infant daughter was able to understand the communications of her animal neighbors. Paul does not appear nor is he mentioned in this work. Both Salten and his publisher Paul Zsolnay were convinced that this book, like his other animal stories, would do especially well in America. Zsolnay had the book printed and bound, but when it was ready for distribution, the larger world intervened, throwing Salten's *Perri* into a state of literary limbo.

Chapter 22: A Change in Homeland

During his period of dictatorial rule, Kurt Schuschnigg used every means available to stave off Austria's absorption into Germany. In January 1937 he had made his first attempt at appeasing the Germans by granting a general amnesty to those National Socialists who had participated in the 1934 coup attempt against the Dollfuss government. He tried to counterbalance this attempt in February by proclaiming his willingness to restore the Habsburg throne, in the hope that such a move would reinforce a strong feeling of Austrian national identity. Several months later, he even took the preliminary step of restoring the Habsburg family properties.

Salten supported this move, but it enraged the German and Austrian National Socialists and set off a series of violent demonstrations throughout the country. By now Benito Mussolini and Adolf Hitler had formed the Rome-Berlin Axis, and, at a meeting with Schuschnigg in April 1937, Mussolini warned the chancellor that Austria could no longer count on Italy's support against a German takeover. He urged Schuschnigg to drop both his ideas of allying himself with Czechoslovakia and seeking to restore the Habsburg throne.

The situation grew increasingly dire. Schuschnigg was unable to create an alliance of nations willing to defend Austrian independence, and, at a state visit to Berchtesgaden in February 1938, Hitler bluntly demanded that Schuschnigg give the National Socialists in Austria greater freedom of movement and that he take the party's members into his government. Schuschnigg was forced to submit and named a Nazi, Arthur Seyss-Inquart, as the new Minister of the Interior. At the same time, however, he reaffirmed the independence of Austria and called for international support so that he could resist future German demands for Austrian concessions.

For Salten, Austria's uncertainty and fear was reflected on the professional and the home front, as he learned for the first time just how serious his wife's heart condition really was. On January 17, 1938, Salten wrote in his diary: "At home: the doctor forbids Otti to leave the house for a week. Apparently, her heart is now a cause for worry, after her having held out heroically until now. What must she endure? What do I endure? The two of us just remain silent to protect one another." And, on February 16: "Worries because of Austria. Also worry about my position at the Neue Freie Presse!"

On March 9 Schuschnigg announced that he would hold a plebiscite so that Austrians could decide for themselves whether they wanted to remain independent of Germany. Because of a rigged voting procedure (*yes* votes would be available to all voters, while those voting against continued Austrian independence would have to follow procedure in producing their own negative voting form), Hitler mobilized troops on the Austrian border and demanded that the plebiscite be cancelled and that Schuschnigg resign. Schuschnigg had no options left. His last statement on the radio was "God protect Austria."[1] Seyss-Inquart was named chancellor as German troops marched across the frontier. The Austrian president also resigned as tens of thousands of Austrians jubilantly greeted the Germans armies. Hitler came to Vienna on March 14 to declare Austria's union with Germany and to announce a new plebiscite of Austrian acquiescence. Members of the opposition were rounded up and imprisoned; Schuschnigg was sent to the Dachau concentration camp. The plebiscite, held in April, resulted in overwhelming approval of Austria's incorporation into the German Reich.

When the takeover occurred, it evoked remarkably little protest from Austria's European neighbors. Salten followed the events from his home, where he was suffering from a severe bronchial attack and fever. His diary entries reflect the stunning rapidity of events; on March 16, for example, he wrote:

> No ministers, no legations left. Vienna's international unimportance.
> Huge parade.
> They take Jewish women, without distinction of age, to wash the streets from 11 p.m. to 2 a.m.!
> No message from the [Neue Freie] Presse.
> To the premiere at the Josefstadt theater – no tickets!
> Temperature of 37.8 degrees [100 degrees Fahrenheit].

In the days that followed, word filtered through about the fate of his friends and acquaintances. Many had made a hurried exodus from the country; his neighbor, composer Eric Korngold, had had his house confiscated. Some, like Raoul Auernheimer, were taken to Dachau. Others chose suicide: Egon Friedell leapt to his death from an upper story of his home as the Gestapo came to arrest him. Synagogues and stores were plundered; Jews were arrested and beaten. There were rumors abroad that Salten had emigrated to the United States[2] and others that he had been imprisoned in a Nazi concentration camp.[3] Thomas Mann, who had heard that Salten was taken to Dachau, wrote in his diary, "Memory of Salten's visits last summer in Küsnacht, wearing a silk tie, still in the safety of civilization. It is a bizarre, diabolical fate, rather like that of a young girl from a good home who is carried off to a bordello in Buenos Aires."[4] In June Otti received a letter of condolence from the Norwegian theater director Björn Björnson, who had heard that Salten had died.

Salten, however, was more fortunate than many of Vienna's Jewish population. Since he did not own his Cottagegasse home, it was not immediately confiscated and plundered as many Jewish homes were, and he escaped arrest. Salten hoped that, by keeping a low profile, he could avoid the terror. "I do not think about abandoning my hometown," he wrote, "and do not believe that I will be forced to do so."[5] On March 31 he wrote his last will and testament. On April 6 he returned to his writing. His situation, however, was precarious. The *Neue Freie Presse* published his last piece, a book review, on March 6; now, not even the use of pseudonyms like "Martin Finder" or "Lanzelot" could get him into print. On April 1 his pay was reduced by half; on April 26 he was "fired without notice."[6]

In the meantime, the Gestapo had seized all of Salten's unsold books at the Zsolnay press. Paul Zsolnay had tried desperately to preserve his firm by handpicking the National Socialists who would operate it and, through most of 1938, was able to retain an informal affiliation with the press that he had founded. [7]

Just as Paul Zsolnay struggled to retain some control over his firm, Salten was desperately trying to assure himself of whatever income he could find to see him through this difficult period. He was particularly anxious to complete a contract with the American

Bobbs-Merrill Company in Indianapolis for an English translation of *Perri* that would be published simultaneously in the United States and Canada. He wrote to the new Zsolnay press to explain his situation and ask for its assistance:

> I am temporarily incapable of signing the contract with Bobbs-Merrill and of giving my permission for agreements with any other foreign presses (England, Hungary, etc.) as I have until now.
>
> Circumstances have fundamentally changed. My book *Perri* cannot appear with your press. After many successes achieved jointly with you, I see myself not only excluded from my dear German mother tongue but also cut off from any earnings at all.
>
> But now I must try at least to eke out an existence for myself and my family.
>
> For this reason I now urgently request that you give me your binding assurance that you will pay me 40 percent of all translation fees and royalties without delay. This would include those payments for work that has been accomplished up until now (Hungary) that are now due.
>
> In addition I request that you free the inventory of the book *Perri* as well as the other inventories of my works for a foreign German press; this is, after all, also to your advantage. By no means do I mean by this one of the emigrant presses, because I am not an emigrant.[8]

The last line of Salten's letter indicates Salten's belief that he could outlast the German annexation and remain a resident of his beloved home city. In its response the Zsolnay press urged Salten to sign the contract with Bobbs-Merrill and assured him that he would get his 40 percent payment for all translations. Salten had no way of knowing that by continuing his relationship with the Nazi-run Zsolnay press he was getting himself into legal difficulties that would haunt him later. Still, *Perri* did appear on the American market later that year, with an introduction by the nature writer Donald

Culross Peattie. It also appered in England, where Paul Zsolnay had made arrangements for the British author Beverley Nichols to write a foreword to it, similar to that which John Galsworthy had written for *Bambi*.

As things turned out, Paul Zsolnay and Felix Salten were both naive regarding their plans to retain control over their lives and work. Zsolnay lost prestige with many of his fellow publishers, who believed that he had willingly sold out to the Nazis, while Salten played into Nazi hands by giving the newly constituted Zsolnay press the authority to sell his forbidden works in foreign countries. Although Salten's home and possessions were left untouched, he was required, as all Jews were, to give a full accounting of his wealth to the authorities in late April.

Salten's financial concerns weighed on him doubly because of Otti's continued ill health. Her heart condition now required that she spend many days in bed. Salten hoped that by firing the chambermaid and by subletting the children's rooms he could temporarily cover basic expenses. He and Otti still had a fairly large circle of friends in Vienna: the actor Otto Tressler and his wife Helene Wagener, attorney Josef Hupka and his wife Minnie, his hunting companion Felix Koessler and his wife Helene, Wally Strakosch, Arthur and Lotte Rewald, Grete Bauer, and Dora Breisach, to name but a few, but many of these friends were thinking of emigrating. Salten first realized the seriousness of his position when he learned that the *Neue Freie Presse* was not going to pay him the eighteen-month salary to which he was entitled for his twenty-five years of service at the newspaper. At first Salten deluded himself into believing that he could get these monies through a lawsuit, but by August his financial situation had become so critical that he applied to the Society of Authors, Composers, and Music Publishers for monetary assistance. When asked to supply documentation regarding his financial situation, Salten wrote, "I am in fact totally without any means of support. Since May 1 of this year, I have not drawn *one* pfennig of salary. ... Meanwhile the 66.67 Marks that I have received from you constitute my *only* income." That fact alone, he added, "is already sufficient proof to you of my distress." [9]

Salten turned to Stefan Zweig for assistance; this younger colleague was now living in London, and Salten sent him his novel *Sträfling Nummer 33* and one of his newer novellas in the hope that

Zweig might find a suitable publisher for him in England. He also sent the novel to Alexander Korda, hoping that this great film director would find it worthy of filming. After Korda claimed to have "lost" Salten's manuscript twice, even though he received one copy from Salten and one from Zweig, Salten gave up hope, finding the situation "shameful" for Korda and "humiliating" for himself.[10]

Anti-Semitism had been introduced into Germany over a five-year period. In Vienna, however, things moved much more quickly. Despite the fact that Vienna's 170,000 Jews made up nine percent of the city population,[11] harsh anti-Semitic laws were quickly introduced that governed all aspects of Jewish life. Suddenly, no Jews were allowed to sit on park benches or go to the city movie houses. The American consulate in Vienna was flooded with applications from Jews desperate to emigrate to the United States. Fortunately for many of them, the consulate proved to be more sympathetic to the Jews' plight than the United States Department of State was. Salten was one of its beneficiaries. Without even making an inquiry at this office, Salten was contacted by the American consul, Leland Morris, who expressed his personal admiration for Salten's *Bambi* and said that, if Salten's situation should become serious, Salten should come to him at once and he would facilitate his emigration to the United States.

This letter would be Salten's salvation on November 9-10, the notorious *Kristallnacht*, or "Night of Glass Shards," in Germany and Austria. That night he and Otti had spent the evening with their neighbor, Wally Strakosch. At eight o'clock the following morning, Salten was precipitately awakened from sleep by a man in his bedroom "whose rudeness I respond[ed] to with calmness." Salten declared himself "under the protection of the American general consulate"; as a result, he and Otti were left alone, although their landlord, their loyal Aryan housekeeper Josefa (Pepi) Wik, and her brother Robert were arrested and held for several hours.[12] Salten commented on the fact that during that night "synagogues were burned and stores were ransacked, retaliation for the disastrous deed of a single reprobate in Paris." In spite of the day's menace, Salten was able to spend an evening of "boredom" and even to do some writing.[13] Salten was convinced that it was because of Leland Morris's promise of protection that he was "spared from insult and physical torture."[14]

It was the Americans who kept Salten's hope alive during these dark days in Vienna. On August 1, for example, Simon and Schuster wrote in its royalty report to the Zsolnay press that, in spite of the strict agreement between the two presses requiring all royalty payments to be divided between Salten and Zsolnay, "we have received reports that he [Salten] is in need, and in view of our always cordial and friendly relationship, we have undertaken to send him a check for $300.00 against his royalties," adding, "in view of the urgency of the matter, we felt that you would have no objection to our making this arrangement."[15] Zsolnay accepted this as a one-time arrangement but told the American press that, in the future, only 40 percent of royalties should go to Salten, with 60 percent being sent directly to Zsolnay. In fact, the Zsolnay press did continue to represent Salten's interests abroad. When, for example, it learned that Winfield R. Sheehan was selling his film rights for *Florian* to Metro-Goldwyn-Mayer, Zsolnay wrote to the studio at once, emphasizing Salten's "own hard-pressed material situation" as a reason why the film studio should recognize Salten's – and Zsolnay's – legal rights to the book and asking them to make a "reasonably appropriate offer."[16]

Salten was no longer able to go to the theater, the Rotary Club, the city restaurants and concert houses, and in town he had to endure the humiliation of watching former friends hurriedly cross the street when they saw him approaching. He continued to socialize in the evening, but only at the homes of loyal Jewish friends. In late May, he began burning most of his correspondence. In June and July, he sold half his library and several larger pieces of furniture so that he and Otti could move into a smaller, less expensive apartment down the street at 26 Cottagegasse. He now confessed in a letter to Stefan Zweig that he had been wrong not to see the seriousness of the political situation long before the Nazi takeover. "If I could offer an excuse for this," he reflected, "it would be simply my obsession with the theater, art, and literature, which one might well call willful, my fanatic deep-rootedness in the native soil of Vienna and Austria, in the music that has poured from this soil, Mozart, Schubert, Johann Strauss and Bruckner, my attachment to the forest and its animals, an attachment that had something animal-like about it."[17] He now avoided his old hunting grounds; as he wrote to his daughter in late June, he missed getting out into the fresh air of the forests, but that he was probably "right, all in all" to stay at home.[18] There he took out the manuscript of *Ein Gott erwacht* (A God Awakens), which he had begun soon after the First World War.

That tale, set in twelfth-century Rome, dealt with the pagan god Apollo reawakening and returning to Christian Italy during its darkest days to usher in a new age of artistic rebirth, the Renaissance. To the interaction between the dominant Christian culture of the Dark Ages and the forgotten joy and beauty of classicism – an interaction that resulted in a lofty renewal of mankind, Salten added a sub-theme in the person of Ahasver, the Wandering Jew. As Salten relates it, he, like Apollo, had endured a harsh punishment by the Christian God: Apollo had been sentenced to a dreamless sleep, but Ahasver had been condemned to eternal wandering. Salten had seen how Nazi propaganda seized upon the legend of the Wandering Jew to remind Christians that Ahasver was being punished for mocking Christ on the way to the Crucifixion. Salten, however, presented the Jew as a poor cobbler who had always followed God's commandments and simply failed to recognize Christ as God's son when He came to his door. Salten's Ahasver tells Apollo that God "outwitted me in my trust and my simplemindedness! He broke the old covenant that he once made with our ancestors!"[19] Both Apollo and Ahasver are now forced to bow to the superior power of Christ; at the same time, both bring with them the cultural impulses of their own backgrounds to enrich the Christian tradition. As Ahasver tells Apollo, the gift he brings is "not, like yours, sublime beauty, but rather the exalted beauty of loyalty to the Almighty, never-tiring endurance in misfortune, holding out in spite of terrible mistreatments, faith in that which was revealed and promised."[20] When Apollo says that he is tired of mankind, Ahasver responds that he can never stop loving "[a]ll of them, all of them! Even though they push me back and despise me … one day they will understand me."[21]

This work is a remarkable statement of faith on Salten's part in the powers of beauty and endurance in a bleak world. "I very well know," he said, "that this book, if it appears at all during my lifetime, can appeal only to a narrow circle of especially distinguished readers."[22] Writing the book had been for Salten one way to keep "the pernicious spirit of the present at a distance"; it was an intellectual exercise "that anesthetized me, as it were."[23]

During this first year of the Austrian annexation, Salten had seen the city that he knew and loved undergo a terrible transformation. In a letter to an emigrant friend in New York, Salten would write one year later, "The Viennese whom we knew, with their talent, with their musicality, with their charm, arose from the racial mixture of Hungarian, Czech, Italian, Spanish, and Jewish blood. These people do not exist any more. The outrageous nonsense of a Germanic racial theory has put an end to this unique Viennese character."[24]

Paul Zsolnay had officially gone "on vacation" from his press in March;[25] in August he resigned from its board and in November left the country for England. That fall and winter, more and more of Salten's friends left the country. The Hupkas' son Robert left for New York; his old hunting companion Felix Koessler moved with his wife to London. One day in September, Salten was surprised to get a glimpse of Rauel Auernheimer in the streetcar. He had been released from Dachau and emigrated to the United States two months later.

Salten, too, had begun casting around for ideas on how to manage his future. For a while he seriously considered taking up Leland Morris's offer of protection and moving to the United States. There he would be better able to negotiate his American book and film contracts, and he was confident that he would be more successful in getting his stories into magazines and his plays onto the American stage. On the other hand, he and Otti did not want to put an ocean between themselves and their daughter. Anna was tied to Switzlerland, where she and her dying husband shared a home with Hans's widowed sister in Langenthal, outside of Bern. Through her marriage Anna had acquired Swiss citizenship, and with her Swiss passport, she was able to make several trips to Vienna to visit her parents. Both were very proud of her; as Otti wrote to her brother, "I not only admirte Annerl but directly revere her, for I don't know any one who is as self-sacrificing as she and at the same time does everything with such cheeriness."[26] In addition to helping her parents, Anna aided Jewish friends in getting valuables out of the country; on May 29 she even got Schnitzler's grandson out of Austria and safely reunited with his parents. "She risked every danger," Salten wrote proudly.[27] In September the Saltens began the lengthy process of applying for entry permits into Switzerland. The Swiss police asked for character references from Anna's father-in-law, Johann Rehmann, who lived in Zurich, and from Dr. Carl Naef, who served as Secretary of the Swiss Writers' Union, or *Schriftstellerverein*. Naef responded in November with a complete listing of Salten's works, most of which, he noted, had been published by "first-class publishers." As for the union's own evaluation of Salten, he stated:

> Felix Salten is a very well known, much-read author, who can be considered a representative of the light, charming, and often somewhat superficial Viennese character. His works lack poetic fervor and intellectual depth, but they are all the expression of a decent attitude and a well-meaning humanity. It is not to be expected that Felix Salten will seriously enrich the intellectual life of our country – he is too removed from our way of life. However, his presence in Switzerland will also not bring harm to anybody.

The Writers' Union had no problem with Salten's moving to Switaerland for a year, but set three conditions. First, he should be forbidden to work for any Swiss magazines or newspapers; second, he should not be allowed to accept any position as editor, editorial staff member, or writer; and finally, his situation should be reviewed at the end of the year. It had no objection to Salten's writing books, nor to their being published or sold; it also had no objection to his plays being performed in Switzerland or to his writing for foreign newspapers.[28]

The caveats expressed by the Swiss Writers' Union suggest a fear of competition from a man of formidable journalistic talents. Still, these were conditions that Salten was willing to accept. The financial hurdle was somewhat more difficult to deal with, since the Swiss officials noted that, because of Hans Rehmann's severe illness, he and Anna had virtually no income. Eventually, however, the family was able to put together the required security payment of nearly 16,000 francs. Over 6000 francs came from Anna and

Hans Rehmann, 5000 came from Hans Rehmann's sister, Louise Roth, and the Saltens made a cash payment of 4,430 francs.[29] In anticipation of their move, Salten bought his wife a dyed fur coat for Christmas. Finally, after days of tormented waiting and uncertainty, on January 20, 1939, the Saltens were granted the Assurance of Conferral of Permission for Residency by the Confederate Foreign Police Office in Bern.[30] The Saltens made arrangements to have their furnishings and books sent after them, got their passports, got a permit for their dachshund Flipsi, visited their doctors and dentists, bought enough medications to tide them over their first months in Zurich, and paid their last visit to their son Paul's grave. As a precautionary measure, Salten also paid a last visit to the United States consul general, Leland Morris, to reassure himself that he and Otti could, if necessary, move to the United States. On March 1 Anna wrote that she had procured a two-room apartment for them in Zurich for 65 francs a month. Two days later the Saltens took a "tearful departure" from the small group of friends who accompanied them to the train station.[31] They had reserved a private first-class compartment for themselves and their dog Flipsi for the long trip to Zurich and entered Switzerland by way of Buchs. At the border Otti was subjected to a complete body search, but all was done, Salten noted, "very politely." A friend of Anna's met them at the train station in Zurich with 300 francs to help tide them over. They then went, in a state of "befuddled exhaustion," to their apartment, which they found to be "primitive, but clean." [32]

Salten settled well into his new life. He and Otti could again move around freely, attend the theater and the cinema, and eat out in public. From this new vantage point, Salten aired his bitterness towards his old homeland in a letter to a friend:

> All my life I have greatly overestimated the people of Vienna, and there are now no human beings whom I disdain so much, whom I condemn as much as I do the Viennese and the Austrians in general. ... I have never fallen out with a person, but I have also never reconciled with anyone who forced a state of enmity upon me. I maintain this position with the city that was once

dear to me, and with the people whom I once loved. From there, from this city and from these people, the most contemptible hostility, the most disgusting and most criminal spitefulness was actively and forcibly directed against me and my kind. I will never set foot on the soil of that land again.[33]

Until July the Saltens lived in the tiny furnished apartment that Anna had secured for them in Zürich-Hottingen, at 10 Englisch Viertelstrasse; then, when their art objects, books, and furniture arrived from Vienna and their housekeeper Pepi Wik was able to join them, they moved to a larger firstfloor apartment at 4 Wilfriedstrasse, also in Hottingen. During this transition period, Thomas Mann's daughter Erika secured a small stipend for Salten from the scholarship committee of the American Guild for German Cultural Freedom in New York.

The Saltens' transition to a new life in Zurich was certainly made easier by the fact that they already had friends there, both among Swiss writers and in Swiss emigrant circles. Siegfried Trebitsch and his wife had settled into a spacious suite in Zurich's Grand Hotel Dolder, and, when they were not on frequent trips to Paris and London, they visited the Saltens regularly. The Saltens met up with Salten's old publisher at the *Neue Freie Presse*, Ernst Benedikt, with fellow journalist and author Roda-Roda, and with Salten's old classmate Eugen Jensen. Grete von Urbanitzky, now thoroughly disillusioned by Nazi politics, had herself become an exile and moved to Lugano, and she and the Saltens exchanged frequent visits. Otti's brother Richard came for longer visits, and Wally Strakosch made a longer stopover in Zurich on her journey to safety in the United States. The Saltens could be fairly confident that Switzerland was a safe haven since, in the previous summer, the League of Nations had accepted Switzerland's appeal for unconditional neutrality, and Switzerland had exchanged diplomatic notes with Germany and Italy confirming this status.

On August 10 Hans Rehmann passed away, and there was no longer anything preventing Anna from moving to Zurich to be with her parents. That same month Richard Beer-Hofmann and his wife Paula, who had spent the past year in hiding, came to Zurich on the first stage of their journey to America. Anna went to visit them, and Salten learned, upon her return, that Beer-Hofmann had never inquired about her loss. This confirmed again for Salten that Beer-Hofmann thought only of himself, never of others. In reality Beer-Hofmann had grave personal concerns of his own; his wife was in extremely poor health, and, during their stay in Zurich, she suffered a fatal heart attack. A broken-hearted Beer-Hofmann bought two burial lots, buried her in Zurich, and then departed alone for the United States.

Paula's death shook Salten, and he wrote a conciliatory note to Beer-Hofmann, noting that they had, after all, experienced "a whole, long lifetime" together. "Of course, we don't presume anything from you," Salten added, "However, we want, in any case, to say that we are ready with all our hearts to see you, to come to you or to have you come to us, if you have even the slightest desire for that. … You will find in the two of us old, unchanged admirers."[34] Beer-Hofmann, in his state of grief and turmoil, never responded to Salten's letter.

Salten's immediate concern in Zurich was to find a way to guarantee his future income; this meant first securing the foreign rights for his animal novel *Perri*. He was soon in touch with Paul Zsolnay, who had founded a new firm called Continental Department under the auspices of A. M. Heath and Company in London. Through this agency Zsolnay hoped to mediate and facilitate contracts for books and film rights between the German- and English-speaking worlds. Zsolnay himself knew that this was an admittedly risky business since, once war broke out, Germany would ban new English literature and English readers would regard all literature coming from Germany as "Nazi."[35] Furthermore, the exile presses, such as Gottfried Bermann-Fischer's in Stockholm,[36] were struggling for their own survival and angling for new contracts with former Zsolnay authors. Franz Werfel had already jumped ship and signed on with Bermann-Fischer. Salten was justifiably nervous about his own prospects, but, unlike Werfel, he decided to break with the Zsolnay Verlag in order to sign on with Paul Zsolnay as an individual, in London. His legal argument for the break with the Vienna publishing house was that it had neither brought *Perri* to the home market nor released it in German for publication abroad. Paul Zsolnay supported him in his break with the publishing house in the belief that Salten had the legal right to become a free agent for his own works.[37] Salten's case, however, was far more complex than Franz Werfel's had been. First, he still had substantial debts to Zsolnay that the publishing house claimed were owed to it. Second, and more importantly, Salten had signed a contract with the Zsolnay publishing house *after* its takeover by the Germans. Since it was eager to hold Salten to his prior contracts in order to benefit from his foreign earnings, the press refused to accept Salten's claim of justifiable termination.

The American firm of Bobbs-Merrill was confused by the conflicting assertions made to it by Salten and by the Zsolnay press, with which Bobbs-Merrill had signed the original contract for the English-language version of *Perri*. The situation was further complicated by Paul Zsolnay's assertions that he and his London office were now Salten's sole representative for the international rights to his works. Letters flowed between Indianapolis, London, Zurich, and Vienna that tested the patience and tempers of all parties. Bobbs-Merrill finally took the matter to court, and on March 22, 1940, an American arbitration tribunal decided fully in Salten's favor.

This decision was a happy one for Salten, but Paul Zsolnay did not benefit from it. During the months of uncertainty, Salten had sought advice from Stefan Zweig, who advised him to break off all his earlier contracts and to transfer the German rights for his books to the exile presses of Bermann-Fischer or Allert de Lange. From his post in London, Zweig cautioned, "As for Mr. Paul v. Z., I believe that, especially in America, where one is adamant in matters of Nazi compromises, people are strongly biased against him" and that "the danger of confusing the Z[solnay] publishing house in Germany with him as an individual still exists." Zweig added, in parentheses, that "one really does not know whether he still retains certain ties with his earlier firm; … people allege this, at least."[38] This caution was enough to dissuade Salten from continuing to use Zsolnay as his agent beyond a single, one-year contract, and he began to look for a new German-language publisher. He considered going with Bermann-Fischer, then with the Rascher firm in Zurich, before finally settling on another Zurich publishing house, that of Albert Müller.

The first new Salten novel that this firm published was *Bambis*

Kinder (Bambi's Children), a work designed to capitalize on Salten's greatest commercial achievement and to assure Salten's continued success by taking up where *Bambi* left off and relating the story of Bambi's twin offspring, Geno and Gurri. While the work remains faithful to nature in its depiction of the beauty and danger of forest life and seasonal changes, it is also a charming depiction of Salten's and Otti's relationship to Paul and Anna when they were small. Paul, like Geno, had been cautious and fearful, while Anna, like Gurri, was outgoing and slightly reckless. Unlike real woodland roebucks, Bambi takes an active role in the lives of his children, rescuing them from danger and teaching them to develop their finer traits. Geno grows up to be wise, serious, and brave, while Gurri becomes even more charming and earns a special spot in Bambi's heart.

When Salten's American publisher said that one scene of the work appeared "improbable," Salten argued that this was an example of "poetic license," much as the scene in *Bambi* where the old stag frees a hare from a noose. As to this newer work, he commented, "After all, the nightly visit by Bambi to the captured Gurri is also improbable, it is improbable that he leads his family to safety behind the hunters' roundup of game, and Gurri's behavior towards the bellowing elks is improbable." In fact, Salten commented, if one were to examine his text for probability, *Bambis Kinder* would be "just as improbable as the Bambi book, or Perri, or Florian." Still, he noted that the scene that disturbed his publisher – Bambi's attack on a young hunter – was not impossible, either: "It is something that I myself experienced in September when a buck, frightened by who knows what, almost ran me over.... If Bambi's improbable paternal solicitude for his children can be accepted, then this act caused by fear for his family can also stand."[39]

Salten was wise in not taking the easy route of publishing this story with a children's press. Not only did this free him from the constraints placed on works of children's literature,[40] he protected himself from being identified as "just" an author of juvenile fiction. This was a point that he had to make over and over again with his American publisher, who wanted Salten to soften his emphasis on animal sexuality for the sake of his juvenile readers. Salten responded quickly, saying "your intention to 'soften' the mating period of the deer horrifies me a little," adding:

294

> At this time I beg you most urgently, quite apart from softenings, *not* to advertise my work as a children's book or to launch it otherwise in such a way. This would close the door from the very beginning to the larger world of adults, friends of nature, women, young girls, and so on. Excuse me when in this point too I support my request with my Bambi experiences. *Bambi* found its way from adult readers to children to such a degree that right up until today American children and adults write me letters. The path from children to adults is much longer and much more difficult.[41]

It was, in fact, the many fan letters from American readers that bolstered Salten's spirits during these difficult times. On September 6, 1939, he spent his first birthday in exile. It was, in fact, his seventieth birthday, and he could not help but compare the occasion with the tumultuous reception the Viennese had given him ten years before. He turned down suggestions from friends that the day should be recognized in any public fashion and celebrated instead with his family and a small circle of friends.

Chapter 23: Life in Exile

Anna was now living with the Saltens and contributed to the family income by writing short stories for the newspapers and translating literary works from English into German. Theoretically, the Saltens were free, if they wished, to emigrate to the United States, and Salten played with this idea for some time. He was dissuaded, however, by the difficulty of getting to Portugal and the prospects of a long and difficult sea voyage that he feared Otti would not survive, given her serious heart condition. Another dissuading factor was news that filtered back to him about the difficulties faced by many of his emigrant friends in America. Thomas Mann, for one, applauded Salten's decision to stay in Switzerland. "The way matters lie, you are in far better hands than you would be in this country, where the living conditions for German writers are so difficult that I discourage everyone who is not immediately threatened in Europe from coming here," he wrote. The United States was not the safe refuge that many Europeans imagined. "[German writers] have to beg for support from overburdened committees one dollar at a time," Mann stated, "and the illusion that people were waiting for them [here] is quickly destroyed."[1]

Although Salten was frustrated at first by the fact that his works were not being published or performed in America as he had hoped – his play, *Louise von Koburg*, which seemed to him to be a guaranteed success on a New York stage or in a Hollywood film, languished with well-wishers who had promised him help – Salten slowly resigned himself to living out his days in Zurich. He followed a regular schedule, taking care of his correspondence and working on his literary production in the morning. Two or three afternoons a week, he dictated from his notes to his secretary, Gertrud Schattner. Most of his literary activity centered on his animal stories and other works of fiction, but he also began dictating portions of his memoirs. On Sundays the Saltens joined a small circle of friends who met regularly for dinner at the Tannenbaum Restaurant near their home. They also frequented other restaurants, had numerous small dinners and evening gatherings at their apartment, called on friends from emigrant and Swiss artistic circles, went to the cinema, and attended theatrical productions and concerts. The Wednesday Club gatherings at the home of Lily Reiff-

Sertorius were a special treat; Lily had been a piano student of Franz Liszt's and had made a considerable name for herself as a concert performer and composer. Her Wednesday social gatherings and concerts drew the most illustrious visiting writers, musicians, and artists to her spacious home. The Saltens were regular attendees and delighted both in the company and in the music.[2] Many refugees from German and Austrian theaters had sought refuge in Switzlerand, and the Zurich Schauspielhaus thrived with this infusion of new talent. Salten's daughter recalled that her parents frequently invited members of the Zurich Schauspielhaus to their home, such as the dramaturg Kurt Hirschfeld and actor Heinrich Gretler. Salten developed particularly strong friendships with the socialist politician Kurt Düby and with the theater critic Paul Pereszlenyi, while the feuilleton editor for the *Neue Zürcher Zeitung*, Jakob Welti, lived in the same house as the Saltens. Because of foreign book sales, especially Salten's income from America, the family was, in fact, able to live quite comfortably.

The Saltens, therefore, had an easier time than many exiles. Salten enjoyed the companionship of his pet dachshund, Flipsi; his daughter recalled that when Salten grew lonely in exile, "this loyal companion of his strolls in the forest, gladdened its master, with its mild-mannered mirth and intelligent seriousness."[3] The unswerving loyalty of dogs was evidently much on Salten's mind, for, while noting that "war stories are not my thing at all,"[4] he composed two stories that focused on the positive qualities of dogs in wartime.

The short story "How War Came to Zorek" was motivated by the 1939 Nazi takeover of Poland. It tells of a mongrel dog owned by Polish peasants that happens to be away from the house when it is bombed and all its inhabitants killed. For two days the dog remains by the ruins of its former home, whimpering over the loss of his human family and suffering pangs of hunger. Finally, a patrol of soldiers appears, and the dog runs to greet them, "wagging his tail enthusiastically for them, dancing around the group" because, as a dog, he "knew nothing about war. He could not distinguish between friendly and enemy troops." One of the soldiers draws his pistol and kills him. When the others protest, the soldier shrugs and answers, "What of it? It was only a Polish dog!"[5]

The other work was *Renni der Retter* (Renni the Rescuer), a new novel that traced the life of a rescue dog, its training and its service on the battlefield. In preparing this work, Salten requested of the sixth division of the Swiss army that he be allowed to spend a half day with its dogs as part of his research into their functions in war.[6] Salten divided the book into three parts: Renni's life as a puppy, his first training and work in army maneuvers, and his work on the battlefield. Georg is the model dog owner because, contrary to all expectations, he manages to train his dog to search for the wounded without ever beating him or even speaking to him harshly. The dog is the model pet: loving, loyal, and eager to please his master. Together, Renni and his master are idealized figures in a world of blood and chaos, although Georg does occasionally allow his temper to flare when he sees an animal mistreated or people discriminated against because of their social class. Georg describes to Renni their role in the war effort: "With every wounded man that we rescue, we do some good. Whether he's a friend or a foe, it's all the same to you, partner, isn't it? And to me. We have no enemies."[7] The book is full of reflections on war. When Georg and Renni cross the border into enemy country, Georg remarks: "These villages, these fields, these meadows!... So that was what the enemy country was like. It looked much like home."[8] Georg despairs sometimes over the fact that, in the massive slaughter of war, he and Renni are able to save only a few individuals. This leads him to what are perhaps his deepest insights into the nature of war:

> In war people cease to be persons, separate individuals. So long as men are under fire, can keep on their feet, can go on shooting and charging like robots, they're not themselves at all; they forget they have a life of their own, they forget their work, their hopes, their sorrows, their joys. ... They're only senseless atoms. Atoms in a strange and terrible compound. But a mighty will runs through them, a sort of mass intoxication, a compelling force to overcome the power of the enemy, to reach an objective, and this force melds them all into one living whole... victory, fame![9]

Georg and Renni, however, are concerned with the other side of war: "We care for the poor fellows who lie wounded on the ground. We carry them out, and they... well, when they wake up, when they're put to bed, they cease to be atoms then. They're men again, persons, individuals... with a fate of their own... all too often a fate distorted out of all semblance of itself." Georg concludes, "War leaves all its victims wrecked in body, soul, or spirit, or all three. ... Only a very few, only the most robust come out of this mad horror unscathed. Or do any do so? Who knows?"[10]

Because the novel dealt with a contemporary war, Salten was concerned about its reception, noting, "Never have I been so worried about a book as I have been this time."[11] He was careful to avoid identifying the war in the novel with the present European conflict by changing the circumstances of the war and by talking only about its economic, not its political origins. In spite of this, the novel clearly takes place in the present: the characters talk about the First World War, and Georg becomes friends with a family of refugees from the Russian Revolution. Salten took meticulous care to avoid giving any indication of partisanship in the present conflict. Although the names of his human characters are German, Salten played around with several dog names, using Bosco,[12] then Forto,[13] before settling on Renni as a more neutral name less likely to be associated with the Italian language and, through it, with the present German-Italian axis. Unlike his earlier novel *Florian*, where Salten bemoaned the passing of Imperial Vienna, Salten names no towns or cities, and no known figures appear in the work. The novel is, in fact, as ahistorical as his earlier *Sträfling Nummer 33* (Prisoner 33).

As in the case of *Perri* and *Bambis Kinder*, *Renni* was published in the United States before it appeared in Switzerland. Because of this, several weaknesses that his Swiss publisher eliminated from the German version are evident in the earlier edition. In the American novel, Renni and another war dog, Hector, question the reasons for the war in which they are forced to serve. Walter de Haas quite correctly disputed the need for such a conversation, and Salten, while protesting that animals did, in fact, converse with one another, agreed to cut this particular passage. He also agreed to cut the subplot of a carrier pigeon that is traumatized by the war and seeks refuge by riding around on Renni's head, saying, "Let this bird lead its life only in America."[14]

At least one critic has pointed out that Salten's political outlook had changed since the beginning of the war, that, whereas he had glorified the splendor of the old Habsburg empire in *Florian*, he now addressed the necessity of equality for people of all social classes.[15] Salten reiterated his old views from the previous war, however, when he said, "This world of ours is coming to an end." He was surely speaking of himself and his generation when he added, "And the new world which will come into being is a world we'll never live to see, a world we can't even imagine."[16]

In truth, Salten had had enough difficulty understanding the political currents of his own age. He and Otti were both in frail health now; Salten reported, "I am writing, and, instead of occupying myself too much with events, I strive to make the best of them in the conviction that not much more life is left for me and I do not need to worry about things all too much."[17] He tried to help other refugees whenever he could. He decided against joining the P.E.N. Club in Exile, but did join the Augustin Keller Lodge of the B'nai B'rith and wrote letters to distant friends, offering advice and, whenever possible, modest financial support. His old journalist friend Bertha Zuckerkandl was one of those to whom he sent money during these hard times.[18]

Salten's sister Rosalie was still living in Vienna and was of particular concern. She had supported herself through the years by housing and caring for the elderly; now she herself was an "elderly, also somewhat feeble-minded woman" in need of care. The Nazis had ordered her to vacate the small garden house in which she had been living by the end of 1939, but she had appealed and managed to get a delay until May 31 of the following year. Salten tried to help her from abroad, looking for some way to reverse this notice and to get her permission to stay in her home.[19] Her situation continued to worsen, however, as Salten received reports that she "cannot even buy the medicine prescribed by the doctor" and "is starving and freezing because she is not receiving any money."[20] Salten had already committed himself to sending regular payments of 100 Reichsmarks to help cover her expenses. Fortunately, philanthropic organizations were also able to provide some assistance to people in Rosalie Salzmann's situation. The Swedish Mission helped out until it was dissolved in May 1941, then the Quakers, and finally the Welfare Action Committee for Christian and Non-denominational non-Aryans of the Ostmark [Austria] took up

Rosalie's case and oversaw her care in a communal dwelling in the city's second district. Still, matters continued to deteriorate. Rosalie reported to Salten in February 1941 that "the people who are in my neighborhood are extremely upset, almost deranged, and every day transports leave for Poland, carrying people to an uncertain fate." The Galician Jews had been the first to go; now they had begun rounding up other groups of Jews as well: *"all the others, I among them, this danger cannot be stopped any more."*[21] On June 28, 1942, Rosalie Salzmann was deported to Theresienstadt, where she died on August 30.[22]

Salten also had concerns closer to home. In October 1940, Anna's glands were swollen, her left eye swelled alarmingly, and she came down with trigeminal neuralgia, which caused her intense pain that could be treated only with morphine injections. Fortunately, Salten was able to send her on a five-week course of treatment to a spa in Engadin. Anna returned to Zurich after the new year; Salten noted that she still had traces of the disease, but that the doctors were hopeful that these would eventually disappear. At the same time, he noted proudly that, in addition to paying for Anna's treatment, he had now been able to pay Paul Zsolnay half the long-standing debt that he and his son had incurred with Zsolnay's father some ten years earlier.[23] The report to the Swiss police of January 1941 stated, "In regards to his tax obligations, it should be mentioned that Salten does not want to incur any debts. ... Rather than worsening, his income has gotten somewhat better. The remittances from America always arrive regularly."[24]

However, Salten suffered his own economic shock when, in June 1941, the American government suddenly shut down all transfers of funds to Europe, out of fear of unwittingly contributing to the German war effort. The timing was especially bad for Salten since his American agent, Sanford Greenburger, and the publishing firm Simon and Schuster were still negotiating with Disney to assure fair payment to Salten for his various animal works. Greenburger assured Salten in mid-June that special royalty licenses would soon be made available and that the delay would be temporary. The situation remained difficult, however, and in April 1942 Greenburger wrote that he would try to get a royalty license for Anna, since she, as a Swiss citizen, could more easily be approved to receive payment from America.[25]

In spite of these personal and financial worries, Salten expressed optimism in August 1941 about his life in exile. Otti was doing "astonishingly well" under the treatment of Doctor Hämmerli-Schindler, the man who had treated Rilke in his final illness and whom Salten described as "angelic" and having "an artist's nature," and Anna was recovering from the aftereffects of her inflamed trigeminus. "We have very pleasant contacts here with extraordinarily cultivated Swiss," he reported, and, except for the difference in Swiss and Viennese accents, "I do not notice at all that I am away from home."[26] In the meantime, Salten produced another animal book for Bobbs-Merrill which he called *A Forest World* (German title: *Kleine Welt für sich*). In it he summarized his views of the proper relations of humans to wild and domesticated animals while stressing that there would always be an invisible wall between man and animal because of their failure to communicate with one another. In addition, he fleshed out the contrasting inducements for animals of a safe life of servitude to man and a perilous life of freedom in the forest, thereby making it possible, once again, for "readers to find whatever each one chooses: a dramatic and timely warning or purely a delicious tale."[27] Salten summarized the book's message a bit differently, condemning his own escapism into nature by saying, "that this story tries to portray human and animal cohabitation, as well as the impossibility of shutting oneself off from the world and remaining alone in the simple state of nature." Because this book brings together all of Salten's views regarding man's relationship to nature, the author felt that the novel belonged "to the most difficult of all my efforts."[28] His American agent, Sanford Greenburger, co-translated the novel for Bobbs-Merrill, who published it in 1942. It appeared in Switzerland two years later.

Salten was prohibited from writing for the Swiss newspapers, but this did not prevent him from giving occasional lectures, usually to Jewish circles. He lectured twice before Zurich's Zionistische Ortsgruppe, once on Heinrich Heine, once on Theodor Herzl. The 1940 Heine lecture was the most noteworthy, since in it Salten elaborated on his theory of the two basic strains in Judaism, the Mosaic and the Davidic, which he had first developed in the 1920's and written about in 1932,[29] calling Ferdinand Lassalle, Karl Marx, and Leon Trotsky representatives of the insurgent Mosaic impulse and British politicians Benjamin Disraeli, Rufus Isaacs, and Leslie Hore-Belisha conservative and artistic Davidic figures.[30] Salten went on to say that, whereas the country one lived in generally determined the dominance of one of these impulses, Heine uniquely combined both. He fought "against the servitude of all mankind with formidable wit, with powerful earnestness" but was at the same time a master stylist of prose and poetry, "one of the three, four greatest, if not the very greatest poet Germany has ever had." And because he joined both the Mosaic and the Davidic elements in his person, he was truly a representative "of all Jewry."[31]

In the summer of 1941, Salten went to Basel to speak to the city's Rotary Club "About Old Vienna" [*Vom alten Wien*]. He refused a fee for this presentation, stating proudly that "it will be one Rotarian speaking to [other] Rotarians."[32] Then, in November, Salten delivered a lecture in the Jewish Community Center in Zurich entitled "We and the Theater," which was doubtless a reworking of the speech he had given in Vienna in 1935 with the sardonic title "The 'Destructive Influence' of the Jews in the Life of the Theater." This speech would have had particular resonance in Zurich, since so many Jews from German and Austrian theatrical circles had sought refuge there. Ironically, the Saltens had just lost their "German" (Austrian) citizenship and were now stateless.

Salten continued to be plagued by the difficulty in getting money from America. He was also angry with the Walt Disney Studios because he believed that they were trying to cheat him out of his due. Whereas he had previously been careful not to antagonize Disney, he now found the newest contract that his agent was negotiating highly detrimental to himself. "The only thing still missing" from this contract, he wrote Greenburger with pointed sarcasm, "is … that I would have to pay Disney something extra in case he decides to acquire one of my books or short stories." Anyone could see "that an options contract that binds me makes sense only if this obligation is paid for through appropriate remuneration," that is, it would make sense only if it stated that "the purchase price is negotiated from case to case."[33]

This dispute did not prevent him from writing, however. Bobbs-Merrill had been so pleased with his latest animal novel that it requested a new one as soon as possible, and Salten went quickly to work on a work about a cat.

In many ways *Djibi* was a contrast work to *Renni*, which had shown dogs as loyal and obedient servants even to the cruelest of masters. Djibi is a thoroughly independent cat; as soon as she is rebuffed by the boy who had raised her, Djibi leaves his home forever. Eventually, she settles into the home of a kindly teacher, where she and the teacher's dog Tasso become loving companions. Salten's alter ego, the teacher who adopts Djibi, praises her as "a free being ... untamed and untamable." In this she resembles her larger relatives, the lions and tigers, who "adapt themselves" to captivity with some difficulty and "are grateful if one is kind to them."[34] Djibi has strong hunting instincts that have nothing to do with hunger; she simply kills for the delight of it. This proves to be her undoing, for after the neighboring farmer loses several of his rabbits to the cat, he kills her.

Djibi is the last of Salten's animal novels. It appeared in Switzlerland and in England in 1945 and in America in 1948.[35] Salten began another novel bearing the title *Der Kater Rustan...* (The Tomcat Rustan...), but it remained a fragment of thirty-nine pages.

By constantly writing, Salten was able to live through the difficulties of the war and the health problems that plagued the family. In April 1942 he and Otti quietly celebrated their fortieth wedding anniversary. In anticipation of the event, Otti wrote to their friend Wally Strakosch: "In these days I have also had many cares and worries, but I have experienced only good things from my husband. Not many women can say that."[36] Her heart condition had grown more critical. Salten had been careful not to tell her of her brother Richard's death, out of fear of the effect it would have on her. Although he held out little hope for her, the doctor found Otti's condition "somewhat better" on June 13, and the family celebrated by going to the Apollo theater to see the MGM film version of Salten's novel *Florian*. Salten knew the requirements of writing for an American film audience and was tolerant of the changes the writers had made, noting in his journal that "although the story is butchered, the basic intent of the book is well brought out; [it is] tasteful, lovely."[37]

It had been an enjoyable respite and was Otti's last outing. By June 16, the doctor told Salten she had no hope of recovery. She was then heavily sedated. Family friends – the actor Eugen Jensen, Siegfried Trebitsch, and Lily Reiff – helped Salten keep watch at her bedside. She died early on June 22 and was buried in the Lower Friesenberg cemetery in Zurich. A large crowd gathered for the ceremony. Besides family members and the rabbi, Siegfried Trebitsch and Eugen Jensen spoke at her graveside. Salten noted in his diary that Jensen was "very moved and poignant."[38] Kurt Hirschfeld of the *Schauspielhaus* spent much of the day with Salten; when a guest came by that evening, Salten was "too tired and sad" to converse for long and took to his bed.

Salten remained inconsolable over the loss of his wife in the days that followed. "*I am alone,*" Salten wrote in his diary, "*alone!*"[39] He became a virtual recluse, refusing to leave his home and trying, with little success, to bury himself in his writing. Anna grew more and more concerned about his mental state, and Eugen Jensen wrote to him a month after Otti's death, saying that he had heard "that you are inaccessible, that you say life holds nothing for you and that you wish you wouldn't wake up anymore. ... For God's sake! Felix! What kind of thoughts are those? ... Life still holds much beauty for you and you have responsibilities to it, especially to Anna, and then to the world and to your friends." He tried to move Salten by telling him, "when you retreat so forcibly, your flight into your work will bring about no fruitful result, the pulse, the heart of your work will be lacking." Jensen called on him to recognize that, "in spite of war and all the bitterness, life still has so much beauty," adding that he personally rejoiced in life and gave thanks to God every day: "the old Lord God in whom you don't want to believe. ... Think about the time when you slung your gun on your shoulder and went out into the forest. Didn't you ever sense Him? The forest remains, even if we old lads can no longer shoot bucks any more." He suggested Salten go up to the top of Zurich's Uetliberg and spend an evening there: "You will see how refreshed and energized you will be when you come home."[40]

Salten eventually began to socialize within a small circle of friends and, after some weeks, to attend Lily Reiff's Wednesday Club, but he avoided going to the theater for a full year after Otti's death; he returned only in June 1943 to see a production of Hofmannsthal's *Der Turm* (The Tower). He returned to the movie theaters in November 1942 to see the long-awaited Disney production of *Bambi*. The movie audience applauded him, and Salten found the film "very nice!" but noted despondently that "Otti should have seen it."[41]

Anna was a great comfort. She was starting to get some recognition for her translations and was giving frequent readings of them. Her major triumph was a translation for the stage of John Steinbeck's *The Moon is Down*, a work presenting a devastating picture of the effects of the German invasion of Norway. She completed it that summer, and in December 1943 it was performed in the Zurich Schauspielhaus.

It also looked, for a time, as though Salten would succeed in finally getting his novel *Sträfling Nummer 33* into print in Switzerland. In anticipation of this, the Swiss newspaper *Baseler Nachrichten* published the work in serial form during the fall of 1942. Unfortunately, the plan to publish the book was ultimately scrapped.

Salten himself had begun to fade and was living more and more in the past. Otti's death had turned him into an old man. He developed severe leg pains, and now, when he went walking with his dog, his gait was a slow and painful shuffle. He reminisced more and more about his life in prewar Vienna, speaking "masterfully" and "with quiet humor" with his friends about the Habsburg royalty and about the many writers, actors, and artists that he had known.[42] When the news came that Max Reinhardt had died, the Zurich Schauspielhaus organized a memorial service in his honor, and Salten was one of those asked to share the speakers' podium. This speech, which was held in the theater on November 14, 1943, was published the following year in a volume entitled *In memoriam Max Reinhardt*, along with the speeches of Oskar Wälterlin, Wolfgang Langloff, and Eugen Jensen.

By September 1944 Salten's health was too poor for him to partake in any elaborate celebration of his seventy-fifth birthday. The day was marked by the publication on the front page of the *Neue Zürcher Zeitung* of one of his old feuilletons, in which he had written about the blessings music, literature, and nature provide in helping one momentarily forget one's anxieties.[43] The Augustin Keller Lodge of B'nai B'rith organized a low-key birthday celebration for him at which Eugen Jensen and his actress wife Alice Lach read from Salten's works, and Salten received letters, telegrams, and flowers from friends and readers scattered around the world.

Salten no longer kept a diary, so there is no record of his reaction to the birthday celebration, nor to December 13, when his daughter married a prominent young lawyer named Veit Wyler, whom she had first met in Saint Moritz through a mutual friend. Wyler was four years Anna's junior and was extremely active in Zionist circles – from 1940-1943 he had served as President of Zurich's Zionistische Ortsgruppe, and he had won a name for himself in 1936 for his defense of David Frankfurter, who had assassinated the German leader of the Swiss Nazi party. He was most effective, however, in helping Jewish refugees steal across the Swiss border, supplying passports and visas to many of them, and arranging their further flights into safe territories. Wyler was able to take over Salten's legal affairs. And, in 1945, he and Anna presented Salten with his first grandchild, Judith.

Unfortunately, Salten was by now too worn down to take full pleasure in these events or to socialize even in small circles; as Anna stated in her annual report to the Zurich police in December 1944, Salten could "no longer work much as a writer" and was "confined to bed much of the time."[44] Anna and her husband came to the apartment for daily visits, but Salten found even these visits tiring and said to Wyler one day, "I am happy when you come and even happier when you leave."[45] The last months of his life were spent quietly at home with his housekeeper, Pepi Wik, and with Flipsi, the dachshund that he had brought with him from Vienna. On October 8, Salten "quietly and willingly" passed away.[46] Rabbi Taubes, Kurt Hirschfeld from the Schauspielhaus, Anna, and Siegfried Trebitsch spoke at his burial. Trebitsch noted later that "with Felix Salten's death, the last friend whom I have had since youth had been snatched away from me," asserting, "we were actually brothers-in-arms." The sad thing about reaching an advanced age, he said, was that "one sees one's comrades falling to [the] right and to [the] left of one in the battle that life is."[47]

Salten would probably have agreed with Trebitsch about the loss of old friends. He had outlived his closest friends from the Young Vienna circle, including Beer-Hofmann, who had died in September. He had also outlived his enemies. He had even survived Adolf Hitler, the Third Reich, and the annexation, terror, and destruction of Vienna. It is doubtful that Salten took much pleasure in Hitler's death; the Nazis had, in his opinion, already destroyed the multicultural climate of Vienna that had been the source of so much music, art, and fine literature. Salten had, to be sure, found a safe haven in Switzerland, and Zurich had come to hold a special place in his heart as a place where "there is an honest fraternization that creates a single people above every racial difference." As he had written to a friend several years earlier, "nobody lets me feel that I am an outsider, and I forget it myself at times, and yet at times I feel this outsider status with gentle melancholy."[48]

In visiting other countries, Salten had waxed ecstatic about Palestine, although he felt that it was a state only for the young and vigorous, and about the United States, although he was puzzled by the naiveté and the Puritanism of its people. Next to Austria, Switzerland had come the closest to his ideal of a homeland but, until the very end, Salten had felt himself an outsider there. One might say that he had become Ahasver, the Wandering Jew, whom he had featured in his early attempt at establishing a Viennese cabaret, who had figured so prominently in the anti-Semitic literature of the Nazis, whom he had introduced into *Ein Gott erwacht*, his last great unpublished novel of the early Renaissance. At the end of that novel, the god Apollo tells Ahasver that, because he is a mortal, Ahasver is still looking for "some blissful ending." Apollo goes instead to the forests, to the mountaintops, "where the gods are": there "they are all alive, they wander on the earth as I do." Ahasver calls, "Perhaps we will see each other again in hundreds, perhaps in a thousand years!" "Perhaps," Apollo answers but has already disappeared into the brilliant sunrise.[49]

Salten ended this novel as he had ended *Florian*, with the allegorical title figure refusing to dwell in pathos and turning away instead into the silent beauty of nature. This had, after all, been one of the great lessons of Salten's works: that there is nothing to be gained by mourning the past; one can only, like Salten's deer and rabbits, live as best as one can in the present, snatching those small pleasures to be found in wood and field. This lesson was Salten's legacy. One who recognized and spoke of it was Ernst Lothar, former head of the Theater in the Josefstadt, who wrote from his exile in New York to tell Salten: "In the midst of the crowd of destroyed, embittered, and despairing men, your figure towers up consolingly, a man who, behind his work, always stands before it, an advocate of life even where things seem hopeless. You have always shown the way. Now you show the way out."[50]

Chapter 24: The Disney Transformations

When Walt Disney acquired the film rights to *Bambi* in 1937, Salten had to be pleased. By then *Bambi*, like all of Salten's novels, had been banned in Germany, and he was desperate to maintain his income. Disney paid Salten $5000 for these rights and made of *Bambi* what is arguably the best of his full-length animated films. Disney went on to acquire film options to all of Salten's future writings and used two more novels, *Perri* and *The Hound of Florence*, as the basis for popular live-action films. The Disney studios also made sequels and/or new creations based on themes and concepts from these novels.

To date the Disney output includes two *Bambi* films: the full-length animated cartoon *Bambi* (1942) and its sequel, the direct-to-video animation, *Bambi II* (2006); one "true-life fantasy" film, *Perri* (1957); and four live-action tie-ins loosely based on *The Hound of Florence*: *The Shaggy Dog* (1959), *The Shaggy D.A.* (1976), a made-for-television movie, *The Return of the Shaggy Dog* (1988), and, most recently, a complete overhaul of the original *Shaggy Dog* with a new story line and characters (2006). In addition, the Disney studios put out illustrated books and/or comics based on two other Salten works, *Bambi's Children* and *A Forest World*.

Salten had to be pleased. What he could not foresee, however, was that the Disney name would quickly supplant his own, that his European settings would be replaced by American forests and towns, and that in bookstores around the world, the simplified Disney texts would greatly outsell his original novels. Disney would benefit from Salten far more than Salten ever benefited from Disney.

Biographically, Salten and Disney had a good deal in common. Neither did particularly well in school, and neither completed a high-school-level education. Both suffered poverty in their childhood and were obliged to take on jobs that held no interest for them in order to contribute to the meager family income. Both had difficult relationships with their fathers. Both were captivated by the charms of the rural landscape and an idealized image of their nations' pasts while also being fascinated by and drawn to the new technologies, especially to the rich potential of the cinema. Both were self-made men. And both worked tirelessly to achieve success.

They differed, however, in several important points. Disney became convinced that he could recreate his idealized vision of small-town America in his films and theme parks while Salten looked back on Austria's glorious past with resignation and sad nostalgia. Because of this difference in world view, Disney infused Salten's works with an optimism lacking in the darker originals. Another point of difference frequently brought up by critics was the different attitudes the two men had towards hunting. As Matt Cartmill recounts it, Disney developed a distaste for hunting when he was five. The family had just moved to a Missouri farm and found the land overrun with rabbits:

> Walt crept into the fields with his older brother Roy to watch them in their springtime mating rituals. Charmed and excited by all the March-hare antics, Walt spent the next few days memorializing them in his very first cartoons: childish sketches of cottontails playing peekaboo in the grass. But when Roy next returned to the fields, he brought along his air rifle and shot the biggest buck bunny he saw. Walt dissolved in tears when Roy broke the thrashing rabbit's neck, and he refused to touch the rabbit stew their mother served up that evening.

The contrast that Disney witnessed that day, "between innocent animal desire and malign human contrivance," would, Cartmill added, "impress that love-and-death opposition on the world with particular force in *Bambi*."[1]

Bambi was the perfect vehicle for showing this opposition since, long before Disney bought the film rights to the novel, Salten's readers had asked again and again how, after writing *Bambi*, Salten could not only continue to hunt but also to defend the practice. Salten responded by pointing out the cruel but necessary predation that occurred within the animal kingdom. He believed that responsible hunting was a necessary and humane way to thin herds and control the animal population. He also pointed out that, on many of his forays into the forest, he went to look rather than to make a kill. For his part, Disney, like Salten, did not set out deliberately to make an anti-hunting film. His primary concern was always to create a good – and marketable – story. As one indication of this desire, Disney tried for several years to include in his animated film Salten's key message about man's and animal's shared vulnerability, until world events made audiences resistant to the image of a dead human being.

Bambi was the only Disney film based on a Salten novel that the author ever saw, and although he liked it, he always referred to it as "Disney's Bambi."[2] The film had had a long gestation period. Sidney Franklin, a producer/director at MGM studios, had bought the rights to the film from Salten in 1933.[3] Franklin had seen the "beauty, poetry, philosophy"[4] in the Salten work and had hoped to film it with live animals. He had recorded Margaret Sullavan and Victor Jory speaking the roles of the two dying leaves (chapter 8 of Salten's novel) and held tryouts for voices for the old Prince before realizing that he could not do justice to the work in a live-action film. Now convinced that the fantasy form of animation might be more amenable to Salten's work, Franklin offered the work to Disney in 1935. Disney's cartoons already featured talking animals, albeit clothed and humanized ones, and Disney was known to be continually experimenting and expanding the genre of animation. Disney liked the book and was intrigued by the idea of putting speech into the mouths of realistically drawn animals. Because of legal issues, it was April 1937 before the contracts were signed between Salten, his publishers, and the Disney studios. Although Disney fully expected to complete the film within a year, he hired Franklin to serve as his artistic consultant for a three-and-a-half year period. Neither man could foresee that it would be another five years before the studios could bring the conflicting elements envisioned by Disney, Franklin, and the Disney artists into harmony.

As two of Disney's animators recalled it, Disney was baffled by the direction the *Bambi* film would take, given the episodic nature of Salten's novel. He decided early on to make the death of Bambi's mother the turning point in the film; at the same time, however, he was determined that there be more humor in the film than in Salten's book and that that humor should come from "additional interesting creatures"[5] and sight gags. Early story ideas included a belligerent skunk, an excitable spider, a weasel, a mole, a possum, and raccoons. (Disney said of the raccoon, "I saw that animal as a kind of nut... the type that wipes off the knife and fork and [is] always wiping out a cup before he pours his tea."⁶) In one sequence that was particularly pleasing to Disney during this period, Bambi accidentally swallows an ill-tempered bee, is advised on how to get rid of it by a squirrel and chipmunk duo, and, while doing so, acquires a case of hiccups; when the bee finally exits Bambi's mouth it, too, is hiccupping wildly. Disney said of this sequence, "I like that situation because I can visualize it with the sound effects of the bee in Bambi's stomach. I think we are getting something that is not just the old type of gag."⁷

Still, these were gags, much in the nature of the short cartoon features his studio was producing with Donald Duck, Goofy, and Pluto as part of its *Silly Symphonies* collection. After viewing the early *Bambi* drafts, Franklin told Disney that the bee sequence should be excluded and that there should be more emphasis on character development, such as the relationship between Bambi and his mother, and on the personality of a philosophical Mr. Hare.

Disney agreed with Franklin that many of the sight gags, however humorous, detracted from Bambi as the main character of the film. Franklin helped Disney see that it was important to draw a long dramatic line so that the audience would identify with and care about the animals portrayed in the work. Franklin also suggested that the film's final scene reflect its opening, with Bambi replacing the old Prince on the hill and Faline and the twins replacing Bambi and his mother in the glade below.

Disney's personal enchantment with the Salten novel made him willing to expend great effort on creating a living setting in which its animal characters moved. Disney's artists studied sketches and photographs of the Maine woods in all seasons of the year, but their drawings looked too "busy" until Tyrus Wong introduced a Chinese aesthetic to the forest drawings, creating a lyrical, stylized background of bold colors and impressionistic forms that made a dream-like setting for the animals. A similar transformation occurred when Disney had his photographer, Maurice Day, shoot studies of deer in those woods, including the birth of a fawn; Day also sent two fawns to the studio as live models for the artists.⁸ Rico Lebrun was a particular help in teaching the artists animal anatomy so that they could authentically capture the various movements of the forest creatures.

At the same time, however, Disney realized that audience members must be made to identify with the animals. The deer would have to show human reactions and emotions, not through human gestures, but through facial expression and body movement alone. Artist Marc Davis achieved a breakthrough when he created a humanized face for Bambi by studying a baby's facial expressions and translating them to the baby deer. Indeed, by exaggerating the sizes of their heads and eyes and by reducing the length of their muzzles, the faces of the Disney fawns even had the proportions of those of human babies[9] and resembled heifers more than deer.

Disney had originally hoped to complete *Bambi* in time for the 1938 Christmas market but decided instead to delay its filming while he made *Pinocchio* (1940) as a successful follow-up to his first feature-length animation, *Snow White and the Seven Dwarfs*. He then made his concert film *Fantasia* (1940) and the less complex animation of *Dumbo* (1941).[10] It was wise to delay production of *Bambi* since these interim projects provided the studio with new artistic insights. Leopold Stokowski's collaborative input on *Fantasia* had a profound effect on the development of *Bambi*. In *Fantasia* the Disney graphics served as illustrations to pieces of classical music, and this music precluded any need for dialogue. This gave Disney new appreciation for the role that music could play in *Bambi*, both in creating mood and in advancing the story. He told his staff that this was a picture "for music..... This *Bambi*. It's a natural for it. More than just background music. The whole winter thing – all music. The whole damn hunt – music. Instead of so many sound effects ... like the fire and everything – do it all with music..."[11] Franklin, too, was enthusiastic about this approach; Disney would now show character and plot development through "music and action, not dialogue" in order "to keep it [the film] from sounding like the book."[12] By the time he was finished, Disney had reduced 10,000 words of Salten's dialogue to fewer than a thousand words,[13] transforming the work into what he called "a symphony" of nature.[14] Stowkowski was enthralled and predicted that *Bambi* would surpass the success of Disney's *Snow White and the Seven Dwarfs*. When this was reported to Salten, he replied modestly, "I will be very content if [it] ... achieves just half the success of the *Snow White* film."[15]

Like Franklin, Disney was eager to preserve the scene of Salten's novel in which the two last leaves clinging to a twig in late fall discuss the mysteries of death and eternity; like Franklin, Disney recognized the difficulty of recreating this dialogue on film. After much discussion, Disney eliminated the philosophical dialogue entirely but created instead a mood of ultimate loss through animation and music alone. The scene is a miniature drama in and of itself and serves as a subtle precursor to the death of Bambi's mother.

Disney also tried, unsuccessfully, to recreate Salten's dialogue between the forest animals and the dog (a pack of them, in the Disney film) that is the obedient servant of Man and turns on his own kind. Eventually that, too, was eliminated; Disney used the occasion instead to focus on Bambi's bravery. The most important scene that had to be eliminated, however, was that in which Bambi's father shows him a dead poacher and explains to him that Man is not an invincible god, as he had thought, but is instead, like the animals, vulnerable to forces larger than himself. The film animators recalled that Disney "had always considered this to be the big finish of his film, the point we had been working toward in all of Bambi's training."[16] But when Disney showed the animated scene with the dead poacher's body to a test audience in 1941, "four hundred people shot straight up into the air" in horror, and he dropped the scene immediately.[17]

The production notes for *Bambi* indicate, again and again, that Disney was sensitive to Salten's message but knew that the medium of the animated film could not deal with the complexities and ambiguities of the novel. As the film became leaner, he narrowed his focus until the film featured a single villain – Man – and simply traced the life cycle of a deer.

The animation process anthropomorphized the forest animals more than Salten ever had. Flower the skunk was a favorite with the Disney staff until the philosophical Mr. Hare was removed from the film and replaced with the outspoken young rabbit, Thumper. Thumper was introduced in part as the solution to an artistic dilemma: the Disney artists were having difficulty drawing Bambi's mother in a naturalistic manner while also having her speak. As a consequence, they limited her speeches to Bambi, and Thumper took over a larger role.[18] As friend and self-appointed mentor, Thumper was made to function much as Jiminy Cricket and Timothy Mouse had in Disney's two *Bambi* predecessors, *Pinocchio* and *Dumbo*. It is Thumper, and not Bambi's mother, who teaches the young deer his first words, helps him to jump, and encourages him out onto the winter ice. In the sequences of Bambi's encounter with a mole and with Bambi's attempts to walk upon the ice, Disney recreated sight gags he had already used in two Pluto cartoons.[19]

With the expanded role of Thumper, the focus of the whole film changed: three-quarters of the finished film now portrayed the world of animal "children," with their parents acting as "supporting players."[20] The childhood friendship between the deer, the skunk, and the young rabbit departed completely from Salten's novel. In fact, the relationship of the Disney animals to one another was a distorted one from the very beginning. In order to keep the storyline and its villain simple, Disney's artists created a forest that was a peaceable kingdom, a place where the forest animals turn against one another only in their rivalries during mating season. This, of course, makes the intrusion of Man all the more threatening. At the opening of the film, Baby Thumper drums on a hollow log to awaken Friend Owl and tell him of Bambi's birth; in Salten's nature novels, owls swoop down and devour young rabbits. Disney reproduced the frightening aspects of severe weather in his film, but not the predatory nature of the forest animals, in part because animation was not a good medium for bloodletting.

These changes affected the allegorical underpinnings of the work. It is possible that neither Salten nor Disney deliberately aimed for allegory, but their audiences read it into both their works. In Salten's novel, readers found clear allusions to the horrors of the First World War and the anti-Jewish pogroms that followed. Those looking for allegories in Disney's film found parallels between the deadly, unseen Man who intrudes into the peaceable forest and the Japanese menace that rained bombs down on Pearl Harbor in December 1941.[21] In the Disney movie, Man, who had been "both a force to be feared and a puzzle" in Salten's novel, is completely demonized by his visual absence and becomes "satanically evil."[22]

Because Disney had determined to make the death of Bambi's mother the turning point of the story, he manipulated scenes to emphasize Bambi's dependence and vulnerability. He disagreed with the suggestion that she be shot during a blizzard, asking,

"Wouldn't it be better to build the feeling [of intense hunger] up and then finally have relief, and just as there's relief, then comes this other thing?"[23] As finally conceived, Bambi's mother finds the first blades of spring grass for Bambi after both have suffered days of severe deprivation. It is then the hunters come. The audience hears the shot, but the doe's death is not shown on screen. Instead, one sees and hears Bambi searching the forest and crying out for his mother. Now the blizzard comes on, and Bambi sees the blurred contours of his mighty father, who informs him that his mother cannot be with him any more.

In Disney's film, this horrific event in the vulnerable young fawn's life transformed Bambi into an icon of the anti-hunting movement. As one scholar has put it, "The anti-hunting message was conveyed on a completely emotional level through sympathy with its characters. It was targeted at children in their most impressionable, formative years."[24] For this reason, the state of Maine declined the honor of hosting the film's premiere. This anti-hunting bias has endured, as generations of children, traumatized by the Disney film, blame hunters for "killing Bambi's mother."

Because *Bambi* was released during wartime, it was not a critical or financial success. Disney himself was strapped for money and deeply involved in making films for the war effort and appeared exhausted by the whole endeavor.[25] It is therefore unlikely that Disney considered making a sequel based on Salten's novel *Bambi's Children*, but he did release a Dell comic book version, illustrated by the Disney artists, in which Salten's twin fawns Geno and Gurri are joined in play by two of Thumper's offspring named Hopper and Patter. This Disney comic is remarkable because it presents a much more differentiated picture of hunting than the film had. Man is no longer an invisible threat; he appears as a kindly gamekeeper, who rescues the injured Gurri, heals her, and then releases her back into the wild. In addition, Disney preserved in the comic book Salten's careful distinctions between responsible and irresponsible hunting and poaching.

From 1941 onward, the Disney studios released a wide variety of products relating to the *Bambi* film: recordings, children's story and picture books, figurines, plush animals, games, children's dinnerware, a lamp, clocks, and watches, with many of these spin-offs continuing to be sold until the present day. Except for Disney's comic book of *Bambi's Children*, the spin-off books veered away completely from the Salten texts. All of them presented Bambi as a vulnerable fawn rather than as a young buck. *Bambi* books appeared under many guises: as trace and color books, as read-along books, as counting books, as scratch and sniff books. *Bambi's Snowy Day* boasted graphics with a fuzzy coating so that one could pet the animals. Other independent Bambi titles included *One Woodland Day*, *Bambi: Friends of the Forest*, *Thumper's Book of Opposites*, *Bambi's Big Surprise*, *Bambi and the Butterfly*, *Bambi: Opossum Problem*. These volumes were geared to preschoolers and introduced situations or characters that had never appeared in Salten's novels. Still, at least the Salten name appeared as the author of the works on which these Disney spin-offs were based, however small the print; the plush beanbag toys, jointed plastic dolls, and porcelein figurines did not. It is small wonder, then, that even in Austria most people believe today that Bambi was an American white-tail deer and a Walt Disney creation.

At the time of *Bambi*'s release, the war was in full swing and the Disney studios had only recently survived an animators' strike; this required Disney to suspend his production of more full-length animated features until 1950. He had acquired a long list of potential projects, however, and several of them involved Felix Salten's animal writings. By now Disney had a contract with Salten that gave him the first film option on Salten's future writings. Because Salten was living in Swiss exile and almost his entire income was dependent on an American market, he was eager not to offend Disney and lose out on potential income from new Disney projects. The Disney studios asked Salten not to use the Bambi name in any of his future titles.[26] Salten agreed to this but regretted that the various Disney spin-off editions of *Bambi* reduced the size of the royalties he had been receiving on his original work.[27]

In 1959, Disney released a new children's book based on another Salten work; entitled *Manni the Donkey in a Forest World*, it was illustrated by the Disney artists and recounted the chapter in Salten's *A Forest World* in which a donkey goes into the forest and meets the forest animals. Once again, Disney changed the emphasis of Salten's text. Most notably, the donkey performs a heroic act in the Disney version, frightening off a fox that was threatening the life of the squirrel Perri. There is no rescue in the Salten novel, and the squirrel that appears in that chapter is not named, but Disney was trying to capitalize on another of his full-length feature films, *Perri*, which had been released two years earlier and was based on Salten's novel about the life of a young squirrel.

Even before he made *Perri*, Disney had begun to capitalize on his *Bambi* success with a series of "true-life adventure" films. These films, Disney claimed, arose directly from the work on *Bambi*: "In *Bambi*, we had to get closer to nature. ... Finally, I sent out some naturalist-cameramen to photograph the animals in their natural environment. We captured a lot of interesting things and I said, 'Gee, if we give these boys a chance, I might get something unique!'"[28] Disney claimed that he had discovered at that time that the "problems and habits of real animals are often funnier and more surprising than the antics we dream up for our cartoon characters."[29] Because of the importance Disney placed on story line, these "true-life adventures," ostensibly documentaries filmed in the wild, had little mini-dramas and mini-gags built into them. And "because all true-life adventures had rhythm," the studios provided a sound track. Like *Bambi*, these films used music to punctuate their drama and gags; in one notable sequence of an early film, tango music was used as background to the stop and reverse motion added to the filmed courtship ritual of two tarantulas, and scorpions performed a square dance to the music and commands of an off-screen caller.[30] More subtle scores traced the moods and changes in the natural cycles of season and growth in the wild. *Perri*, Disney said, was new in that the studios added "the world of fantasy" to "the world of music" and "nature's world,"[31] thereby freeing the film editors to "manipulate the documentary footage to their hearts' content and fashion it into a story."[32] It was the fifth film in the "true-life adventure" series and the first to be filmed from a written script, even though the cycles of nature, the individualization of particular animals, and sight gags and drama of the wild had already given storyline and structure to the earlier films.

Still, *Perri* was the studio's first deliberate attempt to meld documentary with sustained character and plot development. In this film Disney was finally realizing Sidney Franklin's dream of transforming a Salten work into real-life drama. As was the case with its "true-life" predecessors, no human beings appeared in *Perri*. This eliminated immediately one of Salten's main conceits in the novel: that small children have the innocence that enables them to comprehend the speech of animals. But Disney gained as well: by eliminating Man from his film, he restored Salten's emphasis on the predatory nature of wild birds and animals, and the marten replaced Man as the film's main villain. In Salten's novel, humans cut down Perri's tree; in the Disney film, a beaver fells it.

Disney differed further from Salten in that he made no effort to have the animals communicate with one another except through chatter, barks, growls, and yelps. The curiosity, terrors, and joys of the squirrel Perri are revealed through her actions, not through words. Instead of dialogue, an off-screen narrator provides continuity and transitions between scenes. This had been the case for all of Disney's previous nature films, and here, as in those earlier films, Winston Hibler served as both writer and narrator. Perhaps to emphasize the fantasy aspect of *Perri*, Hibler composed most of the *Perri* narration in verse.

The Disney cameramen spent over three years filming in the Uintah Mountains of Utah.[33] Their first assignment was to capture on film the life cycles of all the animals that would be playing a role in the movie. This was already a major departure from the Salten novel but was entirely in keeping with the earlier Disney documentaries: the film would portray the frolicsome childhood not only of the American pine squirrel but of its mortal enemy, the marten. As in *Bambi*, the film infantilized the animals by expending a good deal of screen time on their cute and cuddly stages. A forest fire provided exciting footage of all nature seeking shelter in a beaver pond. Because it was typical of the nature cameramen to blur the lines between fantasy and actuality, it is hard to say how much of that footage was staged.

In the end, Disney's *Perri* bore remarkable similarities to the animated *Bambi*. Both were advertised as love stories. Perri is orphaned after the marten invades the home nest and kills her mother and siblings; Perri meets and frolics with Porro when the two are small, and they mate when they are grown; a forest fire, caused this time by a lightning strike rather than by man's carelessness, threatens all the creatures of the forest; a song called "Together Time" accompanies the joyous mating of the various animal species. Bambi even appears briefly in the film as a real deer, just as he had in Salten's novel.

Salten had described Perri's winter dreams, and the Disney people translated these dreams into a breathtakingly beautiful collage of flying squirrels and snowshoe rabbits sailing through a snowy landscape. Figures metamorphose from – and are transformed back into – clusters of animated snowflakes. This dream sequence is the highlight of the film and gives it a poetic beauty that transcends the genre of the nature documentary. Other techniques used to transcend everyday reality were banal and more conventional. The setting in the Uintah Mountains is renamed "Wildwood Heart," suggesting a non-geographical fantasy location that humans cannot find on any map. Seasons are transformed into the "Time of Beauty," "Time of Beginnings," "Time of Hunting," and so on, compelling one critic to write, "there is ... a cloying and cheapening coyness to some of the basic concepts. Such arch phrases as 'time of beginning ... time of alone ... together time, etc.' are decidedly hard to take."[34]

When, in a Disney television documentary, Winston Hibler implied that the squirrel chosen to play Porro had been selected because he had the special qualities of "leading man and comedian,"[35] he made it appear that Perri and Porro were portrayed by two individual squirrel actors. As one of Disney's cameramen, nephew Roy E. Disney, confessed later, Porro, like Perri, was portrayed by "*many* different squirrels." Some of these squirrels were tame; others were deliberately sacrificed to further the film's plot.[36] As Hibler so soothingly puts it in his film narration, "Death is a necessary evil" in the wild; "some die that others may survive."[37]

The manipulation of the animals disturbed some critics, but, as Leonard Maltin has remarked, the film's "superbly edited pieces of action" were "made possible [only] by the kind of preplanning impossible in the factual nature films." Maltin noted that the film employed nine cameramen, who exposed some 200,000 feet of 16mm film; this was then edited down to 8,000 feet for the finished product, "an incredible ratio of 25 to 1." During the filming process, Disney's crew invented special cameras; they also constructed elaborate blinds and elevator stands, so that they could not only capture close-up shots but also follow the progress of a squirrel or marten up and down a tree trunk. All of this care, Maltin has commented, made the film "a truly dazzling accomplishment. ... There is not a wasted second on screen."[38] As with the Disney animated films, the Disney studios marketed a number of *Perri* products at the time of the film's release: books, comics, plush animals, and even a kit that allowed children to make their own life-size Perri out of plastic and to glue fur to her body. Needless to say, all these products were based on the American pine squirrel, not the European red squirrel of the Salten novel.

As early as 1941, Disney had considered doing something with Salten's *The Hound of Florence*, but his involvement in the war effort and numerous other animated and live action projects caused him to put the work on hold until the late 1950's, when Disney proposed a *Shaggy Dog* television series to the ABC network.[39] When the network rejected the proposal, Disney released *The Shaggy Dog* pilot to movie theaters in 1959 as a low-budget, black and white film. It featured several young actors from his *Mickey Mouse Club* serials: Tommy Kirk, Tim Considine, Kevin Corcoran, Annette Funicello, and Roberta Shore, and cast Fred MacMurray as the hero's laughable father. The film grossed an astonishing $9.6 million and was one of the biggest hits of the year.[40] The enormity of this success inspired Disney to continue making films that blended fantasy with situation comedy, and to continue using the comedic talents of Fred MacMurray. In addition, the studios turned back to the *Shaggy Dog* conceit again and again; the visual gags made possible by having a human being turn into a sheepdog, one that could wear pajamas, brush its teeth, drive an automobile, and even speak, proved a surefire formula for successful comedy.

None of these *Shaggy Dog* films bears much resemblance to Salten's tragic tale of an impoverished Italian artist cursed to experience every other day as the pet of a royal Tuscan tyrant, although the 1959 film did retain the notion of shape-shifting as a phenomenon of Renaissance Italy and, like the novel, made use of a magical ring on which a spell had been cast, "probably by one of the Borgias." The film's hero is an inventive American teenager with a younger brother as his knowing sidekick and a comic father who does not understand most of the events in the film. In point of fact, the film credits say that the plot was only "suggested" by Salten's *The Hound of Florence*. The studios pay passing tribute to the actual novel when the film's young hero, having experienced his first metamorphosis into a sheepdog, goes to ask a museum director for assistance. Professor Plumcutt asks, "Do you remember the

Hound of Florence?" He calls it "the famous story of a young man who was changed into a dog" and goes on to relate Salten's plot, ending with the moment when the hero, in dog form, tries to defend "a beautiful girl" against the attentions of "an evil duke" and is brutally stabbed. The professor concludes, "And then, as the poor little animal lay there with the dagger deep in his heart, he suddenly changed back into a man again." The young teenage hero cries out, "A dagger into the heart! That'd kill me!," to which the professor exclaims, "No, no, you don't grasp the point of the story. What I was trying to say is that it is possible to break such a spell."[41] In the Disney film, the hero proves his valor by rescuing his love interest from the clutches of an East European spy, and it is this act of heroism that restores him – permanently, it seems – to human form.

Bambi, Perri, and *The Shaggy Dog* – all three "Salten" films represented advances in Disney's production techniques. *Bambi*'s artwork has made it a perennial favorite among young audiences; it represents the high-water mark in Disney's animated productions and was Disney's own personal favorite.[42] *Perri* introduced a story line into Disney's nature films and, as such, was his first film to blend fantasy with nature documentary, while *The Shaggy Dog* introduced fantasy into situation comedy to create a successful formula for Disney films made throughout the 1960s.

Unfortunately, Disney took much more from Salten than he ever gave in return. In 1941 Salten complained that, in the one-sided contract Disney had negotiated with his agent, "I have been delivered over to Disney with my hands and feet fettered and a gag in my mouth."[43] The most pressing difficulties – on both sides – were financial. Copyright issues kept Disney and the Salten heirs in court until 1996, at which time a senior district judge, Justin L. Quackenbush, declared that "Bambi learned very early in life that the meadow ... was full of potential dangers everywhere he turned. Unfortunately, Bambi's creator, Mr. Salten, could not know of the equally dangerous conditions lurking in the world of copyright protection ...."[44] One biographer has noted that "the original authors of the stories filmed by Walt Disney Productions ... were often caught in a curious bind. Few other studios were interested in acquiring stories about children or animals, and so there was no one to bid up the prices for them as there often is when a hot best seller goes on the Hollywood market,"[45] adding, "Almost never did the original authors get a cut of the merchandising bonanza the studio habitually generated when the story finally reached the screen." Instead, Disney put his staff of writers to work "Disnifying" the works of these authors; these Disney versions of literary works then outsold the originals, sometimes by a margin of five to one.[46]

This "Disnifying" not only took money away from the authors of the original works; it also rewrote them, shortening them drastically, giving them different emphases and prettying up the story. In the case of *Bambi*, the Disney studios turned a work for adults and older children into a story for first- and second-graders. A prominent children's librarian named Frances Clarke Sayers objected to the Disney bastardization of literary classics, exclaiming,

> I call him [Disney] to account for his debasement of the traditional literature of childhood, in films and in the books he publishes.
>
> He shows scant respect for the integrity of the original creations of authors, manipulating and vulgarizing everything to his own ends. ...
>
> Not content with the films, he fixes these mutilated versions in books which are cut to a fraction of their original forms, [and] illustrates them with garish pictures ....
>
> As for the cliché-ridden texts, they are laughable.[47]

Film critic Richard Schickel has called Disney one of the "most childlike of our mass communicators."[48] He objected to Disney's introduction of "wee creatures" as "a convenient way to brighten and lighten any story [he] feared might grow too serious or unpleasant for audiences," citing Thumper and Flower as examples in *Bambi*.[49] As for the true-life adventure films, especially *Perri*, "The business of individuating animals not only falsifies our understanding of them; in the last analysis, it cheapens experience, substituting patronization for the sense of awe that the truly sensitive observer feels in the presence of nature's enigmas."[50] And in films like *The Shaggy Dog*, "the small-town locale was preserved, and many of the subsidiary characters stayed on in it unchanged, but there was ... a gimmick ... to enliven things," in this particular case, "Hollywood's idea of a typical teen-age boy" turned into a dog.

Unfortunately, the magical Disney touch, even when Disney approached a work with sympathy, tended to relegate the original work to the sidelines. Memories of most films fade, but the Disney studios keep reissuing the old films and hawking related Disney books and toys on the market. To make matters worse, Salten's works had to endure an even greater erosion when sequels and remakes of both *Bambi* and *The Shaggy Dog* were released by the Disney studios in 2006. Neither film bears any resemblance to the Salten novels. Instead, both infantilize the films' characters and have childish plots about distant fathers who learn to appreciate their children. As a "Mom" in Kansas City wrote in one of the reviews for *Bambi II* on the official Disney web site: "It was very heartwarming. My four-year-old loved it."[51] This was Disney's legacy; sadly, it is not the legacy that Salten had hoped for.

Notes

Introduction

[1] Paul Wertheimer, "Felix Salten. Zur Eigenvorlesung am Sonntag, 5. März." The source is unidentified, in the manuscript collection of the ÖNB. The year of the piece is presumably 1932.

[2] "Junge Frauen," *Die Dame im Spiegel*, 26.

[3] "Pirschgang im Gebirge," *Kleine Brüder*, 104.

Chapter 1

[1] "Rückblende: Berühmte Wiener aus Budapest." Part of Salten's protest probably grew out of the fact that Hungarian and Galician Jews were looked down upon in Vienna.

[2] *Neue Menschen auf alter Erde. Eine Palästinafahrt*, 100.

[3] Salten's birth name has various spellings, including Sigmund, Siegmund, and Sziga. His birth certificate has the Hungarian spelling, Szigmund.

[4] "Rückblende: Berühmte Wiener aus Budapest."

[5] "Mein Vater. Aus dem Manuskript: 'Die Währinger Erinnerungen.'"

[6] Ibid.

[7] Ibid.

[8] "Eines Tages...."

[9] *Neue Menschen auf alter Erde*, 101, 100.

[10] "Mein Vater. Aus dem Manusckript: 'Die Währinger Erinnerungen.'"

[11] Ibid.

[12] An eighth child, born when the family still lived in Budapest, died shortly after birth.

[13] "Mein Vater. Aus dem Manusckript: 'Die Währinger Erinnerungen.'"

[14] "Meine Mutter. Aus dem Manuskript: 'Die Währinger Erinnerungen.'"

[15] "Mein Vater. Aus dem Manuskript: 'Die Währinger Erinnerungen.'"

[16] "Meine Mutter. Aus dem Manuskript: 'Die Währinger Erinnerungen.'"

[17] "Die strahlende Frau. Aus dem Manuskript 'Die Währinger Erinnerungen.'"

[18] Ibid.

[19] Salten preferred not to dwell on his aunt's later years when she was tyrannized by her son's "untalented" wife, a "fury" who destroyed the bliss of the family home. See "Die strahlende Frau. Aus dem Manuskript 'Die Währinger Erinnerungen.'"

[20] Ibid.

[21] "Dafnis in Wien."

326

²² See Felix Salten, "Theodor. Ein Porträt aus dem Nachlass," for a touching portrait of this older brother.

²² "Meine Mutter. Aus dem Manuskript: 'Die Währinger Erinnerungen.'"

Chapter 2

¹ *Lehmanns Adressbuch* for 1872 lists the Salzmann home at Taubengasse 6; Géza Salzmann's birth certificate (Dec. 31, 1870) gives Schottenbastei 4 as the family address.

² When the Salzmanns lived there, this house bore the address Wasagasse 10, but the buildings were renumbered a few years later as new construction took place closer to the Ring.

³ "Burgtheater-Jubiläum."

⁴ Again, street addresses are confusing. Lehmann's address books, probably the most reliable listings of the period, along with Salten's school records at the Hernalser Gymnasium, show the Salzmanns living at Theresiengasse 66 from 1876 to 1884 while the Vienna Magistrate's office gives the address as number 66/68. Salten's school records at the Wasagymnasium and Katherine Salzmann's death certificate (Aug. 7, 1883) list the home address as number 64, suggesting that they might have moved in 1882 into an apartment in the building next door.

⁵ "Glanzpunkte einer Kindheit."

⁶ "Spaziergang in der Vorstadt."

⁷ "Aus meiner Kindheit. Nach dem Manuskript: 'Die Währinger Erinnerungen.'"

⁸ "Gewalttätigkeiten. Aus dem Manuskript: 'Die Währinger Erinnerungen.'"

⁹ Ibid. Salten would use this episode of the murdered butcher and the fleeing murderer in his story "Feiertag" (Holiday).

¹⁰ This episode is recorded in Dilly Tante, ed., *Living Authors: A Book of Biographies*, 356.

¹¹ "Aus meiner Kindheit. Nach dem Manuskript: 'Die Währinger Erinnerungen'."

¹² Ibid.

¹³ Josef Lamberg, letter to Salten, May 20, 1906.

¹⁴ *Neue Menschen auf alter Erde. Eine Palästinafahrt*, 102-103.

¹⁵ "Erstes Liebesahnen. Aus dem Manuskript: 'Die Währinger Erinnerungen.'"

¹⁶ Ibid.

[17] "Gewalttätigkeiten. Aus dem Manuskript: 'Die Währinger Erinnerungen.'"

[18] Ben-gavriel, Moshe Ya'akov [Eugen Hoeflich], *Die Flucht nach Tarschisch.* (Hamburg: Hoffmann u. Campe, 1963), 198, cited in *"Ein Dilettant des Lebens will ich nicht sein* by Manfred Dickel,*"* 101. Dickel points out that in Salten's class there were 47 Catholics and seven Jews (102). This book is an excellent work on Salten that focuses on his Jewishness.

[19] *Neue Menschen auf alter Erde*, 103.

[20] ["Erinnerungen"], typescript, 2.

[21] "Wehrlose Jugend."

[22] Ibid.

[23] Stefan Zweig, *The World of Yesterday: An Autobiography*, 37.

[24] K. W.-S. "Zum 100. Geburtstag von Felix Salten am 6. September, Versuch eines Porträts," 181.

[25] ["Erinnerungen"], typescript, 2.

[26] "Erstes Liebesahnen. Aus dem Manuskript: 'Die Währinger Erinnerungen.'"

[27] "Hölle in Omaha."

[28] Siegfried Mattl and Werner Michael Schwarz maintain that Salten didn't actually begin working in the insurance company until the summer of 1893 (see *Felix Salten. Schriftsteller – Journalist – Exilant*, 223-24). They base their argument on a letter to Arthur Schnitzler from July 6, 1893, in which Salten complains that he should never have been persuaded to make his profession in the insurance business. I believe Salten's heavy debts caused him to return to the insurance business at this time since he and his brother Emil were demonstrably employed in 1889 (See *Lehmanns Adressbuch*).

[29] "Die Wiener Straße," *Das österreichische Antlitz*, 18.

[30] *The World of Yesterday*, 15.

Chapter 3

[1] *Lehmanns Adressbuch* lists Michael (Emil) and Zsiga (Sigmund, i.e. Salten) at this address in 1889. There was usually a lag of a year in these listings; not until 1891 is their father "Filipp" included in the listing for this address. Philipp is now listed as "Kaufmann" (merchant) rather than "Agent."

[2] ["Erinnerungen"], typescript, 2.

[3] Cf., for example, Richard Engländer's "Peter Altenberg," Karl Weiss's "C. Karlweis," Friedrich Rosenfeld's "Roda Roda," Gustav Meyer's "Gus-

328

tav Meyrink," and Egon Friedmann's "Egon Friedell." Hofmannsthal hid his identity in his earliest writings as "Loris," Schnitzler as "Anatol."

4 "Aus den Anfängen. Erinnerungsskizzen," 31.

5 See Helmut Schneider, *Felix Dörmann. Eine Monographie*, 4.

6 Goethe, *Faust*, part 1, sc. 6, l. 1700.

7 *An der schönen blauen Donau*, 1888, 5: 110. The complete German texts of Salten's poems have been reprinted in Michael Gottstein, *Felix Salten*, 305-308.

8 "Resignation."

9 "Der Unbesiegbare!"

10 "An Marie von Ebner-Eschenbach."

11 "Der Vagabund. Eine Hundegeschichte," 492.

12 Ibid., 494.

13 Ibid., 493.

14 Arthur Schnitzler, "Felix Salten," 1, DLA.

15 "Aus den Anfängen," 32.

16 Ibid., 33.

17 Richard Specht, *Arthur Schnitzler. Der Dichter und sein Werk*, 33.

18 "Buchbesprechungen. 'Gesammelte Dichtungen,' von Ludwig Eichrodt," *Allgemeine Kunst-Chronik*, XIV (1890): 22, 616.

19 "Felix Salten," 1, DLA.

20 ["Erinnerungen"], typescript, 42.

21 Ibid., 43.

22 Philipp Salzmann, letter to Salten, May 2, 1889.

23 Arthur Schnitzler, *Tagebuch 1879-1892* [Aug. 18, 1891], 345.

24 ["Erinnerungen"], typescript, 42.

25 Salten, letter to Schnitzler, Sept. 12, 1891.

26 In 1890 Salten published five major essays and seven shorter reviews in the *Kunst-Chronik* and in 1891 five major essays, twelve shorter reviews, and a number of aphorisms.

27 Salten, letter to Schnitzler, Mar. 31, 1892, typescript.

28 ["Erinnerungen"], 48.

29 Ibid., 48-49.

30 Arthur Schnitzler, *Tagebuch 1893-1902* [Oct. 25, 1896], 223.

31 Ibid. [Mar. 3, 1900], 323.

32 Ibid., [Dec. 29, 1893], 64.

33 Arthur Schnitzler, letter to Richard Beer-Hofmann, June 15, 1895, in Arthur Schnitzler, *Briefe 1875-1912*, 261.

34 Salten, letter to Arthur Schnitzler, July 22, 1895.

35 Salten, letter to Ottilie Salten, January 21, 1907.

36 Arthur Schnitzler, *Jugend in Wien*, 150.

[37] Arthur Schnitzler, *Tagebuch 1917-1919* [Aug. 12, 1919], 278.

[38] ["Erinnerungen"], typescript, 46, 47.

[39] Kraus, letter to Salten, Sept. 3, 1895, typescript, in private possession. The original handwritten letter is in FSE/LWA.

[40] ["Erinnerungen"], typescript, 47.

[41] Ibid., 48.

[42] Ibid., 47.

[43] Ibid., 48.

[44] Salten, letter to Schnitzler, Aug. 1, 1895. The Beer-Hofmann novella is indeed remarkably like Salten's story and indicates how common such liaisons and secret births were at the time.

[45] ["Erinnerungen"], typescript, 49.

Chapter 4

[1] See Bartel F. Sinhuber, *Die Wiener Kaffeehausliteraten. Anekdotisches zur Literaturgeschichte* for an excellent overview of the development of the coffeehouse as a center for writers and journalists.

[2] Richard Specht, *Arthur Schnitzler. Der Dichter und sein Werk*, 32.

[3] Ibid., 38-39.

[4] Ibid., 39.

[5] Salten, "Ja, damals...."

[6] Sinhuber, 105.

[7] This list of participants is taken from Schnitzler's diaries of the period, from Richard Specht's work *Arthur Schnitzler: Der Dichter und sein Werk*, and from Salten's "Aus den Anfängen. Erinnerungsskizzen."

[8] "Aus den Anfängen," 40.

[9] Ibid., 42.

[10] Hermann Bahr, *Selbstbildnis*, 277.

[11] Ibid.

[12] *Arthur Schnitzler. Der Dichter und sein Werk*, 33.

[13] "Die demolirte Literatur," *Wiener Rundschau*, Nov. 15, 1896, 25.

[14] Lou Andreas-Salomé, *Lebensrückblick. Grundriß einiger Lebenserinnerungen*, 106.

[15] Schnitzler, *Tagebuch 1879-1892* [Oct. 9, 1891], 351-352.

[16] Salten, "Aus den Anfängen," 34.

[17] Specht, *Arthur Schnitzler. Der Dichter und sein Werk*, 33.

[18] Salten, "Aus den Anfängen," 34.

[19] Ibid., 34-35.

[20] "Erinnerung an Hofmannsthal."

[21] Schnitzler, *Tagebuch 1893-1902* [Aug. 22, 1894], 85.

22 "Prolog zu 'Der Tor und der Tod.'" *Gedichte und Lyrische Dramen*, 171, 173.

23 Ibid., 171.

24 Ibid., 172, 173.

25 Ibid., 177.

26 Ibid., 178.

27 No title, ["Salten hat bei Schnitzler geschlafen..."], in letter-folder 2 from Schnitzler to Salten, FSE/LWA.

28 Salten, "Erinnerung an Hofmannsthal."

29 Cited in Salten, "Aus den Anfängen," 45.

30 Ibid.

31 Felix Salten, "Arthur Schnitzler/ Der einsame Weg," *Schauen und Spielen*, 1:173.

32 Bahr, *Selbstbildnis*, 282.

33 Arthur Schnitzler, *Tagebücher 1893-1902* [June 11, 1894], 78.

34 Ibid. [Dec. 21, 1895], 165.

35 Ibid. [Dec. 4, 1902], 387.

36 "Aus den Anfängen," 35.

37 Arthur Schnitzler, "Felix Salten," 2, DLA.

38 Ibid., 4.

39 Salten, "Aus den Anfängen," 44.

40 Ibid., 35.

41 Siegfried Trebitsch, *Chronicle of a Life*, 68.

42 Schnitzler, *Tagebuch 1893-1902* [Jan. 14, 1893], 10.

43 Friedrich Rothe, *Karl Kraus. Die Biographie*, 87.

44 This and the Kraus quotations that follow are taken from a letter that he wrote to Salten on Aug. 22, 1892. I am indebted to Gregory Ackermann for his transcription of this letter. The original is in FSE/LWA.

45 See Friedrich Rothe, *Karl Kraus. Die Biographie*, especially his chapter, "Der Wiener Satiriker und die deutsche Hauptstadt," 64-120, for an excellent treatment of Kraus and his rebellion against the Young Vienna authors.

46 Salten, "Aus den Anfängen," 37.

47 Salten, "Literatur-Schmarotzer," 631.

48 Arthur Schnitzler, *Tagebuch 1893-1902* [May 18, 1893], 32.

49 Ibid. [July 31, 1894], 82.

50 Ibid. [Oct. 24, 1893], 56. Schnitzler is referring here to his play *Liebelei.*

51 Letter to Karl Henckell, Dec. 14, 1891, quoted in *Jugend in Wien. Literatur um 1900*, ed. Bernhard Zeller, ed., 125-126.

52 Arthur Schnitzler, *Tagebuch 1893-1902* [Oct. 14, 1897], 266.

53 Edmund Wengraf, "Kaffeehaus und Literatur," 2.

54 Therese Nickl and Heinrich Schnitzler, eds., *Hugo von Hofmannsthal – Arthur Schnitzler Briefwechsel* [Oct. 17, 1895], 63.

55 "Literatur-Schmarotzer," 631-635.

56 Letter from Mar. 19, 1893, quoted in Hans Christian Kosler, "Karl Kraus und die Wiener Moderne," in *Karl Kraus*, ed. Heinz Ludwig Arnold, 39.

57 Karl Kraus, "Die demolirte Literatur," *Wiener Rundschau*, Nov. 15, 1896, 19.

58 Ibid., 24.

59 Ibid., 22.

60 Karl Kraus, "Die demolirte Literatur, II," *Wiener Rundschau*, Dec. 1, 1896, 68.

61 Ibid., 69.

62 Ibid., 70.

63 "Die demolirte Literatur, III," *Wiener Rundschau*, Dec. 15, 1896, 113.

64 Ibid., 114.

65 Ibid., 115.

66 Ibid., 116.

67 Salten, letter to Maximilian Harden, Dec. 11, 1904.

68 Arthur Schnitzler, *Tagebuch 1893-1902* [Dec. 15, 1896], 229.

69 ["Erinnerungen"], typescript, 5.

Chapter 5

1 The paper was actually called the *Neue Preußische Zeitung* but acquired the more familiar name because of the Iron Cross in its heading.

2 June 2 and 9, 1895.

3 In this book Salten listed "Heldentod" as having been written in November 1895, even though a comparison of the January 1895 and 1900 versions reveals only the most minor modifications in text, and Schnitzler's diary states that Salten already had a version of that story in July 1894.

4 The original 1895 version of the work was published many years later in a book of sketches collected and edited by Marcell Salzer, *Das lustige Salzerbuch. Heitere Lektüre- und Vortrags-Stücke*, 140-166. Here, as in the reworked 1911 publication, the title was shortened simply to *Wurstelprater*.

5 "Fünfkreuzertanz" [Five Kreuzer Dancing], not to be confused with a sketch by the same title that appeared the year before *Wurstelprater* in Salten's volume *Das österreichische Antlitz*, 49-58. The earlier piece describes individuals in the dance hall while the *Wurstelprater* describes types to show the different regions and conditions from which the dancers come.

[6] "Wann I a mal in'n Prater geh', wer' I mi do no untaholt'n derf'n." Felix Salten, *Wurstelprater. Mit 75 Originalaufnahmen von Dr. Emil Mayer*, 58.

[7] f.s. [Felix Salten], "Die XXIV. Jahresaustellung, I. Die Porträtisten."

[8] "Die Schülerausstellung der Akademie." Géza Salzmann was also sculpting busts at this time. Arthur Schnitzler and Adele Sandrock posed for him, and Schnitzler described him as "not without talent." Arthur Schnitzler, "Felix Salten," 2, DLA.

[9] Siegfried Trebitsch, *Chronicle of a Life*, 17-18.

[10] See Kevin McAleer, *Dueling: The Cult of Honor in Fin-de-siècle Germany*, for an excellent survey of the formal aspects of dueling and the rules and regulations that governed it. McAleer points out that "the dueling codes of honor published in Vienna, Budapest, and the German Empire in the last decades before the First World War were very alike" (46). These included the levels of insult, the determination as to who was worthy of seeking satisfaction through a duel, the role of seconds as mediators, and the requirement that the duel take place within forty-eight hours of the sustained insult.

[11] I have found the case mentioned only in two letters that Karl Kraus wrote Salten in July 1894; unfortunately, Kraus provided no names or details. Kraus sympathized completely with Salten in this particular case.

[12] The name of Leopold Jacobson (1878-1943) appears under the variant spellings "Jacobsohn" (see Schnitzler's diary entry for May 29, 1896, in *Tagebuch 1893-1902*, 193-194), "Jacobson," and "Jacobsen" (see Hermann Bahr's diary entry for May 28, 1896, in *Prophet der Moderne. Tagebücher 1888-1904*, 78). The protocol of the affair uses both the Jacobsen and Jacobson spellings.

[13] Written protocol signed by Hermann Bahr and Dr. Julius Sieps on May 28, 1896, FSE/LWA.

[14] Arthur Schnitzler, *Tagebuch 1893-1902* [May 29, 1896], 193-194.

[15] A physical slap counted as a more serious assault on one's honor than mere words. See McAleer, *Dueling: The Cult of Honor in Fin-de-siècle Germany*, 47. Because Kraus had sought – and received – satisfaction through the courts, he was unable to follow up with a challenge to a duel.

[16] His actual name was Otto Werneck or Werncik.

[17] In the summer of 1905, Sor confessed to Salten that this had been the case. Salten described this in a handwritten note, FSE/LWA.

[18] Letter signed by Otto Werneck and published in the *Wiener Rundschau*, Jan. 1, 1897.

[19] Schnitzler, *Tagebuch 1879-1892* [Dec. 31, 1896], 231.

[20] For a more complete account, see the protocols for this case [Jan. 21-23, 1897] in FSE/LWA.

[21] As a foreigner, Van-Jung had to withdraw in favor of Hermann Bahr. The affair was concluded in March 1897. See Hermann Bahr, *Prophet der Moderne. Tagebücher 1888-1904*, 84.

[22] See Salten's ["Erinnerungen"], typescript, 5-6, for his recollections of the conflict with Sor.

[23] Hermann Bahr, however, successfully sued Kraus in 1901 for "venality." See Harry Zohn, *Karl Kraus*, 141.

[24] Arthur Schnitzler *Tagebuch 1893-1902* [Mar. 23, 1895], 131.

[25] For an excellent account of Schnitzler's and Salten's affairs with Sandrock, see Adele Sandrock and Arthur Schnitzler, *Dilly. Geschichte einer Liebe in Briefen, Bildern und Dokumenten*, ed. Renate Wagner, 1975.

[26] *Makkabäer*. See f. s. [Felix Salten], "Theater, Kunst und Literatur: Burgtheater," *Wiener Allgemeine Zeitung*, Apr. 10, 1896.

[27] f. s. [Felix Salten], "Burgtheater," Feuilleton, *Wiener Allgemeine Zeitung*, Mar. 3, 1897.

[28] f.s., "Theater, Kunst und Literatur: Burgtheater" *Wiener Allgemeine Zeitung*, Jan. 6, 1898.

[29] f. s., "Theater, Kunst und Literatur: Burgtheater," *Wiener Allgemeine Zeitung*, Feb. 11, 1898.

[30] *Die Wilddiebe*. See f. s., "Burgtheater," Feuilleton, *Wiener Allgemeine Zeitung*, Sept. 18, 1897.

[31] ["Erinnerungen"], typescript, 1.

[32] ["Erinnerungen"], typescript, 49.

[33] Arthur Schnitzler *Tagebuch 1893-1902* [June 23, 1896], 197.

[34] Ironically, Salten was given an assignment to write a profile of her for the *Wiener Allgemeine Zeitung* at just this time in tribute to her twenty-five years at the Burgtheater. See letter from Salten to Schnitzler, Feb. 8, 1896. The article appeared on February 6.

[35] ["Erinnerungen"], typescript, 1.

[36] Salten, letter to Schnitzler, May 5, 1897.

[37] *Neue Menschen auf alter Erde*, 168.

[38] Ibid., 167.

[39] ["Erinnerungen"], typescript, 1.

[40] *Neue Menschen auf alter Erde*, 103. Salten was won to the cause and to take pride in his race but not to Jewish religious ritual. At about this same time, however, Salten's father returned to the Jewish faith.

[41] And to 147,000 in 1900. These figures are taken from Simon Dubnow, *Weltgeschichte des jüdischen Volkes*, vol. 10, trans. from the Russian by Dr. A. Steinberg, 76.

[42] The text of this resolution can be found in Arthur Schnitzler, *Jugend in Wien*, 360-361. Ironically, this resolution was adopted the same year in which Salten was twice challenged to a duel.

[43] Arthur Schnitzler, *Jugend in Wien*, 328.

[44] See Friedrich Rothe, *Karl Kraus*, 131-135.

[45] Beer-Hofmann, letter to Herzl, March 13, 1896, quoted in Julius H. Schoeps, *Theodor Herzl 1860-1904*, 103.

[46] Cited in Julius H. Schoeps, *Theodor Herzl 1860-1904*, 102.

[47] Simon Dubnow, *Weltgeschichte des jüdischen Volkes*, vol. 10, 83.

[48] ["Erinnerungen"], typescript, 44.

[49] See Egon Schwarz, "Das jüdische Selbstverständnis jüdischer Autoren im *Fin de Siècle*," in *Judentum und Antisemitismus: Studien zur Literatur und Germanistik in Österreich*, ed. Anne Betten and Konstanze Fliedl, especially 21-25.

[50] "Die Woche," *Die Welt*, Oct. 8, 1897.

[51] "Die Woche," *Die Welt*, Oct. 15, 1897.

[52] "Die Woche," *Die Welt*, Oct. 29, 1897.

[53] Erwin Rosenberger, *Herzl As I Remember Him*, 183; Isidor Schalit, *Erinnerungen*, 3 vols., Central Zionist Archives, A 196, 1571. Both works are cited in *"Ein Dilettant des Lebens will ich nicht sein". Felix Salten zwischen Zionismus und Jungwiener Moderne* by Manfred Dickel, 201.

[54] "Das fremde Volk," *Die Welt*, Sept. 1, 8, and 15, 1899.

[55] "'Echt jüdisch.' Bekenntnisse," *Die Welt*, Nov. 10, 1899. It is notable that Salten uses hunting imagery to describe the behavior of his friends and himself.

[56] "Kleine Schauspieler."

[57] Letter to Schnitzler, May 5, 1897.

[58] When printed, this work was renamed "Das Manhardzimmer."

[59] Letter to Schnitzler, May 23, 1897.

[60] Ibid.

[61] Because Salten's journalistic endeavor was so short-lived, Schnitzler published *Liebesreigen* privately in 1900 in a limited reading edition of 200 copies.

[62] Letter to Schnitzler, July 27, 1899.

[63] These sketches appeared in the Sept. 4 and 11 and the Dec. 11, 1899, issues.

[64] In *Variété. Ein Buch der Autoren des Wiener Verlages*, 1902, 108-116.

[65] "(*Geschichten*) aus dem Leben des Herrn Snob." The first work with this title includes the word "Geschichten" and its author is given as "F. F."; the second eliminates this word and gives no indication as to the author.

[66] *WAR*, July 10, 1899.

⁶⁷ See Michael Gottstein, *Felix Salten (1869-1945). Ein Schriftsteller der Wiener Moderne*, 41-44, for an analysis of these tales.

⁶⁸ The fly's desire to get to a warm fire, its death from cold, and its dying vision of warmth resemble Andersen's "Little Match Girl" to a remarkable degree.

⁶⁹ "Andersen," feuilleton, *Die Zeit*, Apr. 2, 1905, reprinted in Salten's collections *Geister und Erscheinungen*, 11-18, and *Geister der Zeit*, 322-328.

Chapter 6

¹ *Die Pflege der Kunst in Oesterreich 1848-1898*, 60-85.

² See, for example, Felix Salten, "Burgtheater, Der Direktor," in which Salten declared Schlenther to be the best of the potential candidates for Burckhard's position.

³ "Dr. Max Burckhard."

⁴ "Burgtheater (Rückblick)."

⁵ ["Erinnerungen"], typescript, 59.

⁶ f. s. [Felix Salten], "Katharina Schratt."

⁷ "Burgtheater," feuilleton, *WAG*, Jan. 18, 1901.

⁸ ["Erinnerungen"], typescript, 59.

⁹ The implication in Salten's unpublished memoirs and in Dietmar Grieser's *Eine Liebe in Wien*, 76, is that Salten and Ottilie Metzl wed soon after her firing. In reality, they did not marry until April 1902.

¹⁰ XIII Watmanngasse 11. The family address at this time was IX Sensengasse 5. *Lehmanns Adressbuch* gives the Hietzing address for "Felix Salten," and the Sensengasse address for "Sigmund" and "Filipp Salzmann."

¹¹ Report of the K.K. Police-Direction L. 3540 in *Felix Salten als Mensch, Dichter und Kritiker* by Kurt Riedmueller, 62.

¹² ["Erinnerungen"], typescript, 4.

¹³ "Vom 'Ueberbrettl zum rasenden Jüngling,'" *Vossische Zeitung*, Oct. 31, 1900, in *Berlin Cabaret* by Peter Jelavich, 39. Wolzogen modeled his theater on the famous Parisian cabaret *Le Chat Noir*.

¹⁴ An announcement to this effect appeared in *Die Welt*, Oct. 18, 1901, 10. For a discussion of the evolution of this pantomime, see Abigail Gillman, *Viennese Jewish Modernism*, 54-76.

¹⁵ Felix Salten, *Extrapost*, Sept. 23, 1901, quoted in "Des Sängers Fluch, Die Geschichte eines Scheiterns" by Iris Fink und Hans Veigl, [13]. This pamphlet offers an excellent historical and critical overview of Salten's theatrical experiment.

¹⁶ Review, Nov. 17, 1901, in Hermann Bahr, *Rezensionen. Wiener Theater 1901 bis 1903*, 191.

[17] Ibid., 194.

[18] Max Burckhard, *Die Zeit*, Nov. 23, 1901, in Fink and Veigl, [18].

[19] *Deutsche Zeitung*, Nov. 17, 1901, in Fink and Veigl, [21].

[20] *Deutsches Volksblatt*, Nov. 17, 1901, in Fink and Veigl, [22].

[21] ["Erinnerungen"], typescript, 72.

[22] "Das Jung-Wiener Theater," feuilleton, *Wiener Allgemeine Zeitung*, Nov. 19, 1901. Fink and Veigl identify the author as Bertha Zuckerkandl; Karl Kraus, too, describes the article as "not signed but written by a Frau Zuckerkandl." ["Sind Sie dabei gewesen?"],19.

[23] Ibid.

[24] Ibid.

[25] ["Erinnerungen"], typescript, 72.

[26] "Jung-Wiener-Theater."

[27] ["Erinnerungen"], typescript, 73.

[28] *Die Insel*, 2, no. 4, 57-117. See Jürgen Ehneß, *Felix Saltens erzählerishces Werk. Beschreibung und Deutung*, 155.

[29] Richard Beer-Hoffmann, letter to Salten, Oct. 26, 1901.

[30] ["Erinnerungen"], typescript, 4.

[31] On occasion, Salten used other pseudonyms as well, although none of these ("Karl Heinrich," "Jeremias Eckenpfeifer," "Iwo," "Graf Traft," etc.) endured as "Martin Finder" and "Sascha" did. He also played with the Salten name, writing it backwards ("netlas") or simply "–ten." When he reviewed one of J. J. David's novels, he went even further and signed the review "–n."

Chapter 7

[1] Stanley J. Kunitz and Howard Haycroft, eds. *Twentieth Century Authors*, 1224.

[2] *Das österreichische Antlitz. Essays*, 167.

[3] Ibid., 170.

[4] "Thomas Theodor Heine."

[5] Two of these works survive only as manuscripts; I can find no indication that the short story, "Liebesreise," was ever published nor that the film, "Der Bauerngraf," was ever made.

[6] "Leiden, Streiche, Kumpaneien. Aus den unveröffentlichten Erinnerungen," 144.

[7] In his memoirs, Salten relates that Leopold was drawn to him initially because of the fact that he was a journalist. Since Leopold had had an intimate relationship with Ottilie in 1890-1891, he was doubtless drawn to Salten also out of curiosity about the man who now held Otti's affections.

Cf. Arthur Schnitzler: "L. F. once had a friendly relationship with Miss M., therefore the acquaintanceship." Schnitzler, *Tagebuch 1893-1902* [Apr. 15, 1898], 283.

8 "Erinnerungen an Leopold Ferdinand," typescript, 19.

9 Ibid., 20.

10 Ibid., 11.

11 Schnitzler, *Tagebuch 1893-1902* [June 22, 1898], 288.

12 "Erinnerungen an Leopold Ferdinand," typescript, 72.

13 Leopold Ferdinand, letter to Ottilie Salten, Dec. 28, 1902.

14 "Leiden, Streiche, Kumpaneien," 147-148. A draft of the letter that Salten helped Leopold write to the emperor is preserved in FSE/LWA.

15 Paul Plaut, *Die Psychologie der produktiven Persönlichkeit*, 297.

16 Huntley Paterson, trans., *The Hound of Florence*, 23.

17 Ibid., 24.

18 "Leiden, Streiche, Kumpaneien," 146.

19 Huntley Paterson, trans., *The Hound of Florence*, 196.

20 In a later version, published in 1928 by Paul Zsolnay, the ending is more ambiguous. There Grassi is still alive when he is found the next morning, and it is left open as to whether he will live or die.

21 "Leiden, Streiche, Kumpaneien," 144.

22 For Leopold's account of his life both at court and in civilian life, see Leopold Wölfing, *My Life Story: From Archduke to Grocer*.

23 "Zweig auf Zweig…."

24 "Erinnerungen an Leopold Ferdinand," typescript, 7.

25 Leopold Wölfing, *My Life Story*, 284-285.

26 "Das Buch der Frau Toselli."

27 See Felix Salten, "Zweig auf Zweig…" Luisa herself never admitted to having taken any men as lovers prior to her flight from Saxony.

28 Salten had used similar arguments with her brother Leopold when the archduke first thought of fleeing Austria in 1898. In an unpublished short story entitled "Liebesreise," Salten portrayed two members of the nobility who flee the court with their commoner lovers, only to return when they are given the opportunity to do so without penalty.

29 "Die Tragödie des schwachen Willens."

30 "Auf Tod und Leben" (To Death and Life), typescript, 26, UOLS. This memoir is not to be confused with Salten's play of the same title, which I refer to by its amended title, *Louise of Coburg*.

31 Goethe, *Faust* part 1, sc. 4, l. 1112.

32 *Die Bekenntnisse einer Prinzessin*, 7.

33 "Erzherzog Otto."

34 *Die Bekenntnisse einer Prinzessin*, 48.

338

[35] Ibid., 188.
[36] Luise von Toscana, *Mein Leben*. This work is a translation of the original English work, Luisa of Tuscany, *My Life Story*, which was published in London in 1911 and which unfortunately was unavailable to me.
[37] Leopold Wölfing, *My Life Story*, 141.
[38] *Die Bekenntnisse einer Prinzessin*, 46.
[39] Ibid., 139.
[40] Ibid., 325.
[41] Ibid., 206.
[42] "Mettachich."
[43] "Auf Tod und Leben," typescript, 26, UOLS.
[44] Princess Louise of Belgium, *My Own Affairs*.
[45] The play was first called *Auf Tod und Leben* (To Death and Life) with the subtitle *Die Liebesgeschichte der Prinzessin Louise von Koburg* (The Love Story of Princess Louise of Coburg) and was published in Berlin-Wilmersdorf by Felix Block Erben in 1932. It was renamed *Louise von Koburg. Das Schicksal einer Liebe* (The Fate of a Love) and was included in Felix Salten's *Vom andern Ufer. Ernste und heitere Theaterstücke*, 9-163. Salten's typed memoir of the Coburg affair was also entitled "Auf Tod und Leben."
[46] *Louise von Koburg*, 130.
[47] "Auf Tod und Leben," typescript, 9, UOLS.

Chapter 8

[1] Kochgasse 32.
[2] Porzellangasse 45. Both this and the Kochgasse addresses are confirmed by the *Lehmann Adressbuch* and by Salten's records at the municipal registration office.
[3] ["Erinnerungen"], typescript, 3, 4.
[4] Arthur Schnitzler, letter to Salten, May 25, 1902, typescript, DLA.
[5] Arthur Schnitzler, letter to Salten, June 11, 1902, typescript, DLA.
[6] Hermann Bahr, "Feliz Salten zum 60. Geburtstag."
[7] "Zolas Lebenswerk von Felix Salten," feuilleton, Sept. 30, 1902, quoted in *Bambis Vater* by Lea Wyler, 31-32. The essay is included in Salten's personal scrapbooks of his articles, but the title of the paper is not given.
[8] William M. Johnston, *The Austrian Mind: An Intellectual and Social History, 1848-1938*, 124.
[9] Ibid., 121.
[10] In "Felix Salten zum 60. Geburtstag," *Jahrbuch. Paul Zsolnay Verlag*, 1930, 104.
[11] Arthur Schnitzler, *Tagebuch 1903-1908* [July 8, 1903,] 35

[12] Arthur Schnitzler, *Tagebuch 1893-1902* [Sept. 14, 1902], 378.

[13] Arthur Schnitzler, letter to Salten, Oct. 16, 1902, typescript, DLA.

[14] See Jürgen Ehneß, *Felix Saltens erzählerisches Werk. Beschreibung und Deutung*, 159-164, for an excellent treatment of this work.

[15] Gustav Klimt. *Gelegentliche Anmerkungen*, 43.

[16] Ibid., 8.

[17] Ibid., 11.

[18] Ibid., 27.

[19] Salten, letter to Arthur Schnitzler, Mar. 3, 1903.

[20] In Arthur Schnitzler, *Briefe 1875-1912* [Nov. 12, 1903], 475-476.

[21] Arthur Schnitzler, *Tagebuch 1903-1908* [Oct. 21, 1903], 46.

[22] Ibid.

[23] Rudolf Jeremias Krentz, "Felix Salten, der Erzähler."

[24] *Der Schrei der Liebe. Novellen*, 1928, 16.

[25] Ibid., 17.

[26] Ibid., 55.

[27] Ibid., 50.

[28] Gustav Klimt. *Gelegentliche Anmerkungen*, 27.

[29] Hofmannsthal, letter to Salten, Dec. 3, 1904, in *Bambis Vater* by Lea Wyler, 9.

[30] ["Erinnerungen"], typescript, 1, in *Feliz Salten. Schriftsteller – Journalist – Exilant* by Siegfried Mattl and Werner Michael Schwarz, 18-19.

[31] *Das Buch der Könige*, 5.

[32] Sascha, "Der Zar," republished in Felix Salten, *Das Buch der Könige*, 11-14.

[33] Karl Kraus, "Ein tüchtiger Mensch," 13-15.

[34] ["Erinnerungen"], typescript, 61.

[35] The play, *Der letzte Knopf*, premiered at the Deutsches Volkstheater in April; Salten gave it a positive review in the April 10 edition of the *Wiener Allgemeine Zeitung*. Salten had made the inquiry as to where he might borrow eight thousand crowns on behalf of the Tuscan Archduke, Leopold Ferdinand.

[36] ["Erinnerungen"], typescript, 63.

[37] Concordia document of May 12, 1907, FSE/LWA.

[38] Salten, letter to Arthur Schnitzler, Mar. 28, 1906.

[39] Salten, letter to Arthur Schnitzler, Mar. 9, 1906.

Chapter 9

[1] Kurt Riedmueller, *Felix Salten als Mensch, Dichter und Kritiker*, 45-46.

[2] Ulrich Weinzierl, "Typische Wiener Feuilletonisten? Am Beispiel Salten, Blei, Friedell, Polgar und Kuh," 74.

[3] Robert Weichinger, "Schluß mit Genuß! Wer schrieb die 'Mutzenbacher'? Wer kriegt die Tantiemen? Felix Saltens Erben wohl nicht."

[4] In his bibliography of selected editions of this work, Michael Farin lists a first private, limited edition of 153 copies as appearing "circa 1917," although most other sources give its original appearance as around 1930. See Michael Farin, ed., *Josefine Mutzenbacher oder Die Geschichte einer Wienerischen Dirne von ihr selbst erzählt*, 548. As Oswald Wiener has pointed out, Paul Englisch's comprehensive 1927 *Geschichte der erotischen Literatur* does not make mention of it, an omission which supports the idea of its having first appeared at a later date. See Josefine Mutzenbacher, *Meine 365 Liebhaber*, 7-8.

[5] Oswald Wiener, "Der obszöne Wortschatz Wiens," *Beiträge zur Adöologie des Wienerischen*, 1969, quoted in Michael Farin, "Die letzten Illusionen – Josefine Mutzenbacher vor Gericht," in *Josefine Mutzenbacher*, ed. Michael Farin, 361.

[6] See Michael Holzmann and Hanns Bohatta, *Deutsches Anonymen-Lexikon* (Weimar, 1909), 5:214.

[7] Arthur Schnitzler, *Tagebuch 1909-1912* [Apr. 4, 1911], 233.

[8] By 1911, the 1909 entry had been revised to list Felix Salten as sole probable author, and by 1928 this work gave Salten as the unquestioned author of the work.

[9] In *Young Vienna and Psychoanalysis: Felix Doermann, Jakob Julius David, and Felix Salten* by Lieselotte Pouh, 182.

[10] Salten, letter to Hugo von Hofmannsthal, July 17, 1892, DLA.

[11] This foreword is not to be found in many of the later editions of the work; in fact, editorial changes to the text occur frequently from edition to edition.

[12] Hilary E. Holt. "Introduction" in *The Memoirs of Josephine Mutzenbacher*, Rudolf Schleifer, trans., 3-12, quoted in "Die letzten Illusionen – Josefine Mutzenbacher vor Gericht" by Michael Farin, in *Josefine Mutzenbacher*, ed. Michael Farin, 515.

[13] Ibid., 518.

[14] Ibid., 516.

[15] Ibid., 525.

[16] This deposition was displayed in a Felix Salten exhibit held at the Jewish Museum in Vienna from Dec. 5, 2006 -- Mar. 18, 2007.

[17] Anton Kuh, "Mutzenbacher kontra Ronacher, Eine neue Salten-Predigt," 3. Cited, quoted in *Josefine Mutzenbacher*, ed. Michael Farin, 476.

[18] Karl Kraus, "Der Nobelpreis," 29, quoted in *Josefine Mutzenbacher*, ed. Michael Farin, 475.

[19] Klaus Pinkus, letter to the editor, "Wer schrieb 'Josefine Mutzenbacher'?" *Frankfurter Allgemeine Zeitung*, May 30, 1970.

[20] Quoted in Michael Farin, ed. *Josefine Mutzenbacher*, 514.

[21] Quoted in Michael Farin, "Die letzten Illusionen – Josefine Mutzenbacher vor Gericht," Ibid., 523.

[22] *Die Gespräche des göttlichen Pietro Aretino.*

[23] Salten, letter to Arthur Schnitzler, Mar. 3, 1903.

[24] Foreword, *Josefine Mutzenbacher oder Die Geschichte einer Wienerischen Dirne von ihr selbst erzählt*, limited private printing, 1906.

[25] Ibid., 9.

[26] Ibid., 9-10.

[27] See, for example, K. H. Kramberg, Foreword, "Steckbrief Mutzenbacher," in *Josefine Mutzenbacher. Die Lebensgeschichte einer Wienerischen Dirne, von ihr selbst erzählt*. Munich: Rogner & Bernhard, October 1969. Reprinted in Michael Farin, ed. *Josefine Mutzenbacher*, 481-484, and in "'Weibsfauna', Zur Koinzidenz von Tiergeschichte und Pornographie am Beispiel von 'Bambi' und 'Josefine Mutzenbacher'" by Dietmar Schmidt and Claudia Öhlschläger, 237-286.

[28] Dietmar Schmidt and Claudia Öhlschläger also point out that, at the time that *Mutzenbacher* was written, sex was traditionally taught to young people through observations of the sex act in nature. Dietmar Schmidt and Claudia Öhlschläger, "Weibsfauna," 244-249. In Salten's novel, Faline seduces Bambi much as Mutzenbacher seduces her lovers.

[29] In Ulrich Weinzierl, "Die Wahrheit ist nackt. Über Josefine Mutzenbachers Lebensgeschichte," in *Josefine Mutzenbacher*, ed. Michael Farin, 29. Originally published in *Frankfurter Allgemeine Zeitung*, Jan. 3, 1985, and reprinted in Marcel Reich-Ranicki, ed., *Romane von gestern – heute gelesen.*

[30] *Die Bekenntnisse einer Prinzessin*, 351.

[31] See Siegfried Mattl and Werner Michael Schwarz, *Felix Salten. Schriftsteller – Journalist – Exilant*, 35-36, for a discussion of Salten's heroines as advocates for the naturalness of lust and desire and for Salten's ironic commentary on bigotry and public sentiments regarding sexuality.

[32] Huntley Paterson, trans., *The Hound of Florence*, 189.

[33] *Josefine Mutzenbacher oder Die Geschichte einer Wienerischen Dirne von ihr selbst erzählt*, 159.

[34] Felix Salten, *Die Geliebte des Kaisers. Novellen*, 44-45.

[35] Ibid., 48-49.

[36] "Nachtvergnügen," republished in *Das österreichische Antlitz*, 83-96.

[37] See a letter from Salten's German publisher, Samuel Fischer, in which Fischer complains that the railway ban is having a serious effect on sales, May 27, 1903, in Dierk Rodewald and Corrina Fiedler eds., *Samuel Fischer, Hedwig Fischer: Briefwechsel mit Autoren*, 683.

[38] Robert Neumann, diary excerpt, 1969, in *Josefine Mutzenbacher*, ed. Michael Farin, 480-481.

[39] Hellmuth Karasek, "Vom Realismus der Pornographie. Zur Neuerscheinung der 'Josefine Mutzenbacher,'" *Die Zeit*, Nov. 21, 1969, in *Josefine Mutzenbacher*, ed. Michael Farin, 7-16.

[40] See, for example, Ernst Seibert, "Felix Salten und die Inszenierung von Kindheit in der Ersten Republik," and Klaus Müller-Richter, "Kindheit als Topografie. Eine Vignette über Felix Saltens Pratervignetten," both in *Felix Salten − der unbekannte Bekannte*, ed. Ernst Seibert and Susanne Blumesberger, 49-61 and 63-70; also Moritz Baßler, "'Einfache Anomalien': Zwerge und Riesen in Felix Saltens *Wurstelprater*," in *Felix Salten: Wurstelprater. Ein Schlüsseltext zur Wiener Moderne*, ed. Siegfried Mattl, Klaus Müller-Richter, and Werner Michael Schwarz, 196-211.

[41] *Josefine Mutenbacher oder Die Geschichte einer Wienerischen Dirne von ihr selbst erzählt*, 199.

[42] Paul Englisch, *Irrgarten der Erotik. Eine Sittengeschichte über das gesamte Gebiet der Welt-Pornographie.*, 86, in *Josefine Mutzenbacher*, ed. Michael Farin, 510.

[43] Salten gives his address as Berlin, Charlottenburg, Kantstr. 34, ÖNB. This was Salten's residence from the end of January through late summer 1906. Because *Josefine Mutzenbacher* [1906] was the only work to appear with the Wiener Verlag after the 1905 publication of *Die Bekenntnisse einer Prinzessin*, one can assume that he is writing about that novel here.

[44] "Vom göttlichen Aretino."

Chapter 10

[1] "Felix Salten," 9, DLA.
[2] ["Erinnerungen"], typescript, 20.
[3] Ibid., 22.
[4] "Die fremde Stadt."
[5] Ibid.
[6] See, for example, the two pieces by Sascha, "Wirklich nur für Reiche?" and "Ja, ein Lokalpatriot...."
[7] "Die fremde Stadt."

[8] Salten, letter to Arthur Schnitzler, May 1, 1906. Salten began learning Spanish for a planned trip to attend the wedding of Spain's young King Alfonso XIII, but the trip never materialized.

[9] Brigitte B. Fischer, *Sie schrieben mir oder was aus meinem Poesiealbum wurde*, 17, 18.

[10] Salten, letter to Arthur Schnitzler, July 6, 1906.

[11] Ibid.

[12] See Salten, "Eine Friedensreise in England."

[13] ["Erinnerungen"], typescript, 19.

[14] Ibid., 20.

[15] Salten variously gives his address there as Armbrustergasse 4 and Armbrustergasse 6-8.

[16] Anna Wyler-Salten, "Introduction," *Felix Salten's Favorite Animal Stories*, v.

[17] Felix Salten, *Bob und Baby*, 5.

[18] Anna Wyler-Salten, "Introduction," *Felix Salten's Favorite Animal Stories*, vi.

[19] Ibid., vi-vii.

[20] Ibid., viii.

[21] Felix Salten, letter to Hedwig Fischer, Dec. 30, 1906.

[22] Arthur Schnitzler, *Tagebuch 1903-1908* [Jan. 14, 1906], 179.

[23] Ibid. [Dec. 8, 1906], 238.

[24] Ibid. [Feb. 20, 1907], 256.

[25] Schnitzler had suggested removing the next-to-last paragraph from the work, since it revealed connections that had already been clearly made in the story and was therefore unnecessary for anyone "who knows how to read properly." Arthur Schnitzler, letter to Felix Salten, May 16, 1906, typescript, DLA.

[26] See letter from Felix Salten to Hedwig Fischer, Mar. 31, 1908.

[27] Schnitzler, letter to Felix Salten, May 16, 1906, typescript, DLA.

[28] Salten, *Herr Wenzel auf Rehberg und sein Knecht Kaspar Dinckel*, 116.

[29] Salten, letter to Arthur Schnitzler, Aug. 15, 1907.

[30] Ibid.

[31] *Künstlerfrauen. Ein Zyklus kleiner Romane*, feuilleton series, *Die Zeit*, beginning Mar. 24, 1907; the last one appeared April 12, 1908. Georg Müller published them in book form in 1908.

[32] Salten, letter to Arthur Schnitzler, Aug. 15, 1907.

[33] Harold B. Segel, trans., "Handwriting and Work," *The Vienna Coffeehouse Wits: 1890-1938*, 191.

[34] Salten, "Leiden, Streiche, Kumpaneien," 146.

344

35 Harold B. Segel, trans. "Handwriting and Work," *The Vienna Coffeehouse Wits: 1890-1938*, 190.

36 Ibid.

37 Ibid., 191.

38 Ibid., 190.

Chapter 11

1 Salten, letter to Arthur Schnitzler, July 3, 1908.

2 "Sterbe-Buch über die in Wien bei der israelitischen Kultusgemeinde vorkommenden Todesfälle," #1191. Record office of the Israelite Cultural Community [Israelitische Kultusgemeinde], Vienna.

3 Salten, letter to Hedwig Fischer, June 21, 1908.

4 See Felix Salten, letters to Hedwig Fischer, Oct. 1, 1908, and July 9, 1909.

5 Brigitte B. Fischer, *Sie schrieben mir*, 73.

6 Salten, letter to Hedwig Fischer, Oct. 9, 1908.

7 Arthur Schnitzler, *Tagebuch 1903-1908*, [July 28, 1908], 347.

8 See Felix Salten, letter to Hedwig Fischer, Oct. 9, 1908.

9 Felix Salten, "Manöverbilder."

10 An eighth, "Der alte Narr," appeared in *Die Zeit* in the Christmas 1910 issue.

11 Felix Salten, *Die Wege des Herrn*. The two that were omitted from any book are "Jugendfreunde" [Friends from Youth], *Die Zeit*, Oct. 31, 1909, and "Seraphine, das Mädchen" [Seraphine, the Working Girl], *Die Zeit*, Dec. 25, 1909.

12 Sascha, "Polizei im Parlament."

13 Sascha, "Lueger."

14 "Vorbereitung zur Schillerfeier," May 7, 1905, clipping in FSE/LWA, title of newspaper unidentified. As early as the Dec. 4, 1899, issue of the *Wiener Allgemeine Rundschau*, Salten had mocked Lueger's application of Christian morality to great works of literature, from Shakespeare's *Othello* to Schiller's *Die Räuber*, from Goethe's *Götz von Berlichingen* to Grillparzer's *Medea*.

15 Felix Salten, "Lueger-Bilder." In an article from April 17, he compared Lueger's life force with that of Theodore Roosevelt.

16 Salten, "Krankenstube."

17 Salten, "Lueger-Bilder."

18 Salten, "Lueger," in *Das österreichische Antlitz*, 129.

19 Ibid., 132.

20 "Erinnerung an Lueger."

21 Freud, letter to Salten, Sept. 20, 1926. See Christfried Tögel and Liselotte Pough, "Sigmund Freud, Felix Salten und Karl Lueger. Ein neuentdeckter Brief Sigmund Freuds," http://www.freud-biographik.de/salten.htm [May 28, 2009].

22 "Wie das Jüdisch-Politische Cabaret entstand," in Oscar Teller, *Davids Witz-Schleuder*, 18.

23 Gerhard Bronner, "Vorwort," *Davids Witz-Schleuder* by Oscar Teller, 13.

24 "Wurstel-Theater. Der Volksaufklärer."

25 "Interpellation."

26 "Lia Rosen." This essay was included in Salten's volume of essays *Gestalten und Erscheinungen*, published by Fischer in 1913.

27 Salten, "Die Juden."

28 Salten, letter to Hedwig Fischer, Dec. 25, 1908.

29 H. Hugo, "Martin Buber und Felix Salten," feuilleton, *Selbstwehr*, Jan. 15, 1909.

30 "Von der Woche. Der Bibelabend Bar Kochbas," *Selbstwehr*, Jan. 27, 1911.

31 Salten, letter to Hedwig Fischer, Dec. 25, 1908.

32 Salten, letter to Hedwig Fischer, Dec. 15, 1907.

33 Salten, letter to Adele Strauss, July 9, 1908. In the manuscript collections of the Vienna Town Hall.

34 Arthur Schnitzler, *Tagebuch 1909-1912* [Feb. 2, 1910], 124.

35 It was performed in England under the title *My Son John*.

36 Salten, letter to Hedwig Fischer, Aug. 6, 1909.

37 "Sterbe-Buch über die in Wien bei der israelitischen Kultusgemeinde vorkommenden Todesfälle." Record office of the Israelite Cultural Community [Israelitische Kultusgemeinde], Vienna.

38 Jürgen Ehneß views the work primarily as a depiction of a family tyrant (Olga's father) and of a heroine, infantile in her desire for acceptance and love. See *Felix Saltens erzählerisches Werk*, 192-197.

39 Brigitte B. Fischer, *Sie schrieben mir*, 75.

40 Letter from Rainer Maria Rilke to Hedwig Fischer, Sept. 6, 1908 in *Samuel Fischer, Hedwig Fischer: Briefwechsel mit Autoren*, ed. Dierk Rodewald and Corrina Fiedler 583.

Chapter 12

1 Alexander von Weilen, "Felix Salten."

2 Karl Kraus, "Pro domo et mundo."

3 Cited in Hans-Albrecht Koch, *Hugo von Hofmannsthal*, 39.

[4] The *Lehmann Adressbuch* is a case in point. From 1899 on it listed "Felix Salten" and "Sigmund (or Siegmund or Zsiga) Salzmann," often giving differing addresses. During the years in Heiligenstadt, for example, "Felix Salten" is listed as living at Armbrustergasse 6, while "Siegmund Salzmann" has the address Armbrustergasse 4.

[5] See chapter 5 of this work for a discussion of the changes Salten made from the 1895 version.

[6] See Siegfried Mattl, Klaus Müller-Richter, and Werner M. Schwarz, eds., *Wurstelprater. Ein Schlüsseltext zur Wiener Moderne* for a reproduction of the 1911 edition plus a number of essays elaborating on this volume as a work of modernity.

[7] Arthur Schnitzler, *Tagebuch 1909-1912* [Nov. 24, 1911], 284.

[8] *Lehmanns Adressbuch* for 1893-1894 lists the Salzmanns as living in Berggasse 13.

[9] Felix Salten, "Der Tunnel."

[10] Felix Salten, "O, du mein Oesterreich. "

[11] In Karl Kraus, "Oder."

[12] His last publication in this area was for a poetry anthology published in 1912: "Verse aus einer Oper," in *Deutsche Lyrik aus Österreich seit Grillparzer*, ed. Camill Hoffmann, 179-184. His last Strauss operetta, *Der blaue Held*, was performed in October of that year.

[13] Salten later undertook a major reworking of the play: he turned the young duke's mistress from a bourgeois seamstress into an impoverished feminist blueblood living on the charity of others. The play also was given a more realistic, if less happy conclusion: the duke and his mistress are not reunited; he accepts his duties while his mistress raises the daughter he has never seen. Finally, Salten added an officer friend to the play in order to mediate between the duke and his mistress as well as an epilogue to demonstrate how the comic self-centeredness of the young duke's mother is, quite unwittingly, passed on to his illegitimate daughter. This later version was published in 1915 by Felix Bloch Erben in Berlin. The original plot is retold in Max Burckhard, "Deutsches Volkstheater," *Fremden-Blatt*, Mar. 17, 1912.

[14] See Felix Salten, "Gerhart Hauptmann."

[15] This information about the play, Salten's opinion of it, the *Fremden-Blatt* review, and the timing of Trebitsch's demand for immediate repayment is taken from several drafts of a letter that Salten wrote Trebitsch in April 1917.

[16] Many of Salten's friends, especially Hofmannsthal and Schnitzler, shared his interest in the cinema, and Salten was by no means a rarity in

trying his hand at film scripts. Felix Dörmann even helped create the Vindobona Film Studio and was prolific as a producer and scriptwriter.
[17] "Kinoprobleme," in Felix Salten, *Schauen und Spielen*, 1:130.
[18] Ibid., 127.
[19] Projektions-AG Union or PAGU.
[20] For a summary of this film, I am indebted to Werner Michael Schwarz, "Felix Salten und das Kino," 51.
[21] Arno Nadel, "Der Shylock von Krakau. Melodrama von Felix Salten," 963-966.
[22] Arthur Schnitzler, *Tagebuch 1913-1916*, [Oct. 7, 1913], 66.
[23] Ibid., [Oct. 30, 1913], 71.
[24] This work did not appear in print until 1937-38, then as a novel *Sträfling Nummer 33* [Prisoner 33], *Pester Lloyd*, Dec. 8 – Jan. 25. It retained a strong dramatic structure and a great deal of dialogue.
[25] Arthur Schnitzler, *Tagebuch 1913-1916* [Oct. 30, 1913], 72.
[26] "Sich einschränken."
[27] *Kaiser Max der letzte Ritter*, 110.
[28] *Gestalten und Erscheinungen*, 61.
[29] The term was created by Hermann Broch. See Hermann Broch, *Hofmannsthal and His Time*, 59.
[30] For an account of this revolt, see Wolfgang Maderthaner and Lutz Musner, *Die Anarchie der Vorstadt. Das andere Wien um 1900*, 17-37.
[31] F.S. [Felix Salten], "Aufruhr."
[32] "Freude im Cottage. Ein Lobgesang."
[33] "Deutsches Volkstheater. Generalversammlung,"
[34] *Selbstwehr*, Jan. 16, 1914, cited by Rahel Rosa Neubauer, "Felix Salten als Autor jüdischer Kinder- und Jugendliteratur," in *Felix Salten – der unbekannte Bekannte*, ed. Ernst Seibert and Susanne Blumesberger, 135.
[35] Ibid., 136.

Chapter 13

[1] "An Bord der 'Vaterland.'"
[2] "Das Große Schiff."
[3] Salten's statement, which contains errors. He did not direct "Der Narr des Schicksals" (The Fool of Fate) until 1916, although the details of the archduke's departure and the crowd's show of displeasure suggest that Salten was witness to the archduke's embarkment and that Salten might have been in Trieste on another mission. Siegfried Mattl and Werner Michael Schwarz believe that this misstatement proves that Salten did not witness the event described here, saying that the Archduke had traveled to

348

Sarajevo by train. In truth, Franz Ferdinand did board the battleship SMS *Viribus Unitis* in Trieste, transferred to the *Dalmat* for the journey up the Neretva River, and boarded the train in Metkovic. However, he met his wife in Ilidze, a spa town near Sarajevo; she was not with him at his Trieste embarkment. Could Salten's memory have failed him in recalling an event many years after the fact? Or was he, as Mattl and Schwarz maintain, following a predilection for associating events in his own life with larger world affairs? See *Felix Salten. Schriftsteller – Journalist – Exilant*, 12.

4 ["Erinnerungen"], typescript, 38.

5 ["Erinnerungen"], typescript, 37.

6 Salten, letter to Arthur Schnitzler, Aug. 10, 1914.

7 "Es muß sein."

8 "Sollen wir Theater spielen?"

9 This was an idea that Salten repeated in a free lecture at the Volksbildungsverein in January 1915. See Arthur Schnitzler, *Tagebuch 1913-1916* [Jan. 24, 1915], 170. He also used it as an argument against raising ticket prices to the Burgtheater and the State opera and against the closing of the National Gallery. See "Erhöhte Preise."

10 "Der Entscheidungstag in Wien," cited in Peter Sprengel and Gregor Streim, *Berliner und Wiener Moderne*, 247.

11 "Das Wiener Problem." See Sprengel and Streim, *Berliner und Wiener Moderne*, 259-276, for a discussion of how Salten, Zweig, Musil, and Bahr responded to the issues of unification and a "separate" Austrian culture.

12 "Leb wohl … komm wieder. Kleine Bilder aus großen Tagen."

13 Published in installments in the *Fremden-Blatt* from Dec. 27, 1914, to Mar. 4, 1915.

14 See Jürgen Ehneß, *Felix Saltens erzählerisches Werk*, 197-204, for a summary of the work and detailed consideration of Schnitzler's critique. The full text of the Schnitzler essay has been published in his *Aphorismen und Betrachtungen*, 482-486.

15 Arthur Schnitzler, *Tagebuch 1913-1916* [Jan. 23, 1915], 170.

16 *Abschied im Sturm*, 87.

17 Ibid., 82.

18 "Das Buch eines Jägers."

19 "Brief an Galsworthy," in *Gute Gesellschaft. Erlebnisse mit Tieren*, 19.

20 Arthur Schnitzler, *Tagebuch 1913-1916* [Nov. 23, 1915], 240.

21 Whittaker Chambers, trans., *Bambi*, 102.

22 "Ein Wort vom Barbarentum."

23 "Studie über Potsdam," feuilleton in two parts, *Neue Freie Presse*, Oct. 21 and 28, 1914.

24 See Felix Salten, "Praterspatzen."

²⁵ *Prinz Eugen der edle Ritter*, 101-102. Salten exaggerated his numbers; today historians set the number of troops at 80,000 for Austria, 150,000 for the Turks.

²⁶ "Begräbnis eines Jünglings."

²⁷ "Besuch in Ischl."

²⁸ Also called *Ein Schuß in der Nacht* (A Shot in the Night). The film was a Berlin production by PAGU.

²⁹ Arthur Schnitzler, *Tagebuch 1913-1916* [Nov. 10, 1915], 237.

³⁰ Also called *Genopstandelsen*. It was directed by Holger-Madsen and released in Austria and Germany under the titles *Auferstehung* and *Die zweimal sterben* and in Great Britain as *A Resurrection*. For film information, I am indebted to Christian Dewald, "Filmografie Felix Salten," in *Felix Salten. Schriftsteller – Journalist – Exilant*, ed. Siegfried Mattl and Werner Michael Schwarz, 177-185.

³¹ "Mit dem ersten Balkanzug."

³² "Fasching 1916."

³³ "Laïs." The poem is cited in chapter 3.

³⁴ The first is a German film, the second an Austrian production.

³⁵ According to Christian Dewald, this is the only film of which it can be established with certainty that Salten was both writer and director. Dewald, "Filmographie Felix Salten," in *Felix Salten. Schriftsteller – Journalist – Exilant*, ed. Siegfried Mattl and Werner Michael Schwarz, 178.

³⁶ Also given the titles *Moritz Wasserstrahl*, *Moritz als Stratege*, and *Aus Moritz Wasserstrahls Soldatenzeit* [From Moritz Wasserstrahl's Time as a Soldier].

³⁷ Manfred Dickel writes that the *Neue Wiener Tageblatt* reported that the film *Moritz Wasserstrahl* inspired "storms of laughter" from the audience. *"Ein Dilettant des Lebens will ich nicht sein,"* 196.

³⁸ ["Erinnerungen"], typescript, 33.

³⁹ Ibid.

Chapter 14

¹ Arthur Schnitzler, *Tagebuch 1917-1919* [May 19, 1917], 46.

² Ibid. From 36,000 to 24,000 crowns. Schnitzler commented that this was "of course untrue" since he knew Salten's proclivity for lying about his true professional and financial situations.

³ "Thronrede."

⁴ Arthur Schnitzler, *Tagebuch 1913-1916* [Nov. 23, 1915], 240.

⁵ "In der Osternacht."

⁶ "Gelegenheitsstücke."

[7] See Felix Salten, "Burgtheater," Feuilleton-Beilage, *FB*, Dec. 11, 1914.

[8] "Verwundet. Eindrücke in einem Truppenspital."

[9] "Besuch in den Skoda-Werken I, II."

[10] "Wer nicht herzlos ist…"

[11] "Salzkammergut. Im dritten Kriegssommer."

[12] "In der Osternacht."

[13] "Ein Brief am Pfingstsonntag."

[14] Karl Kraus, "Eine Friedenstaube."

[15] See Siegfried Mattl and Werner Michael Schwarz, eds., *Feliz Salten. Schriftsteller – Journalist – Exilant*, 49.

[16] "Schweizer Reisetage."

[17] "Gute Botschaft. Ein Brief aus fernen Tagen."

[18] "Geselligkeit und fünfzehn Deka."

[19] "Der Zuckerbäckerladen."

[20] "Kleiderkarte."

[21] "Die kleinen Schneeschaufler."

[22] "Ein Kapitel Zukunft."

[23] Emil Kläger, ed., *Legenden und Maerchen unserer Zeit.*

[24] These plays had appeared in print one year earlier with Felix Bloch Erben in Berlin-Wilmersedorf, a press that specialized in texts for theatrical production.

[25] Arthur Schnitzler, *Tagebuch 1917-1919* [Nov. 12, 1917], 89.

[26] Ibid. [Dec. 23, 1917], 99.

[27] ["Erinnerungen"], typescript, 39.

[28] Arthur Schnitzler, *Tagebuch 1917-1919* [Jan. 1, 1918], 104.

[29] Quoted in Ibid. [July 14, 1918], 166.

[30] See David Rechter, *The Jews of Vienna and the First World War*, 149.

[31] *Esoi*, or "Azoy," is a Yiddish word meaning "such" and has a negative connotation.

[32] See Arthur Schnitzler, *Tagebuch 1917-1919* [Mar. 21, 1918], 123.

[33] The five deleted stories were "Die Wege des Herrn," "Der Hinterbliebene," "Begräbnis," "Sedan," and "Feiertag."

[34] "Bilder aus dem Konzertsaal: Richard Strauß."

[35] "Bilder aus dem Konzertsaal. Arthur Nikisch."

[36] "Ein armer Teufel."

[37] "Sommerfestspiel."

[38] "Sieger und Besiegte. Brief an einen amerikanischen Freund."

[39] Published as a feuilleton in *NFP*, Feb. 23, 1919.

[40] This story may have been the original inspiration for Salten's novel *Florian* (1933) although Salten traces his inspiration to an event that occurred several years later.

41 f.s. [Felix Salten], "Kleine Begebenheit."

42 See Felix Salten, "Deutsches Volkstheater."

43 "Bildung. Die Kundgebung der Mittelschüler."

44 "Abschaffung der Matura."

45 "Verhandlungsformen."

46 "Wienerwald-Elegie."

47 Arthur Schnitzler, *Tagebuch 1917-1919* [May 9, 1919], 251.

48 W., "Burgtheater." Feuilleton, *NFP*, Dec. 14, 1919.

49 Arthur Schnitzler, *Tagebucvh 1917-1919*, 316 [Dec. 12, 1917].

50 "Kleine Dialoge."

51 Molitor's *Novellenschatz*, published by Lyra-Verlag in Leipzig and Vienna.

52 Arthur Schnitzler, *Tagebuch 1917-1919* [Nov. 27, 1919], 312.

53 Ibid. [November 19, 1919], 308.

Chapter 15

1 Article 80, Saint Germain-en-Laye Treaty, Part III, Section 6:11, describes the process in this manner: "Persons possessing rights of citizenship in territory forming part of the former Austro-Hungarian Monarchy, and differing in race and language from the majority of the population of such territory, shall within six months from the coming into force of the present Treaty severally be entitled to opt for Austria, Italy, Poland, Roumania, the Serb-Croat-Slovene State, or the Czecho-Slovak State, if the majority of the population of the State selected is of the same race and language as the person exercising the right to opt." See http://en.wikisource.org/wiki/Treaty_of_Saint-Germain-en-Laye/Part_III. The material in these pages was compiled from the version published by the Australasian Legal Information Institute.

2 "Theaterfrage."

3 "Opernkrise. (Der Protest gegen Richard Strauß)."

4 Published in *Der Neue Tag*, Apr. 12, 1919.

5 *Schauen und Spielen. Studien zur Kritik des modernen Theaters*, vol. 1, *Ergebnisse, Erlebnisse*, 12.

6 In these two volumes, Salten critiques texts, but not performances, of plays. One exception is Ludwig Fulda's *Herr und Diener* (Master and Servant), *Schauen und Spielen*, 2:140-147.

7 *Schauen und Spielen*, 1:407.

8 *Schauen und Spielen. Studien zur Kritik des modernen Theaters*, vol. 2, *Abende/Franzosen, Puppenspiel, Aus der Ferne*, 66.

9 Ibid., 41.

10 Ibid., 87.

352

[11] Ibid., 115.

[12] Ibid., 208.

[13] "Francis de Croisset/Wenn das Herz spricht," *Schauen und Spielen*, 2:244.

[14] "Französische Stunde (1912)," *Schauen und Spielen*, 2:261.

[15] *Schauen und Spielen*, 2:354.

[16] ["Erinnerungen"], typescript, 53.

[17] *Das Burgtheater*, 8.

[18] Ibid., 14.

[19] Ibid., 14-15.

[20] *Schauen und Spielen*, 2:14. This essay first appeared in the *Fremden-Blatt* on Apr. 21, 1914.

[21] Reinhardt had directed Salten's one-act play "Schöne Seelen" [Lovely Souls] at this theater during its 1903/1904 season.

[22] "Reinhardts 'Oedipus.'"

[23] "Das Reinhardt-Problem."

[24] Hofmannsthal's *Jedermann* had premiered under Max Reinhardt's direction in Berlin's Schumann Circus on Dec. 1, 1911.

[25] See "Hofmannsthal: Jedermann," in *Schauen und Spielen*, 2:29-35.

[26] First published as a feuilleton in *Die Zeit*, Aug. 23, 1903.

[27] First published as a feuilleton in *Pester Lloyd*, Mar. 25, 1913.

[28] See Arthur Schnitzler, *Tagebuch 1920-1922* [Dec. 20, 1920], 118. As he so often did, Salten set the manuscript aside for several years and resumed work on it only after the German annexation of Austria in 1938.

[29] See *Ein Gott erwacht* (A God Awakens), typescript, 12.

[30] Felix Salten, "Wien und die Musik," in *Das Mahler-Fest. Amsterdam Mai 1920. Vorträge und Berichte*, ed. C. Rudolf Mengelberg, 32.

[31] Arthur Schnitzler, *Tagebuch 1920-1922*, 63 [June 14, 1920].

[32] In 1921 Fischer called Salten's newly completed *Der Hund von Florenz* "a masterful novella" but objected to the female character's being a courtesan. Letter from Fischer to Felix Salten, in Dierk Rodewald and Corrina Fiedler, eds., *Samuel Fischer, Hedwig Fischer: Briefwechsel mit Autoren*, Letter 784, Apr. 19, 1921, 691-692.

[33] See Arthur Schnitzler, *Tagebuch 1920-1922* [Mar. 15, 1920], 33.

[34] ["Erinnerungen"], typescript, 28.

[35] See Arthur Schnitzler, *Tagebuch 1920-1922* [May 1, 1921], 174.

[36] Felix Salten, "Felix Salten," in *Die Psychologie der produktiven Persönlichkeit* by Paul Plaut, 297. Salten never made this assertion about any of his other works of fiction.

[37] Huntley Paterson, trans., *The Hound of Florence*, epigraph.

[38] Using psychoanalytical techniques, Lieselotte Pouh determines that Cambyses represents Grassi's id with Lucas as his superego and that the

work is a novel of development that describes the hero's maturation process and the attempt to achieve an integrated self. (See Pouh, *Young Vienna and Psychoanalysis: Felix Doermann, Jakob Julius David, and Felix Salten*, 134-139.) Certainly in an age when Freud was analyzing the "Wolfman" and "Ratman," Lucas' doppelgänger in canine form appears to conform to Freud's use of the animal as the representative of a person's subconscious desires, lusts, and shames – this despite Salten's claim that he was not interested in such analyses.

39 ["Erinnerungen"], typescript, 6.
40 Huntley Paterson, trans., *The Hound of Florence*, 110-111.
41 See Manfred Dickel, *"Ein Dilettant des Lebens will ich nicht sein,"* 196.

Chapter 16

1 The name appears to have been suggested by Salten's seventeen-year-old daughter Anna.
2 Arthur Schnitzler, *Tagebuch 1920-1922* [Nov. 6, 1921], 246.
3 See Dietmar Grieser, "Ausgebootet. Felx Salten; 'Bambi,'" *Im Tiergarten der Weltliteratur. Auf den Spuren von Kater Murr, Biene Maja, Bambi, Möwe Jonathan und den anderen*, 17-19. Although Salten began his work on the novel at his summer residence, Salten's daughter has stated that *Bambi* actually "owes its existence" to Salten's "thorough familiarity with and his great love of" the hunting preserve near Stockerau, where he was a frequent visitor. Anna Wyler-Salten, "Introduction," *Felix Salten's Favorite Animal Stories*, vii.
4 Felix Salten, in Paul Plaut, *Die Psychologie der produktiven Persönlichkeit*, 296.
5 Ibid., 297.
6 "Herbstgang."
7 "Das Buch eines Jägers."
8 "Stalking at Dawn," in Felix Salten, *Good Comrades*, 210.
9 Salten, "Bemerkungen zu 'Bambis Kinder,'" in a letter to "Herrn Weldler."
10 "Pirschgang im Gebirge." Also in *Kleine Brüder*, 106.
11 Ibid., 107.
12 "Morgenpirsch," *Gute Gesellschaft*, 89.
13 Salten, "Bemerkungen zu 'Bambis Kinder,'" in a letter to "Herrn Weldler."
14 Ibid.
15 Anna Wyler-Salten, "Introduction," *Felix Salten's Favorite Animal Stories*, vii.

[16] Salten, "Bemerkungen zu 'Bambis Kinder,'" in a letter to "Herrn Weldler."

[17] ["Erinnerungen"), typescript, 37.

[18] John Galsworthy, "Foreword" [Mar. 16, 1928], in *Bambi* by Felix Salten (New York: Grosset & Dunlap, 1931).

[19] William Rose Benet, "The Stricken Deer."

[20] Salten, "Bemerkungen zu 'Bambis Kinder,'" in a letter to "Herrn Weldler."

[21] *Bambis Kinder*, 9.

[22] Margery Fisher, *Who's Who in Children's Books*, 36

[23] Karl Kraus, "Jüdelnde Hasen."

[24] Whittaker Chambers, trans., *Fifteen Rabbits*, 45.

[25] Whittaker Chambers, trans., *Bambi*, 10.

[26] Ibid., 138.

[27] Ibid., 221.

[28] Ibid., 83.

[29] John R. Chamberlain, "Poetry and Philosophy in A Tale of Forest Life."

[30] Paul R. Milton and Sanford Jerome Greenburger, trans., *A Forest World*, 175.

[31] Ibid., 91.

[32] In her book *Young Vienna and Psychoanalysis*, Lieselotte Pouh gives a Freudian reading of *Der Hund von Florenz*. See 134-139.

[33] Barrows Mussey, trans., *Perri*, 14.

[34] Huntley Paterson, trans., *The Hound of Florence*, 47-48.

[35] Ibid., 49.

[36] Whittaker Chambers, trans., *Bambi*, 110.

[37] Ibid., 203.

[38] Ibid., 161.

[39] In contrast, the Disney film version of the novel demonizes man while projecting its positive Christian imagery into Bambi, whom one critic calls "Jesus Whitetail Superstar." In the Disney film, man's hunting of deer becomes "a crime comparable to the persecution of Christ." George Riegler, cited in Matt Cartmill, "The Bambi Syndrome," 12.

[40] Whittaker Chambers trans., *Bambi*, 218.

[41] Ibid., 219.

[42] For readings of *Bambi* as a critique of the European situation, especially the persecution of Jews, see Alfred Werner, "The Author of 'Bambi,'" and Iris Bruce, "Which Way Out? Schnitzler's and Salten's Conflicting Responses to Cultural Zionism."

[43] The German title translates literally as "Tiny Occurrence"; the English title is misleading because of the Christian overtone inherent in its suggestive reference to St. Francis of Assisi.

[44] Paul R. Milton, trans., "Brother Ant," in *Good Comrades*, 19.

[45] Ibid., 21.

[46] Ibid., 23.

[47] From a review in the *Philadelphia Public Ledger*, reprinted on the jacket of a Pocket Book (paperback) edition of the work in 1940.

Chapter 17

[1] See Murray G. Hall, *Der Paul Zsolnay Verlag*, 29. This work was an invaluable source of information regarding the work of the Zsolnay publishing house.

[2] By 1926, when Paul Zsolnay took over the book's publication, it had sold 10,000 copies (see Murray G. Hall, 532).

[3] In Murray G. Hall, *Der Paul Zsolnay Verlag*, 28.

[4] Ibid., 34.

[5] Ibid., 27.

[6] Arthur Schnitzler, *Tagebuch 1923-1926* (Nov. 29, 1923), 101.

[7] "Hugo von Hofmannsthal schreibt," cited in the endpages of *Neue Menschen auf alter Erde* by Felix Salten, 1925.

[8] *Neue Menschen auf alter Erde. Eine Palästinafahrt*, 52.

[9] "'Die Juden.'"

[10] "Bilder vom Zionistenkongreß."

[11] Ibid.

[12] *Neue Menschen auf alter Erde*, 175.

[13] See Rembert J. Schleicher, "Felix Salten als poetischer Zionist. Beobachtungen zum Reisebericht 'Neue Menschen auf alter Erde. Eine Palästinafahrt'" in *Felix Salten – der unbekannte Bekannte*, ed. Ernst Seibert and Susanne Blumesberger, 33-46. Schleicher argues persuasively that the title of Salten's book is a deliberate play on the title of Herzl's novel and that Salten's journey follows the same route as that taken in Herzl's work. Florian Krobb, "Gefühlszionismus und Zionsgefühle: Zum Palästina-Diskurs bei Schnitzler, Herzl, Salten und Lasker-Schüler," demonstrates that in all stages of this journey Salten examines precisely those aspects of the new land that Herzl developed in his utopian novel (160-161).

[14] *Neue Menschen auf alter Erde*, 166.

[15] Ibid., 125-126.

[16] Ibid., 254-255.

[17] Ibid., 254.

[18] Ibid., 269.

[19] Ibid., 270.

[20] Manfred Dickel, *"Ein Dilettant des Lebens will ich nicht sein,"* 381. Dickel provides an excellent reading of Salten's book; see 369-392.

[21] The work continues to be reprinted on a regular basis, including printings in 1986, 1991, and 1999 by Athenäum's Jewish press.

[22] Herman Bahr, "Felix Salten zum 60. Geburtstag."

[23] It appeared as a feuilleton in *Pester Lloyd* on May 25, 1913.

[24] "Verwickelte Geschichte," in *Die Dame im Spiegel*, 123.

[25] *Bob und Baby*, 3.

[26] Ibid., 3-4.

[27] Ibid., 72.

[28] See Salten's ["Erinnerungen"], typescript, 54-58, where he states that he had pledged his support to Herterich even before this appointment and where he relates instances when he gave Herterich advice on casting decisions and on additions to the ensemble.

[29] Karl Kraus, "Ruhe!," 68-69.

[30] Edward Timms, trans., "Aus dem Papierkorb" by Karl Kraus, 12, in *Karl Kraus, Apocalyptic Satirist* by Edward Timms, 53.

[31] See, for example, "Berühmte Wiener aus Budapest. Aus der Bühne vom 21. Jänner 1926," in "Rückblende," *Bühne* (1991), 78. Salten used this code, in part, because of a general boycott of Kraus by the Vienna press.

[32] In Karl Kraus, "Die letzte Nacht," 79.

[33] Ibid., 80.

[34] Ibid., 77.

[35] See, for example, Arthur Schnitzler, *Tagebuch 1923-1926* [Nov. 27, 1924], 208, where Schnitzler writes of Salten's critical review of a play Beer-Hoffmann had worked on that "Richard regards it (and certainly not completely unjustly) as 'Ressentiment.'"

[36] "Die Maschinenstürmer."

[37] Blei first published this work anonymously in 1920; it appeared under his own name in 1922.

[38] *Das große Bestiarium der Literatur*, 60. Blei was equally critical of Karl Kraus, whom he portrayed as the "Fackelkraus," a creature who is "an anti-nature because it is born out of the excrement of that which it wants to destroy, nothing but a voice that consequently lives only as long as one hears it." See Karl Kraus, ["Ganze Ketten von roten…"], *Die Fackel* 24, nos. 601-607 (Nov. 1922): 86.

[39] Manfred Dickel, *"Ein Dilettant des Lebens will ich nicht sein,"* 141.

[40] Nachwort, in Heinrich Mann *Der Tyrann. Die Branzilla. Novellen*, 74.

[41] Karl Kraus, "Die letzte Nacht," 80.

42 "Theodor, Ein Porträt aus dem Nachlass."
43 Salten, letter to Schnitzler, Feb. 8, 1927.
44 Schnitzler, letter to Salten, Feb. 10, 1927, DLA.
45 Arthur Schnitzler, *Tagebuch 1927-1930* [Feb. 28, 1927], 25.

Chapter 18

1 Schnitzler, *Tagebuch 1913-1916* [Mar. 22, 1915], 182.
2 Schnitzler, *Tagebuch 1927-1930* [Apr. 24, 1927], 41.
3 Richard Specht, "Der Roman eines reichen jungen Mannes."
4 From *Illustrierter Filmkurier* in the Filmarchiv Austria, reproduced in *Felix Salten. Schriftsteller – Journalist – Exilant*, ed. Siegfried Mattl and Werner Michael Schwarz, 180.
5 Dr. Mija Marton and a Mr. Incze, both good acquaintances from Budapest.
6 "Dreimal Hochzeit. Die Geschichte einer Uebersetzung," feuilleton, *NFP*, Sept. 29, 1927.
7 –er. "Das Reinhardt-Ensemble im Johann-Strauß-Theater."
8 Ashley Dukes, *The Scene is Changed*, 125. The German title of the play is *Das Wirtshaus zum Pechvogel.*
9 "Ein junger Führer."
10 P.E.N. is an acronym for "poets, playwrights, editors, essayists, and novelists." There was an especially heavy component of journalists in the Vienna P.E.N. Club.
11 Coudenhove left office after a year because of the demands of his Pan-Europa work but retained his membership in the organization.
12 Roman Rocek has pointed out that technically this election could have been declared invalid since seven members of the governing committee were required to select a club president. See *Glanz und Elend des P.E.N,* 62. Much of my information regarding P.E.N. is taken from this comprehensive work.
13 In Roman Rocek, *Glanz und Elend des P.E.N.*, 66 and 67.
14 John Galsworthy, "Der P.E.N.-Club," *NFP*, Jan. 5, 1924, in *Glanz und Elend des P.E.N.* by Roman Rocek, 43.
15 *Der Schrei der Liebe, Die Gedenktafel der Prinzessin Anna, Die kleine Veronika,* and *Olga Frohgemuth.*
16 The title of the English translation of this novel is *Samson and Delilah.*
17 Whittaker Chambers, trans., Preface to *Samson and Delilah*, [1]. He included a second quotation from the "prophetess of Zaphor": "A betrayal such as this is inconceivable, and may not even be conceived."
18 Ibid., 154-155.

[19] Ibid., 71.

[20] Ibid., 18.

[21] Ibid., 19.

[22] Ibid., 177. Although Salten's introduction of a faithful dog into the Biblical epic weakens its grandeur, it is a reflection of how deeply Salten felt about the suffering man inflicted upon apparently dumb animals.

[23] Cited from the book announcement, *NFP*, Oct. 7, 1928.

[24] Rudolf Jeremias Kreutz, "Felix Saltens gesammelte Werke."

[25] "Tagebuchblatt aus diesem Sommer."

[26] Victor Wittner, "Begegnungen mit Felix Salten," *Welt am Montag* 27:5.

[27] *Herr Wenzel auf Rehberg*, a revised *Der Hund von Florenz*, *König Dietrichs Befreiung*, *Die Gewalt der Dinge*, *Das Schicksal der Agathe*, *Die Geliebte des Kaisers*.

[28] A similar epigraph might have been added to Salten's *Simson*, where human characters are frequently referred to as animals and where the stray dog that befriends the captive Samson is referred to as his only friend. This motto was eliminated from later editions of *Fünfzehn Hasen*, perhaps in order to de-politicize the work during Hitler's reign.

[29] Walter von Molo, "Wichtige Bücher. Saltens Hasenbuch."

[30] Gladys Graham, "Outstanding Rabbits," *Saturday Review of Literature* 7 (Aug. 30, 1930): 85

[31] Karl Kraus, "Rabbits with Jewish Dialect," in *The Vienna Coffeehouse Wits, 1890-1938* by Harold B. Segel, 108. Originally published as "Jüdelnde Hasen." Robert Neumann treated the work more gently in a satire called "Sechzehn Ziegen" (Sixteen Goats), in which he mocked Salten's use of odd animal names and his overabundance of animal philosophizing.

[32] Roman Rocek, *Glanz und Elend des P.E.N.*, 78.

[33] Ibid., 79.

[34] Ibid., 80.

[35] Benjamin Crémieux, "Der internationale P.E.N.-Club Kongreß in Wien. Österreichische Eindrücke," *NFP*, June 25, 1929, in *Glanz und Elend des P.E.N.* by Roman Rocek, 80.

[36] "Ein Meister."

[37] "Erinnerung an Hofmannsthal."

[38] Hugo von Hofmannsthal, "Felix Salten zum 60. Geburtstag," *Jahrbuch. Paul Zsolnay Verlag 1930*, 98-99.

[39] Ibid., 99.

[40] Ibid., 100.

[41] Ibid., 99.

[42] Franz Molnar, "Felix Salten zum 60. Geburtstag," in *Jahrbuch. Paul Zsolnay Verlag 1930*, 103-104.

[43] Ibid., 104.

[44] Arthur Schnitzler, "Felix Salten zum 60. Geburtstag," in *Jahrbuch. Paul Zsolnay Verlag 1930*, 106.

[45] At the Reinhardt-Bühne. See *Wiener Bilder*, Sept. 1, 1929, 5.

[46] f., "'Vom andern Ufer.' Salten, der Sechziger."

[47] Diary entry, in *Felix Salten als Mensch, Dichter und Kritiker* by Kurt Riedmiller, 28.

[48] R., "Theater in der Josefstadt."

[49] Arthur Schnitzler, *Tagebuch 1927-1930* [Nov. 30 1929], 294.

[50] Letter from Freud to Sandor Ferenczi, in *The Life and Work of Sigmund Freud*, vol. 3: *The Last Phase, 1919-1939* by Ernest Jones, 102. Similarly, in a 1926 letter to Salten, Freud joked about feeling "like a citizen of Vienna." See Lieselotte Pouh, *Young Vienna and Psychoanalysis*, 125-126.

[51] "Franz Lehar. Zum sechzigsten Geburtstag."

Chapter 19

[1] Felix Salten, "Unterwegs nach Amerika," feuilleton, *NFP*, June 8, 1930.

[2] *Fünf Minuten Amerika*, 11.

[3] Ibid., 20.

[4] See *Fünf Minuten Amerika*, 52-58, where he concludes, "But today no one can know what will happen in fifty or a hundred years."

[5] Ibid., 239.

[6] Ibid., 86.

[7] Ibid., 129.

[8] Ibid., 128.

[9] Ibid., 91.

[10] Ibid., 174.

[11] Ibid., 91.

[12] Ibid., 227.

[13] Ibid., 175.

[14] Ibid., 188.

[15] Ibid., 177. It is ironic how the parallels between humans and the animals led to the slaughterhouse would converge in the Nazi death camps.

[16] Ibid., 178.

[17] See, for example, the essay "Mein Falke" [My Falcon], which appeared as a feuilleton in *Die Zeit* (July 18, 1909) and as an essay in *Die Dame im Spiegel* in 1920.

[18] *Gute Gesellschaft*, 186.

[19] Ibid., 40-41.

[20] *Teppiche*, 7.

[21] Karl Kraus, "Der Nobelpreis."

[22] *Teppiche*, 47.

[23] "Moderne Wunder."

[24] Stefan Zweig, "Die Monotonisierung der Welt."

[25] Salten, "Monotonisierung der Welt?"

[26] "Wunder der Gegenwart."

[27] "Eröffnung eines Theaters."

[28] "Tag in Salzburg."

[29] Arthur Schnitzler, *Tagebuch 1927-1930* [Dec. 3, 1930], 389. The author was Max Mell. Schnitzler felt that, in this particular case, Salten was also motivated by personal antipathy towards Mell, and he was annoyed that Salten had not consulted him in the matter.

[30] "Arthur Schnitzler."

[31] Salten, letter to Anton Wildgans, Nov. 10, 1931, DLA. It would be a year before Salten was able to pay proper tribute to Schnitzler in an essay published in the *Neue Freie Presse* entitled "Erinnerung an Schnitzler," *NFP*, Dec. 1, 1932.

[32] "Proben bei Reinhardt."

[33] "Auf Leben und Tod. Die Liebesgeschichte der Louise von Koburg."

[34] The English translation of this novel was entitled simply *The City Jungle*.

[35] First published on Aug. 23, 1903 as a feuilleton in *Die Zeit* ("In Schönbrunn") and included in the volume *Die Dame im Spiegel*, 1920.

[36] "Bei Gefangenen."

[37] "Der alte Hagenbeck." This essay was reprinted in Salten's *Gestalten und Erscheinungen*, 298-305.

[38] *Freunde aus aller Welt*, 73-74.

[39] Ibid., 74.

[40] "Bei Gefangenen."

[41] Professor Dr. Gustav Brandes, director of the Dresden Zoo from 1910 to 1934.

[42] *Freunde aus aller Welt*, 143.

[43] Ibid., 212.

[44] Cf., for example, his essay written in defense of the protesting proletariat in the 1911 Ottakring rebellion, chapter 12.

[45] "Schwarze Kirschen."

[46] "Mehr Haltung."

[47] "Moses und David," *Der Jud ist schuld...? Diskussionsbuch über die Judenfrage*, 400.

[48] Ibid., 401.

⁴⁹ "Salzburger Glockenspiel."
⁵⁰ "Kongreßtage in Budapest."

Chapter 20

¹ "Tempo, Kino und Gelächter," *NFP*, June 19, 1930; *Fünf Minuten Amerika*, 35-36.
² "Rückkehr zum Lustspiel. Ein Brief."
³ "Die Stadt des Films," *NFP*, July 27, 1930; *Fünf Minuten Amerika*, 109, 110.
⁴ "Rückkehr zum Lustspiel. Ein Brief."
⁵ "Tempo, Kino und Gelächter," *NFP*, June 19, 1930; *Fünf Minuten Amerika*, 35, 34.
⁶ See "Theater und Film: Heute: Eröffnung des Sascha-Palastes," *Die Neue Zeitung*, Mar. 13, 1931. The theater was located in Vienna's third district, Ungargasse 60, in what had once been the military riding academy.
⁷ Walter Wassermann and Walter Schlee were responsible for the basic screenplay, with Salten supplying the dialogue.
⁸ *Die neue Zeitung*, Mar. 15, 1931.
⁹ *Filmwelt* 46 [Berlin], Nov. 5, 1931.
¹⁰ *Scampolo* is the name of the lovable waif of the film and translates as "leftover."
¹¹ Siegfried Mattl and Werner Michael Schwarz call *Scampolo* a "dog's story" and state that the "Salten-Moment" in the story is the waif's "sudden, puzzling and instinctive devotion" to the down-and-out hero. See Mattl and Schwarz, eds., *Felix Salten. Schriftsteller – Journalist – Exilant*, 64.
¹² "Erinnerung an Franz Josef," typescript, 2.
¹³ Erich Posselt and Michel Kraike, trans., *Florian. The Emperor's Stallion*, 122.
¹⁴ Ibid., 123.
¹⁵ Salten remarked how he himself came upon "a noble animal, grown old, superfluous, unusable" on a meadow in the Vienna woods and how, as he watched the animal disappear into the dusk, "It was as the fading of a great, once bright past." Salten, "Erinnerung an Franz Josef," typescript, 2.
¹⁶ Erich Posselt and Michel Kraike, trans., *Florian. The Emperor's Stallion*, 342.
¹⁷ Basil Davenport, "Felix Salten's Story of a Royal Horse."
¹⁸ I. W. L., *Boston Transcript*, Nov. 10, 1934.
¹⁹ Ernst Lothar, "Salten: 'Louise von Koburg.'"

[20] In May 1933 the Akademietheater presented *Feind der Liebe* [Enemy of Love], Salten's translation of the Rudolf Bessie dramatization of the love story of Elizabeth Barrett and Robert Browning.

[21] In a speech delivered at the book burning at the Opernplatz in Berlin on May 10, 1933. From a film clip of the book burning shown as part of the permanent exhibit at the U.S. Holocaust Museum.

[22] Stefan Zweig, letter to Salten, Mai 7, 1933.

[23] Stefan Zweig, *The World of Yesterday*, 229.

[24] Hans Hinkel (1901-1960), journalist and, from 1930-1932, editor of the Nazi newspaper *Völkischer Beobachter* [People's Observer]. When Hitler came to power, Hinkel became the organization leader of the *Kampfbund für deutsche Kultur* (Battle League for German Culture).

[25] Hanns Johst (1890-1978), playwright, SS member, and Hitler propagandist. His propaganda piece *Schlageter* premiered in Berlin on Hitler's birthday, Apr. 20, 1933. He became the Nazi poet laureate.

[26] Salten, letter to Zweig, May 14, 1933, Stefan Zweig Collection, Daniel A. Reed Library, SUNY – Fredonia.

[27] Stefan Zweig, letter to Salten, May 15, 1933.

[28] Salten, letter to Zweig, May 13, 1933, Stefan Zweig Collection, Daniel A. Reed Library, SUNY Fredonia.

[29] Salten had asked that P.E.N. support a motion that a letter be written to Germany's president, Hindenburg, asking him to commute Carl von Ossietzky's prison sentence to "chivalric confinement." *Tätigkeitsbericht über das neunte Clubjahr des Wiener P.E.N.-Clubs*. Wien, 1932, in *P.E.N. Politik, Emigration, Nationalsozialismus: Ein österreichischer Schriftstellerclub* by Klaus Amann, 21.

[30] In Gabriele Maria Reinharter, *Felix Salten. Schriftsteller*, 19.

[31] Ibid., 20.

[32] Minutes of the May 21 meeting held at Salten's home, Grete Urbanitzsky Archive, Vienna City and State Archive, in *Glanz und Elend des P.E.N.* by Roman Rocek, 117-118.

[33] Elster (1888-1983) was a publisher and editor, founder of the Horen publishing house. Busch was a naval officer who wrote about German naval battles; Schmidt-Pauli was the author of the book *Die Männer um Hitler* [The Men around Hitler], 1932.

[34] John Galsworthy died on Jan. 31, 1933, and H. G. Wells was elected to fill his position as president of the P.E.N. International.

[35] In Roman Rocek, *Glanz und Elend des P.E.N.*, 127.

[36] Ibid., 128. Rocek suggests that it would have been nearly impossible, in any event, to avoid discussion of the motion before its passage since it

was almost inevitable that amendments would be suggested that specifically referred to the German situation.

[37] Grete von Urbanitzky stated that those who left the hall were acting not so much in support of the Germans as in protest against Wells's changing the agreed-upon conditions. See Roman Rocek, *Glanz und Elend des P.E.N.*, 134, 136.

[38] Felix Salten, "Die Wahrheit über den Pen-Club-Kongreß." The head of the Swiss delegation, Emanuel Stickelberger, expressed similar sentiments in his speech to the convention. See Werner Berthold and Brita Eckert, eds., *Der deutsche PEN-Club im Exil, 1933-1948: Eine Ausstellung der Deutschen Bibliothek Frankfurt am Main*, 32.

[39] In Volkmar von Zühlsdorff, *Hitler's Exiles: The German Cultural Resistance in America and Europe*, 89. Zühlsdorff then goes on to note that on November 8 of that year the International P.E.N.'s executive committee met in London and, upon Edgar von Schmidt-Pauli's admission that the German P.E.N. had excluded members because of their political conviction, expelled the German P.E.N. for violating the P.E.N. charter.

[40] "Felix Salten für die Nazi," *Das kleine Blatt*, May 25, 1933.

[41] Schiller Marmorek, "Der Verrat der Schriftsteller," in *Felix Salten. Schriftsteller* by Gabriele Maria Reinharter, 21.

[42] "Tagesneuigkeiten," *Arbeiter-Zeitung*, May 28, 1933. See Roman Rocek, *Glanz und Elend des P.E.N.*, 125.

[43] Friedrich Torberg, "Ruhestörung in Ragusa," *Die neue Weltbühne*, June 15, 1933, in *Der deutsche PEN-Club im Exil, 1933-1948: Eine Ausstellung der Deutschen Bibliothek Frankfurt am Main* ed. Werner Berthold and Brita Eckert, 35.

[44] "Die Wahrheit über den Pen-Club-Kongreß."

[45] Felix Salten, "Richtigstellung," *Arbeiter-Zeitung*, June 3, 1922, in *Glanz und Elend des P.E.N* by Roman Rocek, 125.

[46] "Die Generalversammlung des Pen-Klubs," *NFP*, June 29, 1933, in *P.E.N. Politik, Emigration, Nationalsozialismus: Ein österreichischer Schriftstellerclub* by Klaus Amann, 33.

[47] Robert Neumann, "Das mußte aufgeschrieben werden. Aus der Geschichte des Österreichischen P.E.N.," *Blätter des Österreichischen P.E.N. Clubs* 70, no.1, 18, in *P.E.N. Politik, Emigration, Nationalsozialismus: Ein österreichischer Schriftstellerclub* by Klaus Amann, 55. Salten and the publisher Paul Zsolnay were two whom Neumann explicitly included in this group of former P.E.N. Club members.

[48] Letter of Oct. 9, 1933, in *Glanz und Elend des P.E.N.* by Roman Rocek, 145.

[49] Heinrich Eduard Jacob had gently rebuked Stefan Zweig in July for not signing the P.E.N. Club resolution against the Nazi oppression of dissident writers and, when Zweig questioned Salten's future role in P.E.N., responded: "As for Salten, whose tuxedoed presence at banquests and talent at speech-making I truly appreciate, don't you think that Auernheimer can manage that as well, without the unpleasant side effects of critical favor and critical disfavor and personal regimentation?" Heinrich Eduard Jacob to Stefan Zweig, July 5, 1933, in *Finis libri. Der Schriftsteller und Journalist Heinrich Eduard Jacob (1889-1967)* by Anja Clarenbach, 120. Salten briefly considered trying to found a new Friends of P.E.N. Club in Vienna but soon gave up the idea.

Chapter 21

[1] "Der junge David."

[2] Ibid.

[3] ["Erinnerungen"], typescript, 52.

[4] "Wohin soll ich mich wenden?"

[5] "Vor Tau und Tag."

[6] "Herman Bahr – Siebzig!"

[7] ["Erinnerungen"], typescript, 45.

[8] In *Der Jud ist schuld…? Diskussionsbuch über die Judenfrage.*

[9] "Nervenprobe."

[10] Josef Roth, letter to Felix Salten, Mar. 6, 1934.

[11] Hermon Ould, letter to Felix Salten, Mar. 7, 1934, Harry Ransom Center, University of Texas at Austin.

[12] "Erinnerung an Franz Josef," typescript, 1-2.

[13] Oddly, this work is not included among the Salten works listed in the Zsolnay production reports in Murray G. Hall's definitive work on the Zsolnay press, *Der Paul Zsolnay Verlag. Von der Gründung bis zur Rückkehr aus dem Exil*; see 431-432 and 533. Instead, a printing of *Luise von Doburg* [sic] is included in the Salten listing for 1932 but not in Zsolnay's production list for that year. See 533 and 311-312.

[14] Although it had already appeared in 1932, it appears that Mrs. Eichelberger and her board members only became aware of it at this late date. See "Humane Awards Announced Here," *The Oregonian*, Dec. 31, 1934.

[15] In Lea Wyler, "Bambis Vater," 21.

[16] Martin Finder [Felix Salten], "Lerchenjubel."

[17] Published by Georg Marton in Vienna under this title in 1934.

[18] P. W., "'Mädchenhände,' Akademietheater," unidentified newspaper, Apr. 18 1935. File 117/70 in ÖNB, Handschriftensammlung.

[19] o. st. [Otto Stoessl], "Mädchenhände."

[20] Sascha, "Berühmtheit! Brief an einen Jüngling."

[21] "Gang durch Schönbrunn."

[22] "Mako, the Little Bear," *The Delineator* 124 (June 1934): 61. This work had previously appeared in a 1933 collection of banned German authors published by an emigrant press in Amsterdam.

[23] "Ein schneeweißer Hase," in *Kleine Brüder*, 130.

[24] "Herrliche Wohnung!"

[25] Paul Salten, postcard to his parents, n.d. [1933].

[26] Otti Salten, letter to Ludwig Metzl, January 9, 1933.

[27] *Sträfling Nummer 33, Baseler Nachrichten*, Nov. 11, 1942.

[28] f.s. [Felix Salten], "Schlaflose Nacht."

[29] In a production by the *Österreichische Volksbühne* [Austrian Popular Stage], under the direction of Walter Firner.

[30] Rudolph Lothar, "'Kaisertochter' im Deutschen Volkstheater."

[31] In an effort to counteract German claims that he operated a "Jewish press," Zsolnay was now publishing a number of German nationalist authors. He had ceased publishing Heinrich Mann in 1933. See Gerhard Renner, *Österreichische Schriftsteller und der Nationalsozialismus (1933-1940)*, 243-248.

[32] Diary, May 9, 1937.

[33] From an unidentified newspaper, File 227/70 in ÖNB, Handschriftensammlung.

[34] Diary, May 11, 1937.

[35] Ibid., Sept. 12, 1937.

[36] ["Erinnerungen"], typescript, 1.

Chapter 22

[1] In Jürgen Koppensteiner, *Ein landeskundliches Lesebuch*, 48.

[2] To this day, numerous short biographies of Salten state that he moved to the United States before settling in Switzerland in 1939.

[3] A letter to the Zsolnay Press from a Dutch literary agent on July 8, 1939, asserts this (Letter from Gildemeester, Zsolnay files, ÖNB), while a letter to Salten from the Paul Kohner agency in Hollywood states that word has been received in Hollywood that he has gotten out of a concentration camp and made it safely to Switzerland (July 25, 1939).

[4] Thomas Mann, *Tagebücher 1937-1939* [11 Apr. 1938], 206.

[5] Letter from Felix Salten to Stefan Zweig, Apr. 30, 1938, Stefan Zweig Collection, Daniel A. Reed Library, SUNY Fredonia.

[6] Salten's diary, Apr. 26, 1938. *Pester Lloyd* published his last contribution on Mar. 12, 1938.

[7] For a discussion of Paul Zsolnay's status with the press and of Salten's associations and difficulties with it, see Murray G. Hall, *Der Paul Zsolnay Verlag. Von der Gründung bis zur Rückkehr aus dem Exil*, especially 502-504 and 534-547.

[8] Salten, letter to the Zsolnay Press, Apr. 20, 1938, ÖNB.

[9] Salten, letter to the Gesellschaft der Autoren, Komponisten und Musikverleger (A.K.M.), Aug. 23, 1938.

[10] Salten, letter to Stefan Zweig, July 11, 1938, Stefan Zweig Collection, Daniel A. Reed Library, SUNY Fredonia.

[11] In Melissa Jane Taylor, "Bureaucratic Response to Human Tragedy: American Consuls and the Jewish Plight in Vienna, 1938-1941," 244.

[12] Pepi Wik was more like a family member than an employee. During the First World War, the Saltens had taken in her brother Robert for a year after he was wounded at the front. At that time, she had already been in the Saltens' service for some ten years. The Saltens referred to her as "factotum" and "friend." See document IV./3/ in Gabriele Maria Reinharter, *Felix Salten, Schriftsteller. Der österreichische Schriftsteller Felix Salten im Schweizer Exil*, 42.

[13] Salten's diary, Nov. 10, 1938. The anti-Jewish action was ostensibly a spontaneous outburst in reaction to the assassination in Paris of a German embassy official by a 17-year-old Polish Jew.

[14] Salten, letter to D. L. Chambers, Bobbs-Merrill Company, Lilly Library, Bloomington Indiana, in *Der Paul Zsolnay Verlag. Von der Gründung bis zur Rückkehr aus dem Exil* by Murray G. Hall, 531.

[15] Simon and Schuster, letter to Zsolnay Verlag regarding sales of *Bambi*, Aug. 1, 1938.

[16] Zsolnay to MGM, Nov. 28, 1938. See also Zsolnay's correspondence of Nov. 21, 1938.

[17] Salten, letter to Stefan Zweig, June 4, 1938, Stefan Zweig Collection, Daniel A. Reed Library, SUNY Fredonia.

[18] Salten, letter to Anna Katharina Rehmann, June 21, 1938, FSA.

[19] Felix Salten, *Ein Gott erwacht*, typescript, 10-11.

[20] Ibid., 109.

[21] Ibid., 110.

[22] Felix Salten, letter to Walter de Haas, Feb. 8, 1940.

[23] Felix Salten, letter to D. L. Chambers of Bobbs-Merrill Company, n.d., Lilly Library, Indiana University, Bloomington, in *Der Paul Zsolnay Verlag. Von der Gründung bis zur Rückkehr aus dem Exil* by Murray G. Hall, 531.

[24] Felix Salten, letter fragment to an unidentified friend, Sept. 27, 1939.

[25] In reality, as Murray Hall notes, Zsolnay remained part of the daily operations of the press until August of that year. See *Der Paul Zsolnay Verlag. Von der Gründung bis zur Rückkehr aus dem Exil*, 505.

[26] Ottilie Salten, letter to Ludwig Metzl, Jan. 9, 1933.

[27] Salten, letter to Minnie [Hupka], Aug. 19, 1939.

[28] Swiss Writer's Union to the Foreign Police office of Zurich, November 22, 1938, in *Felix Salten, Schriftsteller* by Gabriele Maria Reinharter, Dok. V./2.

[29] See Gabriele Maria Reinharter, *Felix Salten, Schriftsteller*, 42.

[30] Ibid., 43.

[31] Salten's diary, Mar. 3, 1939.

[32] Ibid., Mar. 4, 1939.

[33] Felix Salten, letter fragment to an unidentified friend, Sept. 27, 1939.

[34] Felix Salten, letter to Richard Beer-Hofmann, Nov. 4, 1939.

[35] See Murray G. Hall, *Der Paul Zsolnay Verlag: Von der Gründung bis zur Rückkehr aus dem Exil*, 509, citing a letter to Salten from Oct. 16, 1939, in which Zsolnay confesses that there will be little interest in his branch of Heath operations for the duration of the war.

[36] Bermann-Fischer was Samuel Fischer's son-in-law and took over management of the publishing company after Samuel Fischer's death.

[37] See the chapter, "Das Abenteuer um 'Perri,'" in *Der Paul Zsolnay Verlag: Von der Gründung bis zur Rückkehr aus dem Exil* by Murray G. Hall, 534-547, for a detailed account of the mutual suspicions, charges, and legal complexities of the case.

[38] Stefan Zweig, letter to Felix Salten, May 22, 1939, quoted in *Der Paul Zsolnay Verlag: Von der Gründung bis zur Rückkehr aus dem Exil* by Murray G. Hall, 528.

[39] Feliz Salten, letter to D. L. Chambers, Oct. 8, 1939.

[40] See Verena Rutschmann, "Felix Saltens Zürcher Zeit," in *Felix Salten -- der unbekannte Bekannte*, ed. Ernst Seibert and Susanne Blumesberger, 89-92, where she describes these constraints and the advantages Salten gained by choosing instead a press that published books on marriage and sexuality.

[41] Felix Salten, letter to D. L. Chambers, Aug. 27, 1939.

Chapter 23

[1] Thomas Mann, letter to Felix Salten, Aug. 31, 1941.

[2] Else Lasker-Schüler said that when one listened "to her wonderful playing" one found oneself "in a long since paled past, which now lit up

368

again." Else Lasker-Schüler, *Concert*, Jane M. Snook, trans., 40. Thomas Mann also paid tribute to Hermann and Lily Reiff's Wednesday gatherings in chapter 34 of his novel *Doktor Faustus*.

3 Anna Wyler-Salten, "Introduction," *Felix Salten's Favorite Animal Stories*, viii.

4 Salten, letter to Sanford Greenburger, Sept. 27, 1940.

5 "How War Came to Zorek," *Esquire*, April 1943, 148.

6 This request, dated June 10, 1940, is housed in FSE/LWA.

7 Kenneth C. Kaufman, trans., *Renni the Rescuer*, 250-251.

8 Ibid., 232.

9 Ibid., 239-240. Salten had presented a similar insight in *Abschied im Sturm*.

10 Ibid., 240.

11 Felix Salten, letter to D. L. Chambers, Sept. 27 1940.

12 Salten, letter to Paul Zsolnay, May 1, 1940.

13 Salten, letter to Paul Zsolnay, June 5, 1940.

14 Felix Salten, letter to Walter de Haas, Feb. 10, 1941.

15 See Jürgen Ehneß, *Felix Saltens erzählerisches Werk*, 258. One might note, however, that Salten made a similar case for economic fairness and class equality in *Martin Overbeck*.

16 Kenneth C. Kaufman, trans., *Renni the Rescuer*, 221.

17 Felix Salten, letter to Grete von Urbanitzky, June 19, 1940. On display at the exhibit Felix Salten. Schriftsteller – Journalist – Exilant held in the Jewish Museum of Vienna from Dec. 5, 2006, until Mar. 18, 2007.

18 Selected passages from Bertha Zuckerkandl's letters to Salten during her exile in Paris and later in Algeria are in the FSE/LWA and are selectively quoted in *Felix Salten, Schriftsteller* by Gabriele Reinhardter, 182-185.

19 Felix Salten, registered letter to Herrn Dr. Führer, Jan. 8, 1940.

20 Rosalie Salzmann, written in a different hand on a postcard to Felix Salten, quoted in *Felix Salten. Schriftsteller* by Gabriele Reinhardter, 175.

21 Rosalie Salzmann, letter to Salten, Feb. 1941.

22 Brothers Emil, Ignaz, and Theodor and sister Katherine had all died long before Hitler came to power. I have been able to find no record of the death of Salten's younger brother, Géza.

23 Felix Salten, letter to Paul Zsolnay, Jan. 21, 1941.

24 Graf III. Det. Report of Jan. 15, 1941 to Zurich's Foreign Police.

25 See letters from Sanford Greenburger to Felix Salten, June 19, 1941, and Apr. 14, 1942.

26 Felix Salten, letter to Hedwig Fischer, Aug. 15, 1941, Lilly Library, University of Indiana, Bloomington.

.27 Felix Salten, *A Forest World*, jacket blurb of the 1942 edition.

28 Felix Salten, letter to Sanford Greenburger, May 15, 1941.

[29] Felix Salten, "Moses und David," in *Der Jud ist schuld...? Diskussionsbuch über die Judenfrage*, 399-401.

[30] It may be noted that these Mosaic and Davidic elements correspond roughly to Nietzsche's Dionysian and Apollonian drives. See Nietzsche's *Birth of Tragedy from the Spirit of Music*, 1872.

[31] Typescript, in FSE/LWA.

[32] Felix Salten, letter to Hermann Büchi, May 22, 1941.

[33] Felix Salten, letter to Sanford Greenburger, Apr. 29, 1941.

[34] Raya Levin, trans., *Djibi*, 27.

[35] The American edition of this work has a happy ending.

[36] Quoted in Wally Strakosch, letter to Salten, July 15, 1942.

[37] Salten's diary, June 13, 1942.

[38] Ibid., June 24.

[39] Ibid., Aug. 8, 9.

[40] Eugen Jensen, letter to Salten, July 17, 1942.

[41] Salten's diary, Nov. 13, 1942.

[42] "Felix Salten †," *Neue Zürcher Zeitung*, Oct. 9, 1945.

[43] Felix Salten, "Wohin soll ich mich wenden?" *Neue Zürcher Zeitung*, Sept. 6, 1944. First published in the *Neue Freie Presse*, July 9, 1933.

[44] Graf III Det to police office of the city of Zurich, Jan. 9, 1945, Zurich City Archives.

[45] From a conversation with Lea Wyler, May 29, 2006.

[46] K. W.-S. [Anna Katharina Wyler-Salten], "Zum 100. Geburtstag von Felix Salten am 6. September, Versuch eines Porträts," 183.

[47] Siegfried Trebitsch, *Chronicle of a Life*, 393.

[48] Salten, letter to D. L. Chambers, n.d.

[49] *Ein Gott erwacht*, typescript, 110.

[50] Ernst Lothar, letter to Salten, Nov. 24, 1939.

Chapter 24

[1] Matt Cartmill, "The Bambi Syndrome," *Natural History* 6, no. 93:8.

[2] Salten's diary, Nov. 13, 1942.

[3] In May 1933, M. Lincoln Schuster, of *Bambi*'s American publishing house, Simon and Schuster, urged Disney to make a film of the novel, but Sidney Franklin beat Disney to the punch. That same month Joseph Schenck of United Artsts offered to broker a partnership between Franklin and Disney. See Neal Gabler, *Walt Disney: The Triumph of the American Imagination*, 215.

[4] Ollie Johnston and Frank Thomas, *Walt Disney's Bambi: The Story and the Film*, 106.

[5] Ibid., 112.

[6] Ibid., 114.

[7] Ibid., 115.

[8] Neal Gabler, *Walt Disney: The Triumph of the American Imagination*, 319-320.

[9] See Ralph H. Lutts, "The Trouble with Bambi: Walt Disney's *Bambi* and the American Vision of Nature," *Forest and Conservation History* 36 (Oct. 1992): 160-171. http://www.history.vt.edu/Barrow/Hist2104/readings/bambi.html [June 4, 2008], 8 of 17.

[10] In 1941 Disney also released a film called *The Reluctant Dragon*, which purported to show the process of creating an animated film.

[11] Ollie Johnston and Frank Thomas, *Walt Disney's Bambi: The Story and the Film*, 144.

[12] "*Bambi*: Inside Walt's Story Meetings," from *Bambi*, 2-disc special DVD edition, 2005.

[13] Lea Wyler, *Bambis Vater*, 61.

[14] "*Bambi*: Inside Walt's Story Meetings," from *Bambi*, 2-disc special DVD edition, 2005.

[15] Salten, letter to Robert Wessely, May 6, 1941.

[16] Ollie Johnston and Frank Thomas, *Walt Disney's Bambi: The Story and the Film*, 176.

[17] Ibid., 179.

[18] See Ibid., 147-149. Thumper's personality was shaped in large part by the uniquely self-assured voice of young actor Peter Behn.

[19] See "*Bambi*: Inside Walt's Story Meetings," from Walt Disney's *Bambi*, 2-disc special edition, 2005.

[20] See Ollie Johnston and Frank Thomas, *Walt Disney's Bambi: The Story and the Film*, 148.

[21] See Matt Cartmill, "The Bambi Syndrome," *Natural History*, 6, no. 93:10, where he notes, "On September 1, 1939, the day that German tanks struck across the Polish border and plunged Europe into World War II, the film's story editor Perce Pearce announced that all predators other than *Homo sapiens* had to be excised from the script." The Disney artists continued to sketch figures of Man into the movie, however, until after the bombing of Pearl Harbor.

[22] Ralph H. Lutts, "The Trouble with Bambi: Walt Disney's *Bambi* and the American Vision of Nature," *Forest and Conservation History* 36 (Oct. 1992): 160-171. http://www.history.vt.edu/Barrow/Hist2104/readings/bambi.html [June 4, 2008], 11 of 17.

[23] Ollie Johnston and Frank Thomas, *Walt Disney's Bambi: The Story and the Film*, 170.

[24] Ralph H. Lutts, "The Trouble with Bambi: Walt Disney's *Bambi* and the American Vision of Nature," *Forest and Conservation History* 36 (Oct. 1992): 160-171. http://www.history.vt.edu/Barrow/Hist2104/readings/bambi.html [June 4, 2008], 3 of 17.

[25] Financial reasons forced Disney to cut the film from 8,500 feet to 6,259 feet and to film some scenes in silhouette so that full animation would not be required. See Neal Gabler, *Walt Disney: The Triumph of the American Imagination*, 396.

[26] Salten, letter to Paul Zsolnay, Apr. 3, 1940.

[27] Felix Salten, letter to Mrs. Bleeker, Sept. 8, 1942.

[28] Robert De Roos, "The Magic Worlds of Walt Disney," *National Geographic* 124, no. 2 (August 1963): 178, quoted in *Wildlife Films* by Derek Bousé, 64.

[29] "Tribute to Winston Hibler," *Walt Disney's Legacy Collection: True-Life Adventures*, DVD, vol. 4: *Nature's Mysteries*, disc 2, 2006.

[30] The film is *The Living Desert* (1953). See Leonard Maltin, *The Disney Films*, 114.

[31] Walt Disney, speaking in 1957. "Adventure in Wildwood Heart," *Walt Disney's Legacy Collection: True-Life Adventures*, vol. 4: *Nature's Mysteries*, disc 2, 2006.

[32] See Leonard Maltin, *The Disney Films*, 142.

[33] Leonard Maltin notes that some of the winter footage was shot at Jackson Hole, Wyoming, *The Disney Films*, 144.

[34] John Beaufort, cited in Ibid., 144.

[35] "Adventure in Wildwood Heart" (1957), included in *Walt Disney's Legacy Collection: True-Life Adventures*, vol. 4: *Nature's Mysteries*, disc 2, 2006.

[36] From an interview in the CBS documentary *Cruel Camera* [*The 5th Estate*, 1984], in *Wildlife Films* by Derek Bousé, 226, n. 79.

[37] In Leonard Maltin, *The Disney Films*, 143.

[38] Ibid., 144.

[39] Review of DVD, "*The Shaggy Dog: The Wild & Woolly Edition*," http://www.ultimatedisney.com/shaggy.html [July 3, 2008].

[40] Neal Gabler, *Walt Disney: The Triumph of the American Imagination*, 586. Gabler points out that, in comparison, the color comedy feature *Pillow Talk*, featuring the popular duo Doris Day and Rock Hudson, grossed only $7.4 million.

[41] Cited from Disney's *The Shaggy Dog*, 1959. Walt Disney Film Classics: The Comedy Favorites Series, DVD, vol.1.

[42] Ollie Johnston and Frank Thomas, *Walt Disney's Bambi: The Story and the Film*, 192.

[43] Salten, letter to Robert Wessely, May 6, 1941.

[44] "U.S. 9th Circuit Court of Appeals: Twin Books v. Disney, Opinion," http://caselaw.lp.findlaw.com/cgi-bin/getcase.pl?court-9th&navby=case&no=9515250 (Aug. 4, 2008), 1-2.

[45] Richard Schickel, *The Disney Version: The Life, Times, Art and Commerce of Walt Disney*, 344.

[46] Ibid., 345.

[47] Cited in Ibid., 350-351.

[48] Ibid., 12.

[49] Ibid., 234.

[50] Ibid., 290.

[51] http://disney.go.com/disneyvideos/animatedfilms/bambi2/index_flash.html. (July 8, 2008).

Bibliography

ABBREVIATIONS

DLA	*Deutsches Literaturarchiv*, Marbach
FB	*Fremden-Blatt*
FSE/LWA	Felix Salten Estate/Lea Wyler Archives, Zurich
NFP	*Neue Freie Presse*
NZZ	*Neue Zürcher Zeitung*
ÖNB	Österreichische Nationalbibliothek
SBD	*An der schönen blauen Donau*
UOLS	Division of Special Collections and University Archives, University of Oregon Library System
WAG	*Wiener Allgemeine Zeitung*
WAR	*Wiener Allgemeine Rundschau*

Unpublished Cited Manuscripts by Felix Salten

"Auf Tod und Leben." Typescript. UOLS.

"Bermerkungen zu 'Bambis Kinder.'" In letter to "Herrn Weldler."
    April 25, 1940. FSE/LWA.

"Der Bauerngraf." Handwritten manuscript and typescript.
    FSE/LWA.

Ein Gott erwacht. Phantastisches Märchen. Typescript. FSE/LWA.

"Erinnerung an Franz Josef." Typescript. UOLS.

["Erinnerungen"]. Typescript. FSE/LWA.

"Erinnerungen an Leopold Ferdinand." Typescript. FSE/LWA.

"Liebesreise." Typescript. FSE/LWA.

["Salten hat bei Schnitzler geschlafen..."]. Manuscript. Schnitzler letters
    to Salten, Folder 2. FSE/LWA

Cited Articles by Felix Salten in Newspapers and Journals

"Abschaffung der Matura." Feuilleton. *NFP*, Apr. 12, 1919.
"An Bord der 'Vaterland.'" Feuilleton-Beilage. *FB*, May 24, 1914.
"Andersen." Feuilleton. *Die Zeit*, Apr. 2, 1905.
"An Marie von Ebner-Eschenbach." *SBD* 20 (1890): 463.
"Arthur Schnitzler." Feuilleton. *NFP*, Oct. 22, 1931.
"Auf Leben und Tod. Die Liebesgeschichte der Louise von Koburg." *NFP*, Dec. 25, 1931.
"Aufruhr." Feuilleton [F.S.]. *Die Zeit*, Sept. 19, 1911.
"Aus den Anfängen. Erinnerungsskizzen." *Jahrbuch deutscher Bibliophilen und Literaturfreunde* 18/19 (1932/33): 31-46.
"Aus meiner Kindheit. Nach dem Manuskript: 'Die Währinger Erinnerungen.'" Feuilleton. *NFP*, May 27, 1928.
"Begräbnis eines Jünglings." Feuilleton. *NFP*, Apr. 28, 1915.
"Bei Gefangenen." Feuilleton. *NFP*, Feb. 6, 1927.
"Berühmtheit! Brief an einen Jüngling" [Sascha]. *NFP*, June 9, 1935.
"Besuch in den Skoda-Werken I." Feuilleton. *FB*, May 14, 1916.
"Besuch in den Skoda-Werken II." Feuilleton. *FB*, June 18, 1916.
"Besuch in Ischl." Feuilleton. *NFP*, July 18, 1915.
"Bilder aus dem Konzertsaal. Artur Nikisch." Feuilleton. *NFP*, June 2, 1918.
"Bilder aus dem Konzertsaal: Richard Strauß." Feuilleton. *NFP*, Apr. 28, 1918.
"Bilder vom Zionistenkongreß." Feuilleton. *NFP*, Aug. 28, 1923.
"Bildung. Die Kundgebung der Mittelschüler." Feuilleton. *NFP*, Dec. 22, 1918.
"Ein Brief am Pfingstsonntag." Feuilleton. *FB*, May 23, 1915.
"Buchbesprechungen. 'Gesammelte Dichtungen,' von Ludwig Eichrodt." *Allgemeine Kunst-Chronik* 14 (1890): 22, 616.
"Burgtheater." Feuilleton [f.s.]. *WAZ*, Mar. 3, 1897.
"Burgtheater." Feuilleton [f.s.]. *WAZ*, Sept. 18, 1897.
"Burgtheater." Feuilleton. *WAZ*, Nov. 23, 1898.
"Burgtheater." Feuilleton. *WAZ*, Jan. 18, 1901.
"Burgtheater." Feuilleton-Beilage. *FB*, Dec. 11, 1914.
"Burgtheater, Der Direktor." Feuilleton. *WAZ*, Dec. 19, 1897.
"Burgtheater-Jubiläum." Feuilleton-Beilage. *FB*, Oct. 14, 1913.
"Burgtheater (Rückblick)." Feuilleton. *WAZ*, June 26, 1898.
"Dafnis in Wien." *NFP*, Jan. 28, 1917.

"Das Buch der Frau Toselli." Feuilleton. *Die Zeit*, Sept. 17, 1911.
"Das Buch eines Jägers." Feuilleton. *NFP*, Oct. 30, 1915.
"Das fremde Volk." *Die Welt*, Sept. 1, 8, 15, 1899.
"Das Große Schiff." Feuilleton. *NFP*, May 26, 1914.
"Das Mozartdenkmal." *Moderne Rundschau. Halbmonatsschrift* 3:1 (Apr. 1, 1891): 35-36.
"Das Reinhardt-Problem." Feuilleton. *NFP*, July 10, 1921.
"Das Theater und die Juden" [F.S.]. *Die Welt*, Feb. 17, Mar. 3, Apr. 14, June 9, 1899.
"Das Wiener Problem." *Berliner Tageblatt*, Jan. 18, 1915.
"Der Abfall vom Judentum." *Selbstwehr*, Jan. 22, 1909.
"Der alte Hagenbeck." Feuilleton. *NFP*, Apr. 19, 1913.
"Der Entscheidungstag in Wien." *Berliner Tageblatt*, July 27, 1914.
"Der junge David." Feuilleton. *NFP*, Dec. 21, 1933.
"Der Tugendbund." *WAZ*, Feb. 19, 1899.
"Der Tunnel." Feuilleton. *NFP*, June 5, 1913.
"Der Unbesiegbare!" *SBD* 21 (1889): 492.
"Der Vagabund. Eine Hundegeschichte." *SBD* 21 (1890): 491-494.
"Der Zar." Feuilleton. *Die Zeit*, Oct. 4, 1903.
"Der Zuckerbäckerladen." Feuilleton. *NFP*, Nov. 18, 1917.
"Deutsches Volkstheater." Feuilleton. *FB*, Jan. 6, 1915.
"Deutsches Volkstheater. Generalversammlung." Feuilleton-Beilage. *FB*, Apr. 13, 1913.
"Die XXIV. Jahresaustellung, I. Die Porträtisten." Feuilleton [f.s.]. *WAZ*, Apr. 19, 1896.
"Die elf Scharfrichter und noch Einer." Feuilleton. *WAZ*, Aug. 21, 1901.
"Der Entscheidungstag in Wien," *Berliner Tageblatt*, July 27, 1914.
"Die fremde Stadt." Feuilleton. *Die Zeit*, May 13, 1906.
"Die Juden." Feuilleton. *Die Zeit*, June 17, 1905.
"'Die Juden.'" Feuilleton. *NFP*, May 13, 1923.
"Die kleinen Schneeschaufler." Feuilleton. *NFP*, Feb. 11, 1917.
"Die Maschinenstürmer." Feuilleton. *NFP*, June 7, 1923.
"Die Schülerausstellung der Akademie." *WAZ*, July 21, 1896.
"Die Stadt des Films." Feuilleton. *NFP*, July 27, 1930.
"Die strahlende Frau. Aus dem Manuskript 'Die Währinger Erinnerungen.'" Feuilleton. *NFP*, July 19, 1931.
"Die Tragödie des schwachen Willens." *Die Zeit*, Feb. 15, 1903.
"Die Wahrheit über den Pen-Club-Kongreß." *NFP*, June 2, 1933.

"Die Woche" [Anon.]. *Die Welt*, Oct. 8, 1897.
"Die Woche" [Anon.]. *Die Welt*, Oct. 15, 1897.
"Die Woche" [Anon.]. *Die Welt*, Oct. 29, 1897.
"Dreimal Hochzeit. Die Geschichte einer Uebersetzung," Feuilleton. *NFP*, Sept. 29, 1927.
"Dr. Max Burckhard," Feuilleton. *WAZ*, Feb. 4, 1898.
"'Echt jüdisch.' Bekenntnisse" [F. S–n.]. *Die Welt*, Nov. 10, 1899.
"Ein armer Teufel." Feuilleton. *NFP*, Aug. 18, 1918.
"Ein Engagement. Aus einem Schauspieler-Roman." *WAR*, Dec. 11, 1899.
"Eine Friedensreise in England." Feuilleton. *FB*, Dec. 25, 1914.
"Eines Tages....." *FB*, Mar. 31,1918.
"Ein junger Führer." Feuilleton. *NFP*, Feb. 4, 1923.
"Ein Kapitel Zukunft." Feuilleton. *NFP*, June 10, 1917.
"Ein Meister." Feuilleton. *NFP*, Oct. 13, 1929.
"Ein Wort vom Barbarentum." Feuilleton. *NFP*, Sept. 10, 1914.
"Erhöhte Preise." Feuilleton. *NFP*, Jan. 31, 1915.
"Erinnerung an Hofmannsthal." Feuilleton. *NFP*, July 18, 1929.
"Erinnerung an Lueger." Feuilleton. *NFP*, Sept. 19, 1926.
"Erinnerung an Schnitzler." *NFP*, Dec. 1, 1932.
"Eröffnung eines Theaters." Feuilleton. *NFP*, Sept. 20, 1931.
"Erstes Liebesahnen. Aus dem Manuskript 'Die Währinger Erinnerungen.'" *NFP*, May 29, 1932.
"Erzherzog Otto." *Die Zeit*, July 31, 1904.
"Es muß sein." Feuilleton. *NFP*, July 29, 1914.
"Fasching 1916." Feuilleton. *NFP*, Feb. 6, 1916.
"Freude im Cottage. Ein Lobgesang." Feuilleton-Beilage. *FB*, July 14, 1912.
"Gang durch Schönbrunn." Feuilleton. *NFP*, July 20, 1935.
"Gelegenheitsstücke." Feuilleton-Beilage. *FB*, Oct. 4, 1914.
"Gerhart Hauptmann." Feuilleton-Beilage. *FB*, Nov. 15, 1912.
"Geschichten aus dem Leben des Herrn Snob. Eine fatale Sache" [F.F.]. *WAR*, Aug. 21, 1899.
"Geschichten aus dem Leben des Herrn Snob. II. Eine Taktlosigkeit" [F.F.]. *WAR*, Oct. 16, 1899.
"Geselligkeit und fünfzehn Deka." Feuilleton. *NFP*, May 6, 1917.
"Gewalttätigkeiten. Aus dem Manuskript: 'Die Währinger Erinnerungen.'" Feuilleton. *NFP*, Aug. 14, 1932.
"Gute Botschaft. Ein Brief aus fernen Tagen." Feuilleton. *FB*, Dec.

24, 1916.
"'Habsburgerlegende.' Burgtheater." Feuilleton. *NFP*, Oct. 12, 1933.
"Heldentod." *WAZ*, Jan. 1, 1895.
"Herbstgang." Feuilleton. *Die Zeit*, Sept. 23, 1906.
"Herman Bahr – Siebzig!" Feuilleton. *NFP*, July 16, 1933.
"Herrliche Wohnung!" Feuilleton. *NFP*, Jan. 19, 1936.
"Hölle in Omaha." Feuilleton. *NFP*, Oct. 26, 1930.
"Ihre Herkunft. Aus einem Schauspieler-Roman." *WAR*, Sept. 4, 1899.
"In der Garderobe. Aus einem Schauspieler-Roman." *WAR*, Sept. 11, 1899.
"In der Osternacht." Feuilleton. *FB*, Apr. 4, 1915.
"In Schönbrunn." Feuilleton. *Die Zeit*, Aug. 23, 1903.
"Interpellation." *WAZ*, Nov. 13, 1899.
"Ja, damals...." *Pester Lloyd*, Feb. 12, 1911.
"Ja, ein Lokalpatriot...." Feuilleton [Sascha]. *Die Zeit*, Aug. 19, 1906.
"Jugendfreunde." *Die Zeit*, Oct. 31, 1909.
"Jung-Wiener-Theater." Feuilleton. *WAZ*, Jan. 5, 1902.
"Katharina Schratt." Feuilleton [f.s.]. *WAZ*, Sept. 30, 1900.
"Kleiderkarte." Feuilleton. *NFP*, Sep. 30, 1917.
"Kleine Begebenheit." Feuilleton. *NFP*, Jan. 12, 1919.
"Kleine Dialoge." *FB*, Mar. 22, 1919.
"Kleine Schauspieler." Feuilleton. *WAZ*, Sept. 5, 1896.
"Kongreßtage in Budapest." Feuilleton. *NFP*, May 22, 1932.
"Krankenstube." Feuilleton. *Die Zeit*, Mar. 6, 1910.
"Laïs." *Moderne Dichtung. Monatsschrift für Literatur und Kritik*. 1. Jahrgang, 2:1 (July 1890): 464.
"Leb wohl ... komm wieder. Kleine Bilder aus großen Tagen." Feuilleton. *NFP*, Aug. 12, 1914.
"Lebenszeit." *WAR*, July 24, 1899.
"Leiden, Streiche, Kumpaneien. Aus den unveröffentlichten Erinnerungen." *morgen* 53/87 (1987): 144-148.
"Lerchenjubel." Feuilleton [Martin Finder]. *NFP*, May 30, 1937.
"Lia Rosen." Feuilleton. *Die Zeit*, Sept. 22, 1907.
"Literatur-Schmarotzer." *Neue Revue* 5, no. 20 (May 2, 1894): 631-635.
"Lueger." Feuilleton [Sascha]. *Die Zeit*, Oct. 23, 1904.
"Lueger-Bilder." Feuilleton. *Die Zeit*, Mar. 11, 1910.
"Manöverbilder." Feuilleton. *Die Zeit*, Sept. 11, 1909.
"Mehr Haltung." Feuilleton. *NFP*, Oct. 11, 1931.

"Meine Mutter. Aus dem Manuskript 'Die Währinger Erinnerungen.'"
Feuilleton. *NFP*, May 24, 1931.

"Mein Vater. Aus dem Manuskript: 'Die Währinger Erinnerungen.'"
Feuilleton. *NFP*, Jan. 1, 1931.

"Mephistophela." *Moderne Rundschau. Halbmonatsschrift* 3, no.2 (April
15, 1891): 74.

"Mettachich." *Die Zeit*, Mar. 27, 1904.

"Mit dem ersten Balkanzug." Feuilleton. *NFP*, Jan. 28, 1916.

"Moderne Wunder." Feuilleton. *NFP*, Jan. 1, 1925.

"Monotonisierung der Welt?" Feuilleton. *NFP*, Feb. 8, 1925.

"Nachtvergnügen." Feuilleton. *Die Zeit*, Jan. 26, 1908.

"Nervenprobe." Feuilleton. *NFP*, Feb. 18, 1934.

"Nuance." *Moderne Rundschau. Halbmonatsschrift* 3, no.7 (July 1, 1891):
282-284.

"O, du mein Oesterreich." Feuilleton. *NFP*, July 13, 1913.

"Ohne Wunsch." *SBD* 5 (1888): 110.

"Opernkrise. (Der Protest gegen Richard Strauß)." Feuilleton. *NFP*,
Apr. 12, 1919.

"Pirschgang im Gebirge." Feuilleton. *NFP*, June 29, 1935.

"Polizei im Parlament." Feuilleton [Sascha]. *Die Zeit*, Nov. 12, 1902.

"Praterspatzen." Feuilleton. *NFP*, Dec. 22, 1914.

"Proben bei Reinhardt." Feuilleton. *NFP*, Feb. 27, 1932.

"Quer durch den Wurstelprater." *WAZ*, June 2 and 9, 1895.

"Reinhardts 'Oedipus.'" Feuilleton. *Die Zeit*, May 6, 1911.

"Resignation." *SBD* 19 (1889): 445.

"Richtigstellung." *Arbeiter-Zeitung*, June 3, 1922.

"Roosevelt." *Die Zeit*, Apr. 17, 1910.

"Rückblende: Berühmte Wiener aus Budapest. Aus der Bühne vom
21. Jänner 1926." *Bühne*, 1991: 78.

"Rückkehr zum Lustspiel. Ein Brief." Feuilleton. *NFP*, Jan. 8, 1933.

"Salvator-Medaille." *WAR*, Oct. 23, 1899.

"Salzburger Glockenspiel." Feuilleton. *NFP*, Aug. 21, 1932.

"Salzkammergut. Im dritten Kriegssommer." Feuilleton. *NFP*, Aug. 6,
1916.

"Schlaflose Nacht." Feuilleton, [f.s.]. *NFP*, June 26, 1936.

"Schwarze Kirschen." Feuilleton. *NFP*, May 5, 1932.

"Schweizer Reisetage." Feuilleton. *NFP*, Dec. 8, 1916.

"Seraphine, das Mädchen." *Die Zeit*, Dec. 25, 1909.

"Sich einschränken." Feuilleton. *NFP*, Nov. 9, 1913.

"Sieger und Besiegte. Brief an einen amerikanischen Freund."
   Feuilleton. *NFP*, Feb. 2, 1919.

"Sollen wir Theater spielen?" Feuilleton. *NFP*, Sept. 3, 1914.

"Sommerfestspiel." Feuilleton. *NFP*, Sept. 6, 1918.

"Spaziergang in der Vorstadt." *Die Zeit*, May 29, 1904.

"Studie über Potsdam." Feuilleton. *NFP* , Oct. 21 and 28, 1914.

"Tagebuchblatt aus diesem Sommer." Feuilleton. *NFP*, Aug. 26, 1928.

"Tag in Salzburg." Feuilleton. *NFP*, Aug. 2, 1931.

"Tempo, Kino und Gelächter." Feuilleton. *NFP*, June 19, 1930.

"Theaterfrage." Feuilleton. *NFP*, Mar. 23, 1919.

"Theater, Kunst und Literatur: Burgtheater" [f.s.]. *WAZ*, Jan. 6, 1898.

"Theater, Kunst und Literatur: Burgtheater" [f.s.]. *WAZ*, April 10,
   1896.

"Theater, Kunst und Literatur: Burgtheater" [f.s.]. *WAZ*, Feb. 11,
   1898.

"Theater, Kunst und Literatur: Carl-Theater" [f.s.]. WAZ Sept. 19,
   1901.

"Theodor. Ein Porträt aus dem Nachlass." *Neue Zürcher Zeitung*, Oct.
   7, 1985.

"Thomas Theodor Heine." *NFP*, Mar. 1, 1927.

"Thronrede." Feuilleton. *NFP*, June 1, 1917.

"Unterwegs nach Amerika." Feuilleton. *NFP*, June 8, 1930.

"Vater und Söhnchen." Feuilleton. *Die Zeit*, Oct. 18, 1908.

"Verhandlungsformen." Feuilleton. *NFP*, June 19, 1919.

"Verwickelte Geschichte." Feuilleton. *PL*, May 25, 1913.

"Verwundet. Eindrücke in einem Truppenspital." Feuilleton. *NFP*,
   Sept. 16, 1914.

"Victor Tilguer †." Feuilleton. *WAG*, Apr. 17, 1896

"Vom göttlichen Aretino." Feuilleton. *Die Zeit*, Mar. 15, 1903.

"Vom 'Ueberbrettl zum rasenden Jüngling.'" *Vossische Zeitung*, Oct. 31,
   1900.

"Vor Tau und Tag." Feuilleton. *NFP*, June 17, 1934.

"Wann ruht der Geist?" *SBD* 2 (1889):33.

"Wehrlose Jugend." Feuilleton. *NFP*, Feb. 26, 1930.

"Wer nicht herzlos ist...." Feuilleton. *NFP*, June 25 1916.

"Wienerwald-Elegie." Feuilleton. *NFP*, Dec. 13, 1919.

"Wirklich nur für Reiche?" Feuilleton [Sascha]. *Die Zeit*, July 24, 1906.

"Wohin soll ich mich wenden?" Feuilleton. *NFP*, July 9, 1933; *NZZ* ,
   Sept. 6, 1944.

"Wunder der Gegenwart." Feuilleton. *NFP*, Jan. 1, 1932.

"Wünsche." Feuilleton. *FB*, Dec. 16, 1917.

"Wurstel-Theater. Die Cäsarenkrone" [Anon.]. *WAR*, July 10, 1899.

"Wurstel-Theater. Der Volksaufklärer" [Anon.]. *WAR*, Dec. 11, 1899.

"Zweig auf Zweig...." *Die Zeit*, Dec. 25, 1902

Works by Felix Salten and Cited Contributions to the Works of Others in German

Abschied im Sturm. Langens Kriegsbücher. Munich: Albert Langen, 1915.

Auf Tod und Leben. Die Liebesgeschichte der Prinzessin Louise von Koburg. Fünfzehn Bilder. Berlin-Wilmersdorf: Felix Bloch Erben, [1932].

"Aus den Anfängen. Erinnerungsskizzen." In *Jahrbuch deutscher Bibliophilen und Literaturfreunde*, vols. 18/19. Edited by Hans Feigl, 31-46. Berlin: Zsolnay, 1932/33.

Bambi. Eine Lebensgeschichte aus dem Walde. Berlin: Ullstein, 1923.

Bambi. Eine Lebensgeschichte aus dem Walde. Berlin: Zsolnay, 1926.

Bambis Kinder. Eine Familie im Walde. Zurich: Albert Müller, 1940.

"Begegnung mit den Bettelmusikanten." In *Jahrbuch. Paul Zsolnay Verlag 1927*, 83-93. Berlin: Zsolnay, [1926].

Bob und Baby. Illustrated by Anna Katharina Salten. Berlin: Zsolnay, 1925.

Das Buch der Könige. Illustrated by Leo Kober. Munich: Georg Müller, [1905].

Das Burgtheater. Naturgeschichte eines alten Hauses. Vienna: WILA, 1922.

"Das Bürscherl." In: *Menschen auf der Strasse. Zweiundvierzig Variationen über ein einfaches Thema*, 165-172. Stuttgart: J. Engelhorns Nachf., 1931.

Das lockende Licht. Pantomime in vier Bildern. Berlin: Harmonie, 1914.

Das österreichische Antlitz. Essays. Berlin: Fischer, 1910.

Das Schicksal der Agathe. Novellen. Leipzig: Insel, 1911.

Das stärkere Band. Drei Akte und ein Epilog. Berlin-Wilmersdorf: Felix Bloch Erben, 1915.

Der alte Narr. Novellen. Berlin: Rudolf Mosse, 1918.

Der Gemeine. Schauspiel in drei Aufzügen. Vienna: Wiener Verlag, 1901.

Der Hinterbliebene. Vienna: Wiener Verlag, 1900.

Der Hund von Florenz. Vienna: Herz, 1923.

Der Schrei der Liebe. Novelle. Vienna: Wiener Verlag, 1905.

Der Schrei der Liebe. Novellen. Berlin: Zsolnay, 1928.

Die Bekenntnisse einer Prinzessin [Anon.]. Vienna: Wiener Verlag, [1905].

Die Dame im Spiegel. Illustrated by Gräfin Christine von Kalckreuth. Berlin: Ullstein, 1920.

"Die Einzige." In *Schwarz auf Weiss. Wiener Autoren den Kunstgewerbeschülern zu ihrem Feste am 6. Februar 1902*, 105-118. Wien: Adolf Holzhausen, 1902.

Die Gedenktafel der Prinzessin Anna. Novelle. Vienna: Wiener Verlag, 1902.

Die Gedenktafel der Prinzessin Anna – Der Schrei der Liebe. Zwei Novellen. Munich: Georg Müller, 1913.

Die Geliebte des Kaisers. Novellen. Berlin: Zsolnay, 1929.

Die Geliebte Friedrichs des Schönen. Novellen. Berlin: Marquardt, [1908].

Die Jugend des Eichhörnchens Perri. Vienna: Zsolnay, 1938.

Die Jugend des Eichhörnchens Perri. Illustrated by Hans Bertle. Zurich: Albert Müller, 1942.

Die kleine Veronika. Berlin, Fischer, 1903.

Die klingende Schelle. Roman. Berlin: Ullstein, 1915.

Dies kleine Mädchen. 6 Bilder. Vienna: Georg Marton, 1934.

Djibi das Kätzchen. Illustrated by Walter Linsenmaier. Rüschlikon-Zurich: Albert Müller, 1945.

"Felix Salten." In *Die Psychologie der produktiven Persönlichkeit* by Paul Plaut, 296-299. Stuttgart: Ferdinand Enke, 1929.

Florian. Das Pferd des Kaisers. Berlin: Zsolnay, 1933.

Freunde aus aller Welt. Roman eines zoologischen Gartens. Mit 16 Tiefdruckbildern. Berlin: Zsolnay, 1931.

Fünf Minuten Amerika. Berlin: Zsolnay, 1931.

Fünfzehn Hasen. Schicksale in Wald und Feld. Berlin: Zsolnay, 1929.

Geister der Zeit. Erlebnisse. Berlin: Zsolnay, 1924.

Gestalten und Erscheinungen. Berlin: Fischer, 1913.

Gustav Klimt. Gelegentliche Anmerkungen. Vienna: Wiener Verlag, 1903.

"Gute Botschaft. Ein Brief aus fernen Tagen." In: *Legenden und Märchen unserer Zeit*, Emil Kläger, ed., 7-13. Vienna: Artur Wolf, 1917.

Gute Gesellschaft. Erlebnisse mit Tieren. Berlin: Zsolnay, 1930.

"Handschrift und Arbeit." In: *Jahrbuch deutscher Bibliophilen und Literaturfreunde.* Edited by Hans Feigl, 90-94. Zurich:

Amalthea, 1931.

"Hans Kaltneker." In: *Dichtungen und Dramen*, by Hans Kaltneker, Edited by Paul Zsolnay, 7-14. Berlin: Zsolnay, 1925.

Herr Wenzel auf Rehberg und sein Knecht Kaspar Dinckel. Berlin: Fischer, 1907.

Im Namen des Kaisers. Eine historische Erzählung. Molitor's Novellenschatz No. 8. Leipzig: Lyra (H. Molitor), 1919.

Josefine Mutzenbacher oder Die Geschichte einer Wienerischen Dirne von ihr selbst erzählt [Anon.]. [Vienna:] Private printing, 1906.

Kaiser Max der letzte Ritter. Berlin: Ullstein, 1913.

Kinder der Freude. Drei Einakter. Berlin-Wilmersdorf: Felix Bloch Erben, 1916.

Kinder der Freude. Drei Einakter. Berlin: Fischer, 1917.

Kleine Brüder. Tiergeschichten. Vienna: Zsolnay, 1935.

Kleine Welt für sich. Zurich: Albert Müller, 1944.

Künstlerfrauen. Ein Zyklus kleiner Romane. Munich: Georg Müller, 1908.

Mädchenhände. Sechs Bilder. Vienna: Georg Marton, 1935.

"Mako, der junge Bär." In: *Novellen deutscher Dichter der Gegenwart*, Hermann Kesten, ed., 311-326. Amsterdam: Allert de Lange, 1933.

Martin Overbeck. Der Roman eines reichen jungen Mannes. Berlin: Zsolnay, 1927.

Mein junger Herr. Operette in 3 Akten. Von Ferdinand Stollberg [Felix Salten]. Musik von Oskar Straus. Leipzig: W. Karczag & K. Wallner, 1910.

Mizzi. Novellen. Berlin: Zsolnay, 1932.

"Moses und David." In: *Der Jud ist schuld...? Diskussionsbuch über die Judenfrage*, 399-401. Basel: Zinnen-Verlag, 1932. Republished in *Gegen die Phrase vom jüdischen Schädling* by Heinrich Mann, Arthur Holitscher, Lion Feuchtwanger, Richard Coudenhove-Kalergi, Max Brod, etc. Prague: Amboss Verlag, 1933.

"Nachwort." *Der Tyrann. Die Branzilla. Novellen*, by Heinrich Mann, 73-77. Leipzig: Reclam, 1929..

Neue Menschen auf alter Erde. Eine Palästinafahrt. Berlin: Zsolnay, 1925.

Olga Frohgemuth. Erzählung. Fischers Bibliothek zeitgenössischer Romane, vol. 9. Berlin: Fischer, [1910].

Prinz Eugen der edle Ritter. Berlin: Ullstein, 1915.

Reiche Mädchen. Operette in drei Akten. Von Ferdinand Stollberg [Felix

Salten]. Music by Johann Strauß. Vollständiges Regiebuch. Leipzig: W. Karczag & C. Wallner, 1910.

Renni der Retter. Das Leben eines Kriegshundes. Rüschlikon-Zurich: Albert Müller, 1941.

Schauen und Spielen. Studien zur Kritik des modernen Theaters. Vol. I, *Ergebnisse, Erlebnisse.* Vienna: WILA, 1921.

Schauen und Spielen. Studien zur Kritik des modernen Theaters. Vol. II, *Abende/Franzosen, Puppenspiel, Aus der Ferne.* Vienna: WILA, 1921.

Schöne Seelen.... Brünn: K. und F. Hofbuchdrucker Fr. Winiker & Schickardt, n.d.

Schöne Seelen.... Lustspiel in einem Akt. Leipzig: Reclam, 1925.

Simson. Das Schicksal eines Erwählten. Roman. Berlin: Zsolnay, 1928.

Sträfling Nummer 33. Serial publication in *Pester Lloyd,* Dec. 8, 1937–Jan. 25, 1938. Reprinted in *Basler Nachrichten,* Sept. 21 –Nov. 11, 1942.

Teppiche. Allen Freunden dieser unentbehrlichen Gewebe. Vienna: Verlag Prof. Emanuel Fischer, 1930.

"Verse aus einer Oper." *Deutsche Lyrik aus Österreich seit Grillparzer.* Edited by Camill Hoffmann, 179-184. Berlin: Meyer & Jessen, 1912.

Vom andern Ufer. Drei Einakter. Berlin: Fischer, 1908.

Vom andern Ufer. Ernste und Heitere Theaterstücke. Berlin: Zsolnay, 1934.

"Vorwort." In: *Ignaz Brüll und sein Freundeskreis. Erinnerungen an Brüll, Goldmark und Brahms* by Hermine Schwarz, 3-14. Vienna: Rikola, 1922..

Wiener Adel. Großstadt-Dokumente no. 14. Berlin: Hermann Seemann Nachfolger, [1905].

"Wiener Theater (1848-1898)." In: *Die Pflege der Kunst in Österreich 1848-1898,* 60-85. Vienna: Moritz Perles, 1900.

"Wien und die Musik." In *Das Mahler-Fest. Amsterdam Mai 1920. Vorträge und Berichte.* Edited by C. Rudolf Mengelberg, 29-33. Vienna: Universal-Edition, 1920.

"Wurstelprater (1895)." In: *Das lustige Salzerbuch. Heitere Lektüre- und Vortrags-Stücke.* Edited by Marcell Salzer, 140-166. Hamburg: Anton J. Benjamin, 1921.

Wurstelprater. Mit 75 Originalaufnahmen von Dr. Emil Mayer. Vienna: Brüder Rosenbaum, [1911]

Translations/Adaptations by Felix Salten

Dreimal Hochzeit. Ein New Yorker Schwank. Translation of *Abie's Irish Rose* by Anne Nichols. Berlin: Drei Masken-Verlag, 1929.

Der gute König Dagobert. Lustspiel in 4 Aufzügen. Translation of *Le bon roi Dagobert* by Andre Rivoire. Berlin: Bloch, 1910.

Works by Felix Salten Translated into English

A Forest World. Translated by Paul R. Milton and Sanford Jerome Greenburger. Illustrated by Bob Kuhn. Indianapolis: Bobbs-Merrill, 1942.

"As A Friend Knew Him: A Reminiscence of Herzl and His Influence in Literary Vienna." In: *Theodor Herzl: A Memorial.* Edited by Meyer W. Weisgal, 239. New York: New Palestine, 1929.

"A Shot in the Forest." In: *The Bedside Esquire.* Edited by Arnold Gingrich, 317-328. New York: Tudor Publishing, 1940.

Bambi. Translated by Whittaker Chambers. Illustrated by Kurt Wiese. New York: Grosset & Dunlap, 1928.

Bambi's Children: The Story of a Forest Family. Translated by Barthold Fles. Edited by R. Sugden Tilley. Illustrated by Erna Pinner. New York: Grosset & Dunlap. 1939.

Djibi. Translated by Raya Levin. Illustrated by Walter Linsenmaier. London: Transatlantic Arts, 1946.

Fifteen Rabbits. Translated by Whittaker Chambers. Illustrated by Kurt Wiese. New York: Grosset & Dunlap, 1930. Revised and enlarged edition, 1942. Page references are to the 1942 edition.

Florian, The Emperor's Stallion. Tranlated by Erich Posselt and Michel Kraike. Indianapolis: Bobbs-Merrill, 1934.

Good Comrades. Translated by Paul R. Milton. New York: Grosset & Dunlap, l942.

"Handwriting and Work." In: *The Vienna Coffeehouse Wits 1890-1938.* Translated and edited by Harold B. Segel, 188-191. West Lafayette, IN: Purdue University Press, 1993.

"How War Came to Zorek." *Esquire,* April 1943, 59, 148.

Jibby the Cat. Illustrated by Fritz Kredel. New York: Julian Messner,

1948.

"Judgment of Orestes." *Esquire*, October 1939, 72, 120, 122.

"Mako, the Little Bear." *The Delineator* 124 (June 1934): 13, 60-61.

"Moral Courage (The Gravity of Life)." In: *Fifty More Contemporary One-Act Plays*. Edited by Frank Shay, 453-463. New York: D. Appleton, 1928.

Perri. Translated by Barrows Mussey, with a Foreword by Donald Culross Peattie. Illustrated by Ludwig Heinrich Jungnickel. Indianapolis: Bobbs-Merrill, 1938.

Perri: The Youth of a Squirrel. With an Introduction by Beverley Nichols. London: Jonathan Cape, 1938.

"Peter Altenberg." In: *The Vienna Coffeehouse Wits 1890-1938*. Translated and edited by Harold B. Segel, 171-177. West Lafayette, IN: Purdue University Press, 1993.

"Pleasures of the Night." In: *The Vienna Coffeehouse Wits 1890-1938*. Translated and edited by Harold B. Segel, 183-188. West Lafayette, IN: Purdue University Press, 1993.

Prisoner Thirty-three: A Fantasy of Today. Translated by Hildegard Nagel. n.p., n.d.

Renni the Rescuer: A Dog of the Battlefield. Translated by Kenneth C. Kaufman. Illustrated by Diana Thorne. Indianapolis: Bobbs-Merrill, 1940.

Royal Highness: A Play Adapted from the German. Translated by Mary Ashton. n.p., n.d.

Samson and Delilah: A Novel. Translated by Whittaker Chambers. New York: Simon and Schuster, 1931.

The City Jungle. Translated by Whittaker Chambers. Illustrated by Kurt Wiese. New York: Simon and Schuster, 1932.

"The Emperor and the Gladiator." *Esquire*, June 1936, 39.

The Hound of Florence: A Novel. Translated by Huntley Paterson. New York: Simon and Schuster, 1930.

The Love of Life. Adapted by Joseph H. Nube. Typescript. Chicago: n.p., 1910.

The Memoirs of Josephine Mutzenbacher. Attributed to Felix Salten, author of Bambi. Translated by Rudolf Schleifer. North Hollywood: Brandon House, 1967.

"The Vienna Route." In: *The Vienna Coffeehouse Wits 1890-1938*. Translated and edited by Harold B. Segel, 177-183. West Lafayette, IN: Purdue University Press, 1993.

Works about Felix Salten

Bahr, Hermann. "Feliz Salten zum 60. Geburtstag." Feuilleton. *NFP*, Sept. 6, 1929.

Bartsch, Rudolf Hans. "Das Paradies." Feuilleton. *NFP*, Dec. 10, 1931.

Benet, William Rose. "The Stricken Deer." *Saturday Review of Literature*, July 14, 1928, 1032.

Bruce, Iris. "Which Way Out? Schnitzler's and Salten's Conflicting Responses to Cultural Zionism." In: *A Companion to the Works of Arthur Schnitzler.* Edited by Dagmar Lorenz, 103-126. Rochester, NY: Camden House, 2003.

Burckhard, Max. "Deutsches Volkstheater." *FB* 17 Mar. 1912.

——. "Jung-Wiener-Theater 'zum lieben Augustin.'" In: *Theater. Kritiken, Vorträge und Aufsätze.*" Vol. 1 (1898-1901), Vienna: Manz: 1905, 336-343.

Chamberlain, John R. "Poetry and Philosophy in A Tale of Forest Life." *New York Times Book Review,* July 8, 1928, 5.

Davenport, Basil. "Felix Salten's Story of a Royal Horse." *Saturday Review of Literature,* Nov. 3, 1934, 262.

Dickel, Manfred. *"Ein Dilettant des Lebens will ich nicht sein."Felix Salten zwischen Zionismus und Jungwiener Moderne.* Heidelberg: Winter, 2007.

Ehneß, Jürgen. *Felix Saltens erzählerisches Werk. Beschreibung und Deutung.* Edited by Bernhard Gajek. Regensburger Beiträge zur deutschen Sprach- und Literaturwissenschaft. Reihe B/Untersuchungen, vol. 81. Frankfurt/Main: Peter Lang, Europäischer Verlag der Wissenschaften, 2002.

Eipper, Paul. "Erlebnisse mit Tieren." Feuilleton. *NFP*, Dec. 11, 1930.

-er. "Das Reinhardt-Ensemble im Johann-Strauß-Theater." *Wiener Zeitung,* Oct. 2, 1927.

f. "'Vom andern Ufer.' Salten, der Sechziger." *Wiener Zeitung,* Sept. 8, 1929.

Farin, Michael, ed. *Josefine Mutzenbacher oder Die Geschichte einer Wienersichen Dirne von ihr selbst erzählt. Ungekürzter Nachdruck der Erstausgabe aus dem Jahr 1906, Mit Essays zum Werk....* Stuttgart: Parkland Verlag, 1992.

"Felix Salten †." *NZZ*, Oct. 9, 1945.

"Felix Salten für die Nazi." *Das kleine Blatt*, May 25, 1933.

Gottstein, Michael. *Felix Salten (1869-1945). Ein Schriftsteller der Wiener Moderne.* Klassische Moderne, vol. 4. Edited by Achim Aurnhammer, Werner Frick, Frank-Rutger Hausmann, Dieter Martin, Mathias Mayer. Würzburg: Ergon, 2007.

Graham, Gladys. "Outstanding Rabbits." *Saturday Review of Literature*, Aug. 30, 1930, 85.

Grieser, Dietmar. "Ausgebootet. Felx Salten: 'Bambi.'" *Im Tiergarten der Weltliteratur. Auf den Spuren von Kater Murr, Biene Maja, Bambi, Möwe Jonathan und den anderen*, 16-32. Munich: Langen Müller, 1991.

——. "Die Kündigung. Felix Salten und Ottilie Metzl." *Eine Liebe in Wien*, 71-82. St. Pölten: Niederösterreichisches Pressehaus, 2003.

Hofmannsthal, Hugo von. "Felix Salten zum 60. Geburtstag." In *Jahrbuch. Paul Zsolnay Verlag 1930*, 98-99. Berlin: Zsolnay, 1929.

——. "Prolog zu 'Der Tor und der Tod.'" *Gedichte und Lyrische Dramen*, 171-178. Stockholm: Bermann-Fischer, 1946.

Hugo, H. "Martin Buber und Felix Salten." Feuilleton. *Selbstwehr*, Jan. 15, 1909.

"Humane Awards Announced Here." *The Oregonian*, Dec. 31, 1934.

K. W.-S. [Anna Katharina Wyler-Salten]. "Zum 100. Geburtstag von Felix Salten am 6. September. Versuch eines Porträts." *Das neue Israel* 22 (September 1969): 179, 181, 183, 185.

Karasek, Hellmuth. "Vom Realismus der Pornographie. Zur Neuerscheinung der 'Josefine Mutzenbacher.'" *Die Zeit* (Hamburg), Nov. 21, 1969.

Kraus, Karl. "Aus dem Papierkorb." *Die Fackel* 11, no. 289 (Oct. 25, 1909): 3-16.

——. "Der Nobelpreis." *Die Fackel* 32, nos. 847-851 (May 1931): 28-30.

——. "Die letzte Nacht. Wien. Vom Mut vor der Presse. Gesprochen am 15. Februar." *Die Fackel* 25, nos. 613-621 (Apr. 1923): 59-91.

——. "Eine Friedenstaube." *Die Fackel* 19, nos. 454/455/456 (Apr. 1, 1917): 55-56.

———. "Ein tüchtiger Mensch." *Die Fackel* 12, nos. 319/320 (Mar. 31, 1911): 13-15.

———. "Jüdelnde Hasen." *Die Fackel* 31, nos. 820-826 (Oct. 1929): 45-46.

———. "Oder." *Die Fackel* 18, nos. 360/361/362 (Nov. 7, 1912): 35.

———. "Pro domo et mundo." *Die Fackel* 13, nos. 326/327/328 (July 8, 1911): 40.

———. "Rabbits with Jewish Dialect." *The Vienna Coffeehouse Wits 1890-1938*. Translated and edited by Harold B. Segel, 106-108. West Lafayette, IN: Purdue University, 1993.

———. "Ruhe!," *Die Fackel* 25, nos. 632-639 (Oct. 1923): 68-75.

———. ["Sind Sie dabei gewesen?"]. *Die Fackel*, 3, no. 86 (Nov. 1901): 19-23.

Krentz, Rudolf Jeremias. "Felix Salten, der Erzähler." Literaturblatt. *NFP*, Sept. 8, 1929.

———. "Felix Saltens gesammelte Werke." Feuilleton. *NFP*, Oct. 18, 1928.

Krobb, Florian. "Gefühlszionismus und Zionsgefühle: Zum Palästina-Diskurs bei Schnitzler, Herzl, Salten und Lasker-Schüler." In: *Sentimente, Gefühle, Empfindungen. Zur Geschichte und Literatur des Affektiven von 1770 bis Heute. Tagung zum 60. Geburtstag von Hugh Ridley im Juli 2001*, Anne Fuchs and Sabine Strümper-Krobb, eds., 149-163. Würzburg: Königshausen & Neumann, 2003.

Kuh, Anton. "Mutzenbacher kontra Ronacher. Eine neue Salten-Predigt." *Die Stunde* (Vienna), Feb. 12, 1924: 3.

Kunz, Ingrid. *Felix Salten als Theaterkritiker zwischen 1902 und 1910*. Lizentiatsarbeit, Univ. of Zurich, July 1983.

Lothar, Ernst. "Salten: 'Louise von Koburg.'" Feuilleton. *NFP*, Jan. 15, 1933.

Lothar, Rudolph. "'Kaisertochter' im Deutschen Volkstheater." *Neues Wiener Journal*, Oct. 20, 1936.

Marmorek, Schiller. "Der Verrat der Schriftsteller." *Arbeiter-Zeitung*, June 3, 1933.

Mattl, Siegfried, and Werner Michael Schwarz, eds. *Felix Salten. Schriftsteller – Journalist – Exilant*. Wiener Persönlichkeiten, vol. 5. Commissioned by the Jewish Museum of the City of Vienna. Vienna: Holzhausen Verlag, 2006.

Mattl, Siegfried, Klaus Müller-Richter, Werner M. Schwarz, eds. *Wurstelprater by Felix Salten. Ein Schlüsseltext zur Wiener Moderne.* Edition Spuren. Vienna: Promedia, 2004.

Molnar, Franz. "Felix Salten zum 60. Geburtstag," In *Jahrbuch. Paul Zsolnay Verlag 1930*, 103-104. Berlin: Zsolnay, 1929.

Molo, Walter von. "Wichtige Bücher. Saltens Hasenbuch." Feuilleton. *NFP*, Dec. 17, 1929.

Nadel, Arno. "Der Shylock von Krakau. Melodrama von Felix Salten." *Ost und West* 13 (1913): 963-966.

Neumann, Robert. "Sechzehn Ziegen." In: *Unter falscher Flagge. Parodien*, 181-183. Berlin: Zsolnay, 1932.

o. st. [Otto Stoessl]. "Mädchenhände." *Wiener Zeitung*, Apr. 20, 1935.

Pinkus, Klaus. Letter. "Wer schrieb 'Josefine Mutzenbacher'?" *Frankfurter Allgemeine Zeitung*, May 30, 1970.

Pough, Liselotte. *Young Vienna and Psychoanalysis. Felix Doermann, Jakob Julius David, and Felix Salten.* Series on Austrian Culture, vol. 31. Edited by Harry Zohn. New York : Peter Lang, 2000

R. "Theater in der Josefstadt." *Wiener Zeitung*, Nov. 24, 1929.

Riedmueller, Kurt. "Felix Salten als Mensch, Dichter und Kritiker." PhD diss., Univ. of Vienna, 1949.

Reinharter, Gabriele Maria. "Felix Salten. Schriftsteller. Der österreichische Schriftsteller Felix Salten im Schweizer Exil. Materialien zu seiner Biographie von 1939 bis 1945." Diplomarbeit. Graz: Karl-Franzens-Universität, 1992.

Schmidt, Dietmar, and Claudia Öhlschläger, "'Weibsfauna', Zur Koinzidenz von Tiergeschichte und Pornographie am Beispiel von 'Bambi' und 'Josefine Mutzenbacher.'" In: *Hofmannsthal Jahrbuch zur Europäischen Moderne* 2 (1994): 237-286.

Schnitzler, Arthur. "'Die klingende Schelle' von Felix Salten." *Aphorismen und Betrachtungen.* Edited by Robert O. Weiss, 482-486. Frankfurt am Main: Fischer, 1967.

——. "Felix Salten." Typed manuscript, Aug. 14, 1917. DLA.

——. "Felix Salten zum 60. Geburtstag." *Jahrbuch. Paul Zsolnay Verlag 1930*, 106. Berlin: Zsolnay, 1929.

Schwarz, Werner Michael. "Felix Salten und das Kino." *filmarchiv* 39 (December 2006/January 2007): 48-57.

Seibert, Ernst and Susanne Blumesberger, eds. *Felix Salten — der unbekannte Bekannte*. Kinder- und Jugendliteraturforschung in Österreich, vol. 8. Vienna: Praesens, 2006.

Tögel, Christfried and Liselotte Pough. "Sigmund Freud, Felix Salten und Karl Lueger. Ein neuentdeckter Brief Sigmund Freuds." http://www.freud-biographik.de/salten.htm

"U.S. 9th Circuit Court of Appeals: Twin Books v Disney, Opinion." FindLaw. 4 Aug. 2008 <http://caselaw.lp. findlaw. com/ scripts/getcase.pl?court=9th&navby=c…>.

"Von der Woche. Der Bibelabend Bar Kochbas." *Selbtwehr* 27 Jan. 1911.

W. [Hugo Wittmann] "Burgtheater (Drei Einakter von Felix Salten)." Feuilleton. *NFP* 14 Dec. 1919.

Wagener, Hans. "Franz Josef I. für alt und jung. Das Bild des Kaisers bei Felix Salten." *An meine Völker. Die Literarisierung Franz Joseph I.* Ed. Leopold R. G. Decloedt. Bern: Peter Lang, 1998. 53-70.

Weichinger, Robert. "Schluß mit Genuß! Wer schrieb die 'Mutzenbacher'? Wer kriegt die Tantiemen? Felix Saltens Erben wohl nicht." *Die Presse* 2/3 Feb. 1991.

von Weilen, Alexander. "Felix Salten," *Das literarische Echo* 13 (1910-1911): columns 1724-1731.

Weinzierl, Ulrich. "Typische Wiener Feuilletonisten? Am Beispiel Salten, Blei, Friedell, Polgar und Kuh." *Literatur und Kritik* 191/192 (1985): 72-85.

Werner, Alfred."The Author of 'Bambi.'" *Saturday Review of Literature* 3 Nov. 1945: 17-18

Weyss, Barbara. "Felix Salten als Burgtheaterkritiker der Direktion Paul Schlenther 1898-1910." Diplomarbeit. Vienna: U Vienna, 2001

Wittner, Victor. "Begegnungen mit Felix Salten." *Welt am Montag* 27:5

Wyler, Lea. *Bambis Vater. Eine Collage über Felix Salten 1869-1945, erzählt von seiner Enkelin.* Radio DRS – Studio Zürich. Dir. Hans Jedlitschka. Copyright 1983 Lea Wyler

Wyler-Salten, Anna. "Introduction." *Felix Salten's Favorite Animals Stories.* Illus. Fritz Eichenberg. NY: Julian Messner, 1948

Zuckerkandl, Bertha. "Das Jung-Wiener Theater." Feuilleton. *WAG* 19 Nov. 1901

General Works

"Adventure in Wildwood Heart" [1957]. *Walt Disney's Legacy Collection: True-Life Adventures 4: Nature's Mysteries.* 2006. Disc Two

Amann, Klaus. *P.E.N. Politik, Emigration, Nationalsozialismus. Ein österreichischer Schriftstellerclub.* Vienna, Cologne, Graz: Hermann Böhlaus Nachfolger, 1984

Andreas-Salomé, Lou. *Lebensrückblick. Grundriß einiger Lebenserinnerungen.* Frankfurt am Main: Insel, 1968

Aretino. *Gespräche des göttlichen Pietro Aretino.* Trans. Heinrich Conrad. Leipzig: Insel, 1903

"Art Design: Impressions of the Forest." *The Making of Bambi. Bambi.* 2-disc special DVD edition, 2005

Bahr, Hermann. *Prophet der Moderne. Tagebücher 1888-1904.* Selection and commentary by Reinhard Farkas. Vienna, Graz, Cologne: Böhlau, 1987

---. *Rezensionen. Wiener Theater 1901-1903.* Berlin: Fischer, 1903

---. *Selbstbildnis.* Berlin: Fischer, 1923

Bahr, Hermann, ed. *Briefe von Josef Kainz.* Vienna, Berlin, Leipzig, Munich: Rikola, 1922

"*Bambi*: Inside Walt's Story Meetings." *Bambi.* 2-disc special DVD edition. 2005

Berthold, Werner and Brita Eckert, eds. *Der deutsche PEN-Club im Exil, 1933-1948: Eine Ausstellung der Deutschen Bibliothek Frankfurt am Main.* Frankfurt am Main: Buchhändler-Vereinigung, 1980

Betten, Anne, et al. *Judentum und Antisemitismus. Studien zur Literatur und Germanistik in Österreich.* Berlin: Erich Schmidt, 2003

Blei, Franz. *Das grosse Bestiarium der Literatur.* Frankfurt am Main: Insel, 1982 [1924]

Borchmeyer, Dieter, ed. *Richard Beer-Hofmann: "Zwischen Ästhetizismus und Judentum."* Collected Contributions from the Public Symposium at the Akademie der Wissenschaften in Heidelberg on October 25-26, 1995. Paderborn: Igel Verlag Wissenschaft, 1996.

Bousé, Derek. *Wildlife Films.* Philadelphia: U Pennsylvania, 2000

Broch, Hermann. *Hofmannsthal and His Time: The European Imagination, 1860-1920.* Chicago, U Chicago, 1984

Bruce, Iris. *Kafka and Cultural Zionism: Dates in Palestine*. Madison: U Wisconsin, 2007

Bülow, Ulrich von, ed. *"Sicherheit ist nirgends": Das Tagebuch von Arthur Schnitzler*. Marbach am Neckar: Deutsche Schillergesellschaft, 2000

Clarenbach, Anja. "Finis libri. Der Schriftsteller und Journalist Heinrich Eduard Jacob (1889-1967)." Diss., U Hamburg, 2003

Crémieux, Benjamin. "Der internationale P.E.N.-Club Kongreß in Wien. Österreichsiche Eindrücke." *NFP* 25 June 1929

Disney, Walt. *The Shaggy Dog*, 1959. Walt Disney Film Classics: The Comedy Favorites Series. Volume I.

Dubnow, Simon. *Weltgeschichte des jüdischen Volkes* 10. Transl. Dr. A. Steinberg. Berlin: Jüdischer Verlag, 1929

Dukes, Ashley. *The Scene is Changed*. Obscure Press, 2006 [London: Macmillan, 1942].

Ehrlich, Anna. *Auf den Spuren der Josefine Mutzenbacher. Eine Sittengeschichte von den Römern bis ins 20. Jahrhundert*. Wien: Amalthea, 2005

Englisch, Paul. *Geschichte der erotischen Literatur*. Stuttgart: Julius Püttmann, 1927

Fiedler, Leonhard M. *Max Reinhardt. Mit Selbstzeugnissen und Bilddokumenten*. Reinbek bei Hamburg: Rowohlt Taschenbuch, 1994 [1975]

Fischer, Brigitte B. *Sie schrieben mir, oder was aus meinem Poesiealbum wurde*. Munich: Deutscher Taschenbuch, 13. Auflage, 1992

Fisher, Margery. *Who's Who in Children's Books: A Treasury of the Familiar Characters of Childhood*. New York: Holt, Rinehart and Winston, 1975

Gabler, Neal. *Walt Disney: The Triumph of the American Imagination*. New York: Vintage Books, 2007

Gillman, Abigail. *Viennese Jewish Modernism. Freud, Hofmannsthal, Beer-Hofmann, and Schnitzler*. University Park, PA: The Pennsylvania State University, 2009

Hall, Murray G.. *Der Paul Zsolnay Verlag. Von der Gründung bis zur Rückkehr aus dem Exil. Studien und Texte zur Sozialgeschichte der Literatur*. Vol. 45. Ed. Wolfgang Frühwald et al. Tübingen: Max Niemeyer, 1994

Hofmannsthal, Hugo von. *Gedichte und Lyrische Dramen*. Stockholm:

Bermann-Fischer, 1946

Holzmann, Michael and Hanns Bohatta. *Deutsches Anonymen-Lexikon.* Weimar 1909

Jelavich, Peter. *Berlin Cabaret.* Cambridge, Massachusetts and London, England: Harvard University, 1993

Johnston, Ollie and Frank Thomas. *Walt Disney's Bambi: The Story and the Film.* New York: Stewart, Tabori & Chang, 1990

Johnston, William M. *The Austrian Mind: An Intellectual and Social History, 1848-1938.* Berkeley, Los Angeles, London: U California, 1972

Jones, Ernest. *The Life and Work of Sigmund Freud.* Vol. 3: *The Last Phase, 1919-1939.* New York: Basic Books, 1961 [1957]

Koch, Hans-Albrecht. *Hugo von Hofmannsthal.* Munich: Deutscher Taschenbuch Verlag, 2004

Koppensteiner, Jürgen. *Österreich. Ein landeskundliches Lesebuch.* Vienna: Edition Praesens, 2001

Kosler, Hans Christian. "Karl Kraus und die Wiener Moderne." Ed. Heinz Ludwig Arnold. Munich: text + kritik, 1975. 39-57.

Kraus, Karl. "Die demolirte Literatur." *Wiener Rundschau.* 15 Nov. 1896, 1 Dec. 1896, 15 Dec., 1896, and 1 Jan. 1897: 19-27, 68-72, 113-118, 153-157

---. ["Ganze Ketten von roten..."]. *Die Fackel* 24.601-607 (Nov. 1922): 84-90.

Kunitz, Stanley J. and Howard Haycroft, eds. *Twentieth Century Authors. A Biographical Dictionary of Modern Literature.* New York: H. W. Wilson Co., 1942

Lasker-Schüler, Else. *Concert.* Trans. Jean M. Snook. Lincoln, Nebraska: U Nebraska, 1994

[Lehmann, Adolphe]. *Lehmanns Adressbuch, Lehmanns Allgemeiner Wohnungsanzeiger für die Stadt Wien,* 1869-1939. Microfiche. ÖNB, Vienna

Lothar, Ernst. *Das Wunder des Überlebens. Erinnerungen und Ergebnisse.* Vienna, Hamburg: Zsolnay, 1961

Lutts, Ralph H. "The Trouble with Bambi: Walt Disney's *Bambi* and the American Vision of Nature." *Forest and Conservation History* 36 (October 1992): 160-171. 4 June 2008 <http://www.history.vt.edu/Barrow/Hist2104/readings/bambi.html>

[Princess] Louise of Belgium. *My Own Affairs.* Trans. Maude M. C. Ffoulkes. New York: George H. Doran, 1921

Luise von Toscana. *Mein Leben.* Vienna: Carl Ueberreuter, 1988

Maderthaner, Wolfgang and Lutz Musner, *Die Anarchie der Vorstadt. Das andere Wien um 1900.* Frankfurt am Main, New York: Campus, 1999

Maltin, Leonard. *The Disney Films.* New, updated edition. New York: Crown Publishers, 1984

Mann, Thomas. *Tagebücher 1937-1939.* Ed. Peter de Mendelssohn. Frankfurt am Main: Fischer, 1980

McAleer, Kevin. *Dueling: The Cult of Honor in Fin-de-siécle Germany.* Princeton, New Jersey: Princeton University, 1994

Mutzenbacher, Josefine. *Meine 365 Liebhaber. Die Fortsetzung meiner Liebensgeschichte.* Mit einem neuen Beitrag von Oswald Wiener. Munich: Regner & Bernhard, 1970

Nickl, Therese and Heinrich Schnitzler, eds. *Hugo von Hofmannsthal – Arthur Schnitzler Briefwechsel.* Frankfurt am Main: Fischer, 1964

O'Brien, George M. "The Parks of Vienna." *Journal of Popular Culture* 15.1 (Summer 1981): 76-86

Rechter, David. *The Jews of Vienna and the First World War.* London; Portland, Oregon: The Littmann Library of Jewish Civilization, 2001

Renner, Gottfried. *Österreichische Schriftsteller und der Nationalsozialismus (1933-1940). Der "Bund der deutschen Schriftsteller Österreichs" und der Aufbau der Reichsschrifttumskammer in der "Ostmark."* Frankfurt am Main: Buchhänder-Vereinigung, 1986

Rocek, Roman. *Glanz und Elend des P.E.N. Bioraphie eines literarischen Clubs.* Vienna, Cologne, Weimar: Böhlau, 2000

Rodewald, Dierk and Corrina Fiedler, eds. *Samuel Fischer, Hedwig Fischer: Briefwechsel mit Autoren, with an introduction by Bernhard Zeller.* Frankfurt am Main: Fischer, 1989

Rosenberger, Erwin. *Herzl As I Remember Him.* New York: Herzl, 1959

Rothe, Friedrich. *Karl Kraus. Die Biographie.* Munich, Zurich: Piper, 2003

Sandrock, Adele and Arthur Schnitzler. *Dilly. Geschichte einer Liebe in Briefen, Bildern und Dokumenten.* Ed. Renate Wagner. Vienna, Munich: Amalthea, 1975

Schickel, Richard. *The Disney Version: The Life, Times, Art and Commerce of Walt Disney.* New York: Simon and Schuster, 1968

Schneider, Helmut. *Felix Dörmann. Eine Monographie.* Vienna: VWGÖ

[Verband der Wissenschaftlichen Gesellschaften Österreichs], 1991

Schnitzler, Arthur. *Aphorismen und Betrachtungen.* Ed. Robert O. Weiss. Frankfurt am Main: Fischer, 1967.

---. *Briefe 1875-1912.* Ed. Therese Nickl and Heinrich Schnitzler. Frankfurt am Main: Fischer, 1981

---. *Tagebuch 1887-1892.* Ed. Peter Michael Braunwart, Susanne Pertlik, Reinhard Urbach. Vienna: Österreichische Akademie der Wissenschaften, 1987

---. *Tagebuch 1893-1902.* Ed. Peter Michael Braunworth, Konstanze Fliedl, Susanne Pertlik, Reinhard Urbach. Vienna: Österreichische Akademie der Wissenschaften, 1995

---. *Tagebuch 1903-1908.* Ed. Peter Michael Braunwarth, Susanne Pertlik, Reinhard Urbach. Vienna: Österreichische Akademie der Wissenschaften, 1991

---. *Tagebuch 1909-1912.* Ed. Peter Michael Braunwarth, Richard Miklin, Maria Neyses, Susanne Pertlik, Walter Ruprechter, Reinhard Urbach. Vienna: Verlag der Österreichischen Akademie der Wissenschaften, 1981

---. *Tagebuch 1917-1919.* Ed. Peter Michael Braunwarth, Richard Miklin, Susanne Pertlik and Reinhard Urbach. Vienna: Österreichische Akademie der Wissenschaften, 1985

Schoeps, Julius H. *Theodor Herzl 1860-1904. Wenn Ihr wollt, Ist es kein Märchen. Eine Text-Bild-Monographie.* Vienna: Christian Brandstätter, 1995

Segel, Harold B., ed. *The Vienna Coffeehouse Wits 1890-1938.* Trans. Harold B. Segel. West Lafeyette, Indiana: Purdue University, 1993

Sinhuber, Bartel F. *Die Wiener Kaffeehausliteraten. Anekdotisches zur Literaturgeschichte.* Vienna: Dachs-Verlag, Edition Wien, 1993

Specht, Richard. *Arthur Schnitzler. Der Dichter und sein Werk.* Berlin: Fischer, 1922

Sprengel, Peter and Gregor Streim. *Berliner und Wiener Moderne. Vermittlungen und Abgrenzungen in Literatur, Theater, Publizistik. Mit einem Beitrag von Barbara Noth.* Vienna, Cologne, Weimar: Bohlau, 1998

Taylor, Melissa Jane. "Bureaucratic Response to Human Tragedy: American Consuls and the Jewish Plight in Vienna, 1938-1941." *Holocaust and Genocide Studies* 21.2 (2007): 243-267

Teller, Oscar. *Davids Witz-Schleuder. Jüdisch-Politisches Cabaret. 50 Jahre Kleinkunstbühnen in Wien, Berlin, London, New York, Warschau und Tel Aviv.* Darmstadt: Darmstädter Blätter, 1985

"Theater und Film: Heute: Eröffnung des Sascha-Palastes." *Die Neue Zeitung* 13 Mar. 1931

"*The Shaggy Dog: The Wild & Woolly Edition* DVD Review." *The Ultimate Disney DVD Index.* 3 July 2008 <http://www.ultimatedisney.com/shaggy.html>

Timms, Edward. *Karl Kraus, Apocalyptic Satirist: Culture and Catastrophe in Habsburg Vienna.* New Haven and London: Yale University, 1986

Trebitsch, Siegfried. *Chronicle of a Life.* Trans. Eithne Wilkins and Ernst Kaiser. Melbourne, London, Toronto: William Heinemann, 1953

"Tribute to Winston Hibler," *Walt Disney's Legacy Collection: True-Life Adventures,* Volume Four: *Nature's Mysteries.* 2006. Disc Two

"Twin Books Corporation v. Walt Disney Company," No. 95-15250. United States Court of Appeals, Ninth Court. Decision 20 May 1996. OpenJurist 9 August 2009 <http://openjurist.org/83/f3d/1162>

Walt Disney's Legacy Collection: True-Life Adventures, Volume Four: *Nature's Mysteries.* 2006

Wengraf, Edmund. "Kaffeehaus und Literatur," *Wiener Literatur-Zeitung* II:7 (May 15, 1891): 2

Wölfing, Leopold. *My Life Story: From Archduke to Grocer.* New York: E. P. Dutton, 1931

Zeller, Bernhard, ed. *Jugend in Wien. Literatur um 1900.* Munich: Insel, 1974

Zohn, Harry. *Karl Kraus.* New York: Twayne, 1971

Zühlsdorff, Volkmar von. *Hitler's Exiles: The German Cultural Resistance in America and Europe.* Trans. Martin H. Bott. London, New York: Continuum International Publishing Group, 2005

Zweig, Stefan. "Die Monotonisierung der Welt." Feuilleton. *NFP* 31 Jan. 1925

---. *The World of Yesterday. An Autobiography.* New York: Viking Press, 1943.

400

Franz Josef, Emperor 2, 66, 86,
90, 95, 110, 138, 162, 172,
173, 174, 253, 269, 273
Freud, Sigmund 141, 152, 225,
233, 235, 240, 255
Freund, Fritz 71, 72, 77, 83,
106, 120, 121
Freytag, Gustav 189
Die Journalisten 189
Friedell, Egon 112, 281
Friedrich II, King of Prussia
(Frederick the Great) 169
Friedrich, Archduke 165
Frischauer, Otto 61
Fulda, Ludwig 188
Der Dummkopf (The Idiot)
188
Herr und Diener (Master and
Servant) 188
Funicello, Annette 321

G

Galsworthy, John 202, 210, 225,
226, 232, 233, 257, 259, 264,
283
Ganghofer, Ludwig 80
Gans-Ludassy, Julius von 58,
65, 109, 123, 128, 129, 130
George, King of Saxony 93
George, Lloyd 125
George, Stefan 53
Géraldy, Paul 233
Germaine, Auguste 71
Geyer, Emil 191
Ginzkey, Franz Karl 71
Ginzkey, Ignaz 239
Girardi, Alexander 139, 146
Glas, Charlotte (Lotte) 39, 40,
41, 58, 63, 76
Glas, Emma 39
Gluemer, Marie (Mizzi, Mz.) 38
Godowski, Leopold 124

Goebbels, Joseph 255
Goethe, Johann Wolfgang von
55, 92, 169
Faust 31, 63
Tasso 136
Goldberg, Heinz 251
Goldmann, Paul 31, 33, 44, 70,
71, 99
Goldschmidt, Adalbert von 44
Graham, Gladys 231
Greenburger, Sanford 270, 300,
301, 302
Gretler, Heinrich 296
Grillparzer, Franz 12, 176
Grimmelshausen, Hans Jakob
Christoffel von 115
Die Lebensbeschreibung der
Erzbetrügerin und Land-
störzerin Courage (Life of
the Arch-Deceiver and
Vagabond Courage) 115
Grossmann, Stefan 109, 123,
128, 129, 130

H

Haas, Walter de 298
Haas, Willy 114
Hagenbeck, Karl 158, 245
Hainisch, Michael 232
Halasz, Stefan 209
Halbe, Max 80
Haldane, Richard Burdon 125
Hammer, Victor 165
Hämmerli-Schindler, Theodor
301
Hammerstein, Wilhelm von 58
Handel, Georg Frideric 15
Handl, Willi 83, 119
Harden, Maximilian 124, 244
Hartleben, Otto Erich 44
Hatvany, Lajos 226, 227, 257
Hauptmann, Gerhart 51, 52, 63,